CONTENTS

LIST OF FIGURES AND TABLES

FIGURES

TABLES

FOREWORD

At the United Nations Conference on Environment and Development (popularly known as the Earth Summit) in Rio de Janeiro in 1992, the consensus was that the greatest challenge facing society today was the need to find a more sustainable way of life, based on a more careful use of resources and reduced environmental emissions. Signatories to the Earth Summit agreements called for a fundamental shift away from the view that environmental protection has to be sacrificed for economic gain, towards a model in which environmental enhancement is fully integrated and compatible with economic development.

Political declarations, though indispensable, must be followed by practical action. If we are to achieve sustainable development, we will have to reconsider many aspects of public policies, business strategies and individual lifestyles and behaviour. This in turn will require a better understanding of the functioning of the biosphere, the environmental impact of human activities, and of the role of new technologies as well as policy and information tools.

The European Union (EU) has taken up this challenge. Its commitment to sustainable development is one of the most important features of the Treaty of the European Union agreed at the Amsterdam Council of Heads of State and Government in 1997. In particular, under Article 3d, environmental protection requirements must now be integrated into many European policies.

The EU's fifth Framework Programme on Research, Technological Development and Demonstration Activities (1998–2002) therefore lays strong emphasis on improving the knowledge base in order to develop the technologies and devise the tools needed to achieve sustainable development. The need to improve the general quality of life and strengthen our ability to manage natural resources pervades most of the specific actions under the programme (for example the moves to promote the integrated development of rural and coastal areas and better management of water and biodiversity resources, and to develop and promote cleaner products and energy).

Considerable progress has been made over the past decades; we have deepened our understanding of the environment, and many new, cleaner, production techniques and processes have been developed. European Union research and technological development (RTD) programmes have provided substantial contributions to the advancement of science in these areas. However, in the early 1990s it became clear that the uptake of innovative technologies was still slow. The EU Environment and Climate RTD Programme therefore included a specific research theme on the measures needed to promote more rapid diffusion and wider adoption of cleaner technologies, as part of its work on the

'Human Dimensions of Environmental Change'. This supported the substantial cross-national comparative study that forms the basis of this book.

The research was conducted by scientific teams from four European countries, coordinated by Dr Robin Williams of the University of Edinburgh. Through detailed comparisons between different regions and different sectors, the study explored the 'drivers' and the 'barriers' to the implementation of cleaner technologies, and showed that the problems with the acceptance and adoption of cleaner approaches are socio-political and economic as much as technical in nature. The project identified the combination of policy measures that would be needed to enable industries to reconfigure their production systems to reduce their environmental impact.

The publication of the results will make a valuable contribution to the various European Commission initiatives on cleaner technology and innovation. It will also serve as a timely and important source of information for a number of related projects being developed under the EU's fifth Framework Programme on Research, Technological Development and Demonstration Activities. More generally, this book provides a well-documented basis for action, and can thus make an important contribution to the search for more environmentally sustainable patterns of development.

Christian Patermann
Director, RTD Action Environment
European Commission

ACKNOWLEDGEMENTS

This book is based largely on a report to the European Commission Directorate-General for Science, Research and Development (DG XII). The report, titled *Implementation of Cleaner Technologies: a Cross-regional Comparison*, summarized the main findings of a two-year research project, funded by DG XII,* into the social, economic and technical factors that could encourage or obstruct the development and dissemination of cleaner technologies and production systems across Europe.

The project was designed and led by a team based at the University of Edinburgh. The core of the project consisted of a series of detailed comparative case studies which were undertaken by teams in each of the four regions in the study. This book therefore has a number of contributors. Each chapter lists only the main authors, but every member of the original research consortium carried out and wrote up case studies, undertook part of the analysis of the data, generated text and contributed intellectually to the source report. Each team was also responsible for one or more of the sectoral studies, and the cross-national comparisons of similar firms in different settings.

Robin Williams, Anthony Clayton and Graham Spinardi, as project leaders, were responsible for the overall analysis of the findings, for formulating the conclusions and identifying the implications for policy, and for editing and collating the final report (though we are pleased to acknowledge helpful comments here from the network and especially from Leo Baas and Søren Kerndrup). In all other respects the report was a collective product, reflecting contributions from every research team. The authors (in alphabetical order, listed by research centre) were as follows:

Scotland
University of Edinburgh: Anthony Clayton, Graham Spinardi and Robin Williams.
Heriot-Watt University: Ian Thomson, with additional contributions from Olwyn Duncan.

Robin Williams was the project coordinator and Anthony Clayton served as the scientific consultant throughout the study.

* The original research project was funded by DG XII under the European Commission's Environment Programme, Socio-Economic Research on the Environment (SEER) (Contract EV5V CT94 0364).

Ireland
Cork Institute of Technology, Clean Technology Centre: Noel Duffy and Brendan Ryan, with assistance from Pat Griffin and Pierette O'Shea.

The Netherlands
Erasmus University: Leo Baas, with additional contributions from Frank Boons.

Denmark
Roskilde University: Associate Professor Børge Klemmensen and Dr Søren Kerndrup, of the Department of Environment, Technology and Social Studies, were the coordinators of the team at Roskilde University, which also involved: Birgitte Steen Hansen, Ole Erik Hansen, Birgitte Larsen, Ulf Nielsen, Inger Stauning and Jacob Hass Svendsen.

This book was written by Anthony Clayton, Graham Spinardi and Robin Williams. Dr Clayton is currently the Alcan Professor of Caribbean Sustainable Development at the University of the West Indies Centre for Environment and Development, Dr Spinardi is a Senior Research Fellow and Dr Williams is a Reader and Director of the Research Centre for Social Science at the University of Edinburgh.*

We would like to express our sincere thanks to all the members of the research team, to Andrew Sors and William Watts of DG XII for funding and support throughout the original study, to Moyra Forrest and Barbara Silander, the information officer and project adminstrator, and to all the other support staff at the institutions that undertook the research, to Jonathan Sinclair Wilson, Rowan Davies, Ruth Coleman and Frances MacDermott at Earthscan, and – above all – to the companies who allowed us generous access to their plants, their files and their people.

The final form and content of this book and any errors are the sole responsibility of the three authors.

Anthony Clayton, Graham Spinardi and Robin Williams, 1999

* Please address any enquiries relating to the research to:
Dr Robin Williams, Director, Research Centre for Social Science, University of Edinburgh, Old Surgeons' Hall, High School Yards, Edinburgh, EH1 1LZ, Scotland, UK.
Email: R.Williams@ed.ac.uk. Fax: +44 (0)131 650 6399. Tel: +44 (0)131 650 6384.

1 CLEANER TECHNOLOGY AND THE GREENING OF INDUSTRY: AN INTRODUCTION

Anthony Clayton, Brendan Ryan and Robin Williams

INTRODUCTION

Polluted rivers, contaminated ground, acid-damaged trees, eroding soils, disappearing species, ozone depletion, global warming ... it now appears that human activity can, potentially, affect the global ecology in ways and to an extent not previously thought possible. There is a growing consensus about the need to reduce the environmental impact of human activities, and about the failure of current approaches to deliver the necessary improvements. Our technology, for example, has become very much more sophisticated and efficient during the course of this century, but consumption of fossil fuels has still increased some 50-fold since 1900 as growth in demand has dramatically outpaced the rate of technological improvement. It has been suggested that we must now reduce our wastage of energy and materials at least by a factor of four if we are to achieve environmentally sustainable development (Weizsäcker et al, 1997). But how can this level of improvement be achieved? This is not just a question of which technical means might be available but, more importantly, how to bring about the necessary changes in our economic and social systems.

This book explores these questions by addressing the scope for adopting technologies and production systems that are fundamentally 'cleaner' in terms of the resources they use and the wastes they generate. Cleaner technology seems to offer a more effective approach to environmental improvement than traditional methods of applying 'clean-up' or 'end-of-pipe' controls to existing 'dirty' industrial processes. This is partly because many end-of-pipe controls displace problems, rather than solving them,[1] and partly because end-of-pipe controls themselves consume energy and resources, and can thus increase the total energy and resource demand associated with a particular industrial process. Cleaner solutions, on the other hand, aim to solve problems at or near their source, with the goal of eliminating problems entirely or even of converting them into positive assets.

Cleaner technology has come to be seen as an economically attractive approach, allowing firms to save costs through more efficient resource utilization and reduced waste-disposal charges, and to reduce pollution, thus offering a 'win–win' solution. In addition, it has become clear that the integration of pollution prevention with process design can help firms to reduce the risk of making an inefficient investment in pollution control technology. End-of-pipe pollution control costs tend to escalate as environmental standards become more stringent. If environmental standards become significantly more stringent, it may become necessary to upgrade or replace existing end-of-pipe controls before the end of their design life, thus writing off part of that earlier investment. Waste problems that are solved by being eliminated, however, generally remain solved, thus protecting that investment.

Thus cleaner technology appears to offer a way of reconciling economic and environmental objectives. This is why the Report of the World Commission on Environment and Development (the Brundtland Report, 1987) argued that it was essential to develop and disseminate such solutions if the people of the world were to make a transition to a more sustainable way of life.

But if cleaner technology does indeed represent a 'win–win' solution, why has it not been adopted more widely? What is impeding the universal uptake of such solutions? Is this a case of market failure? Are there factors – or forces – inhibiting these solutions? Alternatively, is there still a gulf between rhetoric and reality in terms of what cleaner technologies can actually offer industry? What are the types and sources of cleaner technology and industrial systems, and where are these new solutions actually being generated? And what measures could be adopted to promote their wider development and uptake?

Much of the focus to date has been into the research and development of new technologies that might enable cleaner and more efficient industrial processes. More recently, however, a number of studies have suggested that the real impediments to the widespread adoption of cleaner technologies may be social and economic as much as technical in nature. This is significant, as it indicates why support for technical development alone has not been sufficient to promote the adoption of cleaner technologies.

It is clearly important, therefore, to analyse and explicate the socio-technical and socio-economic factors that determine, in practice, whether cleaner technologies are developed and adopted. This can be resolved into three key issues:

- What are cleaner technologies, and how are they developed and adopted?
- What are the motives and incentives for their development and adoption, and what are the obstacles?
- What are the sources of relevant innovation?

We set out to examine these issues in a set of 31 comparative case studies of innovations in firms in nine selected industrial sectors in four regions of Europe (the regions containing and adjacent to the cities of Cork, Edinburgh, Roskilde and Rotterdam). By comparing the behaviour and performance of firms in particular regions and sectors, we hoped to explicate the factors that shaped the relevant decision making by the firm, including its internal constitution, its commercial context, its relationship to broader innovation systems and the regional regulatory setting.

CONTENTS

Chapter 1 explores what we mean by clean technology, sets out the debates that form the background of this study, then explains the methodology adopted in our detailed study of the implementation of cleaner technology. An important element here, discussed in Chapter 2, is a cross-regional comparison, highlighting in particular the influence of the regulatory setting.

Chapters 3 to 11 present the detailed findings of our case studies in our selected industries, respectively:

- oil refining,
- petrochemicals,
- fine chemicals,
- pharmaceuticals,
- dairies,
- brewing,
- sugar,
- paper mills,
- plating.

Chapter 12 analyses these findings to identify the factors that may promote or impede the adoption of cleaner technologies and makes some policy recommendations.

Finally, Chapter 13 explores the wider implications for understanding cleaner technologies, including the uneven economic pressures to improve resource efficiency, the scope for initiatives across the product supply chain and the stimulation of innovation.

THE TRADITIONAL CONFLICT BETWEEN THE ENVIRONMENT AND THE ECONOMY

Economic needs and environmental concerns have often been seen to conflict. Many aspects of our current economic system were established with little apparent regard to the long-term effects of human activity on the environment. Some have therefore suggested that long-term sustainability will require far-reaching changes to our current systems of production and consumption. The particular significance of cleaner technology in this regard is in the potential that it appears to offer to reconcile the traditional conflict between the environment and industrialized society, and thus to enable a move towards a more genuinely sustainable economy.

A key cause of environmental degradation is that many direct and indirect environmental inputs into economic processes have been significantly undervalued. Forests have been felled with no allowance made for their function in maintaining biological diversity. The pollution absorption capacity of the atmosphere has been partly consumed by the generations who have enjoyed the benefits of cheap fossil fuel, and who have not met the full cost of this consumption. In general, inputs that are undervalued will tend to be used to excess. There is little incentive to economize on the use of resources that are apparently cheap and plentiful. There is now evidence, however, that some resources – such as atmospheric pollution absorption capacity – may have become seriously overstretched as a result of this failure to recognize the value of these resources.

Some have argued that environmental damage arises from the pursuit of profit.[2] Indeed many environmentalists have seen unsustainable use of resources as deeply rooted in the system of capitalist competition. The historical evidence does not entirely support such a simplistic analysis. It is now known that environmental damage in countries with centrally planned economies has been more severe than in capitalist economies (for example, some 16 per cent of the geographical area of the former Soviet Union has been very severely environmentally damaged (Mnatsakanian, 1992)). However, the history of corporate operations in relatively unregulated environments, such as in developing nations, is not dissimilar. Some of the more rapacious mining, timber and other resource extraction and processing operations in Southeast Asia or South America, for example, have clearly inflicted immense environmental damage. The fact that environmental problems have arisen in diverse political and economic conditions – in both Western and Eastern Europe, for example – implies that different political and economic systems can generate some similar problems, and that these outcomes may therefore be related to particular patterns of industrial production and consumption per se.[3] Given the importance of economic growth to both capitalist and socialist states, it is perhaps not surprising that, at times, the state's industrial promotion role has taken precedence over protecting the environment. The key question then concerns the separation of powers and the extent to which the state's environmental regulation functions are unbundled from its economic role and are effectively enforced. As we see in Chapter 2, the latter depends, in part, on how well these roles are institutionalized, and also upon public scrutiny and whether there is a broader social contract about the need to protect the environment.

It is hard to deny, however, that the profit motive has provided an incentive to many firms to externalize as many of their costs of production as possible, by operating with minimal environmental controls, paying the lowest possible prices for raw materials, and avoiding payment for any wider environmental costs that the use of these materials might entail. In this way firms have transferred part of their production costs to the environment, thus securing a hidden subsidy. Society has, however, suffered a general loss of welfare as a result. Some of this loss is immediate and obvious, as in the severely reduced environmental quality and increased rates of respiratory disease in heavily industrialized areas, but much is less obvious, such as with the long-term changes in soil structure associated with acid deposition, or the increased risk of climate change and the associated consequences for future generations.

There has been a dramatic increase in the rate of environmental damage during the course of the 20th century, largely driven by the remarkable increase in the rate of global economic development. Over the last century global industrial production has increased some 100-fold (Graedel and Allenby, 1995). This unprecedented economic growth has brought widespread social improvements. There are, however, serious questions as to whether these developments can continue indefinitely, because of the serious environmental costs involved. As Graedel and Allenby (1995) point out, the increases in global industrial production and in the volume of international trade have been strongly correlated with increased consumption of resources. For example, between 1950 and 1997, fossil fuel consumption quadrupled, while the consumption of timber tripled, partly driven by the increase in the consumption of paper, which rose six-fold over the same period (Brown et al, 1998). Some resource bases are now seriously overstretched as a result, while the Earth's pollution absorption capacity has been partly consumed and reduced by the flows of waste generated by these activities.

The process of economic development has also led to the creation of entirely new categories of pollution (Graedel and Allenby, 1995). Global output of synthetic organic chemicals, for example, was minute in 1900, but by 1995 some 225 billion pounds per annum were produced in the US alone. The rate of development and manufacture of these new compounds is now such that it greatly exceeds the current capacity to carry out a full assessment of potential environmental and health impacts (National Academy of Science, 1984).

THE TRANSITION TO AN ENVIRONMENTALLY SUSTAINABLE ECONOMIC SYSTEM

If we are to meet expectations that living standards will be maintained and improved, and in particular meet the growing aspirations of the developing world, without escalating levels of environmental damage, far reaching changes will be needed in our current system of industrial production and patterns of consumption. Substantial reductions in the resource costs of our activities will be needed before they could be sustainable in the long term. Weizsäcker et al (1997) argue that we need to increase energy and resource-use productivity by a factor of four, in order to double total wealth while simultaneously halving total resource use. This will necessitate profound changes to the technologies and production processes currently deployed as well as in broader patterns of consumption and waste management. Some see environmental sustainability as requiring a shift to radically different sets of technologies and ways of meeting human needs. This might imply the need to conduct basic research and development to develop industrial processes that are radically different to those currently deployed and cleaner in terms of resources used and wastes created. However there are serious questions about how, and indeed whether, such a radical transition is achievable. Amongst those who accept the need for far reaching change, there are questions about whether this idea of a quantum jump represents the best path towards sustainability. In particular, studies of the development of our existing technologies and practices show that these have become deeply *entrenched* in society and our industrial system, and cannot be readily changed by *fiat*.

'*Entrenchment*' refers to the ways in which particular technological solutions and designs come to dominate and so constrain subsequent developments. This arises because new technology tends to develop cumulatively over time, incorporating earlier technical advances, and because an increasing array of actors become closely tied up with, and committed to, the production and use of certain artefacts. As economies develop skills and sink capital into particular solutions, the cost (in terms of risk, time and capital) involved in moving to a fundamentally different approach becomes a serious deterrent (Miles and Green, 1994). Sunk investment, alignments of views about the nature of problems and how they may be solved, standards, decision-making criteria can all contribute to 'lock-in' to particular approaches (Williams and Edge, 1996) and to dominant techno-logical regimes. Thus an economy can become *path dependent*; locked into just one of the possible paths of development which it could have followed (Goodstein, 1999). Relatively major perturbations may be required to shake an economy or an industry out of a deeply established mode (Miles and Green, 1994; Kemp et al, 1998).

A striking example of entrenchment is the emergence in the developed nations of the transport system based largely on the use of private cars. This 'large scale technological system' has arisen through the activities of a range of players (vehicle builders, developers of engines, oil companies, road builders etc) developing and promoting products around a shared view and interest in the petrol/diesel-powered private car. In the US, for example, the government's decision to construct the interstate highway system after the Second World War enabled suburban development, which required mass individual car ownership, which then locked in this particular development pathway (Goodstein, 1999). Any 'head on' attempt to reduce the role of the motor car and reverse its deeply entrenched technological trajectory must confront a powerful alliance of interests, and is very unlikely to succeed, especially in the short term, as current products, available technologies, and customer views as to what products might be suitable and desirable are mutually reinforcing. There are many interlocking barriers to change including current urban geography, the availability of alternative technologies, price, performance in relation to customer expectations and the culture that surrounds the car (Sørensen, 1994). The continued failure of 'the electric car' over recent decades provides a case in point (Callon, 1980). A gradualist and multi-level strategy may therefore be required to reverse the existing processes of 'lock-in' and re-orient the system around a different paradigm incorporating ideas of cleaner engines, electric cars and cleaner transport systems (Schot, 1992; Kemp et al, 1998).

Similarly, Miles and Green (1994) have argued that a transition towards environmentally cleaner industrial systems will not come about through 'tech-nology push' alone (ie the development of new generic core technologies), but will depend on an iterative process involving 'societal and demand pull' as much as technology push. There is evidence that technological trajectories may be reversed as a result of changing circumstances, particularly if the array of forces that tended to sustain and reinforce it become fragmented and disrupted (Fleck et al, 1990; Williams and Edge, 1996). This raises the possibility of reshaping existing technological trajectories through external pressures and incentives, gradually shifting design criteria and market signals and establishing a new development pathway (Schot, 1992; Miles and Green, 1994). In this way a new technological regime could be created involving different priorities in relation to resource utilization and waste reduction.

Not all technological regimes are as deeply entrenched as the motor car system (and today even that is beginning to change). Other areas may offer more immediate opportunities for changing technological paradigms and trajectories. For example, McMeekin and Green (1994) have found a number of 'buried' technological development trajectories within firms with more environmentally benign products and processes, which had not been developed previously when environmental concerns were not a priority. There may be a reservoir of untapped innovation within industry, and processes and products that could be developed, given the right external signals.

Though the kinds of change needed are substantial, some have argued that it is feasible. Weizsäcker et al (1997) underpin their call for a fourfold increase in resource efficiency by more than fifty examples of similar or greater improvements in energy and resource-use productivity, including several examples of ten to hundred-fold improvements, from a wide range of industries. They point out the vast scope for savings. For example some 97 per cent of the fuel energy employed for lighting is wasted, and some 99 per cent of the original materials contained in or used in the production of goods made in the US becomes waste within six weeks of the sale of the finished product. The authors estimate that this inefficiency costs the US about US $1 trillion per annum and that, globally, the figure could be as much as US $10 trillion per annum.[4] The authors conclude that enhancing resource productivity and reducing this level of wastage could bring multiple benefits including an improved quality of life, reduced pollution and resource depletion, enhanced profitability, improved market and business efficiency, better use of scarce capital, greater equity and increased employment.

THE GREENING OF INDUSTRY?

Recognition of the scale of change needed for sustainability, and the urgent need for such change has led environmental advocates to move away from their traditional oppositional stance towards industry – in which industry is seen as solely a source of environmental 'problems' – towards a model of constructive engagement which seeks to involve industry around more proactive strategies of pollution prevention. There is evidence of the start of a new synthesis between industry and the environment, captured in the slogan 'the greening of industry'.

This perspective sees the involvement of industry as not just desirable but crucial if the world is to achieve such sustainable development.[5] Industry possesses many of the key resources needed for achieving such change (Hawken, 1994). Furthermore many sectors of industry have accepted that environmental regulation is now a permanent feature of the business landscape, and are potentially open to environmental concerns (Irwin and Hooper, 1992). The idea of greening of industry implies that firms accept environmental goals as intrinsic to their activities rather than as an externally imposed obligation. What is needed is to get firms to move beyond their reactive stance towards environmental concerns and regulations and take on a proactive, and indeed leading, role in achieving sustainable development (though it is clear that most firms are not yet anywhere near this position) (Hawken, 1994).

An important element of this new approach involves using market forces to provide incentives to change the behaviour of firms and individuals (Hawken, 1994; Porter and van der Linde, 1995). Porter and van der Linde (1995) in particular have argued that the idea that economic development must inevitably be at the expense of resource consumption and environmental degradation is fundamentally incorrect, because enhanced resource productivity can lead directly to enhanced economic competitiveness – the 'win–win' scenario. This is linked to the idea – which we return to in Chapter 2 – that regulation and other policy instruments could be used to promote innovations that are more efficient in resource use, and thus more competitive as well as 'cleaner'. This is, clearly, an attractive suggestion, as it implies that market forces can drive business and industry in the direction of ever greater resource efficiency, thereby reducing environmental impacts. It also implies that economic development and environmental protection can be genuinely reconciled, and that the same factors will drive firms to improve both their economic and their environmental performance.

This view is not universally accepted. For example, Welford (1997) offers a radical critique of the greening of industry approach. Taking a traditional green view that industry alone cannot or will not make a transition to more sustainable practices and that only a profound reconstruction of industry and attendant social relationships and political structures will enable society to make a transition to a genuinely sustainable development path, he suggests that industry has in fact pre-empted and neutered the debate by capturing and restructuring the environmental agenda, excising radical elements in ways which are compatible with the exigencies of a liberal capitalist economy frame of reference.

Many commentators are not convinced that business and industry, historically responsible for many of the worst pollution problems and still driven primarily by the need to make profits, can really be expected to reform to the extent required. For example, some European steel manufacturers avoided the additional costs of complying with relatively stringent environmental standards adopted in Germany during the 1980s (which added about 50 DM to the cost of manufacturing a tonne of steel compared to 25 DM per tonne under the relatively low environmental standards in Spain and Italy) by shifting operations to southern European states. Similarly, with the creation of the North American Free Trade Association (NAFTA), a number of US companies saw the opportunity to move out of the relatively tough US regulatory regime, and to take advantage of the much laxer environmental standards then operating in Mexico. The US companies switched the most dangerous and polluting parts of their operations south of the border, then re-imported their own finished products back into the US market, thereby evading environmental and health and safety regulations.[6]

In addition to such deliberate avoidance, and probably more typical, there appear to be many instances in which firms simply neglect the potential benefits of improving resource efficiency and reducing waste. Weizsäcker et al list some of the institutional and other factors that appear to be effectively preventing progress, including the lack of relevant skills, transaction costs and organizational inertia, unwillingness to write off the capital sunk in old technologies, discriminatory financial criteria, split incentives (so that the benefits of an action do not accrue to the person bearing the cost), distorted prices, lack of organizational time (so that one large project can be easier to manage than many little projects, even though the little projects might offer greater gains overall), obsolete regulatory requirements and inappropriate reward schemes (utilities, for example, are rewarded for selling more energy or resources, so have an incentive to promote inefficiency).

TECHNOLOGY AND THE CONTROL OF ENVIRONMENTAL HAZARDS

Many of the currently available environmental technologies were developed during the 1960s and 1970s in response to increasing regulatory pressure, which was in turn based on growing awareness of the damage that pollution (discharges of gas and liquid in particular) could do to local air and water quality. Most of them resulted from the application of traditional separation processes to waste gases and liquids. Gases were scrubbed with appropriate solvents to remove undesirable materials. Dust was removed by filtration, centrifugation or precipitation. Liquids were cleaned up by distillation, liquid extraction processes or by the precipitation of undesirable dissolved solids. Biological waste water treatment plants were used to convert organic material to carbon dioxide, water and so on. In many cases dilution or dispersion of existing waste was the preferred solution. Stack heights were increased and pipelines were extended out to sea or into deeper or faster flowing water.

It gradually became apparent, however, that the standard methods of treating effluents left significant residual problems. Much of the treatment basically involved a simple transfer of the material from one medium to another. When effluent gases were scrubbed with solvent, the clean gas could be discharged but the contaminated solvent remained. This would then require further treatment, which might involve either some form of water treatment plant or perhaps incineration. The former process could involve the incidental evaporation of volatile material from the liquid into the atmosphere, while the latter, particularly at the relatively low temperatures that were used in the early days, could involve the discharge of highly toxic dioxins and other pollutants into the atmosphere. Either method would usually result in the generation of solid waste which could be contaminated with residual toxic materials and which would still present a disposal problem.

It also became clear that dilution and dispersion was not a satisfactory solution, with the growing recognition that long-term exposures even to low levels of pollutants could damage the environment. There was increasing evidence of acid deposition with its transnational impact on buildings and forests. Many industrialized countries started to become aware of problems with their ground water quality, and there was also evidence of accumulation of toxic material in many marine environments, with associated biological impacts. Baas et al (1990), for example, reviewed the additional problems that can arise when a number of countries share a common waste sink, in this case the North Sea which receives the discharges from a large number of different national sources. They concluded that a twin track approach was required, and that this would involve both promoting cleaner production across Europe and designating the North Sea an 'environmental clean-up demonstration area' in order to focus sufficient attention on this common problem.

The dilution/dispersion approach also stored up problems for industry. As environmental standards rise over time (which they generally do), the acceptable levels of discharge are progressively reduced, thus causing treatment costs to escalate (Clift, 1995). The basic principles of thermodynamics mean that the cost of separation, for example, starts to increase exponentially at low concentrations. It may be relatively easy to remove 90 per cent of a contaminant, for example, but much harder to remove 99 per cent, and very hard indeed to remove 99.9 per cent. Translated into economic terms, a distillation column designed to extract 99.9 per cent of a material could (depending on equilibrium relationships) be perhaps ten times more expensive than a column which achieved 99.0 per cent extraction. The same underlying relationship between thermodynamics and economics explains why it would cost about $50 per kilowatt to remove 70 per cent of the SO_2 from coal fired generating station effluent gases, $2200 per kilowatt to remove 95 per cent of the SO_2, and $4270 per kilowatt to remove 99.9 per cent of the SO_2 (Commoner, 1994).

The dilution/dispersion approach also appeared to fail to achieve the desired results, and concern about levels of pollution has continued to rise. A number of local and national environmental issues started to become more pressing during the 1970s and 1980s. Many authorities started to feel that, however defined, the limits of assimilative capacity were being reached and exceeded in many cases. There was growing concern about acid deposition and leachate. Several nations started to experience problems with landfill as a disposal option; existing sites were starting to reach capacity and it was becoming increasingly difficult to find new sites. Opposition to waste incinerators became particularly intense following fears about dioxin discharges. Some firms began to be concerned about whether their waste disposal routes would be secure, especially in the longer term. Toxic waste became an internationally traded commodity as firms and city authorities tried to find a country somewhere that was prepared to accept their waste for burial. Some firms started to export their waste to developing nations for landfill via unscrupulous operators who were prepared to relabel drums of toxic waste and give assurances that they contained only inert material.

In addition, what were previously seen as essentially local pollution issues came to be regarded as instances of globally unsustainable trends and changes. Global warming and ozone depletion, for example, are now acknowledged to be truly global issues, which have elevated environmental concern to a new and unprecedented level of political significance. The majority of the nations of the world sent their heads of state to the Earth Summit in Rio de Janeiro in 1992, indicating the level of political attention now being given to these matters.

THE TRANSITION TO CLEANER TECHNOLOGY

The concept of cleaner production arose out of these combined demands for pollution-free, resource-efficient and sustainable modes of production (Huisingh, 1990). A number of partly interlocking considerations tended to favour the idea of waste minimization at source, and changes to industrial processes to improve resource efficiency, as an alternative to conventional control strategies of capture (or dispersal) of emissions and wastes generated by industrial activities.

In particular, during the 1970s and 1980s, three factors led to a gradual evolution in approach to the control of pollution:

- The established procedures for dealing with waste were becoming increasingly difficult and costly.
- The number of pressing environmental issues and problems was growing, which was starting to generate increasing pressure on firms and governments.
- Public awareness and concern was also growing, and the public debate was becoming increasingly sophisticated, which was making a number of previously acceptable and established 'solutions' increasingly untenable.

These factors led to a fundamental reappraisal of existing practice, which initiated a paradigm shift in environmental management thinking (Hirschorn et al, 1993). It had gradually become apparent that innovative pollution prevention strategies, involving elimination of problems at source or minimization of the output of pollution, could be a viable and attractive alternative to the increasingly costly pollution abatement technology.

The new emphasis on pollution prevention also reflected growing concern about how to control the increasing number of diffuse, non-point sources of environmental hazards. Industry started to become more aware, for example, of fugitive and other previously unrecorded emissions. Some of the findings, however, broadened the focus beyond the factory itself. The main source of heavy metals in sewage treatment plants in the UK, for example, proved to be the storm drains that received the water running off roads and hard standings for vehicles (which would thus carry the used sump oil, brake fluid and so on leaking from vehicles), rather than manufacturing or process plants. Thus transport was an example of a source of environmental damage that could not be remedied by pollution abatement technology alone. Similarly, one of the main sources of nitrates in aquifers proved to be agriculture, partly as a result of the ploughing-up of grassland during and after the last world war in order to plant crops which released stored nitrates to start migrating towards the water table, and partly as a result of a progressive increase over the post-war years in the use of nitrogenous fertilizer, with an attendant increase in fertilizer run-off. So this problem also proved to have extensive multiple sources, and to be beyond the reach of any one pollution abatement technology.

Thus it started to become apparent that pollution was no longer exclusively – or even primarily – a phenomenon related to industrial production alone. It was increasingly acknowledged that every stage of the production cycle (extraction, refining, processing, manufacture, consumption, degradation and dispersion (Van Weenen, 1990 p155)) added to the total environmental burden. The demand for improved environmental performance, therefore, expanded to require a review of every stage of the production cycle. This then started to fuse with the growing concern about the finite nature of most natural resources. Thus general environmental concern, initially focused on the elimination of the various threats from pollution, was increasingly subsumed into a much wider debate about sustainability and sustainable development.

The search for cleaner production may therefore call for an assessment of the entire life cycle of a product, addressing resource extraction, every stage of production, to final use and waste disposal. Within this, cleaner *technology* is understood to refer more specifically to the changes which are made to the production process in order to meet the necessary condition of pollution prevention, which in turn represents one stage in the progress towards the desirable objective of cleaner *production*. As 100 per cent energy or resource-conversion efficiency is thermodynamically impossible, no process can be defined as absolutely 'clean' and the concept is usually expressed relatively, in terms of 'cleaner' technology.

Cleaner technology, however, is still a very broad concept, used generally to describe the entire range of responses by firms to the need to prevent or reduce the generation of environmentally hazardous material. There is at least a basic consensus that if an action is to be called 'cleaner technology', it must involve improving overall energy and resource-use efficiency, typically by minimizing or eliminating wastes at source or by using them as inputs into other processes. This can be contrasted with the traditional 'end-of-pipe' approach to the control of environmental hazards, in which the production process remains unchanged, and the waste streams it generates are processed before they are released into the environment. The end-of-pipe approach is, typically, addressed primarily to local pollution control rather than to overall energy and resource-use efficiency. Cleaner technology, by contrast, seeks to reduce environmental impact by eliminating rather than by detoxifying or diluting waste streams.

This still leaves room for a great deal of debate as to which solutions and techniques should be called cleaner technology. The UK Department of Trade and Industry (DTI), for example, has tended to see the search for cleaner technology primarily in terms of new and innovative engineering solutions, which might, for example, emerge from research and development into fundamentally cleaner technologies. In practice, however, many cleaner solutions only involve the application of already known technologies, and may often simply require the reorganization of production processes without the introduction of any new technology at all (Remmen, 1995). Thus cleaner technology has to be seen as an approach rather than a specific type of solution.

The production process, of course, is still crucial, as it is the point within which most *resource transformations* take place. These transformations – defined as the processes by which natural resources are converted into useful products – are usually accompanied by the intensive use of energy, and the generation of both unsaleable by-products and residual raw material so contaminated as to render it no longer commercially valuable, both of which represent waste.

Jackson (1993a) points out that the concept of cleaner production is based on three principles:

- precaution (assume reasonable worst case scenarios);
- prevention (look at the production process as a whole and eliminate as many areas of potential risk as possible); and
- integration (protect the environment across all areas of activity by factoring it in to all decisions).

The search for cleaner production may thus involve two elements:

- increasing resource-use efficiency and reducing material flows; and
- substituting less hazardous materials where possible.

The goal is to handle *smaller quantities* of *less hazardous* materials. Jackson notes that substitution is often a better option than recycling for particularly hazardous materials, as it is impossible to eliminate all risk of leakage or contamination. The goal is not 100 per cent elimination of all hazardous materials – which would be unrealistic, and might prove counterproductive (as most materials can be hazardous in the wrong circumstances) – but to remove wherever possible the most generally dangerous elements and compounds.

Resource-use efficiency can be achieved both within and beyond the firm. Production processes can be improved by eliminating leaks and spills, closing internal materials loops and upgrading plant and equipment. Product cycles can be made more efficient by reusing, reconditioning and recycling products. Consumption patterns can be reformed by designing for longer service life, or for disassembly, with sub-components then being streamed for refurbishing and reuse or recycling.

There are limits, of course, to the extent to which it is possible to improve efficiency in this way; improvements in efficiency at one point in the system are often only achieved at the expense of an increase in the total consumption of resources at another point (recycling, for example, consumes energy).

A variety of definitions of cleaner technology have been advanced in this debate. Despite some minor differences in emphasis and (in particular) scope,[7] cleaner technology responses can be seen as including:

- changes in processing techniques which result in a reduction in the use of raw materials;
- changes in processing techniques which result in a substitution of environmentally hazardous by less hazardous process materials;
- changes in operating systems and processing techniques which result in a reduction in either the environmental toxicity or volume of waste streams; and
- process energy integration which results in more efficient use of energy (eg 'pinch' technology).

Similarly, a recent report for the EU states that 'cleaner technology is the conceptual and procedural approach to the development, purchase, and use of processes and products preventing and reducing internal and external environmental problems throughout a product's life cycle by integrating options to:

- minimize volumes and hazards of gaseous, liquid and solid wastes;
- minimize the risk of accidents involving chemicals and processes;
- minimize consumption of raw materials, water, and energy; and to
- use substitute chemicals and processes less hazardous to human and ecological health.' (Rendan, 1994 p2)

Zwetsloot (1995) has broadened the scope of this discussion, arguing that cleaner production programmes are no guarantee of continued progress towards higher environmental standards, and that they must themselves form part of a larger commitment to systemic environmental management. Zwetsloot also suggests that the most relevant lessons are frequently those learned in quality management issues and in the management of working conditions.[8] Jackson has extended this argument further by pointing out that, broad though the above definitions are, the term clean production is still used largely in a fairly technical, goal-oriented context, and cannot therefore by itself provide answers to questions about some of the wider technological, economic and social choices that are at least equally important. It is important, therefore, to continue to see clean production as a part of a wider process of social change.

Table 1.1 identifies the characteristics of various, increasingly comprehensive, responses to environmental pressure. These responses are located on a spectrum that ranges from traditional (eg end-of-pipe) pollution control to a comprehensive societal review of the entire production chain, thus integrating across the range of technical, managerial and social options, and locating all responses in a single matrix.

Some technological responses to environmental pressure nevertheless remain difficult to classify. In particular, not everyone agrees that *external reuse and recycling* – which involves sending material on to another firm or into another

Table 1.1 *Elements of various (increasingly comprehensive) environmental responses*

	Best available technology BAT/BPT	Clean(er) technologies	Pollution prevention and waste reduction	Cleaner production
Pollution control	x			
Prevention		x	x	x
Technological	x	x	x	x
Non-technical			x	x
Process oriented		x		x
Product oriented			x	x
Strategic management			x	x
Society oriented				x

Source: adapted from Baas, 1996 p216

process for utilization – are really cleaner options.[9] Some have argued, for example, that external reuse reduces the pressure on firms to address problems at source. These arguments tend to be inconsistent, however, for three reasons:

- Internal reuse and recycling is universally regarded as mainstream cleaner technology, which makes it difficult to argue that external reuse and recycling should not be seen in this way. Why should the (often circumstantial) question of the boundaries of firm ownership determine whether a process is considered 'clean'?
- If a market is found for a material which would otherwise have to be treated and dumped, then (a) the environmental impact associated with the disposal of the waste is reduced and (b) there will a reduction in the demand for the raw material for which the waste is being substituted, which means that there will be a reduction in the environmental impact associated with the supply of the raw material.
- The concept of industrial ecology, itself a significant extension of current models of cleaner technology, largely revolves around the attempt to find secondary recycling opportunities for every material for which primary recycling is inappropriate.

It may be important, here, to distinguish between different kinds of external reuse and recycling, as some of the criticisms are more valid than others. It would be possible, for example, to count the incineration of hazardous waste in an incinerator run by another firm as a case of external reuse provided that the incinerator was being used as, say, a source of energy.[10] Many would not, however, regard this as a cleaner technology response. The issue is whether the overall balance of energy and resource use and waste creation of the set of activities is improved and whether such a route holds out the prospects of further improvements in future.

FACTORS PROMOTING AND IMPEDING THE ADOPTION OF CLEANER TECHNOLOGY

The rhetoric of cleaner technology mainly paints a very positive picture of how industrial economies can be more environmentally sustainable. There is a growing body of supportive case studies. Many of these are associated with particular public initiatives, however, and have been carried out by people closely associated with these programmes. This book subjects the concept of cleaner technology to an independent and perhaps more critical appraisal. We seek to explore the reality of cleaner technology implementation, and in particular to address the key factors promoting or discouraging its adoption. One key question, as noted in the introduction, stands out above all: Given that cleaner technology apparently offers such a range of seemingly attractive and readily attainable benefits, why are not more businesses spontaneously initiating such improvements? Why, in fact, do many companies still treat pressures to improve the environment as a potential cost which should be avoided if at all possible?

Clearly, there is substantial support for the idea that clean technology does indeed represent a win–win scenario, offering cost savings as well as reduced environmental burdens. There is a growing body of case-study material which supports such a view. The Centre for the Exploitation of Science and Technology studies (1995a, b) of the Aire and Calder Project (one of the most extensively studied waste minimization projects in the UK), for example, revealed that the 11 participating companies were able to identify some 671 resource saving measures, which reduced the total volume of discharges to the river by 36,000 cubic metres, to sewer by 623,394 cubic metres, to landfill by 4842 tonnes and to air by 30 tonnes, and generated some £3,350,000 in direct savings in the first two years of the project. Some two-thirds of these identified financial savings resulted directly from reductions in input use. Some of the measures could be adopted at very low cost, and the majority had short payback periods. Good housekeeping measures (simple improvements in basic practice) generated about 40 per cent of the savings and reuse of previous waste material accounted for a further 12 per cent, while technical modifications generated some 42 per cent. These findings of course, bring us back to the paradox of why the companies involved had not implemented some of these improvements before the start of the project, given that 52 per cent of the savings required no technical modifications at all.

In contrast, Howes et al (1997) offer a more sceptical account of cleaner technology, pointing out that many of the advantages of cleaner technology are simply asserted in the literature without hard empirical data, and that this portrayal of clean technology as offering cheap and easy 'win–win' financial and environmental outcomes has created some unrealistic expectations. They argue that pollution prevention does not invariably pay (at least not for the company concerned), which will be a major obstacle since cost pressures are still by far the most important determinants of particular courses of action. Buriks (1989) similarly points out that the implementation of waste reduction technology may involve costs and in particular uncertainties about whether the proposed change will work or represents the most cost-effective solution and the best use of the company's money. Moreover, some industrial waste reduction technologies may present challenges to established patterns and views of industrial production and its development. This kind of radical innovation may require the development of particular management strategies, structures and technical skills within an organization (Geffen, 1995). Such factors can encourage resistance to change, including cleaner innovation, and deter many less committed firms (Buriks, 1989; Geffen, 1995). Thus many firms appear to require an initial regulatory stimulus before they will even search for cost-saving opportunities.

It is known that levels of uptake and awareness of cleaner technology vary considerably between different regions of Europe, between industrial sectors and between firms. This raises some fundamental issues. Traditional (eg neo-classical) economic theory would suggest that all firms should seek to maximize their profits by adopting cleaner innovations that offered financially beneficial improvements in resource efficiency. Assuming that people in different regions of Europe, industrial sectors and firms are equally rational, why do some take advantage of the opportunities offered by cleaner technology while others do not?

Certain national differences are clearly quite important. For example, McMeekin and Green (1994) found that the general level of understanding of clean technology in UK industry was still low. Though there did appear to be some slow movement towards a greater uptake of waste minimization and source reduction ideas, there was little awareness of the potential commercial gains. Remmen (1995), in contrast, notes the broad political consensus in Denmark on the need to move to cleaner technologies, as opposed to end-of-pipe solutions (for example the Danish Ministry of the Environment switched its policy to support cleaner technologies as far back as 1986). Despite these historical differences a clear consensus has emerged during the 1990s across Europe and beyond about the importance of pollution prevention, which represents a significant change over the last decade.

State intervention has played an important role here, not only through measures directed towards raising awareness, but also, and it appears most significantly, through direct intervention. For example, Sweeney and Mega (1996) found that compliance with regulation and the requirements of grant aid for restructuring had been the primary determinants to date of environmental responses in Ireland. Similarly, Conway and Steward's (1998) comparative study of environmental innovation in the UK and Germany pointed to the importance of regulation (of products and processes), particularly in Germany where environmental requirements were institutionalized to a much greater extent. This draws attention to international differences in the content and manner of enforcement of regulation. For example, much environmental regulation has explicitly or implicitly been focused upon remediation and treatment technologies rather than pollution prevention technologies (Geffen, 1995, in the case of the US).

Furthermore, industry is not homogeneous, and firms can respond in a very wide variety of ways to regulatory pressures and public concerns (Howes et al,

1997).[11] For example, some firms tend to react defensively to change, while others will adopt a more proactive response (Fischer and Schot, 1993). Where some firms seek specific solutions to environmental problems, others will attempt a more profound assessment of their products and operations, and will consider more radical or otherwise cleaner technological solutions.

This highlights the extent to which the actual response of the individual firm is shaped by an internal array of social, economic and technical factors. There may be a degree of inertia to be overcome before firms will switch into new development paths (Duncan, 1996). Regulation may play a role in stimulating a reassessment of current activities and methods of operating. On the other hand, regulation can sometimes encourage the adoption of traditional environmental control strategies. Some have therefore suggested that cleaner innovation may best be promoted by focusing on the core business and technical innovation strategies of the firm, rather than on environmental compliance (Zwetsloot, 1995; Geffen, 1995).

One of the key organizational factors addressed in the literature concerns firm size and structure. Some have pointed to a growing divide between large and small companies, suggesting that many large companies are now becoming more environmentally proactive, moving to implement environmental management systems, more ready to perceive common interests, and more willing to move into partnership arrangements with other firms, regulatory bodies and others to help to resolve problems. In contrast, small and medium sized enterprises (SMEs) are generally seen as less likely to be proactive, to implement environmental management systems or to participate in wider schemes, for example in waste management (Howes et al, 1997).

This appears to be because many SMEs have limited technical and financial resources, and just do not have the expertise or the spare management time to look beyond their immediate horizons and examine the scope for improved practice (Partidario, 1997). Even in Denmark (a relatively advanced state in this regard) many SMEs were found to lack the information and understanding of material flows needed to carry out even basic environmental audits (Christensen and Nielsen, 1993).[12] This has important policy implications since some 99.8 per cent of all companies (and 80 per cent of industrial firms) in Europe are SMEs, and they account for 66 per cent of total employment and 65 per cent of total business turnover (Partidario, 1997).

THE RESEARCH PROJECT

Numerous successful cases of cleaner technology adoption point to the potential of cleaner technology, particularly in certain regions and sectors. However this unevenness in uptake points to the existence of barriers to implementation. Progress in implementing cleaner technologies in countries such as Denmark and The Netherlands indicates the importance of regulation and public policy initiatives directed towards this goal. However cleaner innovation is neither uniformly adopted in, nor restricted to, these countries. This underlines the complex range of factors shaping corporate decision-making over industrial processes and environmental responses.

If we wish to assess and unlock the potential of cleaner technology, therefore, one key task is to identify the social and economic factors that might encourage or obstruct the development and uptake of cleaner technologies. One way to explore these factors is by examining systematic differences in firm behaviour between sectors and regions, while keeping other factors (such as the function of the firms) as similar as possible. Such a comparative study would allow us to contrast the culture, strategies, attitudes and responses of otherwise similar firms in different regional and national settings, and examine the effects of these factors on the process of decision-making in the firm.

This study was conceived from the outset as an interdisciplinary research project. Expertise in assessing the environmental impact of industrial operations was combined with expertise in socio-economic analysis of technology. The primarily technical focus of the former was combined with the theoretical and policy insights of the latter (drawing especially upon studies of technological innovation and of the implementation of new technologies within organizations). This research, particularly from the *social shaping of technology* perspective, provided valuable concepts for understanding the detailed processes of innovation; the interplay between social and technical factors (indeed the 'socio-technical' character of innovation); and factors promoting and inhibiting social and technological change (Williams and Edge, 1996).[13] One finding from this research, of potential relevance to cleaner technologies, is that industrial technologies may embody features from the context in which they emerged, such as the research and development laboratory, and may need to be further innovated and adapted to fit them to the particular circumstances and requirements of industrial users (Fleck et al, 1990). This suggested two of the hypotheses explored in this study:

1   that there might be difficulties in implementing radical clean technologies arising from the efforts of suppliers or public sector research institutes; and
2   that industrial users might constitute an important reservoir of expertise relevant both to adapting external cleaner solutions and developing them in-house. A further implication concerns the need to avoid the adoption of prior conceptions of what is clean technology, that is, of the most appropriate types and most significant sources of cleaner innovation. Cleaner innovation may take different forms, and is not necessarily restricted to those developments typically promoted as exemplars of cleaner technology.

Objectives

The objectives of the study can be summarized as follows:

■   To assess the different types of environmental response and cleaner innovation and their contribution to waste minimization and resource efficiency (for example contrasting incremental improvements developed in-house with radical innovations, based perhaps upon external research and development effort); to examine the compatibility of the various technological options with the productive and commercial circumstances and policies of firms, and in this way to develop a more comprehensive understanding of the *sources of cleaner innovation.*

- To improve understanding of industrial decision-making and of *the behaviour of the firm* in relation to cleaner technologies, focusing both on the environmental responses and strategies of firms and their selection/development / adoption of particular industrial technologies, processes and practices.
- To identify the socio-economic factors affecting the adoption and dissemination of cleaner technologies, including the internal culture and strategy of the firm, its products and markets, financial and technical resources and its regional, national and global context, including competitive and regulatory pressures and public concerns.
- To explore the policy measures best able to promote the adoption of cleaner responses by identifying the barriers to and drivers of particular kinds of change.

These objectives were pursued through a tightly controlled set of case studies of firms in selected process industries in four regions of Europe (including regions with well-established clean technology programmes and policies, and regions that are less well developed in this regard). Differences between cases could be related to features of the firm, its sector and product market and its broader economic, political and regulatory context. Detailed comparison between the outcomes in different cases revealed some of the forces inhibiting and promoting the adoption of cleaner technology. In particular, the regional comparison drew attention to the range of policy instruments – from formal regulation to informal pressures – and their effects on the environmental performance of firms. This in turn pointed to some of the policy measures through which the development and adoption of cleaner technologies could be encouraged in particular settings.

These factors are summarized in Figure 1.1.

Methodology

The research programme was focused on process industries and on their liquid wastes, although the full range of resources used, wastes produced and shifts in disposal media were taken into account. Process industries were chosen because they are more homogeneous in their production processes than, for example, manufacturing industries, which makes it easier to characterize their technologies. A sample of firms was chosen from nine sectors:

- oil refining,
- petrochemicals,
- fine chemicals,

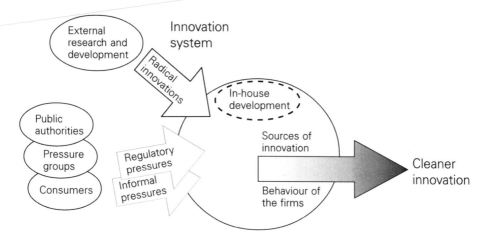

Figure 1.1 *Model of factors that may affect the adoption of cleaner responses*

- pharmaceuticals,
- dairies,
- brewing,
- sugar,
- paper mills,
- plating.

These sectors were chosen because of their economic importance and environmental significance, because there was sufficient representation of these industries in the four regions of the study to enable comparisons to be made, and because they usually generate significant flows of liquid wastes.

We chose to focus on liquid wastes because they are easier to measure than airborne effluents, because reasonably extensive and reliable records are – in general – publicly available, because there have been important recent changes in various national and EC regulations which have stimulated various reactions from industry, and because it is usually possible to make relatively clear distinctions between end-of-pipe control and cleaner technologies in regard to the treatment of liquid wastes.

The company case studies were drawn from four regions in four different EU member states: Storstrøms county (amt) in Denmark, Cork county in Ireland, the Zuidholland region in The Netherlands and Lothian region in Scotland.[14] These regions either contained or were adjacent to the cities of Roskilde, Cork, Rotterdam and Edinburgh.

THE CASE STUDIES

Eight detailed case studies were developed in each region from the selected process industries. Firms were chosen on the basis that they had introduced some significant change which had improved their environmental performance (irrespective of whether it involved cleaner technology or end-of-pipe pollution control, or whether it was motivated for environmental or commercial reasons). A few cases were included not primarily because of their intrinsic interest but to ensure that a sector was represented in a particular region – to provide a cross-match with firms in other sectors or regions, or to provide an indication of the industry norm. This allowed us to include at least three regions in each of our sectors, except the paper processing sector (which was not represented in every region) and the plating sector (which was developed in the course of the study as a reserve candidate[15]). A slightly different approach was adopted in two sectors: oil refining and brewing. Here the high level of integration of plant and the basic similarity in operations between cases created the possibility of developing a benchmark study of the overall technological configuration of a plant and its implications for environmental performance, so particular projects were addressed as part of a broader assessment of overall operations.

A total of 31 detailed case studies were made.[16] Table 1.2 shows how these broke down across the nine sectors and four regions. The cases have been anonymized, here and in the chapters that follow.

DATA COLLECTION

The empirical research involved four phases:

1   Background enquiries and screening surveys to select firms for detailed study.
2   Detailed case studies based on company-level interviews to elicit the general corporate position on environmental issues, and to explicate the decision-making processes in relation to production processes and environmental responses. This also included the identification of recent projects affecting the firm's environmental performance and selection of one for detailed study.
3   Detailed studies of selected projects, focusing on the factors shaping the choice of techniques and technologies.
4   A study of the regional and sectoral context of each case.

The detailed company case studies (phase 2 and 3) included several series of semi-structured interviews with managers with responsibility for environmental performance, managers and technologists in research and development and production, and senior managers, as appropriate. Information from both internal and external sources was collected over a period of some 20 months.

Phase 2 interviews and data collection focused on such issues as:

■   detailed information on the commercial and environmental performance of the firm, its products and markets;
■   the history of the selected firm, with particular reference to its environmental behaviour and its choice of industrial processes;

Table 1.2 *The case studies and their distribution by country and sector*

Sector	Country	Case study (anonymized)
Refining	Denmark	DK Refinery 1
	Denmark	DK Refinery 2
	Ireland	IRL Refinery
	UK	UK Refinery
Petrochemicals	Ireland	IRL Chemicals
	The Netherlands	NL Chemicals 1
	The Netherlands	NL Chemicals 2
	UK	UK Chemicals
Fine chemicals	Denmark	DK Fine Chemicals
	Ireland	IRL Fine Chemicals
	UK	UK Fine Chemicals
Pharmaceuticals	Denmark	DK Pharmaceuticals
	Ireland	IRL Pharmaceuticals 1
	Ireland	IRL Pharmaceuticals 2
	The Netherlands	NL Pharmaceuticals
	UK	UK Pharmaceuticals
Dairy	Ireland	IRL Dairy
	The Netherlands	NL Dairy
	UK	UK Dairy
Brewing	Ireland	IRL Brewery
	The Netherlands	NL Brewery
	UK	UK Brewery
Sugar	Denmark	DK Sugar 1
	Denmark	DK Sugar Corporation[17]
	Ireland	IRL Sugar
	The Netherlands	NL Sugar
Paper	Denmark	DK Paper Mill
	UK	UK Paper Mill 1
	UK	UK Paper Mill 2
Plating	Denmark	DK Plating
	The Netherlands	NL Plating
Total = 9 sectors	Total = 4 regions	Total = 31 case studies

- detailed examination of its managerial structures, product markets, industrial processes, technologies and practices, the environmental strategies and policies of the firm;
- information was collected on recent projects within the firm that affected its environmental performance (of which one was subjected to detailed study in phase 3).

For the specific project selected for in-depth study (phase 3) we traced the sequence of events through the life of the project. The interviews sought to explicate the detailed processes of managerial decision-making and the selection/ design of technology and industrial processes. The key points included:

- The definition of the problem, and the approaches considered for resolving the problem. What factors led to the project being initiated and underpinned the general approach adopted by the firm? (These could include, for example, the adoption of end-of-pipe or cleaner responses to environmental concerns, or process enhancements adopted for other, eg commercial, reasons that improved environmental performance.)
- The identification of the objectives and decision-making criteria adopted (including financial, environmental and other assessments), the identification of outcomes, and the assessment of the extent to which the project objectives were achieved.
- The managerial division of labour and knowledge and its effects on choice and implementation of technologies and practices, the extent to which different technological solutions (with different environmental implications) were available within the industry, and the reasons for their adoption or rejection, and the sources of knowledge, ideas and expertise and of technical solutions, within the firm and beyond.

The (phase 4) study of the context of the firm involved a parallel series of semi-structured interviews with a range of relevant actors, including officials from national and local government, regulatory agencies, and trade associations and industry research bodies, which documented the external milieu of each case and sector. The interview data was further supplemented by literature reviews and a search of databases and other sources of information on relevant technological and commercial developments.

ANALYSIS

Empirical research continued until 1996. The fieldwork was followed by a detailed process of comparative analysis, which drew also upon a broader review of the array of industrial activities, product markets, competitive dynamics, patterns of innovation and environmental response in the sector, and the range of cleaner technologies available. These sectoral studies form the main empirical basis of the book, and are included as Chapters 3–11.

There were important variations between cases, even in the same sector. These could be related both to differences in the internal context and traditions of the firm and to its broader socio-economic and regulatory setting. The empirical findings were then subjected to an overall analysis, both comparing the broad patterns that had been identified in the different sectors and comparing the overall patterns of cleaner innovation across all 31 cases as a whole.

Different types of environmental response

An important aspect of the study was to distinguish between rhetoric and industrial reality, by examining the range of types and sources of cleaner innovation, rather than restricting the scope of enquiry to some pre-defined archetype, or to those projects that were explicitly recognized as cleaner technology. A key analytical task was therefore to categorize different types of response. Thus, in responding to a given environmental challenge, a firm might choose:

- to ignore the problem and resist all pressure to change;
- to implement an end-of-pipe solution, typically based on a set of well-established control technologies for physical separation and/or neutralization of contaminant – for example a waste water treatment plant;
- to adopt cleaner innovations in its processes and practices geared (or otherwise leading) to waste minimization and increasing resource efficiency.

The range of possible cleaner responses can be classified as follows:

The range of cleaner responses

- To improve operating techniques and *working practices* and upgrade house-keeping.
- To implement *internal recycling* mechanisms to reintroduce waste materials into production processes.
- To implement *external recycling* systems to recover and sell waste materials on to another party.
- To introduce *incremental improvements* in the process technology aimed at reducing waste.
- To introduce *radical changes* in the process technology aimed at reducing waste.
- To *develop new products* or services.
- To become involved in a wider process of *product chain management*, where environmentally oriented change takes place across a number of producing and consuming firms in a supply chain.

The study then focused on two key issues affecting these choices: the process of *decision-making in the firm*, and the processes of *technological innovation* and related changes that gave rise to cleaner technologies and approaches.

2 REGULATORY FRAMEWORKS: A CROSS-NATIONAL OVERVIEW

Anthony Clayton, Børge Klemmensen and Robin Williams

INTRODUCTION

Regulation comprises one of the main influences on the environmental and related behaviour of firms. It is important to consider, therefore, how regulation – conceived in its broadest sense, to comprise not simply formal legal rules and public policies, but also the manner of its implementation, and the way that this is buttressed by a broader set of values in civil society – might be encouraging or inhibiting the adoption of cleaner or otherwise more fundamentally satisfactory solutions. The search for cleaner technology involves encouraging firms to integrate improvements in their products/processes with improvements in environmental performance. It implies a search for innovative approaches that link these two goals, although these may range in scope from small changes in working practices to the research and development of radically new production systems. How can regulation promote such innovation and better coupling between commercial and environmental considerations?

The traditional response to environmental pollution has been to use regulation to stimulate firms to change their behaviour. Various different regulatory models have developed in different countries. The relationship that has developed between regulatory authorities and industry in the majority of countries has tended to be adversarial. Industry has tended to see environmental regulation as an imposition of unnecessary costs, while some regulatory bodies have tended to see industry as recalcitrant – resisting their attempts to police environmental standards – and as a source of environmental problems rather than of solutions.

In some cases it appears that regulation can have negative effects. Rothwell (1992), for example, noted that high costs of regulatory compliance could inhibit innovation by diverting resources away from research and development. In relation to environmental regulation, a number of studies have suggested that some of our existing models of regulation may not encourage industry to take risks with the kind of technological innovation that could lead, eventually, to fundamentally cleaner solutions. There have been suggestions, for example that regulatory pressures for immediate compliance may force firms to seek short-term responses, which may take the form of known technological solutions, such as end-of-pipe waste treatment plants (Bonifant and Ratcliffe, 1994). Recognition that regulation, under certain circumstances, can have undesirable and unintended consequences, such as the further embedding of ultimately unsatisfactory solutions, has promoted interest in two key questions: the first concerns the possibility of different models of regulation and their different costs and benefits; the second follows from the observation that firms may vary in their responses to regulation (Laughlin, 1991). The outcomes of regulation, in terms of its effects on industrial performance, are not solely a product of the regulatory system but depend upon how signals from the regulatory system are taken up within the firm. This draws our attention to the interaction between regulatory pressures and corporate governance which in turn will be shaped by the internal politics of the firm, its access to technology and finance and its market situation and location in the supply chain and region (Bonifant and Ratcliffe, 1994; Holm et al, 1994).

Today, therefore, the search is for a regulatory system that provides an incentive to solve environmental problems at source. Without undermining the importance of meeting environmental standards, there have been attempts to move away from the adversarial model and the traditional concept of the regulator operating at arms-length as an environmental 'policeman', monitoring and enforcing compliance with regulatory requirements, towards models involving more collaboration between regulator and regulated firm around environmental goals (Holm and Stauning, 1994). The Danish model of local authority regulation (Larsen and Olsen, 1989) and the National Environmental Plan in The Netherlands represent interesting initiatives in this connection. The experience in Denmark and The Netherlands to date suggests that partnerships with regulators and sector-wide agreements can play a key role in enabling firms to respond more positively and constructively to regulatory pressure. Firms are encouraged to collaborate in research projects and share the benefits of the associated investments and developments by participating in formal and informal agreements to share the costs and risks of developing new and more fundamental solutions to their common environmental problems.

The cross-national and cross-regional comparative element of our investigation allows us to explore these questions in some detail in relation to four different regions within the European Union. There were important differences in the content, enforcement and context of regulation between these four regions. The research methodology revolves around comparisons between sector and region. Holding constant sectoral features (such as products, markets and production processes) leaves *regulation*, broadly conceived, as the most important difference between the regions, in terms of environmental behaviour of firms and their propensity to search for cleaner solutions.

Regulation is thus of double importance to this study; *substantively*: as the primary means whereby society seeks to change the behaviour of industry with regard to environmental, health and safety and related issues, and *methodologically*: as a key component of the regional comparative analysis. This chapter therefore seeks to elucidate the nature and operation of the regulatory agencies (and their insertion within broader underlying value systems and structures) in the four regions in the study, and to start to draw out some of their implications for the environmental responses and behaviour of firms (in particular regarding the possible contribution to the search for cleaner technology). This introduction is followed by four sections. The first examines the outcomes of regulation, both intended and unintended, on the environmental and economic performance of regulated industries, and considers the kind of regulatory system that might favour the development of innovatory cleaner approaches. The second section examines the different kinds of regulatory instrument and standards which have been adopted and their potential consequences for environmental responses (cleaner or otherwise). The third section provides a cross-national overview of the different regulatory frameworks in the regions studied. As a prelude to the comparative analysis, the fourth section seeks to characterize these different regulatory options; it develops a schema of the different approaches possible and how these may constitute particular regulatory regimes. This forces us to touch upon some broader questions about the administration of regulation, and in particular the relationship between the regulator and the wider political system.

THE OUTCOMES OF REGULATION: INNOVATION, COMPETITIVENESS AND THE BEHAVIOUR OF FIRMS

The need for state intervention

The profit motive tends to provide an incentive for firms to externalize as many of the costs of production as possible. This could mean operating with minimal environmental controls, or paying the lowest possible prices for raw materials, or avoiding liability for any wider environmental costs that the use of these materials, or the disposal of consequent waste, might entail. By transferring these costs to society, the environment or to future generations, firms may avoid meeting the full environmental costs of their activities (Clayton and Radcliffe, 1996). State intervention may thus be necessary to redress the failure of the market to protect the environment (particularly, for example, where the costs of waste disposal or raw material prices are low). The need for state intervention is most marked in relation to the potential broader and longer-term effects of industrial activities, in which players encounter the consequences of their actions only indirectly and diffusely.[1]

In principle, societal pressures may operate upon firms without the use of formal legal mechanisms enacted by government agencies. Local communities may be able to put some pressure on industry in their midst where effluent emissions are particularly unpleasant or damaging. Likewise campaigning environmental pressure groups may trigger a response in firms. Depending on the nature of a firm's market, on the visibility of its brand name, and on general public perceptions of the environmental threat posed by that industry, there may also be different levels of sensitivity about the potential for consumer boycotts of products. These effects may not simply reflect the actual hazards associated with an area of activity, but may be filtered through uneven perceptions of the level and acceptability of certain kinds of risk. For example, it would appear that industries producing traditional goods (notably the food sector, such as breweries or dairies) are widely perceived as being less environmentally hazardous than, in particular, the chemical industry, and as a result they appear to be less sensitive to public or consumer pressures about their environmental performance. In practice, however, resistance both to change and to spending money means that firms will react only a little if at all to these generalized public pressures. Most change in the environmental policy of firms comes either as a direct response to enforcement of legal requirements or as proactive anticipation of foreseeable requirements. On the other hand, public perceptions of hazard may influence the behaviour of politicians and regulators in both developing and implementing regulation.

So although growing environmental concern seems to be the underlying driver for change, this does not primarily act directly upon firms, but seems instead to operate through its effects on legislation and the implementation of regulation. Public perceptions and pressures may be an important influence, and we return to them at the end of this chapter. However, *regulation* and other kinds of public policy intervention and regulatory pressure, including the *expectation of changes in regulation*, appear to be the most immediate influences on the environmental behaviour of firms. There is, of course, a range of different policy instruments through which such regulatory pressures may be applied. There are also different approaches to the implementation of regulation. We will explore these below. Critically, some mechanisms and approaches seem to have a particular role in encouraging firms to adopt cleaner approaches rather than traditional end-of-pipe engineering control.

The impacts of regulation on innovation and competitiveness

The introduction of new regulatory requirements has typically been associated with a debate about the costs and benefits of regulation, with industry, which has to bear them, particularly worried about the technical difficulties and costs of compliance.[2] There have been particular objections to the idea of using regulation as a driver of technological change. One of the key problems in legitimating regulatory proposals has concerned their technical feasibility. These are particularly acute in relation to 'technology forcing' regulation, where improvements are required in a context where proven solutions do not yet exist or are not widely agreed (Williams, 1984). In such a situation, the uncertainties regarding both the technical feasibility of compliance and their imputed costs could be especially high. These uncertainties present particular difficulties, for industry about whether, how quickly, and at what cost regulatory requirements could be met and for regulators about how to assess these claims (Schot et al, 1994). Such approaches tend to be associated with conflict between regulators and industry (Wallace, 1995).

There has been a gradual extension in the scope and stringency of regulation (to protect consumers, workers and the environment) in most developed countries since the 1960s, reflecting growing popular concern about, and increasing knowledge of, the environmental impacts of many industrial activities which had hitherto been presumed to be 'safe' (Irwin and Hooper, 1992). However, in the harsher economic climate of the 1970s and 1980s many industries (particularly the chemical industry) mounted an aggressive counter-attack, suggesting that excessive regulation imposed undue costs on industry and was having negative effects on economic growth. In the US and the UK in particular, policy discussions began to be increasingly influenced by laissez-faire views, in a context of a resurgence of neo-liberal perspectives and growing economic globalization. Debates about the negative impacts of regulation on industry emerged in two related areas. The first concerned the potentially high costs that regulation imposes on industry and its consequences for national competitiveness, particularly in the face of growing competition from less-strictly regulated economies in the developing world. The estimates that have been advanced by regulated industries of the costs of regulatory compliance have, however, been disputed.[3] The second and perhaps more far-reaching argument was that regulation could make firms more risk averse and inhibit innovation by diverting investment from new product and process development (Irwin and Hooper, 1992). An influential OECD report (1985) argued that excessive regulation could indeed hinder economic development by increasing the financial and other risks of innovation, creating uncertainties for developers, and adding to the delay between expenditure on research and development and getting commercial returns from successful product launch. This could inhibit technological innovation and thereby undermine longer-term competitiveness and growth (Rothwell, 1992).

Although the critique of regulation has been strongly voiced, a number of studies have argued that the relationship between regulation, competitiveness and innovation is rather more complex than this critique suggests. For example environmental regulation can itself become a key competitive factor, creating new markets and new opportunities to make profits (OECD, 1985). Regulation also shapes markets and may favour some players, able to meet particular regulatory requirements, over others (Bonifant and Ratcliffe, 1994; Howes et al, 1997). The presumption that there is a zero-sum game between environmental improvement and economic development has come under increasing criticism. In particular, Porter and van der Linde's (1995) influential account argues that:

> *Properly designed environmental standards can trigger innovations that lower the total cost of a product or improve its value. Such innovations allow companies to use a range of inputs more productively – from raw materials to energy to labor – thus offsetting the costs of improving environmental impact and ending the stalemate. Ultimately, this enhanced* resource productivity *makes companies more competitive, not less.*

This suggests that the key to such win–win scenarios is regulation that enables better coupling between environmental protection and resource use. As discussed in the previous chapter, cleaner innovation can encompass a range of solutions, from small changes in working practices, to more far-reaching innovations such as the research and development of radical new process technologies, or the redesign of production systems. Innovation, geared towards improving resource efficiency or waste minimization, can thus result in improved industrial competitiveness. This view therefore calls into question traditional presumptions about the tension between wealth creation and the environment, and between risk and profit, and holds out the possibility of a virtuous circle of improved resource efficiency, competitiveness and environmental improvement.

From this perspective, regulation needs to promote improved environmental responses in a way which encourages (or at least does not stifle) industrial innovation, and shapes it in the direction of greater resource efficiency. In a context where organizational inertia and other factors constitute a barrier to innovation within firms, the question arises of whether regulatory pressure could even be an important stimulus for change. The challenge, therefore, is to design ways of applying regulatory and public policy pressures in a way which encourages innovation geared towards improvements in the efficient use of resource *and* reduced environmental impact.

Considering these points, Holm and Stauning (1994) have noted that the traditional 'policing' approach to industrial regulation has not been very successful in promoting pollution prevention. They argue that the emphasis must shift to policies to stimulate a more positive, proactive response by firms, engaging them in the search for solutions. They, and a number of other writers, broadly agree around three features that may be important in regulatory regimes for cleaner innovation:

1 The need to stimulate and harness the firm's capacity for innovation encouraging them to search for and implement cleaner solutions. In order to mobilize tendencies within industry, it is important to pay attention to ongoing *processes of innovation* and encourage *positive self-regulatory tendencies* (Holm and Stauning, 1994; Holm et al, 1994; Cramer et al, 1994). This is perhaps the sine qua non. However, this aim has other implications for the regulatory setting.
2 The importance of dialogue between firms and government, both to solve problems and to ensure that cleaner solutions may be more generally disseminated and adopted. Critically, such dialogue may allow firms to disclose important information about their operations to regulators and in turn allow regulators to utilize the expertise and innovative ability of industry in formulating solutions. Joint-problem solving may thus avoid a key difficulty with 'technology-forcing' regulations (ie that promote change in situations where technical solutions are not well-established) – that the regulator is not well-placed to subject to critical scrutiny claims by industry about the economic or technical unfeasibility of change. However such a cooperative relationship would be hard to maintain under the adversarial model of regulatory enforcement, but would instead depend upon the development of a high degree of trust between firms and regulators (Wallace, 1995).
3 The need for regulatory pressures that can provide a consistent incentive for improvement within firms. An important part of this would be policy and

regulatory *stability*. Instability in the regulatory environment creates serious risks for industry, for example if it promotes investments by firms that are subsequently revealed as inappropriate, or where industry faces additional costs from the need to meet new and unanticipated regulatory requirements. Policy stability, conversely, reduces these risks and costs (Johnston, 1992). It would also seem to be an important prerequisite for developing dialogue and high-trust relations between firms and regulators. (Wallace, 1995).

What is implied is a shift in the mode of regulation, from seeing it as an external force compelling firms to adopt certain behaviours, to seeing it as promoting and reinforcing a shift in the internal climate and perspectives of the firm (leading to a culture in which environmental goals are intrinsic and linked to competitive goals). From such a perspective, one important role of the regulator may be in promoting and organizing exchanges of information amongst firms and between firms and other sources of knowledge such as research and advisory bodies and regulators themselves (Johnston, 1992; Allen, 1994; Cramer et al, 1994).

The complex and diverse outcomes (planned and unintended) of regulatory actions suggest that regulatory measures need to be carefully considered. Moreover, the outcomes of regulation are never just a product of the content of regulation but depend on the way in which it is implemented, and the social, economic and technological setting of the regulated firm/industry. One of the key concerns of this study is to explicate these complex relationships. We will explore this further, below, starting by examining some of the possible instruments that have been adopted for environmental regulation.

POLICY INSTRUMENTS

We can distinguish three main types of policy instrument for regulating and shaping the environmental behaviour of industry (Baas et al, 1990, p12):

1 **Direct regulation**, in which the firm's consent or permit to operate depends on meeting environmental standards. These standards may be set as *compliance standards*, setting out permissible levels of substances in the firm's discharges or as *procedural standards*, for example, requiring a firm to adopt best practice, or as a combination of these two.
2 **Voluntary instruments**, such as the covenants used in The Netherlands, in which firms are enrolled in an interactive dialogue with regulators, and emphasis is given to the sharing and dissemination of expertise.
3 **Economic instruments**, such as waste taxes or subsidies which shift the financial calculations of firms towards environmentally beneficial approaches.

In practice, varying combinations of all three types of instrument are typical, but direct regulation has so far been predominant. We will briefly discuss each in turn.

Direct regulation

Historically, one of the first areas of state intervention in industrial activities was direct regulation of industrial hazards, based on the premise that the state should intervene directly to set standards for the environmental behaviour of firms, dating back to the early 19th century factories legislation. This presupposes direct, purposive control by the state. The first such regulations stipulated the particular precautions to be followed in certain (highly polluting) industrial activities. For example, the 1864 Alkali Act in Britain required the use of scrubbers for acid gaseous emissions and tall chimneys to effect dilution of emissions. Such *prescriptive standards* were largely superseded over the last century by *compliance standards*, which set limits for the emission of environmentally damaging substances. Compliance standards, by focusing on the outcomes of industrial activities and their attendant risks, left it largely to the regulated firm to determine how to meet regulatory requirements. The state therefore did not need to become engaged with industry's choice of production and control methods. Compliance standards thus provided a more rapid and flexible method of implementing regulation than prescriptive standards. They proved better able to cope with continuing changes in industrial and control technologies and the accelerating rate of technological development, and have been increasingly adopted in the 20th century. However, recently, regulators have again become interested in going beyond this narrow model of regulating outcomes (eg through emission limits), seeking instead to influence directly the behaviour, and environmental performance, of the firm in particular kinds of ways. This has seen the increasing adoption of procedural *standards*, which seek to promote specific kinds of change in the firm. The difference from earlier prescriptive regulations is that procedural standards today more usually take the form of general duties on the firm and its members to pursue certain goals. In relation to the environment this typically takes the form of a requirement to adopt what is perceived as best practice or best available technology.

Compliance standards and effluent limits

The need to protect ecosystems (and human health) has meant that much environmental regulation has focused on setting legal limits for the discharge of harmful substances. This type of regulation can be implemented in a variety of ways. First, discharge limits for liquid effluents may be set as absolute amounts of contaminant leaving the site in the waste stream. Second, the limits may be set as concentrations relative to the diluting capacity of the water body (ie concentrations that will arise after the waste is diluted by the recipient water body). This difference is sometimes described as being between 'source oriented' and 'recipient oriented' regulations, since in the latter case the standard is set relative to the carrying capacity of the recipient waterway. Third, in some instances regulation of discharge levels will not be by setting particular maximum limits, but will be through applying charges according to the level of discharges, on the polluter pays principle.

Source- and recipient- oriented standards represent different philosophies and strategies for hazard control. Emission standards are defined in relation to the toxicity of specific substances. However, different environments have varying abilities to absorb different kinds of waste. There has been a debate about the extent to which these abilities should be exploited. Some regulatory bodies took the view that permissible levels of pollution should be defined in terms of the *assimilative capacity* of or *critical load* for the recipient environment. The need for such recipient-oriented approaches seemed perhaps self-evident in the initial stages of regulation, when there was a concern with the acute (ie immediate, local) effects of pollution, and have prevailed until recently in the UK and Ireland. However with growing understanding of the effects of low-level pollution and global pollution issues there has been a shift, notably in countries such as The Netherlands, Germany and Denmark, towards an alternative approach based on the *precautionary principle*. The presumption is that the default option should always be to avoid environmental damage, especially where there is uncertainty as to the extent of the environmental impact (Baas, 1996).

Because 'recipient-oriented' regulations take into account effluent dilution and the carrying capacity of the disposal medium, regulatory pressures will fall unevenly. This means that the firm's location becomes critical. A manufacturing operation that happened to be situated beside, and discharge into, a major estuary with a large dilution capacity might thus be under far less pressure than an otherwise identical firm that happened to be situated beside, and discharge into, a small stream or enclosed waterway.[4]

One of the most important historical regulatory differences between the regions studied has been between those setting absolute, 'source oriented' and relative, 'recipient oriented' standards. As indicated above, the difference is particularly significant for industries in estuarine locations where large diluting capacity allowed relatively large waste discharges under recipient standards. As we see below, European Community harmonization of regulations has prompted a shift towards absolute limits, requiring firms in these regions to move rather quickly to meet the stricter standards that have been applied elsewhere (reflecting either precautionary regulatory standards or recipient-oriented standards in more enclosed waterways).

Compliance standards are concerned only to set maximum levels (whether absolute or relative) for substances discharged, not how those discharge levels are achieved. They are geared to achieving some change in the behaviour of firms that exceed the limits (assuming that the limits are actually enforced). Compliance standards do not, per se, prioritize waste reduction over end-of-pipe controls. However, where regulation demands rapid improvement in effluent quality, there can be pressure to adopt end-of-pipe solutions because they can be implemented relatively quickly, offer apparently straightforward and reliable generic solutions, and do not require (potentially uncertain and disruptive) changes to industrial processes.

Procedural standards, the promotion of best practice, and the transfer of expertise

Where environmental problems and solutions are well known, the role of regulators can be simply to police emission standards and ensure that they are met. However, underpinning the principle of cleaner technology is the notion that some ways of meeting environmental goals may be more beneficial and desirable than others. This may suggest the need to go beyond simply regulating the outcomes of industrial activities to seeking to influence the way in which those activities are conceived and carried out. Attempting to lay down the detailed methods of industrial operation in detailed legislation or regulatory codes would not be feasible on a wide scale, given the diversity and rate of change in industrial processes today. The effort of monitoring and assessing industrial activities would be enormous, though systems of licensing, particularly for hazardous activities, do go some way in this direction. More generally, therefore, we see such goals pursued by imposing general regulatory requirements and duties, with which organizations and their members must then comply. In relation to the environment this has often taken the form of requirements to use Best Available Technology (see below).

Determining whether such general requirements have been met clearly involves an important task of interpretation. How can it be established (and agreed between firm and regulator) that a particular solution does indeed constitute 'best practice'? To overcome this, regulators may issue generic guidelines about best practice in an industry. At the end of the day, however, much will depend upon expert judgement.

Compared to emission standards, monitoring compliance with best practice procedural standards requires much more extensive communication between regulator and regulated firms. This may also mandate in favour of a shift in the relationship between regulator and firm from adversarial confrontation to cooperation. Indeed what may be needed is a joint problem solving approach, particularly where there are uncertainties about how to define and implement best practice. This is because the regulator can, under such circumstances, be an important resource for the firm, helping it to comply by acting as a source of guidance on best practice, and a conduit to other sources of expertise. This is significantly different from the conventional arms-length policing role, in which the regulator simply enforces certain standards of environmental performance by a firm. Equally, for the regulator, the firm can then become an important source of specialist expertise and experience about what approaches are possible in practice and their costs and benefits. Regulatory relationships of this nature, which are based on guiding a firm's environmental performance over a number of years – rather than setting short-term legal requirements for emission reductions – appear to enable the implementation of incremental waste minimization programmes, facilitate fundamental reappraisal of all aspects of the business, and allow capital investments in cleaner plant to be scheduled accordingly. The Danish regulatory system, for example, favours dialogue with companies. Danish experience, as we shall see later, shows that this model has had some considerable success.

On the other hand a number of difficulties can be anticipated around the enforcement of 'best practice' procedural regulations. In some cases, the regulator might not have sufficient expertise to subject industry proposals to critical examination. A more subtle but potentially more profound problem is that the adoption of some particular notion of what currently constitutes the best available technology might well overlook the potential for innovation within the firm itself, and thus might stifle more innovative approaches and thereby suppress more satisfactory solutions (see Porter and van der Linde, 1995).

Voluntary instruments

We have already noted that, although the underlying driver of environmental improvement is growing scientific understanding and public awareness of environmental problems, regulation seems to be the most immediate motivator to change within the firm. However this is only part of the story, since the attitudes and behaviour of an organization's members may be an important influence over how it reacts to external regulatory and other pressures. The effects of internal culture can be seen in the varied ways in which otherwise apparently similar firms can react to the same external pressures, with responses that vary from resistance to regulation to conspicuous and early compliance with new requirements.

The way that environmental concerns may be taken on board within the organization is particularly significant in relation to cleaner technology, as this can involve taking strategic, financial and marketing issues as well as environmental concerns into account, which may in turn require the involvement of a broad range of organization members (such as board members, production managers, marketing and research and development staff), rather than just environmental managers. The importance of mobilizing 'self-regulatory' tendencies, therefore, and seeing these goals as intrinsic to the organization and its commercial future suggests that there may be a role for different kinds of intervention other than just direct regulation.

An important illustration here is provided by the Dutch National Environmental Policy Plans of 1989 and 1990, which provided for voluntary agreements (covenants) about environmental targets to be negotiated by groups and sectors. This initiative seems to have provided an effective way of mobilizing firms around quite challenging long-term objectives. This framework provides spaces, within which self-regulation will be adopted. However, it would be unhelpful to see this as a retreat from state regulation, but rather as a pointer to what can be achieved in a context of substantially shared agendas between regulator and industry.

We can also consider under the heading of voluntary instruments the range of national and regional public initiatives to promote increased awareness of clean technologies through advice centres, networks and clubs. In general such initiatives seem to have been very effective in enlisting involvement of industries, though improvements in environmental awareness and performance often seem to be short-lived once the initiative comes to an end. In terms of the concerns of this study such instruments seem more likely to be *facilitators* than *drivers* of improvement.

Economic instruments

Many inputs into economic processes have been historically undervalued and as a consequence have tended to be used to excess. This applies both to 'direct inputs', such as usage of raw materials and 'indirect inputs', the environment's capacity to absorb waste. For example, if producers are allowed to use low-cost waste disposal options, this will encourage them to produce more waste and pollution than they otherwise would. Additional natural resources will be appropriated, and additional pollution will be generated, which will cause some loss of amenity or perhaps more serious damage. The widespread adoption of direct regulation over industrial activities has sought to redress this area of market failure. Recently, however, there has been some debate as to whether it would be more efficient to use economic instruments to correct these market failures and thereby achieve environmental goals. Taxes on inputs, disposal charges and subsidies could be used to bridge the gap between private and social costs, and thereby correct the misallocation of resources.

Environmental taxes seem very attractive; environmental economic theory suggests they would, almost uniquely, correct an existing misallocation of resources. They are also an attractive option for the practical reason that they could be very cost-effective. Though they do not eliminate the need for monitoring and enforcement, they arguably reduce enforcement costs by making it in the economic interest of players to change their behaviour. Finally, environmental taxes should yield a positive income stream to government, whereas effective traditional regulation requires significant expenditure.

Moreover, unlike direct regulation, which motivates improvement up to the currently applicable standard, economic instruments in principle create an incentive to achieve further improvements in order to reduce costs by further reducing the use of those inputs or outputs for which a charge is incurred and thus create signals that could promote a wider reorientation of the economic system.

Experience with the development and application of economic instruments is growing (Grasl, 1997).[5] However, debates continue about their costs, benefits, effectiveness, wider impacts and political acceptability, and some doubts remain whether they really would offer a cheaper and more effective way to achieve a given social and environmental goal than direct regulation. For example environmental taxes would need to be part of a fiscally neutral redistribution of the tax burden if they were not to deflate the economy, and it would be important to ensure that they did not significantly reduce national competitiveness. Equally, economic instruments have very immediate implications for competition, as they

– even more, arguably, than direct regulations – can reshape markets to the benefit of some players (whether nations, sectors or firms) over others (Howes et al, 1997). Their immediate impacts on cost structures and the relative prospects of different industries gives them very direct social and economic significance, making it essential to maintain transparency, accountability and care when such instruments are drafted to ensure that they are not seen, for example, to have been captured by one interest at the expense of another.

In considering how to design regulatory regimes to promote cleaner innovation, the counterposition between economic and direct regulatory instruments may not be helpful. It is notable that all societies that have introduced economic instruments have used them as part of a larger package of measures, alongside direct regulatory systems. It seems likely, therefore, that environmental taxes will probably represent a very valuable addition to the range of tools for changing behaviour, but also that they are unlikely to provide a solution to all environmental problems in all circumstances (Rothwell, 1992; Howes et al, 1997).

REGULATORY FRAMEWORKS: A CROSS-NATIONAL OVERVIEW

The question of the effectiveness of regulation and of the way in which different systems generate different outcomes is, of course, of general concern. There is currently a great deal of experimentation with regulatory systems and structures: The Netherlands adopted a National Environmental Policy Plan (NEPP) in 1989 which, with amendments adopted in 1990, now informs regulatory programmes. The UK and Ireland have recently moved to adopt an Integrated Pollution Control (IPC) strategy, and are now moving to integrate previously disparate structures and control measures. Denmark and The Netherlands passed through that stage some time ago, and are now starting to make greater use of in-firm expertise in a more interactive model of regulation. The focus in Denmark is on continuous improvement, however, while the focus in The Netherlands is on the operationalization of the national plan in covenants with firms and sectors of industry. These covenants specify reduction goals and timeframes in order to deliver an equivalent process of continuous improvement.

The UK regulatory bodies, in particular, underwent significant reorganization during the course of the study. One of the most obvious features of the UK regulatory environment was, until 1996, the number of regulatory agencies. Not only were there a number of organizations, but also their areas of responsibility were divided up on a number of different bases. Some agencies were allocated responsibilities in terms of the substance involved, some in terms of the medium of disposal, and some in terms of the geographical region of responsibility. The approach that these agencies took, in terms of the frequency of inspection, severity of penalties and so on was not uniform. This created scope for some firms to switch between waste disposal media to a less stringently regulated or well-policed medium. In 1976, therefore, the fifth report of the Royal Commission on Environmental Pollution recommended that the UK move to a system of integrated pollution control. In April 1996 the UK merged a number of agencies into two integrated pollution control agencies, one for England and Wales and one for Scotland.

Thus the four countries in the study represent two different schools of thought and regulatory traditions on environmental protection issues. The approach in the UK and Ireland to the protection of surface water was, until recently, 'recipient oriented', focusing on the extent to which the recipient body of water could absorb, dilute and disperse pollution without undue harm. Standards and requirements for waste water discharged therefore varied, according to the ability of the recipient waters to cope with different types of waste. As a result the stringency of requirements would depend on plant location and the nature of the waters to which they discharged. For example, the UK petrochemical industry was mainly located on estuaries, where the enormous dilution capacity presumed for the receiving waters meant that, until recently many of these plants did not need to have sophisticated waste water treatment facilities.[6]

The Netherlands and Denmark used to work on the same basis. However, during the 1980s both countries switched to a 'source oriented' approach, based on a philosophy of reducing the environmental load, rather than allowing emissions to increase towards the threshold at which environmental harm could be detected, and influenced by concern about build up of pollutants in inland waterways and in shallow and enclosed seaboards. This approach also involved applying standards and requirements for waste water, which were usually based on a reference to 'best available technology' (BAT) – often subject to the further qualification 'not entailing excessive cost' (BATNEEC) – including requirements in some cases for clean technology or clean production systems (Larsen and Olsen, 1989), which were usually specific to an industrial sector. These technology based standards were enforced through emission limits set as concentration values but based on what is currently achievable through best practice; direct criteria for performance standards are still rare. These developments were also associated with the adoption of a more *holistic* or integrated approach to the environmental impact of a firm, so that a problem with a nitrogen surplus in the waste water, for example, could not be 'solved' by washing it out and sending it up through the chimney as NO_x.

The difference between the two groups of countries can also be seen in their relation to EU directives on environmental issues. Denmark and The Netherlands, usually with support from Germany, have generally supported or even pushed for tighter regulations for waste water. This is because they have already incorporated some of these regulations in their national legislation, and are therefore under domestic pressure from public opinion and industry (who would like to see their competitors across Europe obliged to meet similarly stringent standards) to have these national rules applied across the EU. The UK and Ireland have, by contrast, been more reluctant to countenance such changes. For example, many in the UK chemical industry saw EU standards as appropriate for inland waterways and shallow seas but not for UK estuarine waters, and thus saw the shift from recipient- to source-based standards as reflecting competitive and political exigencies rather than environmental improvement. The recent changes and general raising of standards in the UK and Ireland, the move away from the recipient-oriented strategy and the introduction of the technology based approach to waste water standards have been largely driven by the need to accommodate EU accords.

Recent developments

The change in Scotland in April 1996, which was part of a larger programme involving parallel changes in England and Wales, was to a system of comprehensive regulation based on IPC. The responsibility for administering the regulatory system was vested in the Scottish Environmental Protection Agency (SEPA), which was created from a merger of the seven River Purification Boards and Her Majesty's Industrial Pollution Inspectorate (HMIPI). SEPA also assumed control over water pollution, taking over this power from the three Island Councils, and waste regulation and air pollution control from the 53 district councils and Island Councils. This meant that virtually all significant powers in relation to the regulation of industrial pollution were vested in one organization. Part of the authority for the regulation of air pollution was retained by local government.

A parallel move was made in Ireland in July 1993. All regulation of industrial pollution in industrial sectors associated with significant environmental impacts was centralized, and authority vested in the national Environmental Protection Agency. This has gradually taken over responsibility for certain specified sectors of industry from the County and City Councils. The Environmental Protection Act determined and specified the sectors of industry to be regulated by the EPA. The non-listed sectors remained the responsibility of the County or City Councils.

Integrated approaches to environmental regulation are more established in the regulatory systems of Denmark and The Netherlands. Denmark, for example, introduced an integrated (or 'comprehensive') approach to the regulation of industry in the 1970s, and the model has been gradually evolving since then. Similar developments have taken place in The Netherlands. For example, in the 1970–1980 period new environmental regulation involved media-specific approaches, starting with the 1970 Law on Surface Water Pollution. Though media-specific approaches were still dominant at the level of Dutch regional EPAs, more integrated approaches began to emerge in the late 1980s. The National Environmental Policy Plans (NEPPs) of 1989 and 1990 involved a profound shift. They revolved around covenants – agreements based on private law – between national government and companies and/or sectoral industrial organizations about the implementation of environmental targets defined in the NEPPs. These agreements are implemented within 'target groups', covering key sectors chosen on the grounds of their environmental impact. This new approach allows the incorporation of explicitly political criteria and judgements into what were previously seen as purely technical assessments. This does not imply that some sectors can force the regulators into derogation; the idea is that companies that undertake to invest in R&D and meet more stringent targets in the future can be encouraged by allowing them temporary derogation in the interim. However, the achievements and outcomes of this policy initiative to date indicate that this may be particularly successful in encouraging a positive response from industry. A number of covenants have been developed in target industries such as the chemical industry. These include specific agreements such as the Hydrogenated Carbons-2000 Program and a covenant on the reduction of noise between the regional authorities and the regional chemical sector representatives in the Rijnmond area, as well as general provisions. In particular, the implementation of the covenant between the Ministry of Environment and the Dutch chemical industry involved the adoption of Company Environmental Action Plans by 1995. These required companies to develop 4-year programmes for improving environmental performance, with budgets allocated for activities planned in the first year and less concrete plans for longer-term developments. The plans have to be revised annually, and the firms have to have each successive plan approved by the environmental regulators. The plans allow for more integrated approaches in place of end-of-pipe solutions.[7]

This overview reveals some elements of convergence between the four countries in terms of their regulatory strategy, including their choice of legislation and key policy instruments. This is, undoubtedly, largely a result of the increased importance given to environmental issues in the EU. Environmental issues were explicitly acknowledged in the 1986 treaty, and subject to majority decision as part of the Maastricht treaty in 1992. The timing and nature of the recent changes in Ireland, Scotland and the rest of the UK, therefore, strongly suggests that they are EU-driven.

Despite some convergence across the EU in the choice of regulatory strategies and instruments, differences remain. One difference concerns the structure of regulatory apparatuses. The recent introduction of Integrated Pollution Control in Britain and Ireland has entailed restructuring the associated administrative apparatus, with the most extensive reorganization required in the UK. This was, in both cases, accompanied by a degree of centralization of decision making, control and implementation of regulation. Denmark, by contrast, has maintained a relatively decentralized system of implementation, in which the elected municipal and regional councils are the key decision making and control bodies. The Netherlands has a slightly different model: implementation is decentralized apart from the regulation of surface waters (including licensing and control of discharges), which is managed by regional Water Boards. These are state organizations, albeit organized into regional offices. Reform may be shifting in divergent directions. Moreover, despite the recent changes and the harmonization goals of EU regulation, differences still prevail between the countries (eg about the shift from recipient- to source-based standards and in particular, about the administration and implementation of waste water regulation).

Regulatory systems and their implementation and their consequences have to be understood in relation to their particular intricate histories and administrative settings. Despite these differences, the question arises of how far we can, for analytical purposes, distinguish different types or regimes of regulation.

REGIMES OF REGULATION

As already noted, the formal regulatory instruments adopted only tell us part of the story about the regulatory pressures encountered. We now consider how these different instruments may be deployed in particular regulatory regimes. First we consider the difference between 'single factor' approaches where regulation applies separately to particular materials or disposal media, and those where a holistic regulatory approach is considered. Second we consider a further distinction between regulation directed towards general environmental goals and regulation based on specific emission standards. Combining these two distinctions yields a taxonomy of regulatory regimes. We consider some implications of these different regimes, both for the relationship between regulator and industry and for the administration of regulation.

Environmental regulatory agencies have often emerged separately in relation to different media (eg water, air, land). Emission standards are typically set for particular pollutants. As a result, the regulatory regime is often enforced on a *single factor basis* (media by media and substance by substance). Arguably, such an approach is less conducive to a pollution prevention approach than a more *holistic* regulatory regime, which looks at the full range of environmental outputs of an industrial enterprise.

The second important distinction in regulatory approaches surrounds the way in which regulation is applied and whether this is through setting *general goals* for the regulated industry or setting specific standards with which the regulated firm must comply. This, coupled with the distinction already made between holistic and specific media/compound-based approaches, gives four different combinations in terms of possible regulatory regimes. This allows us to develop a more complex picture of the range of regulatory approaches and their possible implications for the implementation of cleaner technology. We will briefly explore some instances of these four broad possible types of regulatory regime.

Table 2.1 *Possible approaches to regulation of environmental performance*

	Single factor approaches Eg media/compound based	Holistic approaches
Specific environmental standards	1) Strict enforcement	3) Integrated Control
General environmental goals	4) Total load/trade-offs	2) Best practice eg BATNEEC

1 Strict enforcement

Strict enforcement represents the dominant model for environmental regulation and is often found where regulation involves emission standards; it has been historically associated with a recipient-oriented approach to environmental problems (though in principle it could also be adopted with source-oriented standards).

One of the important problems with strict enforcement is that it tends to be oriented towards the control of individual substances and/or individual media. As a result of the latter it may just result in a waste problem being displaced. For example, toxic materials captured from liquid effluent streams may end up as solid wastes that then have to be disposed of.

On the other hand, strict enforcement as a regulatory system does have a number of potential strengths. First, it is usually based upon standards set according to the toxicity of the substances in question. Second, compliance can clearly be monitored and established. These two factors have a third implication: that there is little need for the regulator to make judgements about technical feasibility or the likely commercial impacts of regulation, considerations which might be used by firms to pressurize regulators to reduce the stringency of regulation. Finally, it is left largely to the company to find a solution to the authority's request to comply with the environmental regulation. This allows the regulator to operate at arms-length, policing compliance with environmental standards. It also thus offers the prospect of a clear and uncompromised expression of a need for environmental protection. It may, however, have a key drawback, in that it can tend to lead to end-of-pipe solutions.

2 Best practice: BATNEEC

As already noted, this kind of procedural approach based on best practice (best available technology not entailing excessive cost) has become increasingly adopted. This approach is oriented towards general goals of reducing environmental impact. It may be enforced through source-oriented emission standards, set in relation to what is currently technically (BAT) or commercially (BATNEEC) feasible. Within these general best practice goals for environmental improvement, the company decides on the preferred solution from the range of economic, technically available solutions for implementing these goals. These may include conventional end-of-pipe solutions as well as waste minimization and cleaner technology approaches.

One of the problems with enforcing best practice approaches is that there can be uncertainty (and the consequent need for negotiation and scope for disputes) about what can be achieved under best practice. The idea of best practice approaches depends on collection of information about available approaches and their environmental consequences to determine the targets for the sector and/or region and establish whether firms are meeting these. Best practice models imply that regulators have relatively free access to the information needed to assess corporate proposals, and that information is exchanged within the sector about other comparable plants which could provide a benchmark or demonstrator of best practice.

This model has a number of important advantages. The best practice requirement potentially provides for a 'ratcheting-up' of standards, as what constitutes best practice is likely to improve over time with technical changes. Some have suggested that this approach may be conducive to the adoption of cleaner approaches, particularly by integrating waste minimization considerations into the choice of process technologies. In Denmark and Ireland there are further, explicit requirements to consider waste minimization possibilities in assessing best practice options.

3 Integrated response

Whilst emission standards tend to have been associated with strict enforcement of standards for specific media and materials, it is possible to apply a regulatory regime based on emission standards in a more holistic way, based on a more integrated view of the environmental impact of company activities and an understanding of the interrelated nature of environmental problems. As this comprehensive 'integrated response' is not medium-specific, it can deal with more complex changes in process which may involve some displacement of wastes between media.

Developing such an approach clearly requires some changes to the institutional structure of regulatory agencies, which have tended to be organized on a medium-by-medium basis. This could involve a softening of departmental boundaries within agencies, some sort of formal linking of different agencies, or even moving away from media-based regulatory structures by bringing all into one comprehensive environmental protection agency.

As already noted, Denmark chose this model, with integration of functions into a single comprehensive unit and corresponding organizational changes, during the 1970s. The Netherlands took a similar step with its National Environmental Policy Plans of 1989 and 1990. This was seen as part of a more general move to take more account of the interrelated character of environmental problems. Both of these countries have moved on from this position towards a source-oriented and preventative approach based on 'best practice' concepts. However, the comprehensive response mode still informs a great deal of actual practice. The recent profound organizational restructuring in the UK was addressed, primarily, to the need to bring the dispersed regulatory bodies under one command in order to move towards an integrated response model.

In contrast to best practice approaches, with an integrated response approach, the regulator generally confines their role to the implementation and enforcement of the regulatory requirements. They tend not to enter into technical and practical discussions about the changes to be made, which are left to the firm and its advisers.

4 Total load/trade-offs

The final instance of regulatory regimes is represented by a 'trade-off' model. This is a variant of strict enforcement, but one in which the regulator addresses the overall profile of emissions from a firm, and allows it to make trade-offs between different emissions oriented towards particular environmental goals. For example, the regulator could give priority to the most problematic compounds, insisting that the firm makes progress and improvements in these areas, but also accepting that some standards – for example those applied to less problematic substances – are complied with only to some extent or not at all.

This involves the regulator in deliberate environmental goal-setting, with extensive discretionary powers to determine the order and rate at which particular environmental impacts should be reduced.[8] Such discretionary powers mean that standard setting and enforcement can no longer be presented in a narrow technical role, but include an element of political judgement. This may in turn be shaped by the broader social and economic setting, and the need to take into account the economic situation of the firm and region. In the past, such regulatory discretion has come under criticism, in cases where poor environmental performance has been accepted by a regulator on the grounds of fears about the impacts of regulatory compliance on jobs or on the economic prospects of the firm. Given this concern about a 'political deficit', where the regulator might be (or be perceived to be) unduly influenced by industrial or economic considerations, it becomes important to consider issues of transparency and accountability. One way this can be achieved is through an input from elected representatives. In Denmark, this model of environmental regulation has been carried out within regional government economic planning agencies. This combination of conscious planning and discretion gives this kind of regulation an explicitly political dimension. It may well be that a purely professional state agency would not have had the political context, the public mandate or the political fora to discuss and decide on priorities and to set environmental targets and timetables.

THE ADMINISTRATION OF REGULATION: THE RELATIONSHIP BETWEEN REGULATOR, INDUSTRY AND POLITICAL APPARATUSES

These different models have important consequences for the relationship between regulator and industry, and for the administration of regulation. First we explore the requirements for greater interaction between regulator and industry as regulation moves away from the 'strict enforcement' model to more holistic regulatory regimes directed towards broader environmental goals. Then we consider the implications of these regulatory developments for the structure of regulatory agencies. Both of these are key to understanding the regulatory pressures on the firm and their possible contribution to the development of cleaner responses.

The relationship between regulator and industry

The two actors in the regional context, the firm and the regulator, are forced to communicate, even if they do not adopt a cooperative relationship. They each have a different raison d'être, and thus have quite different reasons for being involved in this relationship. Firms exist to carry out a particular business activity, and thus make money. Regulations impose various constraints on their freedom of action. The regulator is there to protect the environment and/or to provide stable conditions for business activity. There is also a lot of common ground, however, and the relationship can be mutually useful and productive under the right circumstances. The question is, therefore, how and under what circumstances can the relationship be productive? How can the firm and the regulator identify their common ground? This is particularly important in relation to cleaner technology, which takes as its starting point the need to integrate those concerns which are organic to the firm (improving industrial processes, products and performance) and the environmental goals of regulators to reduce waste emissions.

The following simple diagram (Figure 2.1) indicates some of the options for better pollution abatement and their likely outcomes. The horizontal scale distinguishes between regulation directed towards single factors (eg a particular media or environmental aspect) and more holistic approaches, and the vertical scale distinguishes whether the regulation is based on a conventional adversarial approach or is oriented towards the development of consensus between regulator and regulated.

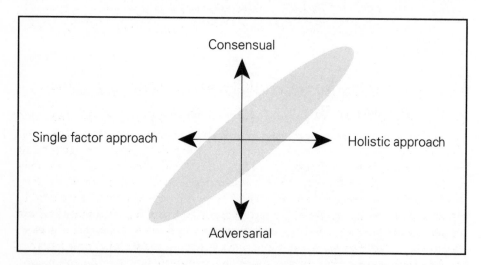

Figure 2.1 *Schema of possible regulatory approaches*

As the shading on this diagram suggests, these two dimensions may be related. Regulatory models tend to be located along a diagonal between adversarial and single factor approaches in the bottom left quadrant, and consensual holistic approaches in the top right quadrant. There is some evidence of a shift towards the latter model, away from the traditional model of strict enforcement on a single factor basis. Under strict enforcement a regulator can restrict its role to policing and enforcement, merely needing to establish that particular environmental standards had been adhered to on a 'compound by compound' basis. An arms-length relationship with the firm could be adopted as the parties would not need to engage in a broader dialogue.

On the other hand the shift to a more holistic regulatory regime (and one oriented to environmental goals) creates the basis, and possible incentives, for greater engagement between regulator and firm. The integrated approach, for example, implies that the regulator addresses the full array of waste streams generated by a firm's activities. The regulatory authority might also be further drawn to explore what balance had been struck between different disposal media. If this was extended to applying judgements about the relative costs and benefits of different regulatory actions, the result would be a trade-off model; one based on a broader view of the activities of a company. A move to a more proactive position might then involve the regulator in making some suggestions as to how the company might improve its performance. As a result of these development the regulator becomes involved in broader strategic judgements about the environmental behaviour of a company. This in turn obliges the regulator to develop some understanding of, and take into account, the technological and commercial context of the firm.

The main advantage of the holistic approach is that it engages the two parties in a dialogue, which may open the way to more creative solutions. The track record of this approach in Denmark and The Netherlands suggests that this more engaged relationship can blossom into an extensive dialogue on a range of issues, and generate a range of ancillary benefits for the firm, such as access to sources of advice and expertise.

The relationship between regulator and political apparatuses

Though the relation between political decision-making on environmental protection and the implementation of policy is a complex question that goes beyond the scope of this book, we can briefly examine the structure and administration of regulation in the four regions studied. We focus here on some related questions concerning: the level of centralization of the regulatory system; the scope for discretion in setting goals and enforcing standards; the extent to which regulation is a technocratic decision within the administration and those which acknowledge a broader political dimension; and the consequent need to include some kind of political representation. We can note differences between the four regions studied, and important changes alongside the implementation of integrated pollution control.

The situation in Denmark, since the beginning of 'integrated' environmental regulation in the early 1970s, is that while legislation is made by Parliament (and in recent years increasingly by the EU Council of Ministers and by the Commission), its implementation is dealt with by regional or county councils and city or municipal councils.[9] Cases are prepared and routines established by the administrators, who may also help to decide in particularly complex cases. The elected council, however (working through sub-committees on the environment and other issues), has to be properly notified, and is responsible for the final decision on environmental consents. This helps to integrate local and regional administration and establishes a close connection between political decision making and implementation. It leaves considerable discretion and some direct regulatory powers with the councils, such as the power to determine regional planning frameworks, which then set regional environmental quality goals and the subsequent necessary level of protection. In Denmark legislation is coordinated at a national level by the Environmental Protection Agency. However the EPA has never been involved in *implementation* (apart from handling appeals).

Paradoxically, Ireland and the UK have both recently moved away from a largely decentralized (and fragmented) system, towards a centralized integrated model. Thus Ireland has just established a nationwide Environmental Protection Agency with some regional offices. This reflected concern that national regulation was not, in practice, being implemented in many areas. The resulting differences in environmental standards between areas were too great (for example, creating potential risks and uncertainties for investors). This change was seen as necessary, therefore, in order to ensure uniform application of legislation and general coordination. Scotland, too, has moved towards a single integrated overarching authority, in place of the pre-existing complex patchwork of agencies, some parts of which were under local authority control. The new Scottish Environment Protection Agency, which is also a national agency with regional offices, has been charged with achieving certain environmental criteria without imposing undue costs on industry, and thus with balancing economic and environmental factors, but must attempt to do so as a largely 'apolitical' technical exercise (as there is no structure of elected bodies in place to oversee a broader and more political regulatory system).[10]

In The Netherlands, finally, there is a long-standing dual system with statutory professional boards for water regulation. A move towards a unified system is only now under way. In other areas, implementation is the responsibility of elected bodies like the regional councils and city councils.

Thus there remain significant differences between those countries that have an explicitly political dimension in their decision-making and a process that allows a wider set of social criteria to be taken into account, and those countries that have set up technical bureaucracies to manage the process of regulatory implementation. With the further development of the National Environmental Policy Plan in The Netherlands, and the further entrenchment of political involvement in the Danish system, these institutional differences appear to be becoming more significant, even though all four countries now have some form of integrated approach and the formal regulatory approaches are therefore now converging. As environmental regulatory functions are increasingly subsumed into the wider debate about sustainable development, this may lead to the development of a 'political deficit' in those countries that have no provision for the incorporation of wider social criteria in regulatory decision making.

THE SOCIAL CONTEXT: THE INFLUENCE OF PUBLIC PERCEPTIONS AND CONCERNS ON REGULATORY SYSTEMS

The development and implementation of regulation is never simply a 'technical' matter, but inevitably involves choices with an explicitly 'political' character about trade-offs between environmental performance and costs of compliance. Moreover it involves balancing different outcomes which are often incommensurable (for example loss of environmental amenity versus costs to industry) and in which the costs and benefits are unevenly distributed between different interested parties (firms, workers, consumers, communities, ecosystems). Regulation thus always involves elements of value judgement, though this may not always be explicitly recognized, as many players involved may wish to stress the 'objective' and 'scientific' basis of their particular propositions.

These observations are very pertinent to environmental regulation. One consequence is that regulation is likely to be influenced by broader public perceptions and concerns about different kinds of risk. Although, as we have seen, the administrative systems in different regions vary in the extent to which they give explicit expression to the political dimension, the behaviour of legislators drafting regulations and regulators implementing them will be influenced by the extent to which they feel their actions are subject to public scrutiny and political campaigns. This is an important aspect of the regional setting. In particular, the more far-reaching and ambitious goals of the Dutch and Danish regulatory systems can be partly related to the strength of popular environmental movements in those countries since the late 1960s. It is therefore important to consider how the operation of the regulatory system may be affected by perceptions of risk.

Perceptions of risk

Risk is conventionally defined as a combination of the probability of occurrence of a defined hazard and the magnitude of its consequences (The Royal Society, 1992). Objective measures of risk, by this definition, obey all the formal laws of combining probabilities. Perceptions of risk, however, are subjective and subject to cultural shaping, and do not necessarily accord with objective measures (Adams, 1995). Most people will rate a situation as being significantly more risky if their exposure to the risk is not voluntary; if it has catastrophic potential; if it has a 'dread' potential (such as carcinogenicity); or if it is not controllable by the risk-taker (Renn, 1990). Risks will be seen as less acceptable, and may be perceived as more serious, if the benefits accrue to one person and the risks to another. For example, it is notable that communities which are highly dependent upon particular firms or industries are willing to accept relatively high levels of environmental impairment (or occupational hazard) if these are seen as needed to 'save jobs'.

These issues also apply to the ways in which industries are perceived. As indicated earlier, some industries are perceived as high risk, or are regarded by many members of the public with some hostility and suspicion, and have a low ratio of perceived benefit to potential cost (such as the nuclear industry). Others are perceived as low risk or benign, with a high ratio of perceived benefit to potential cost (such as the brewing industry). Such perceptions tend to be rather general, and are often based on little hard information about the real environmental performance of the company in question. Few members of the general public are well informed or understand what their local industry does or how it does it. The perceived acceptability of particular activities and the perceived risk attached to certain companies and industries is an important factor in local and national politics, with important consequences for firms and for public regulatory bodies in terms of the extent to which they feel under pressure to accommodate public concerns.

Certain sectors of industry are acutely aware that they are perceived in a generally less benign or forgiving light than others. Some sectors – such as chemicals – are widely seen to be inherently dirty and dangerous. This is, in part, why they are subject to stricter regulation than others – such as food or brewing – which are generally regarded as benign and harmless. There appear to be two elements to such perceptions, relating not only to the extent to which certain kinds of activity are perceived as carrying risks, but also to the extent to which these activities are seen as readily understandable. The chemical sector has come to be seen as potentially risky and little understood. In contrast the activities of food processing (eg brewing) tend to be seen as inherently more 'natural', intelligible and thus less threatening. The changing perceptions of the nature and acceptability of chemical industry risks can be seen to have been shaped by a number of widely publicized incidents and events in recent decades.[11] For example, a number of operators in the refining and petrochemicals sectors took steps to upgrade their environmental control systems in the wake of the Exxon Valdez disaster. These differing perceptions of the strength of regulation required, in conjunction with latent public distrust of certain industries, may thus impinge directly upon the behaviour of companies as well as through the pressures on regulators generated by public perceptions about the level of risks and the need to regulate them.

Public perceptions are sometimes reflected in direct action by consumers in their consumption choices, as was the case for example with Shell's attempt to dispose of the Brent Spar oil rig in the North Atlantic (Löfstedt and Renn, 1997).[12] There is a tendency for perceptions to be generalized. Perceived bad behaviour by one member of a sector can therefore affect the perceived acceptability of the behaviour of the other members of a sector, which thus provides some peer pressure for a general raising of standards.

Expectations and values

Civil society is founded on a mix of formal and informal rules and regulations. Many of these norms do not have to be formally enforced, or even discussed, as they form part of the set of common values that then define the more fluid and contested areas where value systems come into conflict. The process of industrial regulation, likewise, rests on both informal and formal values and mechanisms. Individuals and organizations have many options in the face of regulations and rules, for example to conceal or justify transgressions, rather than simply deciding to comply. Which option is chosen may be influenced by a sense of what is and what is not socially acceptable behaviour. The most effective regulatory system will be one in which formal and informal values are consistent and mutually reinforcing, while any regulatory system will be rendered relatively ineffective by significant inconsistencies and conflicts between the formal and informal value systems. Thus the process of regulation is rather more complex and subtle than formal standards and procedures might imply, and regulatory pressures do not work in a consistently predictable way. Such pressures are mediated by other factors, some of which are general to industrial sectors, others of which are specific to particular organizations.

Such factors also inform the attitudes of the different national and local regulatory bodies, which tend to see their roles rather differently. It has been suggested, for example, that regulators in Germany and the US see themselves as having a more overtly political mission on behalf of the public than in France or the UK, where regulators have traditionally been more closely identified with industry (Brickman et al, 1985). The regulators in Denmark and, to an even greater extent, in The Netherlands, see their primary responsibility as being to civil society, but have evolved an intelligent and non-adversarial regulatory style that has become increasingly effective as companies have accepted the need to change. Just as firms have different reference groups, therefore, and vary in the extent to which they will look outside or abroad for ideas and their sense of normative behaviour, so regulatory bodies have a different sense of their constituency and audience.

Thus regulatory systems are informed by a combination of factors. These include not only scientific and technical considerations in, for example, assessing the extent of ecological change and in determining an appropriate set of indicators of that change, but also questions of public concern and perception, which influence the political context within which regulatory systems are ultimately determined (Tait et al, 1991).

3 REFINERY SECTOR

Børge Klemmensen with Leo Baas, Noel Duffy,
Birgitte Steen Hansen, Brendan Ryan, Graham Spinardi and
Robin Williams

Four companies were examined in this sector, two in Denmark, one in Ireland and one in the UK.

THE SECTORAL CONTEXT

Main industrial processes

The word 'refining' captures the essence of the core process in this industry. It is primarily about separating out all the different components of crude oil. This is done by both atmospheric and vacuum distillation, followed by 'cracking' processes for the heaviest or thickest parts of the crude to turn some of these heavy fractions into lighter fractions (such as naphtha and kerosene). This part of the process has become more and more important over the last 10 to 15 years, as the market for heavy fuel has decreased. Distillation is the main process, but heating the crude oil is also essential to make the distillation and the cracking possible. There is also a cleaning element in this process, as some of the substances in the crude (such as sulphur and phenol) are taken out in order to ensure that the product complies with the environmental limits for these substances. This process-integrated cleaning of the oil is done by passing it over different catalysts, each of which is specific to a particular substance. Sulphur removal is the single most important cleaning activity.

The process is continuous, running for three years without a stop (except for breakdowns). Every third year the process is interrupted for one or two months, when all the major repairs and/or upgrading are carried out. These breaks are therefore very clearly marked events, calculated well in advance. All major investments in the process are carried out during these breaks. Environmentally related investments can be scheduled in and accommodated in the same cycle.

Environmental issues

The very nature of oil refining makes it an unsustainable activity. It is concerned with making an important fossil fuel suitable for consumption for different purposes. The distinction between end-of-pipe and preventive environmental solutions is not particularly clear-cut, since the production process simply comprises the separation of various fractions of the crude oil and removal of toxic substances and other impurities. The difference in environmental terms between, for example, removal of nitrogen in the catalytic process together with sulphur and removal of nitrogen as an end-of-pipe operation in a biological treatment plant may not be significant. What can be done upstream will always be of interest in environmental terms, though, because a waste water treatment plant will inevitably be an add-on installation, implying extra energy and resource consumption.

It is important to note that the biggest environmental impact from the refinery sector does not come from the refining process, but from the consumption of the products that the refinery produces. The pollutants are CO_2, NOx and SO_2 from power generation, heating and the transport sector. The last sector also contributes polycyclic aromatic hydrocarbons (PAHs) from diesel fuel. Some impacts have been reduced by regulation, such as the widespread use of legal limits on the sulphur content in motor fuels, and compulsory cleaning of flue gases from power and heat stations. However, although some of the sulphur is removed (as a result of restrictions in the sulphur content of motor fuels, for example), most of the nitrogen and sulphur from the crude oil stays in the product – particularly in fuel oil used for heating – and is released when that fuel is burnt.

The refining processes affect all media – air, soil and water – and also produce some solid waste. We will look briefly into all of them, but our main focus will be on air and water related impacts, as these can be traded-off (eg in relation to nitrogen removal).

Emissions to the air

The main contribution to the air from a refinery comes from the furnaces and ovens, where fuel is fired for heating the crude oil in connection with the distillation and cracking processes. The most important emissions are SO_2, NO_x[1] particulates and CO_2. The amount of each depends on the quality of the fuel and the cleaning facilities applied, for example fuel-cleaning prior to the burning or smokestack removal of the compounds. A special problem here is that the refineries use quite a lot of the heavy fuel oil from the vacuum-fraction, and a considerable amount of the original sulphur and nitrogen is concentrated here, especially if the refinery uses some of the residuals from the last cracking (the visbreaker cracking) for use in the refinery furnaces. In this case, the only way to keep the emission of SO_2 and NO_x down is by smokestack cleaning, an end-of-pipe technology. Some of these heavier fractions are used by all the refineries in the study with the exception of the Irish case. It is possible for refineries to use cleaner gas streams to fuel their own processes. However, as the fuel oil saved will typically only be sold to be burnt elsewhere, this merely shifts the pollution to another site.

Refineries also have adverse influences on air quality and climate through leakage or evaporation of harmful substances. These VOCs (volatile organic compounds) are well known, but have only recently become an issue in relation to the environmental impact of refineries.

The standards and discharge levels are illustrated by the case material.[2]

Table 3.1 *Emissions to the air*

Parameter (different)	DK 1 actual (t/y)[3]	DK 2 limit mg/Nm³	DK 2 actual mg/Nm³	Irish limit mg/Nm³	Irish actual (t/y)	Reference[4] mg/Nm³
SO$_2$	(2061)	1000	43	1700	(150)	1500
NO$_x$	(418)	225	170	450	(615)	400[5]
Total dust	na	5	<5	50	na	150
VOCs (t/y)	na	(1318)	(1318)	na	na	na[6]

The DK 2 case is the only case in its sector that dealt explicitly with the VOC issue and with the setting of standards for VOCs (see the case study for details).

Soil pollution and threats to ground water

Soil pollution with oil is inevitable with the storage and handling of these enormous amounts of crude and refined products. There are two types of soil pollution:

1 Spills and residuals in relation to the refining and the storage of crude and ready products at the site. Previously, the residuals from tank cleaning and the sludge from waste water treatment were frequently stored or buried at the site.
2 Percolates from sludge farming, which is now commonplace at refineries, including those in this study. This can threaten soil and ground water. Drainage is now normally established and the percolate sent to the waste water treatment plant.

Solid and hazardous waste

Solid waste is generated in various amounts, but some 100 tonnes per year or more is usual. Hazardous waste has special conditions, and they are currently being tightened. Other, non-hazardous waste, goes to the ordinary landfill or to incineration with household waste.

Waste water

The second major environmental issue for the refineries is waste water discharge. This is usually directly to surface water, because of the volume of water discharged. The following table supplies an overview by drawing on some of the cases:

Table 3.2 *Waste water discharge*

Parameters (actual figures)	DK 1	DK 2	Irish	UK	Reference (mg/l)[7]
Crude handled t/y	3,200,000	5,100,000	1,800,000	9,000,000	1,800,000
Waste water m³/day	3000	2900	1726	14,616	(1726)[7]
Total oil, kg/day	11	8.7	15.1	29.2	17.25
pH	7.6–8.2	7.6-8.2	6.8–7.3	na	na
Phenols, kg/day	6.3	0.4	0.15	below 1.4[8]	0.2
Sulphide kg/day	8.2	0.08	na	5.8	0.35
Suspended matter kg/day	na	38.4	44.1	161	na
Total N, kg/day	152.8	57	0.78[9]	73 (NH_4)[10]	25.9
Total P, kg/day	na	0.9	na	na	na
COD, kg/day	na	387–487	259	585	259
Waste water discharge per ton of oil refined (m³/tonne estimated)	0.34	0.21	0.35	0.59[11]	na

The impact on the aqueous environment from the above mentioned compounds is potentially serious, depending on where the wastes are discharged and the kinds of dilution offered by the waterway. Chemical oxygen demand (COD), biological oxygen demand (BOD), suspended matter, nitrogen and phosphorus can lead to water pollution. Phenol is particularly toxic.

The table shows considerable differences in the discharges, indicating very different levels of 'cleanness' in the refinery technology.

The scope for cleaner technology in refining

The configuration of the plant has important consequences for its environmental performance. For example, phenol comes mainly from catalytic crackers used to convert low value waxes into high value feeds such as naphtha and fuel gas (it is formed as an unwanted by-product of regenerating the catalyst by oxidation).

Waterborne impacts comprise toxic substances (such as oil, phenols and sulphur in the form of sulphides) and nutrients. In relation to suspended and dissolved oil content, there is a Helsinki and Paris Convention requirement of a maximum of 5 ppm. Pre-treatment is needed before waste water streams go on to the waste water treatment plant. A variety of solutions are possible, including the use of sand beds, dissolved air flotation and induced air flotation. These allow separation of emulsified oil. Some can be skimmed off and sent back for processing. The remaining oil stays in the sludge and can be treated by sludge 'farming', that is, letting bacteria work on the sludge for a couple of years, 'eating' the oil. Recycling of water in the process will decrease the amount of oil coming to the air flotation plant.

All waste water is discharged via the desalter, taking the salt out of the crude oil at its entrance into the refining process. As phenol is absorbed by the crude in that process and afterwards turned into non-harmful substances in the platformer, along with the light fractions of the crude, some 70–80 per cent of the phenols in the waste water are removed. The remaining can (at present) only be taken care of by a treatment plant which can handle phenols, which means that the BAT solution for the last 15 or 20 per cent left at the end seems to be end-of-pipe technology.

The sulphur contained in the crude is taken out in the strippers and there is (quite complex and expensive) technology available to turn it into free sulphur, which can then be used for fertilizers, for acid production or for gypsum. This technology, which significantly reduces SO_2 emissions, is installed in all but one of the cases in this study.

For the nutrients, nitrogen and phosphorus, the problem depends partly on the type of crude used, but primarily on the kind of refining done at the refinery. The major part of the nitrogen stays in the heavier fractions of the crude oil, and if a market is available for this nitrogen, and if vacuum distillation and cracking are avoided, the problem can be minimized. This is interrelated with the air emissions problem, as the nitrogen can also be disposed of through the flare or discharged through other chimneys as NO_x. However, technology is now available to bring the nitrogen in the waste water down to very low levels while simultaneously reducing the emission to air. This technology is linked to the strippers, and can be combined with the solution to the sulphur problem, resulting in an integrated solution which leaves the nitrogen as free ammonia and the sulphur as free sulphur (see the DK1 case below for more information). However, a biological waste water treatment plant can also take effective care of the waterborne nutrient problem, while leaving the airborne part unresolved. Both solutions – strippers and waste water cleaning – constitute a form of cleaning, but the product coming out of the optimal stripping solution is more readily usable, while this solution solves the air emission problem at the same time.

Industrial context

The oil industry, extraction as well as refining, is a globalized, very capital intensive industry dominated by the large oil multinationals which account for three of our cases. We also have a more special case in the study, IRL Refinery, which is special in the sense that it had a protected role to secure national supply of a strategic commodity and has not needed to get actively involved in the global competition of the oil industry (though this may change). Under these arrangements, distributors of oil products in Ireland were by law obliged to buy a certain percentage of their total purchases from the IRL Refinery, but that obligation was removed in 1996.

The industry has problems with over-capacity and major restructuring has led to closures of many refineries – already some 50 in Europe alone. This is due to a general drop in the market for refinery products in Europe by some 25 per cent in the first half of the 1980s, combined with new demands to maintain the marketability of the products. Many of the refineries are technically not able to handle the heavier fractions of the oil, which makes up some 30–40 per cent of the crude, and as these markets have dropped furthest, these refineries are no longer economically viable. There is still over-capacity in the industry, and more closures are inevitable. This was demonstrated during this study, when the Dutch case was closed in January 1996. This process of adaptation to the market represents, at the same time, a restructuring of the technical capabilities of the refinery sector. The refineries closing first were not only those not able to handle the heavy fractions of the crude oil, but also those with old, inefficient technology and consequently enormously wasteful use of oil resources.

This ongoing restructuring will benefit the environment, not only by a more efficient and complete exploitation of the crude oil and in making environmentally less harmful products like low sulphur diesel fuel, but also because the concentration of the refining capacity will mean more investment in the technology and thereby increased use of cleaner technology, or at least with better controlled discharges to both air and water by more effective end-of-pipe solutions. The options are available as briefly described above, but they are capital intensive. The cases demonstrate this tendency, but they show at the same time that profitability (calculated in terms of payback demand) is still crucial to decision making.

CASE STUDIES

1 DK Refinery 1

Company profile

DK Refinery 1, owned by a multinational, was built in the 1960s. The refinery can process some 3 million tonnes of crude oil per year.

The DK headquarters are situated in Copenhagen and deal with sales and distribution of the products to the Danish market. There is a formal link to the refinery and the refinery director takes part in the monthly board meeting at the headquarters. But in practice the relationship with the refinery/manufacturing department at the European headquarters in London is much more important.

Table 3.3 *Refinery sector cases*

Company	DK Refinery 1	DK Refinery 2	IRL Refinery	UK Refinery
Products		Diesel, fuel oil, petrol etc	Petrol, kerosene, jet fuel etc	Petrol diesel, kerosene
Market	Primarily domestic and nearby countries	Primarily domestic and nearby countries	Primarily domestic and European countries	Primarily domestic and nearby countries
No of employees in firm; in company	250	250	155 in the firm; 200 in the total company	1150 in refinery; 56,650
Ownership/ relation with parent	Branch site of a multinational company	Branch site of a multinational company	State owned firm	Branch site of a multinational company
Regional features	Discharge to shallow waters creates environmental demands, and change to preventive approach from the authority	Participates in a local industrial symbiosis with 3 industries using each other's waste and by-products	Longstanding, traditional firm in the community	Corporate environmental image making prevails

Recently corporate management has launched a green image campaign as well as getting certification to BS 7750 standard for all its sites. A new Environmental Department has been established at the refinery, formalizing the increasing environmental activity which has been developing at the refinery in recent years.

The investment policy of the company, including the policy on environmental investments is, however, unchanged. The normal approach has a short term perspective with a payback period of at most 2 years. Beyond that a special decision from London is required, especially for more significant investments. This makes it important to combine and thereby plan environmental investments in conjunction with other investments for improvements.

Most of the expertise used in relation to the environmental changes comes from London headquarters or the refinery itself, or from consultants (who are used for more specific issues like the strippers).

Environmental profile

The primary focus of the environmental authorities from 1988 has been on the waste water discharge from the refinery. The total discharge is some 900,000 m³/ year, of which some 300,000 m³ is waste water from the refining process. The rest is surface water and water leaking from the ground directly into a shallow and heavily nitrogen-loaded, and therefore vulnerable, recipient watercourse: the Agersø Sound.

The County has focused on oil, sulphide, phenol and nitrogen. Reasonable solutions were found for all of these apart from nitrogen.

Project: removing nitrogen from refinery waste water

From 1987 till 1994 the County pressed for nitrogen removal by biological treatment of the effluent. They tried to make the refinery apply for a waste water licence, arguing that that the nitrogen discharge was above the maximum 66 tonnes year allowed according to the new National Plan for the Aquatic Environment (NPAE). The company resisted making this investment, using all available legal instruments - including an appeal to the National Board of Appeal for the Environment - to avoid complying. They managed to convince the Board of Appeal that the nitrogen discharge was only about 55 tonnes per year, so the County lost the case.

The County then used its regional planning powers to set new standards for the Agersø Sound. These were ready in 1993, and the County immediately warned the refinery about a forthcoming Order (mandate) for a cleaning facility to take the nitrogen discharge to 8 tonnes/year or 15 per cent of the current level.

By 1994, however, the County had moved to a cleaner technology approach. Instead of issuing the Order in accordance with the warning, therefore, the County sent an Order three months later in which they asked the company to take a comprehensive look at the whole production process, applying the standards of best available technology to the refinery, and to come up with proposals for a substantial reduction of the nitrogen discharge. The County requested that the possible solutions be ranked as follows: reduction at source, recirculation, treatment and deposit. End-of-pipe cleaning was not excluded, but it was not the preferred option. The company was given a deadline for implementing the proposals, and asked to give regular 3-monthly progress reports.

This schedule fitted in with the application for a full licence for the refinery, due by 1 January 1997 and with the next production halt for maintenance and update, which was in autumn 1997. Implementation of measures to reduce nitrogen discharge could therefore take place in combination with the other major activities that the refinery was planning.

The County has therefore shifted to an explicit cleaner technology stance, while leaving the company to find the precise solution to the 8 tonnes/year requirement. The nitrogen discharge figure is still in effect, as the County has not given up any core regulatory demands with the new approach.

This shift in the County's position came in conjunction with the growing awareness of the cleaner technology approach, which was introduced in the 1992 revamp of the Danish EPA. They were also influenced by the obligation, established by the same Act, for refineries to apply for a full environmental licence (if they did not have one). This favoured a comprehensive and holistic approach to the management of the environmental impact of their activities.

The timescale was important, as it allowed the company to respond positively. The County accepted the tri-annual closure as the best opportunity for the refinery to install major changes, including those favourable to the environment. The company's response was also shaped by the decision at corporate level to 'go green' and aim at a BS 7750 certification for all their important sites.

What was initially a confrontational relationship between the refinery and the authorities has now developed into a more cooperative relationship, focusing on long-term environmental results achieved by BAT, cleaner technologies, environmental audit and so on. The refinery now sees the County as 'possibly our best consultant'.

The need for a comprehensive approach is demonstrated by the options that the company has for dealing with their nitrogen. Besides better strippers, leading to more NO_x (this entails a trade-off between air and water pollution), and a biological treatment plant (a neighbouring industrial park has surplus capacity, and can take enough to enable the company to meet the 8 tonnes/year requirements), there is also a possibility of a combined solution to the nitrogen removal problem. This option offers the prospect of reducing the discharge to 4 tonnes/year and at the same time reducing both NO_x and SO_2 emissions to the air. It is a very costly solution, however, and will therefore not be pursued unless there is either a major change in – for example – the management of the refinery, or if it is at some later stage required by the environmental authority. Thus, for economic reasons, the initial reduction to 8 tonnes/year will probably be done by discharging part of the waste water from the refinery through the established industrial waste water treatment plant in the neighbourhood.

2 DK Refinery 2

Company profile

DK Refinery 2, owned by a Norwegian company, was built in the early 1960s. The activities of the company are refining, transport and sale. About DKK 500 million was invested in the refinery over six years following a change of ownership in 1986. One of the bigger investments was an extension of the visbreaker/thermocracker and the installation of a hydrocracker plant in 1990. The purpose of these investments was to shift the product profile towards lighter and more profitable products. A part of the investment – some DKK 175 million – was used to address some environmental problems: a desulphurization plant was built and the treatment plant was enlarged.

The refinery is part of an eco-industrial symbiotic network. The network includes a thermal power plant which uses cooling water and surplus gas from the refinery, and gives steam in exchange, a chemical plant which takes the sulphur produced by the refinery, and a plant producing building material which also takes surplus gas from the refinery. Finally, a pharmaceutical firm in the network takes steam from the thermal power plant. The symbiosis offers significant environmental efficiency gains, and is also profitable for the participating firms.

Environmental profile

The emission of SO_2 into the air was reduced by 4000 tonnes/year – one third of the statutory limit – in 1990 by establishing a desulphurization plant. NO_x, dust, H_2S and VOCs are also emitted into the air by the refinery.

The amount of solid waste from the refinery (including the condensate refinery) not suitable for reuse is 210 tonnes/year. The refinery runs a sludge farm, which has recently been extended.

The refinery is situated near an open, but nutrient-contaminated fjord, which is the recipient for the waste water. The refinery discharges about 1.1 million m^3 of waste water annually, including flows from the new condensate refinery. Nitrogen and phosphorus discharge is some 20 t/y and therefore only about one third of the DK 1 case.

The refinery as a whole did not possess the statutory full environmental licence for 'specially polluting industries' covering all activities of the refinery, and was told that it had to apply for the licence by January 1997. This licence will now be further tightened in the light of better knowledge about air emissions and new nutrient regulations (similar to those implemented in the DK 1 case).

Project

In January 1992 the company management decided to invest DKK 3.4 billion to increase the condensate processing capacity of the refinery from 3 to 5 million tonnes/year, consisting almost entirely of the light fractions of crude oil. The decision about the expansion was based first of all on the fact that the company (the oil extraction section in the conglomerate) had a huge quantity of condensate from the crude extraction. The increasingly strict environmental requirements for the refinery products (low sulphur content, low benzene content, etc) were also important, as it was felt that these would be easier to meet with condensate as the raw material than it would with crude oil.

The project thus highlights the role that the clean technology issue plays for the company as well as for the environmental authorities in a situation in which a new section was being added to the refinery, at the point of a substantial investment in production capacity. This can be illustrated in this case by the issue of VOCs, which became a core issue for the first time.

The table shows the emissions *before* and *after* the environmental requirements, including the cleaner technology concept, which was applied to the VOC emissions.

Table 3.4 *VOC emissions*

VOCs from the refinery, sources of emission	Condensate refinery pre-environmental requirements (t/y)	Existing refinery pre-environmental requirements (t/y)	Total, existing and new (t/y)	All refinery after fulfilling environmental requirements (t/y)
Refining process	54	664	718	538
Tanks	34	170	204	140
Waste water treatment	0	100	100	100
Leakages from load/unload at the pier	260	36	296	15
Total	348	970	1318	793

Source: West-Zealand County environmental licence for the refinery.

The licence states that the cleaner technology approach has been applied throughout. This point is illustrated by the VOC emissions. With regard to the process equipment, there was no big difference between the company's perspective and the authority's view. The VOCs were given top priority in the cleaner technology approach in this particular case, due to the inherent risk of high emissions from the existing production process, and due to the financial difficulties of replacing much of the equipment with equipment with lower emissions at a later stage. There was a general acceptance that the company's proposals were environmentally sound.

The areas where views differed can be seen in Table 3.4 on the emission sources for VOCs. For the refining processes, the emissions were expected to drop some 180 t/y, mainly from refitting the valves in the existing oil refinery with an extra set of gaskets. Another important improvement was to come from the tanks, where the company was obliged to supply four existing tanks with floating ceilings within 1 year.

The regeneration plant at the pier, collecting and regenerating the VOCs which evaporate (especially when loading benzene into ships for export) was the main area for improvement in relation to the company's proposal. Benzene is one of the most poisonous VOCs, and benzene made up a high proportion of the total volume of evaporating substances.

This matter caused a major controversy, however, as the investment required was some DKK 35 million, and the running costs of about DKK 1 million/year were about double the value of the regenerated benzene. Furthermore, the EU had been considering a directive on VOCs, which included regeneration on ship-loading, but this was taken out of the directive for a time while the EU waited for the IMO (International Maritime Organization) to decide a standard for ships in this area. This meant that some ships were not allowed to connect to the regeneration plant at all. These factors made the company push to avoid being obliged to build the plant, at least at that stage.

The County made the licence conditional, however, on building the regeneration plant by January 1998, regardless of the IMO decision and the EU directive (which, they argued, could be delayed for years). Without a regeneration plant, the company would have lost some 290 t/year, predominantly benzene, through evaporation, thereby causing the company to exceed the Air Quality Guidelines significantly – a situation which the County found unacceptable. The full benefit of the plant will only come, however, when all ships are able to connect to the regeneration system.

Despite this firm position, the County's licence for the company allowed for an alternative to the regeneration plant: to reduce the evaporation further compared to the licence, and by the same amount from any part of the existing oil refinery. That would have allowed the company to omit the regeneration plant. But no alternatives proved economically viable, so the regeneration plant will have to be built.

The convergence of the company's and the regulator's views on cleaner technology is a significant feature of the case. The company applied a BAT standard, partly reflecting an acceptance of the requirements. In addition, the company's investment in cleaner technology suggests a determination to anticipate future requirements in areas involving major (and sometimes early) replacement of equipment. The case underlines the importance of synchronizing regulatory requirements with the company's major investment cycles.

The case shows that there is no economic incentive to build 'add-on' installations with little economic return. Many companies will resist such impositions, arguing that such 'add-ons' cause a loss of competitiveness. This is particularly true where the requirements are not based on general international regulation, as the companies are likely to perceive purely local restrictions and obligations as particularly disadvantageous.

3 IRL Refinery

Company profile

Founded in 1959, and the only refinery in the state, it was until 1982 a joint venture by four major multinationals. In 1982 the multinationals announced their decision to withdraw from the operation and it was taken into public ownership and kept in operation. The decision was based on the perceived strategic need to have at least some independent national oil supply. Oil companies servicing the Irish market were required to take some of their product from the refinery.

The refinery currently has a throughput of about 2 million tonnes of crude oil and a turnover of about IR£150 million. Its major market is in Ireland (60 per cent of production), where it supplies 35 per cent of the market for gasoline and gas oil/diesel, but it also exports to other European states, and to a small extent to the US. Raw material is currently obtained entirely from the North Sea, predominantly from the Norwegian sector.

Environmental profile

The main environmental concern is change in product specification (eg lead and sulphur content), and much of the company's current capital investment is directed towards this. The firm currently holds air and water pollution licences from the local authority, together with a toxic and dangerous waste permit. The toxic and dangerous waste permit allows on-site land-farming of hydrocarbon contaminated aqueous sludges, landfilling of heavy metal sludges, and landfilling of asbestos wastes. Compliance with these various permits is 100 per cent, and the firm is therefore under no environmental pressure at present from that source. Future plant-oriented pressure is anticipated in the form of an Integrated Pollution Control Licence. The firm has invested IR£50,000 to establish base line data for a future IPC licence application.

In recent years there has been considerable capital investment in the plant. This has been necessitated by market demands, for example for jet fuel, efficiency improvements (distillation tower revamps and energy integration), together with a furnace revamp designed to reduce air emissions, etc. A major sulphur recovery project is currently underway costing IR£6.25 million. This is necessitated by the obligation to reduce fuel sulphur content while at the same time meeting local authority SO_2 licence limits.

The firm has a surprisingly low level of nitrogen in its liquid waste. This arises from this refinery's process configuration, which has neither a catalytic cracker nor vacuum distillation. In addition, the entire plant is air-cooled, resulting in low waste water outputs. Energy for the operation is largely provided by liquid fuel fired furnaces. Seventy-five per cent of the fuel firing is now via low NO_x burners, as the programme of furnace upgrading proceeds. NO_x discharges are about half of the licence concentration limits, although this is similar to the licence limits set for the Danish refineries in this study. The quantity of NO_x discharged is also relatively high by comparison with at least one of the other refineries in this study. The firm is nevertheless happy with its environmental performance and cites comparisons with other European figures which appear to confirm their view. Their major local environmental concerns appear to be minimizing fugitive emissions and assessing the possibility of ground water contamination.

There is a waste minimization/recycling/reuse programme in operation and the firm has had both internally and externally moderated environmental audits.

It hopes to become accredited to ISO 310. An environmental audit of waste disposal contractors was also conducted. The entire workforce has a high level of safety and environmental training.

Project

Refineries produce light naphtha and liquefied petroleum gas (LPG) which can commonly contain traces of hydrogen sulphide and mercaptans that are traditionally removed using a caustic soda solution. Soon after its establishment, this firm sought to reduce the caustic consumption for cost, safety and environmental reasons. A minimization programme was initiated, followed by development and investment in recycling technology in the 1970s. This achieved a 90 per cent reduction in usage. Initial attempts at on-site disposal of the residual spent caustic resulted in odours which generated local complaints, so it was decided to change to sea disposal. Sea disposal of industrial waste was banned by the Oslo Commission in 1992, and spent caustic has been stored on site since then while alternative treatment or disposal routes were investigated. Shipment of the material for external processing was possible, but considered more costly and dangerous.

The firm adopted a procedure used to deal with this problem by a pharmaceutical firm in the region. This involved addition of sodium hypochlorite to the spent caustic to oxidize the hydrogen sulphide and mercaptans to salts followed by the addition of sulphuric acid to adjust pH. The treated solution can then be disposed of in the firm's liquid effluent.

The project was completed in 1994 at a cost of IR£160,000. Similar units in other refineries are claimed to have cost up to IR£2 million. It is regarded as very successful. It produced only a slight increase in effluent flow rate, has not detrimentally affected any licensed parameters, has enabled the firm to meet both its legal requirements and the concerns of the local community, and has removed the negative media coverage which was associated with sea dumping. However, the project does result in a slight increase in sulphuric acid usage and has introduced a new compound, sodium hypochlorite, onto the site.

Regulation of product environmental performance is and will continue to be a major source of pressure. While some initiatives, particularly those with efficiency benefits, are proactive, environmental policy is reactive in general and often regulation driven. The project was necessitated by a combination of local community pressure and international regulation, and involved an end-of-pipe treatment solution to a problem which had been previously greatly reduced by a combination of source reduction and internal recycling.

4 UK Refinery

Company profile

Part of one of the largest global petrochemical firms, this refinery refines oil with some subsequent marketing, supply and transportation. About 9 million tons per year of North Sea crude are piped to the refinery, which differs from the majority of refineries in how it treats the heavier cut of crude fractions. Typically, simple 'hydroskimming' refineries would either sell off this wax cut or convert it to coke, whereas a complex refinery like UK Refinery converts some of it to higher value products.

Environmental profile

The most important by-product of crude oil, in environmental terms, is sulphur. Sulphur is removed as H_2S from the hydrocracker (which converts waxes into higher value volatiles) and the hydrofiner and the distillate hydrotreater (which removes sulphur from low-sulphur diesel and gas streams). UK Refinery has a sulphur recovery plant, which takes the H_2S and converts it to elemental sulphur. It currently extracts 7000 tonnes of sulphur per year, though this will double when they complete four new plants being installed to meet the requirements for low sulphur motor fuels. Currently the price of sulphur is too low for this to be commercially viable, and so recovery is justified on environmental grounds.[12] Sulphur remains in the heavier fractions, particularly the heavy fuel oil, most of which will ultimately be burnt, by UK Refinery or its customers, resulting in atmospheric sulphur emissions. Some of the fuel oil is used, for example, together with any excess gas (which is clean, but more expensive) to run the on-site combined heat and power (CHP) plant, which powers the refinery, an adjacent chemicals plant and other nearby operations.

Heat exchange systems are used throughout the plant to maximize energy recycling, and the energy efficiency of the plant is graded relative to the corporation's other refineries. Computer control systems are widely used, facilitating the recording of performance data as regards temperatures, pressures, flow rates, valve positions, and so on.

In addition to its use in cooling and heat exchanging, water is also used to wash salt out of the crude as it enters the refinery and in various stream stripping processes. In some of the older plant it is not possible to recycle the cooling water. Other sources of waste water are condensation in the distillation columns, and rainwater collecting and running off various parts of the refinery, including roads. When the refinery was built (in the 1950s) it was not the practice, as it would be now, to have separate drains for contaminated process water ('oily water') and for rainwater.

Until recently regulation of liquid effluent from UK Refinery into the Firth of Forth estuary was solely the responsibility of the Forth River Purification Board (FRPB). Recently the refinery has come under the remit of Integrated Pollution Control (IPC), coordinated in Scotland by Her Majesty's Industrial Pollution Inspectorate (HMIPI). Amongst the requirements for licensing under IPC is an obligation for companies to carry out an environmental audit and submit a waste minimization plan. The refinery applied for IPC in May 1992 and received authorization in April 1993. General compliance, as rated by the FRPB, improved from 17 per cent in 1991/92 to 65 per cent in 1992/93 and 71 per cent in 1993/94.

Most of UK Refinery's environmental expertise comes from within the corporate organization, either from experience at other plants and in other countries or from the Technical Centre in England.

Project

The decision to build a new treatment plant stemmed from the growing emphasis given to environmental issues by the corporate group. It conducted a review of all plants with known effluent problems. The waste water treatment plant was chosen as a publicly visible response. The exercise had the goal of bringing them up to the best world standards, based on US plants, beyond what was required by the regulator (FRPB). In this way the company sought to respond proactively to potential future regulatory pressures.

Management in Brussels wanted UK Refinery to be brought up to best European standards. A number of options were considered under the coordination of the Technical Centre. Order of magnitude costings were made for several options, and a sand filter followed by trickle filter approach was recommended to management. They rejected this, however, 'on the basis that it would be regarded as perhaps not "the best technology" and they made a very deliberate decision to go for a more expensive activated sludge system for the biological stage preceded by flotation.'

The outcome of this process was a decision to build a treatment plant costing about £30 million, with an annual running cost of about £2 million, with a further £10 million spent on upstream work. Although the upstream developments could be seen as waste minimization, their rationale was principally to ensure that the waste streams entering the treatment plant would not upset its biological processes. These developments focused on the upstream removal of two pollutants: sulphide and phenol.

Other upstream measures focused on reducing the level of waste water flow and eliminating surges. Recycling reduced water throughput by about 20 per cent. Surge tanks were built to allow the holding back of exceptional peak flows or particularly damaging discharges. The treatment plant's design specification was to reduce oil levels to less than 5 ppm. According to the refinery it typically achieves levels of 1–2 ppm. Some metals are present in the effluent, but in total amount to less than 1 ppm.

Annual waterborne emissions have fallen from 1486 tons in 1990 to 1003 tonnes in 1993 as a result of these works, and with the commissioning of the treatment plant fell by an order of magnitude to 104 tons in 1995.

The project is a long way from the 'pollution prevention pays' concept inherent in the waste minimization approach of cleaner technology. Some waste minimization was carried out prior to the construction of the treatment plant, but the management urgency to build the plant meant that more could have been done. Waste minimization could have reduced the size of the treatment plant by 20 per cent and saved between 5 and 10 per cent of its cost. Hydrocarbon losses throughout the refinery – through leaks, loss of volatile compounds, and flaring – are at the same time losses of potential product. Reducing these losses would probably cost less than the amount gained in extra product over the normal two year payback period required for commercial (not 'stay in business') investments, but very little such capital is available. Reducing hydrocarbon losses would thus not only be good for the environment, it would also be commercially beneficial. To date improvements of this kind – introducing new roof seals, and new designs of pumps and valves that allow less leakage – have been implemented slowly during routine maintenance and replacement of equipment.

The end-of-pipe approach stemmed from the public commitment made by the corporate group to improve its environmental performance. This meant not only that it would be prepared to fund centrally environmental improvements, but also that these improvements needed to be dramatic and highly visible. A treatment plant like that built at UK Refinery is an expensive demonstration of commitment to the environment.

Table 3.5 *Summary of environmental responses of firms*

Company	DK Refinery 1	DK Refinery 2	IRL Refinery	UK Refinery
Regulatory context	Under West-Zealand County Council application for new licence by end of 1996	Under West-Zealand County Council Licence 1992 for the new section	Cork County Council	Recent transfer from the FRPB to IPC and licensed here in 1993
Environmental policy/ management	Formal BS 7750 in progress	Formal	Formal	Formal Green corporate image
Environmental response/ project	High N-discharge End-of-pipe	Capture/ regeneration of lost volatiles Internal recycling	Chemical treatment of spent caustic containing hydrogen sulphide and mercaptans, (stored after dumping prohibition) End-of-pipe	New waste water treatment plant End-of-pipe

Corporate financial organization also favoured a big project rather than incremental improvements. Money is provided from the centre, and winning such money has symbolic significance as an indicator of faith in the future of UK Refinery. At the same time, lack of finance for infrastructure or commercial projects (such as upgrading pipes and seals) inhibited incremental waste minimization. If the organizational units operated as separate cost centres and were required to finance environmental improvements independently, then there could be more incentive for cleaner technology solutions rather than end-of-pipe treatment, which could be cheaper and offer significant savings.

COMPARATIVE ANALYSIS OF CASE STUDIES

This sector is:

- dominated by big multinational companies, acting at global or regional level;
- highly capital intensive;
- very specialized and focused on a production process (refining) which is very well established;
- based on high level internal expertise and experience within each capital group with innovative steps mostly coming from within the respective groups and/or a distinct group of external specialists;
- a key strategic sector, delivering a group of products which are indispensable to industrialized countries.

These characteristics and the accompanying position have for a long time kept the refineries free of (thorough) environmental regulation. This has been the case for virtually the whole industry, apart from land based oil leakages to soil and water and, in particular, regulations in relation to oil tanker disasters.

As a stand-alone state owned refinery – taken over for strategic reasons when closure by the multinational owners was under way – the Irish refinery is an exception from some of these characteristics while underlining the strategic element. Its special status has not, however, meant any difference in an environmental perspective. The strategic position and the state ownership seem to have prevented any strong regulatory pressure being put upon the refinery. The company comes from that same multinational context as the other refineries. It is quite big, specialized and, compared to the regulators, has superior knowledge within the field.

The market situation has been changing over the last couple of decades, beginning with the oil crises of the 1970s and efforts to reduce the high dependence on oil as a source of energy. These changes in terms of a shift of fuels (to coal and natural gas) and savings, were (and are) mainly related to power generation and heating, while transport and a number of industrial products and processes are still very much based on oil products. Consumption here is still growing, especially in transport.

This change in markets has meant over-capacity in the refinery sector and at the same time a need for change of technology at the refineries to turn more of the crude oil into light-fraction products like petrol, jet fuel and diesel fuel. A number of refineries have been closed in this process, including the Dutch case in this study. The two Danish cases show the influence of this shift in the refining process and the technology of the refineries. This is particularly evident in the second Danish case, where the company is building a wholly new section to the refinery intended for refining of condensate, a very light fraction of crude oil.

There are important environmental implications of these changes in products and markets. More substances, especially sulphur and nitrogen, which stay with the heavy fractions, are released in the refining process when the heavy fractions are cracked. Demands for, for example, low sulphur content in diesel fuel means improved stripping and a further increase in the sulphur production at the refinery.

The demand in recent years for low impact oil products demonstrates the increased level of environmental awareness. The Exxon Valdez and Brent Spar cases have made the polluter pays principle a driving force, underlining that protection of the environment is an important issue for the oil industry these days.

This has made a green image an important competitive feature for the oil industry, which can be seen in the case studies. The UK Refinery decided to build a large waste water treatment facility without being obliged to do so, although considerations about anticipated measures were involved. The timing and the character of the decision – a very visible move, including a substantial investment, at a time of no (serious) regulatory pressure – indicates that the desire to develop / maintain a green image and to be perceived to be in a leading role in relation to the protection of the environment were the most important factors behind the decision, which was made at corporate and not at plant level. The move was consistent with a 1990 announcement from the company to reduce aqueous emissions by 50 per cent by 1995 and a commitment to bring all company operations up to the best world standards, which in this case meant reducing the emission levels to the most stringent operating standards in Europe.

In the DK Refinery 1 case a decision at corporate level to give priority to the environmental issue formed part of the explanation for the positive development in the company–regulator relationship, and for the company's concepts of waste minimization. The company also organized Health and Environment Units at each plant as well as making BS 7750 standard obligatory for each site within a couple of years. These measures were company responses to the current trend of consumer demands and a need for green marketing.

This trend is important, but there is nothing to support the view that the market and the increased general environmental awareness and subsequent general pressure upon industry will make the environmental problems disappear. The key role of regulation for protection of the environment comes through very clearly from the case studies, alongside the voluntary or market based initiatives. It is important to note that the requirements to reduce the sulphur content of the oil products are an outcome of regulation to protect the local environment and thereby people's health in cities, and not a market-driven request stemming from car-owners and drivers. But the *regulatory strategy,* the *intensity of the control* and the *level at which the implementation takes place* differ between the three regions.

The regulatory regime has changed in the UK/Scotland over the last few years with primary responsibility moving from the River Purification Board to Her Majesty's Industrial Pollution Inspectorate, followed by the establishment in April 1996 of the new Scottish EPA. This change has been accompanied by a shift in the regulatory strategy from media specific regulation to the new IPC system (integrated pollution control). UK Refinery got an IPC licence in 1993 with standards for all important substances discharged. At the same time problems with compliance with the standards set in the RPB licence – which was as low as 17 per cent in 1991 – illustrates the role of regulation in improving environmental performance. It was one of the reasons why the parent company selected UK Refinery for its initiative to bring plants with known problems up to best world standards.

The parallel Irish restructuring, making a national EPA responsible for the implementation of the regulation while at the same time shifting to the IPC system, has not affected the Irish refinery case very much. It has been regulated by the county council, which has issued a comprehensive licence for both water and air emissions, and the refinery seems to be in compliance. The refinery will continue to be under county council regulation for another couple of years, which will probably mean little or no change in character or intensity of regulation and thereby a continuation of the situation with great company influence on the level and direction of regulatory requirements.

The Danish regulatory system has also been subject to revision in recent years, although mostly in terms of regulatory strategy. The 1991 review of the environmental protection act put the preventive approach firmly into the picture, making a demand for BAT/cleaner technology a standard request on licence issuance. This development influenced the Danish cases, as the cleaner technology approach was implemented by the county council in both cases. This approach means a much closer and a much more direct involvement in the company decision-making process. It should be noted, however, that the authority does not prescribe solutions, it only accepts or refuses the solutions that the company presents.

CONCLUSIONS

The industry is in a process of global restructuring, and change on environmental issues in relation to the refineries is probably not the most important concern for the industry at this stage. The case studies show, as a result, that regulation is essential for environmental protection in relation to refineries. This remains the case despite there being some evidence for proactive measures. The cases also show that the way the regulation is implemented, including the intensity and the effectiveness of implementation and control, influences the response of the company and thereby the level of protection obtained. Regulatory strategy, in conjunction with the structure of the environmental authorities, determines the kind of discretion afforded the companies, and the intensity of control measures. The Danish cases show that the local regulators can influence the environmental decision-making and performance of a refinery situated in the region, even when the owner is a huge multinational company. To do this, however, requires high levels of skill and knowledge in environmental administration as well as a consistent and clear line in county decision making in relation to each company. It is therefore necessary to have environmental departments of some size to ensure that the necessary specialist is always on hand. The moves in Ireland and Scotland towards a more centralized authority structure can be seen as a way to fulfil that requirement. It will, however, take the regional dimension out of the implementation, and thereby out of the protective measures.

4   PETRO-CHEMICAL SECTOR

Leo Baas with Noel Duffy, Brendan Ryan, Graham Spinardi and Robin Williams

---

Four companies were examined in this sector, one in Ireland, two in The Netherlands and one in the UK.

THE SECTORAL CONTEXT

Petro-chemical industry processes

Crude oil refinery products undergo all forms of transformation in organic chemistry, often under special pressure and temperature conditions. The processes can be both continuous (the production quantities are often very large) and in batch production. The chemical products are both end-products and basic materials for special products.

Environmental issues

The chemical industry has always been seen as a high risk industrial sector; many of their chemical substances are flammable, toxic and processed under special conditions. Water, air, soil and surroundings are threatened by polluted effluents, air and soil emissions, stench and noise. After the development of environmental legislation and regulatory agencies in the 1970s and early 1980s, the chemical sector used pollution control measures to meet the new environmental requirements. Because the industry had not previously internalized or even calculated the costs of environmental pollution, however, the process of meeting the new requirements via end-of-pipe technologies like waste water treatment facilities, scrubbers and incinerators imposed new costs on the firms. As a result, the industry did not in general welcome these new environmental requirements. After the industry accepted that the requirements were here to stay, most firms displayed an 'everything under control' attitude until they were faced with a series of disasters including Seveso (1981), Bhopal (1984), Sandoz (1986) and the Exxon Valdez (1990). These events reinforced the widely held perception that the chemical industry is associated with high risks and, as a result, the 'everything under control' attitude started to look less credible.

An initiative of the Canadian Chemicals Manufacturers' Association (CCPA) in 1991 resulted in the Responsible Care Programme adopted by the chemical industry worldwide. Through this programme and by providing more information to the public, the chemical industry is trying to improve its image. Although the chemical industry is an established part of society, public perception of it remains poor because of the high risks and pollution with which it is commonly associated.

Industrial structure and economic context

There are many similarities in the primary features between the companies. All companies are part of multinational corporations. This means that all cases are large companies according to the ownership criterion in the EU definition and by virtue of having net annual turnover of over ECU 38 million.[1] However, this is a capital-intensive industry, and only the UK company also meets the 'big company' criterion of having more than 500 employees.

The annual production ranges from 160,000 tonnes (NL Chemicals 1) to 1,118,000 tonnes (UK Chemicals) per annum. The total number of employees varies between 200 and 1450. Three companies depend largely upon export markets. Although UK Chemicals is a large supplier within the British Isles, and NL Chemicals is supplying a sister company, these companies also face the effects of a global market and strong competition.

In all cases, the plant management is responsible for environmental performance. All the companies are also members of the Responsible Care Programme of the chemical industry.

CASE STUDIES

1 IRL Chemicals

Company profile

The company was formed in 1965, as a state enterprise, and moved to its current location in 1979. Since 1987, the company has been a joint venture between the UK company ICI and the state owned fertilizer company NET. The company processes 918,000 tonnes of different chemicals per annum and has an annual turnover between IRL £ 10 and 50 million. The company exports 59 per cent of its production to Europe.

The Cork plant, one of three production centres in the company, was constructed by NET and commenced production in 1979. It uses natural gas, which is extracted offshore near Cork, to produce ammonia, urea, and liquefied carbon dioxide. It produces about 550,000 tonnes of ammonia, 1500 tonnes of ammonia liquor for the food processing and pharmaceutical industries, 350,000 tonnes of

Table 4.1 *Petro-chemical sector cases*

Firm	IRL Chemicals	NL Chemicals 1	NL Chemicals 2	UK Chemicals
Products	Ammonia, urea, CO_2 liquid	Plasticizer	Phenol	(Poly)ethylene, ethylene glycol
Markets	40% IRL 59% Europe	European market	100% to supply sister company	Mainly UK market
Number of employees	200	430	230	1450
Ownership/ relationship with parent	Joint-venture with British multinational	Branch site of US multinational	Branch site of Dutch multinational	Branch site of British multinational
Regional features	Member of regional association of chemical industries	Member of regional association of chemical industries	Member of regional association of chemical industries	
	Partner member of the Clean Technology Centre	Participant in Industrial Ecology project		

urea and 20,000 tonnes of carbon dioxide per annum. All ammonia and liquefied carbon dioxide is used in Ireland, the majority of the urea is exported.

The ammonia process is a standard production process facilitated in Cork by the unusual purity of the local natural gas. The gas is purchased by NET and sold on to IRL Chemicals at a price which is comparable with other European sources of gas for fertilizer manufacture. Continuous investment has kept the plant efficiency at a high level for a plant of its size and vintage. Projects have included modifying the ammonia converter, modifying the carbon dioxide removal system for energy recovery and recovering hydrogen from a purge stream in the ammonia synthesis section using membrane separation technology.

Urea is produced by reacting ammonia with carbon dioxide to form ammonium carbamate (NH_2COONH_4), which is converted to urea (NH_2CONH_2) and water. High pressure and high temperature are needed. Since not all the carbamate is converted in the reactor, it must be recycled. This is done in a stripper where the carbamate is recycled as ammonia and carbon dioxide. The remaining ammonia, carbon dioxide and carbamate are distilled off at reduced pressure. Pressure is then further reduced to atmospheric and the remaining vapours are flashed off leaving a 75 per cent urea solution. The urea concentration is increased via a two stage evaporator to 99.7 per cent which is essentially a melt of urea. This is sprayed downwards from the top of a high tower in the form of small droplets which cool and solidify to give almost spherical particles. The firm can also granulate to form larger particles.

Environmental profile

The firm operates with separate air and water pollution licences issued by the local authority. These are shortly to be replaced by an integrated pollution control licence from the EPA. Compliance with the water pollution licence has been poor in the past, so the firm is under pressure from the local authority, from environmental pressure groups, from the media, and from the local community group (which is mainly concerned with noise and smells). The firm has therefore invested in new pollution control equipment, has improved its environmental monitoring and is undertaking a comprehensive waste minimization programme. It has undertaken to reduce its liquid mass emission rates by 50 per cent over four years. It proposes to do this by a series of source reduction measures, which will be implemented on a scheduled basis that takes into account the planned maintenance shut-downs of the factory. The firm has assessed the environmental and economic consequences of installing a waste water treatment plant, and has concluded that such a plant would reduce the nitrogen emissions, but consume energy, lime, capital and running costs and produce a sludge for landfill. It believes that the proposed source reduction programme will achieve the same emission reductions without causing other emissions.

The firm expects environmental pressure to increase in the future. It is therefore a member of the Responsible Care Programme and hopes to be accredited to the Irish environmental management system standard, IS 310, within five years. Two senior managers expend a significant amount of time on environmental issues, and 20 per cent of the staff have now been trained in this area.

Project

Environmentally motivated projects that have been undertaken on the urea plant include:

- Extra storage capacity, which will accommodate the drained-down contents of the process in the event of a process shutdown.

- Improved desorption and hydrolysis, which will reduce normal emissions and facilitate the recovery of the stored drain-down material after process re-start. This was achieved by the installation of new trays on the two desorption columns followed by a new heat exchanger on the hydrolyser whereby the exit material from the column was used to heat the inlet stream, thereby improving energy efficiency.
- Improved condensation of the vapours from the rectification column, which will reduce normal air emissions and also facilitate the recovery of drain-down material.

These three projects were interlinked, as the desorbed and recovered condensate has to be stored in the event of a plant shutdown and also in the early stage of process start up. The extra storage capacity and enhanced recovery process have ended the discharge of nitrogen-rich process condensate to the harbour on shutdowns and start-ups, and recover urea and ammonia that would otherwise have been lost as effluent for reuse in the production process. Large deviations from water licence limits due to plant shutdowns were eliminated, and improved desorber performance eliminated condenser overload thus improving air licence compliance. It also enabled the plant to run at full capacity (it was previously restricted by the risk of excessive nitrogen discharge). Other benefits included reduced material costs.

The project, which the company sees as very successful, thus involved a combination of internal recycling, improved techniques, and incremental change in process technology. It involved significant expenditure, which required the approval of the board. It was undertaken in response to pressure, but the idea originated in helpful discussions between the firm and the regulatory authority, with assistance from the original suppliers of the urea plant. The alternative considered, the installation of a waste water treatment plant to treat process condensate from the urea plant, was not pursued because both the economic and environmental cost-benefit assessments were considered to favour source reduction.

This cleaner technology project convinced the company that they could improve their effluent performance without resorting to end-of-pipe treatment options. However, regulatory pressures still force the company to adopt end-of-pipe solutions.

2 NL Chemicals 1

Company profile

The company started in 1978 as a subsidiary of a US multinational corporation to provide plasticizers for a growing market in Europe (before 1978, the plasticizers were shipped from the US). The company, which has been market leader in Europe for a number of years, runs a refinery (760 employees) and four chemical plants on three sites (430 employees) in the Rotterdam industrial area. The Europort site has an oxo-alcohol and a methoxy propyl acetate plant. The Botlek site has a plasticizer plant and a phthalic anhydride plant. The total annual production of the chemical plants in 1995 was approximately 600,000 tonnes. The phthalic anhydride plant was commissioned in 1991 and delivers phthalic anhydride to the plasticizer plant. Before 1991 the plasticizer plant purchased the phthalic anhydride from external sources. The oxo-alcohol plant was an old butyl alcohol plant of a Dutch multinational company, which was modified in 1981 to an oxo-alcohol plant. More recently the market has expanded to include the Far East. The production capacity of the plasticizer plant was extended to three reactors to enable the doubling of the sales of plasticizers in 10 years. The methoxy propyl acetate plant was bought from another chemical company in 1988.

Environmental profile

The plants are regulated by the NWA Zuid-Holland (a regional Directory of the National Water Authorities) for water emissions and the regional EMA (Central Environmental Management Rijnmond Services) for all other emissions and waste. Besides the general regulatory framework, an array of specific covenants has been developed between the national government and chemical sector. The company is a member of the Dutch Chemical Industries Association.

The management committee of the corporation at the Houston headquarters is responsible for strategic decisions worldwide. The European Management Committee in Brussels spends time on viewing collective plans or results, and setting targets for improvement.

In 1989, another branch of the corporation was involved in a major environmental disaster in another country, which received worldwide publicity. Following this, the corporation promoted stronger environmental policies, including a zero-emission approach. In 1990 this zero-emission plan was modified in the corporation's Emission & Waste Reduction Plan. This plan focused on a 50 per cent reduction of emissions and overall waste (by weight) worldwide over 5 years. From 1988 a systematic programme of in-process measures to reduce emissions and waste was undertaken at the plant to allow productivity growth without a corresponding increase of emissions (in terms of inhabitant equivalents (IEs)). At first, the focus was on water use reduction and process control. Subsequently, new technologies (like the catalyst at the plasticizer plant) and interactive education showed remarkable results in the period 1988–1994.

Recently, the corporation developed its Operations Integrity Management System (OIMS), which addresses safety, health and environmental risk-oriented issues, and is based on a pollution prevention/cleaner production approach. The company has had ISO 9002 certification since 1988, and an Environmental Care System since 1993.

In The Netherlands, there is now a covenant between the national government and the chemical industry. The targets in the covenant have to be met by individual Company Environmental Care Plans (CEAP) with a 4 year time frame, approved by the environmental authorities. The plasticizer plant provided its CEAP in November 1994, and formal approval was given in March 1995.

Project

The plasticizer plant started with proven technology and generated a substantial amount of waste (3000 tons). The company invested $10 million in another catalyst, licensed from a Japanese company, which generated a better product and less waste (a two-thirds reduction in the waste stream). Side reactions meant, however, increased pollution in water emissions. These water emissions were treated in the BIOX waste water treatment facility of the corporation's refinery. Implementation thus proved quite difficult, so the whole experience came to be seen as a learning process.

The decision about the investment in the new catalyst was market driven, with product quality improvement the central focus in the decision making process. The anticipated reduction in the environmental load supported the decision. The Vinyls business group of the European Division in Brussels had the final responsibility for the investment decision (as a general principle, the investment plans of the plants have to fit into the strategic plans of the corporation's Chemical Division, Europe).

Water emissions are controlled through permits issued by the National Water Authority. In 1989, a request to revise the permit was sent to the NWA. As the NWA was then in crisis, a temporary permit was granted in 1991. A technical solution was not required in 1991, but was required for the planned enlargement of the plant at the end of 1992. At that time, there was, uniquely, a public subsidy for investments to reduce emissions (DFl 2000 for every IE reduction in historical effluent emission level). However, this subsidy was not intended to cover new plant enlargements. It was also supposed to stop at the end of 1992.

The European Chemical Division management and the plant management developed a plan to ensure that they would get a new permit in time. At a meeting in January 1992, the NWA required a BIOX and a chemical oxidation unit for the reduction of water emissions. At that time, Cobalt-Flash technology was not proven to be adequate for cobalt reduction. To meet the requirements, another technology, NISSAN technology, was therefore considered as a way to achieve the cobalt reduction. The NWA authorities were willing to consult experts for advice.

In several bargaining rounds during 1992, different scenarios provided the basis for environmental and financial feasibility studies. The length of the permit (4 to 10 years) also influenced these considerations. With the subsidy due to be phased out at the end of 1992, time pressure on the decision making processes was mounting. Near the end of the year RIZA, the staff department of the NWA, recommended BIOX and wet oxidation (which was not subsidizable in case of enlargement of the plant) as the best available technology. A 5 year permit until 1 January 1998 was granted. It included the reduction of the cobalt effluent by January 1995 and the operationalization of the BIOX by January 1996.

The total investment costs for these requirements were US$4.4 million for cobalt reduction (no subsidy), and US$9.1 million (subsidy of DFl 2.3 million) for the BIOX unit.

Despite the reduction of IEs by 90 per cent in the period 1986–1994, the NWA insisted on the use of a water treatment facility for the remaining discharges. The company feels rather frustrated by this requirement, because they believe that they can improve their effluent performance without end-of-pipe solutions. The general perception at the company level is that the NWA approach in the permit revision procedure interrupted an integrated organization and technology approach of the reduction of emissions.

Thus the company has responded in various ways to environmental pressures, ranging from improved techniques and good housekeeping to incremental innovations and radical innovation (in the case of the Japanese catalyst system). The incremental innovations/continuous improvement programmes were fairly typical for the chemical sector, but some of the solutions adopted were less typical, the radical innovations and education activities in particular. Though the final decision about investments in cleaner production processes were substantially shaped by economic and technical assessments (and public subsidies played a role in one case), the strategic management's environmental orientation gives relatively greater weight to environmental concerns in decision making in NL Chemicals 1 than in comparable companies.

3 NL Chemicals 2

Company profile

The company started in the 1950s as a subsidiary of a US multinational. After a joint venture with a state-owned Dutch multinational in the 1970s, the plant is now 100 per cent owned by the Dutch corporation. The parent company was originally developed to create employment in Limburg as the coal mines there closed in 1967, but soaring demand for chemical products like nylon over the following decades enabled the corporation to grow into a multinational corporation which now operates worldwide. The plant under study is in Rotterdam, part of the Fine Chemicals division (also linked to the Special Products Business Unit), and produces 160,000 tonnes of phenol each year. The local management is responsible for operational activities, including environmental, safety and health issues.

The plant produces phenol as feedstock for nylon production at the same corporation's Geleen plant. Phenol production is not based on the conventional process of a reaction between benzene and propane gas. Instead, the plant produces phenol from toluene in two process steps, which is cheaper.

Environmental profile

The Rotterdam plant is located at the border of one of the delta streams of the river Rhine in the Rotterdam industrial area. The plant is regulated by the NWA Zuid-Holland (the regional Directory of the National Water Authorities) for water emissions and the regional EPA (Central Environmental Management Rijnmond Services) for all other emissions and waste. During the 1970s and 1980s the usual pollution control approaches like containment floors for toluene storage, a waste water facility and external treatment of chemical waste were developed. By the end of the 1980s, a number of developments at both strategic and division levels within the company were influencing its approach to environmental issues. These included an array of covenants between the national government and chemical sector.

The company, which is in line with others in the sector in its adoption of good housekeeping and incremental cleaner technology, is a member of the Dutch Chemical Industries Association, has a Quality Care System with ISO 9002 certification, and an Environmental Care System is in the final phase of implementation.

In 1988, the corporation's executive board announced that its environmental policy should comply with the highest standards worldwide. It was a statement that symbolized the progressive development of the company's attitude to environmental issues, evolving from a reactive to an integrated approach. Environmental Care Systems (ECS) were developed in all the Dutch plants of the corporation. As the local management is responsible for environmental, safety and health issues, the ECS is the operational platform for integrating these issues. In addition to traditional tasks (such as advising management about environmental issues and the performance of the procedures for environmental permits) the environmental coordinator is responsible for implementing the ECS at the operations level.

In addition, a Company Environmental Action Plan had to be developed by 1995 to implement the covenant between the Ministry of Environment and the Dutch chemical industry. This required the drafting of a four year programme of improvements in the company's environmental performance, with definite budgets for first year activities, which had to be updated annually and approved by the environmental regulators. The plans allow for more integrated approaches (as opposed to end-of-pipe solutions).

Project

In the early 1990s, when the market for chemical products was poor, the board demanded further reductions in production costs. A task group (local chemical and technical staff and the R&D department at headquarters) developed a radical modification to the existing two step process of producing phenol from toluene, using a new catalyst to enable a one step production process. This innovation had the potential to reduce production costs as well as air and water emissions.

The new process was tested on laboratory scale (10 to 25 litres). Funds were then allocated for a pilot production plant capable of processing up to 1000 litres.

After one year of pilot plant tests, however, the project was evaluated negatively, because some probabilities and deviations had been underestimated in the laboratory. The conditions for stabilizing pressure at pilot plant production level are more crucial than at laboratory level, and even harder to manage in normal production process conditions. It was therefore decided not to proceed to commercial-scale operation.

The environmental aspects of the project were evaluated and discussed throughout with the regulatory agencies. The project was part of the company's 4-year CEAP, so alternatives are now under discussion with the regulators.

4 UK Chemicals

Company profile

With 1450 employees on a 500 acre site, UK Chemicals is the third largest of the nine major manufacturing sites run by the chemicals division of a UK-based multinational corporation. It is located at Grangemouth, on the south shore of the Forth estuary. The site manufactures and markets petrochemicals and related products (the main products are ethylene, polythene, propylene, butadiene, polybutenes and benzene). Both bulk and speciality products are manufactured. Total production for 1993 was 1,188,000 tonnes, with a value of UK £ 2,934 million. Some of these products are based on the light gases which are separated from the North Sea crude oil piped ashore at a nearby separation plant. Other products are based on naphtha which is one of the crude fractions produced at the adjacent refinery. The effluent consists of oil from the oil separator and caustics from the wet air oxidation process.

Environmental profile

As a high profile company operating in a field especially susceptible to environmental scrutiny, significant effort is put into maintaining a positive image. The company published its first 'Health, Safety and Environment (HSE) report' in May 1992. This promised that they would report progress against self-imposed medium-term improvement targets each year. The ultimate aim is zero defects in HSE performance. The company takes part in the chemical industry's Responsible Care Programme, and shares best HSE practice with other UK companies through Responsible Care Cells. The company is a member of the Producer Responsibility Group of 28 companies pledged to recover 58 per cent of Britain's packaging waste by 2000. All managers have annual appraisals which include assessment of environmental performance. All site managers have to report to the Chief Executive on their HSE performance improvements during the year, as part of the HSE Assurance Process introduced in 1993.

Discharges from the site to the Firth of Forth estuary have until recently been regulated by the FRPB (Forth River Purification Board). The move to integrated pollution control (IPC) authorization has shifted the prime regulation role to Her Majesty's Industrial Pollution Inspectorate (HMIPI). HMIPI now authorizes consents after taking advice from FRPB. As well as the prospect of additional requirements, the company is concerned about the increase in uncertainty and costs associated with the move. The relationship with the Regional River Purification Board (FRPB) in recent years was thought to work well: 'This allowed flexible and pragmatic solutions'. Another factor underpinning the firm's response was the shift in standards and the environmental principles underlying them, as the UK adopted common European standards based on the precaution-ary principle and critical load considerations. These were more stringent than FRPB standards, which were based on the assimilative capacity of the waterway/ local ecosystem.

Overall compliance, as monitored by the FRPB, was 64 per cent in 1991/92, 92 per cent in 1992/93, and 100 per cent in 1993/94. Recent environmental improvements at the site have been implemented on a case by case basis, depending on the specifics of the process. A single treatment plant was not favoured, partly because the range of differing processes and differing effluent streams meant that individual solutions made more sense, partly because of pride in local scientific and engineering expertise, and partly because of the expense. In many instances, incremental housekeeping improvements provided cheap waste minimization.

Project

A new ethylene cracker was built as part of a programme begun in the late 1980s to increase the capacity of the Grangemouth operations to process a million barrels a day of crude oil. The new cracker uses the traditional steam cracking by which virtually all ethylene is made. Light hydrocarbons (from the nearby separation plant) are heated to about 800°C, cracking their molecular structure and leading to the formation of ethylene and propylene. The cracking process is then stopped by quenching with water.

This process is energy intensive, and design choices are largely concerned with the efficiency of the furnaces and the recycling of energy throughout the plant. The plant was designed using conventional technology, but in a way that would facilitate the retrofitting of a new technology, 'advanced recovery', at some time in the future.

This was to ensure that the plant would not only meet existing environmental regulations, but also that it would meet any likely standards required in ten years time. This was to allow the company to plan its investment over the long term, and avoid having to respond rapidly to regulatory pressure. This proactive philosophy is underpinned by the belief that any costs of over-compliance may be off-set by the increasing importance of good public relations over environ-mental issues.

Thus the 'invitation to bid' document required a basic plant able to produce a certain amount of ethylene, with a range of add-ons to increase energy efficiency, with the proviso that these should provide a return on investment of 15 per cent. The final design of the cracker was a collaborative process between the company and its chosen contractor. The new cracker incorporates several features which reduce emissions compared to the existing cracker, and also provides treatment for other waste water from the site.

Much of the environmental improvement provided by the new cracker over its predecessors is due to good design and engineering practice. For example, hydrocarbon emissions are minimized through the use of best engineering techniques as regards the choice of valves, seals and joints. There is extensive monitoring of fugitive hydrocarbon emission from valves, and no hydrocarbon streams can be vented except through the flare system where they are combusted. This contrasts with the older ethylene cracker, commissioned in 1968, but still in use. Despite some environmental improvements it still allows hydrocarbons to be vented directly to the atmosphere. In practice it is difficult to retrofit systems to channel all the hydrocarbon streams without very fundamental and expensive redesign and reconstruction.

Emissions to water contain two main sources of potential pollution: oil and caustic. Steam is used in the cracking process and results in an oil-contaminated water stream. In the previous generation cracker this stream went to a simple separator, which allowed the oil to float to the surface so it could be skimmed off for recycling. In the new KG cracker this aqueous stream has been reduced to about 10 per cent by the use of a dilution steam recovery system. The 10 per cent left after this recycling loop passes through a further three-stage treatment process.

The other aqueous stream treatment incorporated in the new cracker is for spent caustic. A soda wash tower is used to remove the acid gas impurities in the feedstock – mainly H_2S and CO_2 – which would otherwise greatly reduce the effectiveness of the catalysts used in hydrogenation. The resulting stream thus contains some caustic soda (about 1 per cent), with sodium sulphide and carbonate, and some hydrocarbons. Traditional practice involved the combustion of hydrogen sulphide, which transferred the problem to one of atmospheric emission. Known as wet air oxidation, the new process converts the sulphide to environmentally acceptable sulphate. Aqueous emissions have fallen by over 60 per cent since 1990 as a result of these new developments.

The new KG cracker reduces emissions as compared to previous designs, and also provides treatment for other waste water from the site. These environmental 'add-ons' do not involve any commercial payback, nor were they necessary to satisfy current local environmental regulation. Instead they are the result of UK Chemical's overall corporate policy to reduce emissions to the environment, enhancing the company's environmental reputation, and pre-empting possible future tightening of environmental regulation.

The new KG cracker highlights the importance of new plant in environmental improvements using cleaner technology. Although environmental add-ons have costs that may not be matched by savings from waste minimization, these costs

Table 4.2 *Summary table of environmental responses of firms*

Firm	IRL Chemicals	NL Chemicals 1	NL Chemicals 2	UK Chemicals
Regulatory context	Recent transition from Cork County Council to national EPA	Regional EPA, Regional NWA	Regional EPA, Regional NWA	Recent transition from FRPB to HMIPI
	IPC system applied for	4-year Environmental action plan	4-year Environmental action plan	IPC system in place
Environmental policy/ management	Formal	Formal	Formal	Formal
		Chemical industry and other covenants	Chemical industry and other covenants	
	In transition: IS 310 Environmental management system	ISO 9002 Environmental Care in Total Quality Management	ISO 9002 Environmental Care in Total Quality Management	HSE approach
	Responsible care	Responsible care	Responsible care	Responsible care
Environmental response/ project	Internal recycling (coupled with incremental changes in process technology)	Radical change in process technology	Radical change in process technology developed but not successfully implemented	Incremental changes in process technology with new plant
	Economic /environmental drives towards continuous improvement	Also economic /environmental drives to good housekeeping, incremental improvements	Also economic /environmental drives to good housekeeping, incremental improvements	Waste water treatment plant; economic/ environmental drives towards continuous improvement

will typically be small compared to the overall costs of new plant. However, retrofitting environmental improvements to existing plant will usually be much more difficult and expensive than building it in from scratch. The company's policy of proactively reducing its emissions allows investment to be planned and carried out smoothly at a pace determined by the company, and not as a sudden response to environmental regulation.

COMPARATIVE ANALYSIS OF CASE STUDIES

Clean technology promotion

Though the chemical industry is a focal point in environmental policies, the task of disseminating information regarding cleaner technologies in this industrial sector is not specifically seen as a function of the government in the three countries.

The chemical industry is a highly technology based sector (though not always a 'high tech' sector) and the approach of the industry, as well as the approach of environmental agencies, seems to be that the chemical industry is capable of developing and/or implementing clean technologies itself. Their focus on technology and their orientation to world markets also provides them with opportunities to detect the latest cleaner technology developments. Nevertheless, chemical plants can still be recruited into cleaner technology projects generated by governments or industrial development organizations. As in The Netherlands, they may exploit tax reduction schemes aimed at promoting certain environmentally friendly technologies.

Role of the environmental regulator

Relevant history and environmental perspectives differ between the three countries. The environmental perspective of the UK can be analysed as an 'assimilative capacity' approach (ie based in emissions that can be absorbed by the recipient waterways), while in The Netherlands the 'critical load' approach is dominant (Chadwick and Nilsson, 1993). Regulation in Ireland and the United Kingdom has recently been restructured in anticipation of the EU IPPC proposal.

Irish chemical firms have been subject to air and water pollution licences issued by the local authority. These are shortly to be replaced by an integrated pollution control licence from the EPA. The Environmental Protection Agency Act (EPA Act) 1992 established a new institutional framework for the control of environmental pollution in Ireland, and has essentially been dictated by the need to comply with the relevant EU Directives. The Act was also motivated by concern about the lack of expertise in many local authorities to deal with complex industrial facilities and the need for clear national standards. Within the Act, the chemical industrial sector was singled out for special attention. The Act describes a BATNEEC approach ('the Best Available Technology Not Entailing

Excessive Costs'). A BATNEEC Guidance Note provides guidance to those applying for integrated pollution control licences under the EPA Act, and states that BATNEEC will be used to prevent, eliminate, or where that is not practicable, limit, abate, or reduce an emission from an activity which is listed in the first schedule of the Act.

UK Chemicals' discharges to the estuary were regulated by the regional Forth River Purification Board which had the power to set 'recipient-based' limits for the discharge of harmful substances. The move to IPC authorization has shifted the prime regulation role to HMIPI (Her Majesty's Industrial Pollution Inspectorate) in Scotland, which authorizes consents with advice from FRPB. This includes a requirement for firms to describe their plans for waste minimization and cleaner technology.

The National Environmental Policy Plan (NEPP 1989 and NEPP+ 1990) of The Netherlands included specific arrangements for the chemical industry, such as the Hydrogenated Carbons-2000 Program (50 per cent reduction of hydrocarbons by the year 2000, compared with the year 1985). The actual regulatory responsibilities are divided between Environmental Protection Agencies and Water Authorities. The Dutch chemical companies in the case studies are regulated by the regional EPA, while the regional Directorate of the National Water Board is responsible for the management of the waste water. These regulatory agencies issue permits which have recently been renewed (renewal is now linked to the Company Environmental Action Plans). The regional EPAs are open to an interactive relationship with companies. However, the NWA still follows a more traditional approach of strict regulation. Companies in the region find this inadequate and demotivating.

A rough interpretation of the position of the environmental regulator(s) and the environmental performance of the five companies is laid out in Table 4.3.

Regulation in Ireland has a tradition of less strict enforcement, though the actual situation resembles the UK performance. The Dutch and UK regulatory approaches seem to be helping chemical companies to develop beyond end-of-pipe pollution control towards waste minimization and continuous improvement. These developments seem to be further fuelled by companies' awareness of various economic incentives. In Ireland, this process is now starting to evolve.

Clean technology and decision-making

These cases – the UK case in particular – highlight two aspects of cleaner technology. First, the often mundane, 'low-tech' ways in which existing processes can be significantly improved to minimize waste, often at little overall cost, or even perhaps with some savings. Second, the difficulty of incorporating other more fundamental changes in existing plants, and the need therefore to take the capital investment cycles of companies into consideration when promoting cleaner technology.

Differences in the degree of local autonomy, particularly in financial decision-making were an important influence. However, decision-making in these cases

Table 4.3 *Overview of performance of companies and regulation*

Country	Performance	Regulation	Background CT
Ireland	In transition to more process-integrated approaches	Regulation becoming stricter and moving to stimulate waste minimization	Internal recycling Economic/ environmental pressures towards waste minimization and incremental improvement
UK	Proactive responses to regulation; integration of waste-minimization concepts in new plant installation	Interaction with water regulator; uncertainty about HMIPI	Incremental improvements in process technology as part of installation of new cracker includes explicitly environmental as well as economically driven changes
The Netherlands 1	Integrated approach to process improvement and environmental issues; in transition to 'constructive' approaches	Strict regulation by NWA; interactive regulation by regional EPA; covenants; 4-year environmental action plans	Radical change in process technology Economic/ environmental pressures stimulated programme of incremental improvement in techniques and technologies
The Netherlands 2	Integrated approach to process improvement and environmental issues; in transition to 'constructive' approaches	Strict regulation by NWA; interactive regulation by regional EPA; covenants; 4-year environmental action plans	Radical change in process technology (not fully successful) Economic/ environmental pressures towards improved techniques and technologies

shared certain features. The chemical industry is a high technology sector with the need for specialized expertise and large-scale investments. Decision-making processes are therefore highly structured. This can restrict the scope for more fundamental changes. On the other hand waste minimization projects can sensitize decision-makers to the scope for cleaner technology.

Historical analysis shows that social concern about the chemical industry's polluting practices has been one of the triggers for public environmental policy management. The chemical industry's reaction to such growing concerns tended to be the implementation of reactive solutions. At first, pollution control management often took the form of large investments in end-of-pipe technologies. More recently, however, many representatives of the chemical industry noted that 'Responsible Care Programmes', which essentially require members to adhere to a Code of Good Environmental Management Practice, promote a shift towards more preventive policies.

IRL Chemicals are pursuing improved environmental performance by a waste minimization/recycling/reuse programme, monitoring discharges to air, water and land, and training staff in environmental issues. The main consideration is compliance with environmental requirements and local pressures, but the company may also have been influenced by the environmental policy of the UK joint owners.

In the NL Chemicals 1 case, continuous improvement is being pursued through a mixture of Environmental Care and Quality Management programmes, internal competitions, workers' participation meetings, and goal-setting. A five year 'Emission & Waste Reduction Plan' (initiated at the highest international corporation level after a serious environmental incident) was started in 1992, with the aim of reaching a 50 per cent reduction of all waste and emissions by 1997.

NL Chemicals 2 also pursues policies that comply with the position statement from their international parent corporation; that their environmental policy should comply with the highest standards worldwide. Besides yearly improvements via incremental steps in the performance of the 'Environmental care programme', a radical change in the production process (initiated in order to reduce costs, and justified in those terms) should also lead to substantial reduction of emissions.

In the case of UK Chemicals, the corporate strategy of its international parent is to work towards a more proactive environmental policy. This proactive approach is being operationalized at plant level by a cleaner technology assessment in different plant sectors.

CONCLUSIONS

'Good housekeeping and waste minimization' typify the chemical sector's approach to the management of environmental pollution. The waste minimization approaches show both incremental steps as well as more radical changes in process technology. Either approach may involve substantial investments, particularly given the high costs of retrofitting existing plant (which may favour periodic change as part of programmes of plant replacement, as already noted in the case of refineries).

In recent years, environmental considerations seem to have stimulated the search for more innovative, 'process-integrated' approaches, supplementing economic incentives to enhance process efficiency. Increasingly, companies seem to be initiating educational activities, and generating innovative technological solutions, some of which are radical. Policy statements from the corporate executive on environmental issues, and the arrival of managers who are open-minded to new developments, create the conditions for more environmentally based decisions. Most of these approaches appear at the same time to be cost effective, with a few making a significant improvement to company profitability. This places these chemical industry cases as front-runners (Rogers, 1983) in cleaner production.

The agencies in the three regions are at different levels of development, not only in terms of their attitudes and approaches to enforcement, but also in their relations with companies. In the case studies, higher awareness levels within the local communities seem to engender more sophisticated methods of enforcement. This in turn has a strong influence on the approaches and environmental performance of companies. When companies are developing strategy, especially where environmental issues arise (such as in developing waste minimization programmes), it is clearly useful to involve environmental agencies in the decision making process as early as possible.

The environmental performance in all cases show that waste minimization is evolving in the chemical industry. Three of the four companies set quantifiable goals in terms of percentages in reduction of waste and emissions within a medium-term time frame (up to five years). Though the environmental burden of this sector continues to be high, the pathway from reactive towards proactive approaches is being explored.

5 FINE CHEMICALS SECTOR

Noel Duffy and Brendan Ryan with Leo Baas, Ole Erik Hansen, Ian Thomson and Robin Williams

Three companies were examined in this sector, one in Denmark, one in Ireland and one in the UK.

THE SECTORAL CONTEXT

Main industrial processes

The products and processes of this sector are very wide-ranging. Allied with the organic chemicals sector, it lies between petro-chemicals and pharmaceuticals in terms of the production quantities of products. Processes may be batch or continuous, depending on the production volumes, expected product lifespan and specification variability, and the industry uses all forms of transformation and separation processes. The use of organic chemical solvents is common, and the operations may occur over a wide range of pressures and temperatures.

Environmental issues

The substances involved in production are extremely diverse. Many are flammable and toxic. Wastes and emissions are to all media: water, air and land. End-of-pipe regulation has led to extensive investment in devices such as incinerators, scrubbers, condensers, carbon adsorbers and biological waste water treatment plants. Firms are regulated by national environmental and planning controls, by the Integrated Pollution Prevention and Control (IPPC) Directive (Commission of the European Communities, 1996), and are likely to be affected by the proposed Volatile Organic Compounds (VOC) Directive (Commission of the European Communities, 1997) and suggested Polluting Emissions Register (PER) Directive.

Reputation is important to firms in this sector. They generally attempt to establish a 'quality' reputation with other firms by guaranteeing product performance, price, delivery, after-sales service and so on. Environmental performance is now a part of this image of total quality. The public tends to see all firms in the sector as 'chemical' firms and thus suspect, although this depends on the firm's history and the occurrence of problems such as odours or accidents.

The media can also internationalize local problems, which can then affect the business of other firms in the sector.

Industrial context

Products are differentiated on the basis of performance in use as well as composition. The customer may be the public or another firm. Technical support or product liability issues may distinguish different manufacturers. Technical knowledge or 'know-how' is an important asset, and is protected by patents and secrecy. The cost of manufacturing is a significant part of the product price, and optimization of the manufacturing process is a continuing major concern. Market share is influenced by pricing policy, as well as product quality. Research and development is oriented to new products, improved product quality and process efficiency.

Firms range from small businesses supplying a local market, to global corporations, with many branch plants. Some firms develop niche roles in the market, providing specialist synthesis services, based on expertise and equipment. Others manufacture generic products that are out of patent and whose manufacture is known or can be easily developed. The importance of reputation and marketing, the capital-intensive nature of the sector, as well as the requirement for technical knowledge and skills inhibits new entrants.

The Danish case in this sector is an outlier with interesting similarities. It is not a chemicals firm itself; it produces membrane filters. However, it is both a customer of and a supplier to the industry. On changing ownership, it became part of a chemical multinational, and the extension of the corporate environmental policy of this multinational provides interesting lessons, which are discussed in parallel with the other firms.

Case Studies

1 DK Fine Chemicals

Company profile

This firm was initially set up in 1972 as a spin-off from the research activities of a Danish food processing company. The company was taken over in 1989 by a US multinational seeking a partner for its US subsidiary in the same business line, which gave the firm access to skills and technology from a diverse industrial base. It was integrated into the business unit of Liquid Separations in 1995. The production site has an annual turnover of 189,455 Danish Crowns (1993) and there are 177 employees.

The production site in Denmark produces membrane filtration products and systems for reverse osmosis, nanofiltration, ultrafiltration and microfiltration

Table 5.1 *Fine chemicals sector cases*

Company	DK Fine Chemicals	IRL Fine Chemicals	UK Fine Chemicals
Products	Liquid membrane filtration devices	Liquid ion-exchange reagents & detergent additive	Dyestuffs and other organic fine chemicals
Market	Europe and Asia	Global, with 50% to affiliates in Europe	Global
Number of employees in firm	177	150	800
in whole company	60,000	40,000	31,500
Ownership/ relationship with parent	This firm was taken over and became a branch of a US global corporation	Branch site of an EU multinational. Sole manufacturer of these products within company	Branch site of a UK global corporation
Regional features	Participated in a cleaner technology demonstration project in partnership with regulators	Indirectly influenced by local lobby concerns	

used in a wide range of filtration applications including water desalination and de-alcholization.

The firm is technologically sophisticated and the parent company has invested heavily in the production and research activities in a long-term strategy to become a global forerunner in liquid membrane separation. As a part of this strategy the company became the European centre for separation systems and diaphragm filtration technology within the company.

Environmental profile

Before the takeover the company was in economic crisis and the environmental demands were seen as a threat to the competitiveness of the firm. The company therefore tried to resist environmental demands. Following the takeover, the company changed its environmental profile from a reactive to a proactive waste minimization and pollution prevention strategy. The multinational parent's commitment to eliminate all injuries, prevent adverse environmental and health impacts, and reduce wastes and emissions resulted in a cultural change of environmental behaviour, and many different environmental activities were initiated.

In 1993 the site took part, along with eight other companies, in a regional cleaner technology demonstration project promoted by Storstrøms County, the local authority. The firm had already made some progress in reducing emissions and wastes, and continued to make improvements, but still was not immediately able to meet all the regulatory requirements. The regulators were actually quite satisfied with the company's rate of progress, but the technical breach was not well regarded by the multinational parent, who saw it as a potential embarrassment.

Project

In the regional demonstration project the plant focused on its waste streams resulting from diaphragm production, seeking an economically sound solution for reducing both total water consumption and the volume of waste water that was sent for incineration. Staff were trained, then the firm reassessed its operations. The waste water was identified as coming from three possible sources.

The firm then realized it might be able to apply its own membrane filtration technology to recover organic solvent from its waste water. Two of the firm's own diaphragm filtration plants were used to purify the streams on the two production lines. An average of 55 per cent of the water is now reused, 12 per cent is discharged directly without further treatment and the balance is transferred to the national hazardous waste facility. The projected payback time for the project was 2.6 years. The investment reduced the environmental impact, provided direct financial savings and provided a new potential for sales of the firm's technology. The project also developed a useful dialogue between the company and the public authorities, thereby making cleaner production an integrated element in the regulation of the company, and thus succeeded in a number of respects.

2 IRL Fine Chemicals

Company profile

This firm commenced production in Ireland in 1974, as a subsidiary of a US multinational manufacturing reagents for the mining industry. Ownership transferred to a German company in 1978 and the product range was extended from ion-exchange reagents to include a detergent additive. The firm has a turnover of about IR£50,000,000, exports globally, with 50 per cent going to affiliate plants in Europe, and gets most of its raw materials from within Europe. It employs about 150 people. The manufacturing processes are a combination of batch and continuous operations, many using organic solvents. In 1993 the firm received ISO 9002 certification.

Environmental profile

The firm was, until recently, regulated by Cork County Council from whom it received air and water licences. Environmental control is achieved using what the firm describes as 'standard' technologies though the firm insists that their objective is always to eliminate the problem at source. As far back as 1984 the firm ended the use of chlorinated solvents. Data provided both by the company and by the local authority indicate comfortable compliance with regulatory requirements with the exception of discharge of total nitrogen in liquid waste. The company believes that the licence requirement for total nitrogen is technically unworkable if the biological waste water treatment plant is to work efficiently.

The firm identified legislation and the enforcement of such legislation as the major environmental pressures. It also rates local community pressure, corporate policy and workforce concerns as significant. Five full-time and four part-time staff now work on environmental matters, while 70 per cent of staff have been trained in environmental issues. The firm is a member of the Responsible Care Programme, and expects to be accredited to an environmental management system within three years.

The firm has conducted waste minimization/recycling/reuse programmes together with environmental audits of disposal contractors and suppliers, and invested IR£ 6.5 million in environmental control between 1990 and 1995. The waste water treatment plant represents 25 per cent of total investment on the site, but the firm expects the cost of environmental protection to increase still further in the future because of both regulatory and pressure group demands. Decisions about environmental investment may be made locally if they are within the financial threshold, but larger investments require board approval from Germany though a 'fast track' procedure can apply to environmental and safety projects.

The parent company has a major R&D facility. Local R&D is small scale, but the firm has developed several innovative applications of existing technologies in various collaborative projects.

Project

The firm planned to expand production in 1993. This would have required a substantial increase in acetic anhydride usage. The consequent increase in waste acetic acid being sent to the waste water treatment plant would have necessitated an expansion of the treatment plant. A detailed examination of all streams from the process was therefore conducted. Five contained high concentrations of acetic acid. A sixth contained methanol and sodium acetate in addition to acetic acid. A number of options were developed for this stream. One entailed steam stripping to recover the methanol, combining the residue with the other five streams, but leaving the sodium acetate in the residue. A process breakthrough, using phase transfer catalysis, eliminated the methanol and sodium acetate. It was found that a market existed for acetic acid and therefore it was determined to try to recover and sell the acetic acid waste. A process to do this using liquid extraction with ethyl acetate was developed. The capital investment was IR£3.7 million.

The project, which involved the local R&D department, local project engineering and production staff, consultants, and the parent company engineering department, was an internally inspired innovation which avoided the further use of end-of-pipe treatment facilities and instead resulted in the production of a saleable product which turned out to be considerably more lucrative than expected. The project was initially seen as a way of minimizing needed expenditure by minimizing waste, but it turned out to be commercially successful and provided a useful return on investment. The project has therefore received considerable attention from the rest of the organization. Much of the recovered material is now reused on site, with the balance being used by other firms, as customers of an intermediate chemical supply firm.

3 UK Fine Chemicals

Company profile

This firm was formed in 1993 through the de-merger of a very large UK chemical producer that operated in all sectors from heavy chemicals to pharmaceuticals. The de-merging was aimed at improving performance in some areas and avoiding a threat of takeover. The firm deals exclusively with fine organic chemicals and is organized into three Business Divisions which are responsible for product development, marketing and sales and so on: Pharmaceuticals is the most important, followed by Agrochemicals and Speciality Chemicals. The site is engaged in batch manufacture of a wide range of chemicals, mainly for the Specialities Business Division (mostly organic, especially colours: textile dyes and pigments for paint and plastic products, but also biocides), and materials on contract to the Agrochemical Business. The company operates two manufacturing sites in the UK, this one in Scotland and another in England, for these products.

Expenditure on new projects has to be justified and approved by the Business Divisions. The latter's role in contracting production from the manufacturing sites creates an internal market. The possibility of buying products in or abandoning production of unprofitable lines (in the face of growing international competition, especially from developing nations) creates a degree of competition between these plants. In the aftermath of de-merger, there was a shortage of capital in the firm. The resulting pressure to improve financial performance made it increasingly difficult to justify expenditure, including expenditure on environmental improvements.

Environmental profile

The plant was established before the First World War to manufacture synthetic dyes, utilizing local coal/shale chemicals, and was located beside the Forth estuary because of access to water for processing and to take waste discharges. A pipeline was installed in 1975 to take the waste into deep waters in the estuary, to give better dilution, rather than let it flow down a local stream. Consents were initially very lax, but have become much more stringent (by two orders of magnitude in the case of toxic metals) under the influence of European Directives. The Forth River Purification Board had traditionally framed consents to meet specific local circumstances – in terms of the levels of BOD, pH and so on, that could be absorbed by the estuary without evident environmental harm (eg on biodiversity) – and were quite happy with the plant's performance.

The company has a policy of achieving continuous improvement in safety, health and environment (SHE) performance. A central SHE function sets world-wide corporate standards and 'Good Practice Guidelines'. Every site is required to develop 'Systems and Procedures' for safe operation; their SHE performance is audited annually. SHE is primarily seen as a line management responsibility.

In 1990, the chairman of the parent company announced a policy to reduce waste by 50 per cent by 1995. However, this specific target was not continued after the firm was de-merged (though company reports continue to emphasize waste reduction). The company applies the 'polluter pays' principle internally.

Project

Site managers set up a group in 1988 because of growing internal concern about aqueous effluent discharges. They were aware that the English plant had managed to win a contract to produce certain toxic agrochemicals, partly on the strength of having a water treatment plant (which it had for some years as it discharges to an inland waterway). Local managers felt that they might be vulnerable, without such a plant, to future changes in legislation and working relationships with regulators. They wanted to have more control over their future. Anticipating tighter environmental standards and faced with intense external and internal competitive market pressures, they decided that they needed a waste water treatment plant, but had limited capital.

A small group was established, consisting of staff from the Process Technology Division, SHE and Production Management. The group surveyed liquid effluents and identified 600 different streams. This audit revealed – for the first time – where the components of the waste streams came from. Before the audit, the company had not known where the constituents of many of their waste streams (apart from certain special streams) came from; they only knew the average levels of discharges. The following steps were undertaken:

- segregation of streams, placing 'strong' effluent above ground,
- replacement of drains, some of which had been in place since 1920, and which were therefore aged and failing,
- installing a deep channel multidiffuser,
- installing a containment facility to store accidental discharges.

An extensive waste minimization exercise was undertaken, to be followed by pre-treatment of streams, such as neutralization of acids with lime, finishing with a biological treatment plant.

The waste minimization exercise was stimulated by corporate policy (the target of halving waste emissions by 1995), and then driven by concern to reduce the size and cost of the waste treatment plant. The waste streams were assessed in terms of the volume of waste, legislative pressures, the possibility that current disposal routes might be withdrawn, public complaints, and the potential for achieving rapid reduction in waste. The hundred highest scoring waste streams were examined in detail. After assessing streams that had been omitted because of peculiarities of the scoring systems, and streams that could not really be overcome, 74 projects remained. Each project was then assessed financially, in terms of:

- savings in materials costs,
- savings in construction and running costs for the treatment plant,
- capital and development costs of the project.

This showed that some projects could yield quite significant improvements in environmental performance with modest costs balanced against important savings. They then had to go to the Business Divisions to get approval for the expenditure, as the company applies a 'polluter pays' principle internally, which meant that the Business Divisions would be charged for the capital costs and the running costs of waste treatment.

However, the firm as now constituted, unlike its parent predecessor, was not committed to introducing improvements in areas where there was no legal requirement. Changes were introduced on the basis of legislation or where they offered overall cost savings; waste reduction per se was not a goal for the organization. In addition, once the design of the treatment plant had been completed ('frozen'), it was not possible to include savings in the capital costs of the plant as a factor in the cost-benefit analysis of waste minimization projects.

The most straightforward of these projects have been implemented or are underway. These were the cases that could easily be justified. Some older manufacturing processes have been closed down altogether (eg in the dyestuffs division). These were products at the end of their life cycle, with obsolete plant, and facing strong competition from developing nations.

Waste minimization and segregation, coupled with closure of some older (typically dirtier) product lines will reduce total liquid effluent discharges by 65 per cent from 1990 levels by 1996, when the programme is complete. Total dissolved solids have already (by 1995) been reduced by 65 per cent. The size of waste water treatment plant needed has thus been reduced by 33 per cent, representing a significant cost saving.

It is clear that the emerging structure and commercial strategy of the firm – especially its resort to an internal market – has shaped its response to environmental pressures, and that these commercial pressures have mandated against large-scale environmental works. The firm is seen by regulatory agencies as being relatively slow to respond to requests for improvement. However, paradoxically, this has created space for the adoption of waste minimization under circumstances where this readily yields savings or can be achieved at little cost. The financial constraints, and the need to justify environmental expenditure to Business Divisions, encouraged the search for alternatives to installing a large and expensive water treatment plant, and the steps that followed significantly reduced the scale and cost of the biological treatment plant required.

COMPARATIVE ANALYSIS OF CASE STUDIES

Legislation and its enforcement

The recent changes in the regulatory regime in Scotland and Ireland makes it difficult to give a 'snap-shot' of performance, as the process of assimilation and accommodation of the new regulatory structures confuses the picture. There are differences in the level of pre-existent controls, with stringent requirements in Cork reflected by IRL Fine Chemicals which has a waste water treatment plant, while in Lothian, UK Fine Chemicals discharges directly to the estuary.

The organization of enforcement of the regulations may take different forms. UK Fine Chemicals is controlled by the Forth River Purification Board (FRPB), but under the new Integrated Pollution Control (IPC) system, HMIPI is the primary regulator, but still shares the control of emissions to water with FRPB. The relationship with FRPB is well established, while the attitude of HMIPI is unknown, prompting uncertainty within the company. The prospect of this new IPC system, with an expected emphasis on waste minimization, was a significant stimulus to the examination of their practices.

IRL Fine Chemicals, which was formerly controlled by Cork County Council, is now subject to the recently formed national Environmental Protection Agency (Irish Government, 1992). This decision, applied to a large number of firms throughout the country, was partly due to a lack of resources among local authorities, and partly due to a public concern that the relationship between the regulators and regulated was a bit too cordial and flexible. IRL Fine Chemicals had an allowance to emit organohalogens in their water pollution licence. They had phased out the use of any organohalogens much earlier, but the allowance

Table 5.2 *Summary table of environmental responses of firms*

Company	DK Fine Chemicals	IRL Fine Chemicals	UK Fine Chemicals
Regulatory context	Storstrøms County is the regulator. Recognized as a 'Green County' by UNEP	Recent transfer from county council to national EPA	Recent transfer from the Forth River Purification Board (FRPB) to Her Majesty's Industrial Pollution Inspectorate (HMIPI)
	SPURT project	IPC licence applied for	IPC licence received
Environmental policy/ management	Formal	Formal Parent has signed ICC – BCSD ISO 9002 Working towards IS 310	Formal
	Responsible Care	Responsible Care	Responsible Care
Prior waste water treatment	Firm's biological plant	Firm's biological plant via sewer to estuary	Discharge to estuary
Environmental response/project	Use of firm's own membrane technology to recover organic solvent from waste water	Water usage reduction and recovery and sale of waste acetic acid. National 'Recovery of Waste' award, 1996	Installation of waste water treatment plant, preceded by waste minimization
	End-of-pipe/ internal recycling	Internal plus external recycling	End-of-pipe/ incremental change in process technology

remained, because neither the firm nor the regulator chose to revise the licence. Greenpeace produced a table of emissions from licensed firms in the Cork region, based on their licence limits, rather than their actual emissions. This embarrassed the company. The firm also has a nitrogen limit in their licence, which they argue is technically impossible to achieve, because it is incompatible with the other licence requirements. The experience of the regulators in both Ireland and Scotland with a cleaner technology philosophy is still limited.

In Denmark, the control is devolved to the local authority, which is free to impose its own controls within guidelines established by the national Environmental Protection Agency. Prior to the takeover of DK Fine Chemicals by its new parent, the firm had a poor environmental record with the regulator, Storstrøms County. The change in ownership brought a corporate policy that emphasized compliance with local regulations as a minimum, and sought a standard of excellence. Waste reduction was a corporate goal. At the same time, the County sought to establish a partnership approach to firms, rather than command-and-control. The County started a cleaner production demonstration project with a number of local firms, DK Fine Chemicals being one of them (Storstrøms County, 1993). Working together, the objective was to benefit both the environment and the economy. DK Fine Chemicals identified projects that reduced its use of water, its discharge of pollutants, and had a 2.5 year payback.

Not all of the firm's environmental problems were solved. It was still in breach of its licence, but the regulators were satisfied that the firm's performance was improving. This acceptance by the regulators of current breaches was not understood by DK Fine Chemicals' parent company. This flexibility was seen as an oversight, and the firm's performance was seen as a liability to the company's reputation. Investment and confidence in the local site were threatened by this 'loose' enforcement. The cultural difference between the corporate headquarters and the traditional behaviour of the Danish public authorities made it very difficult for the head office to understand this different regulatory philosophy, and these differences in perception and culture created serious problems for the Danish subsidiary.

Management structure and style

All of the firms in the study are branch plants. Even UK Fine Chemicals may be considered as a production site, segregated from its headquarters. The parent company has introduced a system of business units. The headquarters business units owe little allegiance to the manufacturing sites. Where a company has many sites, it may choose to manage them using a system of benchmarking, or one of internal competition. Benchmarking seeks to identify common performance indicators, and is used to rank sites. This ranking is used to direct support to areas requiring attention. Internal competition seeks to focus on costs alone, and creates an internal market between sites of the same company. It tends to maximize near-term profits, and may encourage a behaviour that merely satisfies minimum environmental requirements, and short-term planning. Since it stimulates a competitive outlook between sites, it inhibits the sharing of good practice or beneficial innovations. UK Fine Chemicals uses this approach. Each site effectively bids against a sister site for production. If it fails to win orders, it will not obtain re-investment, or indeed, income. Ultimately, if it continues to fail, it will be closed down.

Environmental management

Corporate policy can have a significant influence on branch plants. Prior to takeover, DK Fine Chemicals saw environmental controls as a burden and threat. Compliance alone was the objective. The firm reacted to demands. After the takeover, the parent company introduced a policy which aimed for excellence, provided waste reduction targets and sought to be proactive. This pollution prevention approach was in place even before the cooperation with the regulators. Hazardous waste, instead of being emitted, was routed to an approved treatment facility. Next, a waste minimization audit was undertaken. Some benefits were achieved, but the performance did not improve uniformly.

In contrast, there appears to be a reduction in corporate emphasis on waste reduction in UK Fine Chemicals. Prior to the de-merger, a five year target to reduce waste by 50 per cent was published. After the de-merger, this specific target was not continued, though reductions have still been achieved. The site still has a policy to achieve continuous improvement in safety, health and environmental performance, which is annually audited.

IRL Fine Chemicals' parent company has committed itself to the International Chamber of Commerce's Business Charter for Sustainable Development (ICC, 1990). Locally, it has an environmental policy and adheres to the sectoral organization's Responsible Care principles (CEFIC, 1994), which requires members to adhere to a code of good environmental management practice, and prompts a shift to more preventive policies.

Economics of environmental management

Cost minimization has been an important motivator for all the firms studied. IRL Fine Chemicals was faced with the need to expand its waste treatment plant to accommodate a planned plant expansion. It reviewed its operations, and devised an alternative recovery process. Initially this was expected to merely reduce the cost of dealing with this waste, but it was found that the recovered acetic acid commanded a sufficiently high price for the plant to earn a payback. DK Fine Chemicals saved costs by reducing its consumption of raw water and the quantity of waste sent for disposal. It has also, at a corporate level, started to look at the concept of full cost accounting, which includes a cost for the environment.

UK Fine Chemicals decided that it needed a waste water treatment plant as a 'stay-in-business' investment. Capital was scarce, however. Once the decision in principle was agreed, the firm undertook an extensive waste minimization programme. An internal polluter pays system was initiated. Small capital investment projects, changes in operating practices and closure of plants were undertaken. Investments in waste reduction technologies could be offset against the capital and future operating costs of the new waste water plant under design. Once the design was 'frozen', or specified in detail, additional savings could no longer be realized. Investment in this plant provided a window of opportunity;

one that might not be re-opened for many years. This again highlights the significance of investment cycles.

Communications: intra-firm

Some improvement in environmental performance can be directly attributed to particular individuals in firms. A leader of a corporation can set the agenda, targets and general direction. The company chairman prior to UK Fine Chemicals' formation was responsible for establishing quantified waste reduction targets. These were put into effect by many staff implementing this policy, but the lead had been provided. DK Fine Chemicals applied their own technology to process their waste. The same solvents that were used to make the membranes were recovered by the membranes. The initial thought was that the solvents should dissolve the membranes. However, the general manager suggested that they were tried, and the idea was successful. In addition to solving DK Fine Chemicals' own problem, the firm saw a business opportunity in the potential marketing of this new technology to solve similar problems for other firms, which was also a stimulus. The development of this project was carried out primarily at the site. IRL Fine Chemicals by contrast, devised the idea at the local site, but developed it in conjunction with the central corporate engineering. In the case of IRL Fine Chemicals, there is some evidence to suggest that an 'information gate-keeper' played an important role in originating the idea and in championing the project.

Communications: inter-firm

Both UK Fine Chemicals and IRL Fine Chemicals cooperated with other firms to develop their projects. UK Fine Chemicals used a process engineering consultancy to design their waste water treatment plant. Their corporate headquarters preferred a distant relationship between client and contractor (to simplify enforcement of the contract). The local staff preferred to work in a collaborative fashion, drawing on the complementary expertise of the two firms. IRL Fine Chemicals devised their project concept internally. After initial feasibility trials, they turned to external process engineering firms to develop the process and conduct pilot trials. Working cooperatively, the project eventually involved the consultant as well as central engineering. The product is itself sold to another chemical company, which sells it on to other companies. IRL Fine Chemicals has also cooperated with suppliers and customers on packaging issues, for example moving to reusable bulk packaging.

There is a national sectoral organization in each of the regions, for example FDKI in Denmark. In turn, these organizations are affiliated to the CEFIC (European Chemical Industry Council). These organizations have undertaken to follow the principles of 'Responsible Care', originally advocated in North America. While membership of the organization may be contingent on adherence to the principles, application is the responsibility of the individual firm. The primary sanction that applies for non-application is peer pressure.

Communications: public and others

At an international level, the chemical industry has been the subject of considerable media and public interest. The international nature of the business has meant that concerns in one country can be transmitted to the management of an associated operation in another. The parent company of DK Fine Chemicals was very concerned that its reputation would be tarnished by the lack of compliance of this Danish site, even though the local authorities were satisfied. This company publishes a corporate environmental report which lists the emissions from all its European sites. The parent company of IRL Fine Chemicals also publishes an environmental report. This presents the emissions from the main headquarters site in great detail, but does not detail the subsidiaries. These are covered by narrative reports of both bad and good activities. IRL Fine Chemicals has received a high number of favourable reports. UK Fine Chemicals also reports its performance, but no longer compares them with targets, suggesting a lessening in emphasis.

There has been intense local concern about this sector in Cork, prompted by local smell problems, and short term health effects, though no evidence of permanent effects has been substantiated. IRL Fine Chemicals has not been subject to direct criticism from local lobby groups, but was categorized as a poor performer by Greenpeace, and is concerned about its reputation. It therefore now meets with representatives of community groups. Cork County Council has also initiated an Environment Forum to facilitate dialogue between all the parties interested in the region's environment.

CONCLUSIONS

The particular characteristics of this sector are:

- a very diverse range of products and processes;
- that production costs are significant, as well as quality, marketing, etc;
- that innovations are sought in both products and processes.

This sector has similarities with the pharmaceutical sector, and reference should also be made to the conclusions and lessons drawn from that study.

Regulation

Regulation is the primary driving force for environmental performance. If cleaner technology is to be the preferred priority, therefore, direction must be provided by the regulatory framework. Firms need both guidance and a supporting framework. Demanding standards are necessary in order to spur progress, but the industry must be given the time and flexibility it needs to address these standards. These factors will require a level of technical and management competence in the regulatory authorities. Storstrøms County displayed this kind of flexibility, to the benefit of both the firm and the local environment.

Cost minimization

Once a firm has decided to respond to regulatory pressures, cost minimization is the most important determinant of whether or not it opts for a cleaner technology response. It is important to identify the source of the waste, as this is a very useful internal management tool. One example of this is the use of an internal polluter pays system. However, internal competition, which emphasizes cost alone, appears to be less effective than a more sophisticated system which examines the type and impact of the waste, and seeks to support improvement rather than penalize performance.

Public information

The public, as neighbours, can be a major force in sensitizing firms. The suggested Polluting Emissions Register may therefore play an important role in future. However, the public may not be familiar with the benefits of a cooperative approach to regulation, as opposed to a simple command-and-control system, which highlights the need to educate the public in this regard.

Business networks

The three firms studied engaged in considerable cooperation with an outside organization. The regulatory agency was the partner to DK Fine Chemicals. Both IRL Fine Chemicals and UK Fine Chemicals developed their environmental response with the partnership of a consultancy group. This sharing seems to be a productive and efficient model.

While formal environmental management systems are common, the application of accredited standards, for example the Eco-Management and Audit Scheme (EMAS), is at an early stage (Commission of the European Communities, 1993). Although there have been limited production chain effects in these firms, these seem attributable to corporate policy rather than being prompted by these standards. Benchmarking, which attempts to improve poorer performance, can lead to a useful sharing of ideas, which indicates a role for schemes to assist inter-firm benchmarking.

Investment cycles

The influence of investment cycles is considerable. They provide critically important windows of opportunity for environmental improvements. Times of expansion are also opportune points at which to include environmental investments. However, to direct such investments towards cleaner technology requires that the firm or the site is prepared and ready to seize the opportunity, and that there are no overwhelming pressures to install end-of-pipe devices (perhaps because they can offer 'conspicuous compliance'). Many cleaner technology improvements are distributed throughout the plant, and do not have the same visibility. Conversely, it may not be possible to undertake major investment until capital is available and justified. Regulators should be aware of the significance of this cycle, and possibly consider providing 'innovation space', that is, time for a longer-term search for cleaner innovations that can be economically adopted in the next major upgrading of the production process. Some attempts have been made at this in the US (Ashford et al, 1985).

Corporate policy

Key individuals had an important impact in each of the three firms studied in this sector, and corporate policy and peer pressure can be useful motivators. Change in corporate governance had a negative impact on environmental policy in one firm in this study, and a very positive impact in another. The parent of DK Fine Chemicals imposed its standard of excellence. This helped to move the local firm from a reactive to a proactive position. However, the parent company failed to interpret the significance of the local culture, and interpreted flexibility as weakness and failure. Problems can clearly arise in such cases, where a local problem is addressed by distant management. This highlights the importance of good dialogue within the corporate hierarchy in order to ensure that local issues are properly understood at higher levels.

6 PHARMACEUTICALS SECTOR

Noel Duffy and Brendan Ryan with Leo Baas, Frank Boons,
Ole Erik Hansen and Graham Spinardi

Five companies were examined in this sector, one in Denmark, two in Ireland, one in The Netherlands and one in the UK.

THE SECTORAL CONTEXT

Main industrial processes

The pharmaceutical sector tends to pay more attention to the development of products rather than to the means of producing these products. The processes are generally batch. This is justified by the need to maintain flexible operations, where different pieces of equipment may be used for the same purpose. It also preserves batch integrity, whereby a particular medication administered to a patient may be traced to a particular date and time of manufacture. Raw materials and intermediates are initially mixed in a solvent, and then brought to the appropriate temperature and pressure. They are held in this state for the appropriate time to form the desired product. The product is crystallized from solution, separated by centrifugation or filtration and dried. This generic operation is repeated several times. Standard items of equipment such as reaction vessels, centrifuges, filters and dryers, are connected, and operated in a manner typical of bench scale operations, reflecting the origins of the products. Scale-up of production can lead to more by-products than were formed in the laboratory. A waste to product ratio of 10:1 is typically achieved. The final dried product is ground to the desired particle size and then bagged or drummed as desired. The active ingredient is combined with other substances to form the necessary form of the desired end-product, ie tablet, capsule, vial, etc. This is often conducted at a site different from the bulk manufacturer, and the activities are described as primary and secondary manufacturing (Cole, 1990).

Environmental issues

The substances involved in production are extremely diverse. Many are flammable and toxic. Waste is produced at each step of the product synthesis. Therefore, as the number of steps increases, the quantity of waste increases. Waste and emissions are to all media: water, air and land. Most attention has focused on the ancillary materials involved, for example organic solvents and catalysts, rather than the waste intermediate products. End-of-pipe regulation has led to extensive investment in devices such as incinerators, condensers, carbon adsorbers and biological waste water treatment plants. Cleaner technology improvements have centred on improved recovery and recycling of ancillary substances, and substitution of organic solvents with less hazardous ones. More attention is being directed to the fundamental synthesis pathway and successes have been achieved in using safer reagents and achieving the same result via fewer steps and more benign routes (Cunningham et al, 1993). Firms are regulated by national environmental and planning controls, and will be affected by the Integrated Pollution Prevention and Control (IPPC) Directive (Commission of the European Communities, 1996), and are likely to be affected by the proposed Volatile Organic Compounds (VOC) Directive (Commission of the European Communities, 1997) and the suggested Polluting Emissions Register (PER) Directive. There is little linkage between the perceptions of the public as consumers and as neighbours of these firms.

Industrial context

Most companies manufacturing pharmaceuticals operate on the global market (Ballance et al, 1992). Consolidations in the last decade have produced very large companies with many branch plants. Research and development tend to be concentrated in the home country, with a number of branch plants manufacturing the active ingredient in bulk. These supply more plants which produce the product in the finished form of tablets, capsules, vials and so on. These plants are integrated within the company, and may be provided with central support for many issues. A common corporate policy may be applied, initially without reference to the significance of local conditions.

In addition to these large corporations, there are smaller companies which may undertake some of the synthesis steps on a contract basis, 'toll manufacturing'. Often, these develop niche roles in the market, providing specialist synthesis services, based on expertise and equipment. Others manufacture generic drugs or imitations of out-of-patent products developed by the larger corporations.

Research and development of new products is a significant activity. Lead times average 7 to 8.5 years from concept to product launch, while development costs average US$359 million, with a success rate of perhaps 1 in 5000 to 1 in 10,000 for new products (US Food & Drugs Administration, 1995). Global corporations may spend up to 20–25 per cent of their expenses on research. Cost of manufacturing varies between 10 and 40 per cent, with the balance spent on marketing and administration.

Pharmaceuticals, as health-care products, are subject to regulation in excess of the normal workplace safety and environmental controls. Before a pharmaceutical may be sold in a particular country, it must be approved by the local competent body. Since the formation of the European Medicines Evaluation Agency in 1995, companies only need to obtain one licence which is then valid throughout the entire European Union, but they also have the option to seek approval in each of the member states. Firms selling in the United States must seek the approval of the US Food & Drugs Administration (FDA). Some countries will accept the approval of another country, the FDA in particular, as adequate. The FDA's approval procedure extends to the inspection of the manufacturing pre and post approval of a specific product, with additional regular surveillance inspections of the Good Manufacturing Practice (GMP) of a production site. Desired variations in manufacturing practice may require a variation in the approval. Where multiple approvals are held, each must be re-assessed. This produces delays, and is a barrier to change, though not one which is insurmountable, as evidenced by IRL Pharmaceuticals 2's reduction of a six step process to a three step process.

Promotion of the more valuable products is directed to a small number of decision makers in the medical profession, initially senior consultants, followed by general practitioners. When a product is no longer controlled by prescription, promotion to pharmacists accompanies the marketing to consumers.

In conclusion, a highly formalized and structured pattern of product development and manufacture exists. The long lead time in developing and gaining approval of products, the importance of reputation and marketing, the capital-intensive nature of the sector, as well as the requirement for technical knowledge and skills, all help to inhibit new entrants.

CASE STUDIES

1 DK Pharmaceuticals

Company profile

This plant was set up in 1969 by a Danish multinational company and is now the company's biggest production site. The company is the world's largest producer of insulin and industrial enzymes and it has manufacturing sites in nine countries, with major production sites in Europe and the US. There are 13,000 employees and a turnover of 13.723 million Danish krone. There are two business groups: Health Care Group and Bio Industrial Group.

Fermentation is the basic production method for most of the products. In this process selected micro-organisms are cultured in large, closed fermentation tanks using agricultural products as nutrients. The main activities of the site are the production of antibiotics by fermentation, using genetically modified organisms, the recovery of enzymes and insulin, insulin extraction from pancreatic glands, insulin purification, enzyme granulation, and a treatment plant for sludge and waste water. The manufacturing at this site is organized into five units: Enzyme Recovery unit one, Enzyme Recovery unit two, Fermentation unit, Insulin Extraction unit and the Waste Water Treatment unit.

Table 6.1 Pharmaceutical sector cases

Company	DK Pharmaceuticals	IRL Pharmaceuticals 1	IRL Pharmaceuticals 2	NL Pharmaceuticals	UK Pharmaceuticals
Products and market	Insulin, industrial enzymes. World leader	Wide range of finished and intermediate products: anti-fungal, digestive, circulatory, psychiatric. 60% of production goes to an affiliate	Range of finished and intermediate products: in particular, anti-ulcer, antiarthritic and anti-depressant. 99% of product goes to affiliate, mainly UK and France	Intermediates for other companies, including intermediates for antibiotics and cardio-vascular medicines	Fine chemicals, narcotics, opiates, cocaine. One of few legal world manufacturers
Employees in firm in company	1235 12,800	135 81,000	180 57,000	430 (695) 19,000	200
Ownership/ relationship with parent	Main domestic site of Danish multinational	Branch site of a US global corporation	Branch site of UK (formerly US) global corporation	Three site subsidiary of Netherlands multinational	Single site local firm
Regional features	Public concern about use of genetically modified organisms	Indirectly influenced by local lobby concerns, cited favourably by multinational lobby group as a model. Partner member of the Clean Technology Centre	Significant local lobby concern. Partner member of the Clean Technology Centre	Chemical sector covenant	Aqueous discharges regulated by sewage authority. Little local concern or pressure

Environmental profile

The company continuously strives to improve the environmental performance of the production processes. It also supplies other industries with enzymes which will enable them to solve particular environmental problems.

The company has had an environmental policy since 1975 that has been amended several times. The company has signed the International Chamber of Commerce's Business Charter for Sustainable Development, and is a member of the European Partnership for the Environment and the World Industry Council for the Environment. A formal environmental management system is in place, and the company is working towards a recognized system standard, BS 7750. It produces an annual public environmental report.

Several projects have improved environmental performance in recent years, reducing waste to products and reducing emissions. The handling of liquid waste takes place in the central waste water and sludge treatment unit. The waste water treatment unit was set up in 1992/93 and it has reduced the nutrient level by more than 90 per cent. The firm is part of an industrial symbiosis network of firms in the community, which recycles each firm's residual products within the group. The firm takes in process steam from an adjacent refinery and delivers the most concentrated part of their liquid waste as free fertilizer to local farmers. To reduce the transportation and associated environmental effects, more than 50 per cent is now delivered directly to fields by pipeline. Any remaining materials are processed in the firm's own treatment plant. Installation of a biofilter in 1993 reduced the odour emissions to below the permitted level. The yeast slurry is sold as protein supplement for pig feed. Of 5930 tonnes of non-hazardous solid waste, 32 per cent was recycled, while 30 per cent percent of the hazardous waste was recycled.

Project

The growing public demands for minimizing the waste water discharge to the sea, coupled with a demand from the public authorities to separate the sludge from the waste water, forced the company to institute a waste minimization programme, with an internal 'polluter pays' system, and focus on cleaner production. The site developed a three-step approach to minimizing waste production.

1 The first step was to reduce the waste production by waste minimization in the plants themselves. An internal price was applied to nitrogen, which was the limiting factor.
2 The second step was to introduce internal recycling of water between the production units.
3 The third step was to divide the waste streams to establish the possibilities for external waste recycling.

The third step led to the creation of the new fertilizer product, which is now a distinct product with its own unit, budget and brand name. It made sense to give the product away because this route minimizes the discharge of waste water and the content of organic materials, nitrogen and phosphorus. This made it possible to reduce the level of required investment in a waste water plant from Dkr140 million to Dkr40–50 million, while also ensuring good public relations.

2 IRL Pharmaceuticals 1

Company profile

The firm was taken over in 1981 by an EU multinational, which in turn consolidated with a larger US-based global corporation. It is now one of a number of subsidiaries of a large well-known multinational, which comprises 170 firms in 55 countries employing more than 81,000 people.

The Irish facility employs 135 people and has an annual turnover in excess of IR£50 million. Both intermediate and finished products dealing with fungal infections and digestive, allergic, circulatory and psychiatric disorders are produced. These products are destined for markets in Europe (70 per cent), the next most important market being Japan. The reason why Europe predominates is that 60 per cent of the plant's production goes to an affiliate firm within the company. Ninety-eight per cent of raw materials are sourced outside Ireland, 90 per cent of which are from Europe, with 60 per cent of this coming from an affiliate company.

Manufacture is by batch process only. There are two processing plants, the first of which was built in 1980 and subsequently upgraded, the other in 1992–1993. In the former are housed reaction vessels and centrifuges, while the latter houses a powder processing section and a chemical processing section. The chemical processing section is a four storey building, operates a gravity material flow and has state of the art automation and containment. The plant also has a separate hydrogenation building where a single atmospheric hydrogenation reaction takes place. Typically a reaction batch is successively purified by a series of steps which could include filtration, centrifugation and crystallization. Purification can be followed by drying, milling, blending and packaging. Procedure is in accordance with that laid down by the parent company.

Environmental profile

The firm has recently received an integrated pollution control licence from the Irish EPA. It previously held separate air and water licences. The air licence was to 1986 TA Luft standards. The licences incorporate both concentrations and total emissions for a wide variety of materials including a number of organic solvents amongst them: ethanol, acetone, methanol, chloroform and ethyl acetate.

In 1994 the firm had a 100 per cent compliance record with all requirements of its pollution licences and was described by a major environmental lobby group as a model firm whom other firms in the region should imitate. It has been accredited to ISO 9002 since 1992 and plans to become accredited to IS 310. It is a member of the Responsible Care Programme. The firm claims a strong commitment to environmental protection, pollution prevention, and waste reduction. Five per cent of employees have received training in environmental issues, while IR£0.75 million annually has been invested in environmental controls since 1990.

The plant has expanded very significantly, and has also invested heavily in containment and in end-of-pipe treatment, such as an aerobic waste water treatment plant and air emission recovery units which minimize the number of emission points.

For liquid effluent the plant has an aerobic activated sludge waste water treatment plant. Process vapours are collected, go through scrubbers as appropriate and then to a carbon adsorption unit. Only a small proportion of spent solvent is recovered on-site. Virtually all other liquors and waste solvents are collected in bulk tanks or drums and exported to licensed agencies for recovery or incineration.

A number of projects in recent years have improved environmental performance. Production Plant II has an improved powder handling unit. This achieved a significant reduction in losses. However this decision was driven by production quality requirements of Good Manufacturing Practice. Two other significant capital projects were environmentally driven. These were the carbon adsorption plant (IR£2.0 million) and a condenser system upgrade (IR£1 million). The carbon adsorption plant operates at an efficiency in excess of 95 per cent, resulting in a 75 per cent reduction in emissions to atmosphere. In addition the firm has replaced chloroform by other organic solvents and has set itself an objective of eliminating the use of chlorinated organic solvents in the medium term. Unfortunately greater quantities of the substitute solvents are required. This change must also be acceptable to the quality requirements of both customers and the drug regulatory agencies.

Project

This increase in the substitute solvents coupled with the major expansion in production necessitated a further review of liquid emissions. The plant has had an aerobic waste water treatment plant since 1983 which has functioned well, but increased production suggested it might need to be expanded. The firm decided not to do this, however, feeling that restricted capacity would act as a motivation to manage the generation of process effluents more efficiently.

A programme of solvent use reduction coupled with a programme of cleaning solvent substitution was introduced as an alternative to expanding the waste water treatment plant. This initially involved a reduction of alcohol and ketone use for cleaning from 400 to 200m^3 annually by substituting organic cleaning solvents with a water-based 8 per cent acetic acid solution. It is planned to dispense with acetic acid solutions and use a suitable detergent, which will require a determination of the optimum treatment procedure for spent detergent. It is hoped to follow this with a move to the use of water-based detergents. The immediate priority is to minimize the additional water usage resulting from the introduction of aqueous cleaning agents.

The firm identified environmental concerns, and the savings associated with reduced material usage, as the primary motivation for this project. The project idea originated with the visit of an R&D representative from the corporate headquarters to another multinational's plant where similar solvent substitution steps were being implemented. The idea was passed on to the local firm's R&D facility. The firm's small scale and flexibility have led to it functioning as a pilot plant for such innovation within the organization. The firm felt that transfer of this sort of non-proprietary information within the Irish pharmaceutical/fine chemicals sector is inadequate.

Both quality assurance and production departments were involved in the project, largely in order to ensure that the drug regulatory agencies were satisfied, though modifications to cleaning practice are less significant to changes to process solvents.

3 IRL Pharmaceuticals 2

Company profile

This firm is a branch plant subsidiary of a UK multinational. At one stage, it was the primary manufacturing site of the major revenue earner for the corporation. The parent company has about 57,000 employees and sells over 300 branded products in over 130 countries. The Cork plant employs 180 people, and is currently undergoing a major expansion with as many as 600 extra contract personnel on site at one stage.

The firm receives raw materials from within and outside Europe. It exports both intermediates and finished products. These include an anti-ulcer drug, an anti-arthritic, an anti-viral and an anti-depressant. Production, which is exclusively by batch process, follows a generic pattern as follows. Raw materials and intermediates are initially mixed and then brought to appropriate temperature and pressure to form the desired product. The product is crystallized out, separated by filtration or centrifugation and dried. The dried product is ground to required particle size and then bagged or drummed as desired. Ninety-nine per cent of the product goes to affiliate firms within the company, predominantly to the UK and France.

Environmental profile

The firm sees itself as either a design or lead customer in terms of technological orientation and claims that equipment suppliers from both Europe and North

America have used the Cork plant as an opportunity to gain a foothold in new markets in the pharmaceutical sector. The firm also won an award under the EU THERMIE programme. The firm is a member of the Responsible Care Programme, has a quality management system in place and plans to gain accreditation to ISO 14001. All this is undertaken in the context of a corporate environmental statement which heavily emphasizes pollution prevention and waste minimization.

The firm was the first in Ireland to receive an IPC licence from the Irish EPA having been previously licensed by the local authority. During the 1980s (the period during which the site was the major revenue earner for the group) it had an intermittent odour problem resulting from occasional releases of methyl mercaptan, a by-product of the production of the firm's anti-ulcer drug. A combination of reviews of procedures and upgrades of abatement plant reduced this problem to a minimum. The firm's environmental performance is of a high standard, with complaints of odour now rare. In the firm's application for an IPC licence, a local environmental lobby group was also involved in the discussions. The licence, issued in December 1994, was seen as innovative by the firm in that it required a multi-media examination of all emissions and waste, an emphasis on pollution prevention and waste minimization, greater public participation and information, and involvement of all the workforce.

The firm identifies the IPC licence and its enforcement as being the major environmental pressures, followed by local community and environmental pressure groups. It does not see these pressures increasing dramatically in the future particularly since the systematic build up to the introduction of the IPC licence. Nevertheless it anticipates some pressure for greater waste minimization resulting from these licences and also from more demanding corporate standards.

Currently the firm uses a range of measures to ensure acceptable environmental performance. These include an extensive recovery programme, gas scrubbing, chemical treatment, on-site incineration, biological treatment, waste minimization / recycling / reuse programme, environmental audits of both the firm and its waste disposal contractors, improved effluent monitoring, energy efficiency assessment, investment in pollution control equipment and training of the workforce. Twelve staff are assigned to environmental management.

The firm draws on a range of sources for information, and has undertaken a number of environmentally related projects. One, relating to the production of the anti-ulcer drug, involved a 52 per cent overall reduction in waste volumes from the process because of the reduction in the number of process stages (from six to three), elimination of the use of hydrogen sulphide, and a 70 per cent reduction in aqueous effluents.

Project

The extension of the existing waste water treatment plant was a major capital project which emerged from a comprehensive review in 1989. The most important objective was the biological digestion of low strength liquid wastes (high strength wastes are either pre-treated by solvent stripping, or disposed of by incineration). Other objectives, necessary to meet IPC requirements, were reduction of fugitive emissions and reduction in energy and material usage.

The total capital cost of the waste water project was IR£4 million. The plant design was based on pilot level studies of 100 litre units, completed in association with the Irish state agency Eolas and a firm of Danish environmental consultants. There were four stages:

Phase one involved provision of a covered aeration basin with clarifier and acid dosing systems, provision of new blowers and diffuser systems together with the provision of a bio-filter and appropriate controls and instrumentation.

Phase two involved reconstruction and up-grading of the existing aeration system including covers for basins, new clarifiers, TOC analyser, biological filter and de-nitrification system.

Phase three involved the upgrade of pre-treatment storage tanks, provision of steam stripping for input streams with organic content and the provision of a dissolved air flotation unit, together with a 100kg/h sludge dewatering plant.

The final phase involved the provision of an ammonia stripping plant and installation of a control system to integrate the operation of the biological treatment system.

The project looks like an end-of-pipe solution, but the company's view is that the earlier waste minimization exercise together with the innovative technology involved in the project produce a number of consequences which are really cleaner technology. These include odour removal, reduction in chemical usage, reduction in loading, solvent steam stripping, ammonia stripping and membrane disc diffusers.

Thus the firm has undergone a profound change. Initially compliance oriented and with identified environmental problems, it has moved to a proactive pollution prevention stance, involving improved house keeping, process modification, internal recycling, and waste reduction. IPC licensing will move the firm still further in this direction.

4 NL Pharmaceuticals

Company profile

This firm is one site of a three-location company that was purchased by a larger Netherlands based global corporation nearly 10 years ago. The firm was pushed to expand by the parent company, which wanted to expand its range of products. This site has developed expertise in halogenation and enzymatic reactions, with the ability to separate the different optical isomers. Operating in a highly competitive sub-sector, its technical staff are particularly conscious of commercial issues. The firm operates on the boundary between fine chemicals and pharmaceuticals. It supplies intermediates to other firms in the sector, which audit its quality and environmental performance and contractually define its environmental liability. It is also subject to audit by drug regulatory agencies.

Environmental profile

Both the regional EPA and the river authority (NWA) have jurisdiction. The site has a Site Environmental Plan, also known as an Environmental Care System, and is in a voluntary covenant scheme.

Multiple process steps and products and a typical product to waste ratio of 1:10 result in substantial waste generation. Product purity specifications, including a necessity to use only right-hand isomers, make waste reuse difficult though new treatment processes may help. Additional problems arise from both halogenation processes and the widespread use of inorganic materials. Sludge from the waste water treatment plant (with a capacity of 50,000–60,000 IEs) is toxic but can, after further treatment, be transported to official landfill sites. Both production and waste treatment require considerable logistical planning and the latter has generated a dialogue with the local division of the NWA extending back ten years. The variable level and flow of the local river added a further complication.

The firm needed to expand production, but had reached its limit of allowable water emissions. These are seasonal and tightly regulated. The firm also felt that while it could attempt to negotiate a variation in limits with the NWA, any increase in one emission would be traded against a decrease in another. This strict control was balanced by the provision of subsidy for a cleaner production assessment of the firm's operations.

Complexity of regulation and uncertainty of monitoring resulted in a move towards incorporating guidelines for pollution prevention into product development procedures. These guidelines sought both early separation of inactive isomers to minimize further waste generation and an attempt to chemically transform inactive into active isomers. The firm prefers recycling, preferably internal, when waste generation cannot be prevented, with waste water treatment only considered where other steps fail.

Project

The project involved the development of a less environmentally hazardous production process for the 'MEFAT' product. As with all medicines, the development took some years, and involved a formal process. Initial work was undertaken by the R&D department in liaison with the marketing department. A recommendation to proceed beyond the preliminary research was considered by a representative group of senior managers called the Steering Group – New Products & Processes. A separate group, the New Product Decision Group, took the subsequent decision to go into production.

During the early stages of this formal process, environmental concerns are confined to efforts to avoid the use of high-risk materials such as benzene or mercury salts. At a later stage, toxicity concerns come into play, and can result in termination of the development, as can high environmental and safety costs.

Once an optimal synthesis route is identified process scale is increased to 50 litre production units. At this stage safety and environment concerns are crucial, as they are seen as the interface between governmental requirements and R&D, and projects can – and have been – cancelled for environmental reasons. Potential customers for a product exercise further environmental pressure, and in new contracts there is explicit identification of environmental responsibility for the firm's products.

Environmental concern continues as a process matures with production experience. Process modifications are often necessary but because of the tight specification and regulation of pharmaceutical products such modification cannot be too extensive. Nevertheless modifications are initiated for various reasons: R&D can recommend upgrades and recycling; safety and environmental concerns can result in suggestions for solvent substitution; and cost reduction can also be targeted and achieved. At the same time, difficulties in meeting permit requirements can be identified and/or eliminated. Permit requirements can also change and require process modifications.

Traditionally these were dealt with as local process changes but involved all the problems associated with tightly regulated product quality. New products were also accompanied by requests to expand permit requirements. Both scenarios may be seen as reactive approaches. They were unsatisfactory, partly because of the uncertainty associated with a demand for a new permit, and partly because any bargaining for a new permit can raise the possibility of trade-offs, where reduced emissions and hence possible process modifications may be required in other areas.

Now an alternative procedure is used. Both process changes and expansions have to fit into actual permit requirements. These requirements are seen as a fixed agreement between the company and society. Cleaner production research was necessary and was assisted by the regulatory authorities, though production expansion will still generate tension with environmental requirements. The clear market vision of all sectors and the parallel development of a Quality Care System contributed further to a quality orientation in environmental performance.

It was a combination of events and circumstances in this case, including forced growth in production, environmental limits, regulatory and market pressures, customer concerns about environmental liability, quality care certification, assisted cleaner production assessment, a proactive environmental policy, decision making structures and corporate ethos, together with an alliance with another company, that resulted in a successful substitution of water-based solvents and reaction pathways for the organic solvents previously used for the production of 'MEFAT'.

5 UK Pharmaceuticals

Company profile

This firm has a turnover of about £30 million and employs just under 200 people. The core business is the manufacture of controlled drugs, both opiate-derived and synthetic. The firm is therefore subject to particularly stringent regulatory and inventory controls. The company has two plants on immediately adjacent sites in the west of Edinburgh. The company was owned by a UK multinational from 1963 until a management buyout in 1990. Stock Exchange flotation followed in 1995.

Three categories of controlled drugs are produced: opiates, synthetic narcotics and cocaine. The opiates include codeine, dihydrocodeine, morphine and pholcodeine, with the firm accounting for approximately 20 per cent of world production. Opium poppies are the source of these opiates with the firm typically processing the dried poppy capsules known as poppy straw. Morphine is extracted from this material using solvents, followed by chemical conversion and purification to obtain the range of opiates desired. Cocaine is extracted from coca using technology gained by acquisition from Rhône-Poulenc Rorer in 1992. The firm manufactures several synthetic narcotics, including pethidine and methadone. Other standard pharmaceutical and fine chemical processes are also operated.

Environmental profile

The company regards itself – and is regarded by the regulatory bodies (HMIPI and Lothian Regional Council (LRC)) – as a responsible company. The small scale of its operations, and the small amounts of substances involved, means it has never been seen as posing a particularly high risk. Up until the end of the 1980s the aqueous discharge to the sewer was not closely monitored, either by the company or by the LRC. Consent levels for specific substances were introduced in the early 1990s following a discharge of the pungent smelling chemical amyl alcohol into the sewer. Consent limits were set for benzene (0.8 mg/l), toluene (9.5), xylene (9.5), and chloroform (1.8). This made the company realize that it did not know enough about its environmental performance. Monitoring systems and control measures were upgraded with the purchase of two automatic effluent samplers, one for each site.

The firm applied for IPC authorization in October 1993, with authorization granted with effect from 30 November 1994. The IPC authorization introduces a new emphasis on waste minimization, and will impose a time limit on the company to develop a waste minimization programme. The company has registered for BS 5750 (ISO 9002) Total Quality Management system. Environmental control is now the responsibility of the company standards section, which was constituted at the end of 1992.

Project

The company undertakes various solvent extractions, and in recent years the regulatory authority has focused on the residual solvent in the discharge to the sewer system. Although generally considered insoluble in water, these solvents are in fact soluble at the level of about 100–200 ppm, which is well over the consents set by LRC. For most of the solvents in question the solvent level can be brought under the consent concentration by steam distillation. In the case of chloroform this was not sufficient to meet consent levels. An additional hydrolysis step in which the waste is boiled in the presence of alkali was instigated. The project to develop this second-stage of hydrolysis was only considered to be expensive in terms of time; it took about one staff month.

This two-stage treatment is now carried out in all relevant processes. As a result, the company found that its compliance with LRC limits improved, but consent levels have still been exceeded at times. This seemed to be due to two problems. First, the hydrolysis seemed to be reversible, with the chloroform reforming. Second, there was some doubt over the accuracy of the sampling system. It appeared possible that persistent high chloroform readings could be due to repeated sampling of the same stagnant pool.

These circumstances led the company standards manager to conclude that a much better overall understanding of the situation was required as a basis for any further action. A comprehensive review was instigated in late 1995. Particular areas of concern were the performance of the samplers (how well did their readings reflect what was actually in the effluent?) and the efficacy of the distillation treatment to remove solvents (could a more efficient alternative be found?). The concern with the current treatment method is not only that it appears not to work very well in the case of chloroform, but also that it is generally thought to be using more energy and labour than necessary. There is no financial gain in terms of recovering solvent. At the moment, flash distillation followed by carbon adsorption is seen as having high potential.

The emphasis is still very much on treatment prior to discharge, rather than elimination of chloroform from the process altogether. It is acknowledged that it will probably be desirable in the long term to eliminate chloroform, if only because of the way it is perceived. However, there are no short-term plans to seek alternatives to chloroform in the manufacture of the core, narcotic-based products (pholcodeine is one of the main products for which chloroform is used).

For these products, the firm has neither the incentive nor the means to change its long-standing processes. There is regulatory pressure to meet effluent solvent levels, but this can be achieved (it is believed) by an end-of-pipe treatment. While HMIPI would favour a cleaner approach – changing processes to eliminate chloroform – it is recognized that this should be a long-term goal. In the short term it is seen to be too expensive and disruptive, and thus excluded as 'entailing excessive cost'. This perception is based, at least in part, on limited knowledge of potential alternatives to the existing processes. The firm is one of only a few companies in the world making these opiate-based products, and these companies have no history of sharing information about their processes. With no tried and tested exemplar to follow, it is presumed that change will be difficult and expensive. This presumption is reinforced by the fact that the firm has been working at full capacity and has little spare technical expertise to develop new processes. The importance of well-proven and reproducible processes in assuring product quality also means that major customers would expect to be informed if such processes were to be changed, again adding to the preference for end-of-pipe treatment.

Generally speaking this reflects a company attitude which is based around the operation of small, intermittent batch processes for which the chemistry is well known, and the market and profits stable. In recent years the main driver within the company seems to have been to broaden the range of products and to operate the site at closer to its full capacity. With the core products selling in a stable and uncompetitive market there is no incentive for changing production processes, whether for efficiency gains or for environmental reasons.

COMPARATIVE ANALYSIS OF CASE STUDIES

Legislation and its enforcement

The pharmaceutical industry is being affected by the current changes in the regulatory regime in essentially the same ways as the fine chemicals sector (see Chapter 5). There are also similar differences in the level of pre-existent controls. The stringent requirements in Cork are reflected in the existence of waste water treatment plants for example, while in Lothian firms have generally discharged to the local authority sewer collection system, prior to discharge to estuary.

In Denmark, control is devolved to the local authority, which is free to impose its own controls, within guidelines established by the national Environmental Protection Agency. One consequence of this is that the land spreading of spent biomass by DK Pharmaceuticals is allowed by one municipality, West Zealand, but forbidden by another, Storstrøms. In the case of NL Pharmaceuticals, the regional EPA and the river authority (NWA) have been important influences. UK Pharmaceuticals was controlled by the local sewer operator, part of Lothian Regional Council (LRC), but under the new IPC system, HMIPI is the primary regulator, sharing the control of emissions to water with LRC. In contrast, IRL Pharmaceuticals 1 and IRL Pharmaceuticals 2, which were formerly controlled by Cork County Council, are now subject to the recently formed national EPA. This decision was partly due to a lack of resources among local authorities, and partly due to public concern that the relationship between the regulators and regulated was too close. The experience of the regulators in both Ireland and Scotland with a cleaner technology philosophy is still limited.

NL Pharmaceuticals is under particular regulatory pressure. While needing to expand production, it had reached a ceiling on its allowed discharges. It discharges into a river, with limits that vary as the water flow varies. Since it

Table 6.2 *Summary of environmental responses of firms*

Company	DK Pharmaceuticals	IRL Pharmaceuticals 1	IRL Pharmaceuticals 2	NL Pharmaceuticals	UK Pharmaceuticals
Regulatory context	Different regional authorities have different views on acceptability of spreading of spent biomass	Recent transfer from county council to national EPA IPC licence received US-FDA approved	Recent transfer from county council to national EPA IPC licence received US-FDA approved	Strictly limited water emissions IPC system in place; also Environmental Care System required under 'voluntary agreement'	Recent transfer from local sewer regulator to IPC system, administered by both HMIPI and the local sewer regulator
Environmental policy/management	Formal; working towards BS 7750 Signatory to ICC-BCSD, member of EPE, WICE	Formal; working towards IS 310 Environmental Management Programme submitted; ISO 9002 Responsible care	Formal; working towards ISO 14001 Environmental Management Programme submitted Responsible care	Formal, Site Environmental Plan submitted ISO 9001 Responsible care	Informal ISO 9002

Prior waste water treatment	Firm's biological plant via sewer to sea	Firm's biological plant via sewer to estuary	Firm's biological plant via sewer to sea	Firm's biological plant via sewer to river	Via sewer to local authority treatment plant and estuary
Environmental response/project	Distribution of waste fermented biomass to farmers as a soil fertilizer and conditioner;	Substitution of organic solvent cleaning agents by dilute aqueous acetic acid;	Sophisticated waste water treatment plant, preceded by waste minimization steps;	Development of aqueous based chemistry to substitute for organic solvent based one;	Addition of a hydrolysis step to degrade chlorinated waste;
	Incremental change/external recycling[1]	Incremental change in process technology	Incremental change in process technology	Radical change in process technology	End-of-pipe

also has a changing pattern of multiple products, management of emissions is always a difficult task. The firm felt that while it could attempt to negotiate a variation in limits with the NWA, any increase in one emission would be traded against a decrease in another. This strict control was balanced by the provision of subsidy for a cleaner production assessment of the firm's operations. Among the projects examined, NL Pharmaceutical's development of water-based chemistry is probably the most innovative.

IRL Pharmaceuticals 1 also expanded its operations. However, it was granted an increase in its allowable mass emissions, though at an improved performance level. IRL Pharmaceuticals 1 decided to impose a limit upon themselves, by not expanding the existing waste water treatment plant, but instead sought internal improvements, while retaining the facility to export waste. IRL Pharmaceuticals 2, also undertaking a major expansion, chose both internal improvements and a sophisticated treatment plant.

The integrated pollution control (IPC) approach favours, in principle, cleaner technology in each of the regions. Both Scotland and Ireland base this on the concept of best available technology not entailing excessive cost (BATNEEC), defined in Ireland as 'to prevent, eliminate, or where that is not practicable, limit, abate, or reduce an emission from an activity'. Across the regions, as a minimum, control is expressed in the form of emission limit values (ELVs). However, there is also a requirement to prepare some form of plan to reduce emissions, with this plan being agreed between the regulators and the firms. This plan must be regularly updated, and contains rolling targets.

NL Pharmaceuticals has a Site Environmental Plan. IRL Pharmaceuticals 2 was the first firm in Ireland to enter the IPC system, and has submitted its 'Environmental Management Programme', in accordance with its licence. This is a comprehensive plan, documenting the historical and current waste minimization projects, as well as the quantified waste reduction targets, along with their schedule, and makes exhaustive reference to both their licence and the BATNEEC Guidance Notes. NL Pharmaceuticals is subject to a voluntary covenant. The parent company of NL Pharmaceuticals believes that these:

> *are a good way to achieve certain objectives in a specific period of time. They afford industry the time to develop the required technologies and to achieve the agreed goals in the most efficient way. A sector-based, integrated approach often gives the best results. (We are) in favour of such covenants for carrying out government policies.*

Management structure and style

All the firms in the study have been subject to corporate restructuring in the last 10–15 years. Uniquely, UK Pharmaceuticals became an independent firm. It has changed from being a subsidiary of a UK multinational, to being a local management owned firm, to becoming a publicly quoted company in five years. This has imposed particular constraints and priorities on the firm. It has also provided opportunities, by allowing immediate local decision making. The other plants are all branch operations, benefiting from the corporate support structures that are typical of the multinational chemical process sector, but may be inhibited in their freedom to make decisions.

This type of branch operation tends to promote a formal, scientific or hierarchical management system. However, the firms studied seem to have adopted a more consultative approach. IRL Pharmaceuticals 2 applied a team approach to the process improvements carried out in tandem with the design of their new treatment plant. IRL Pharmaceuticals 2, while being a branch plant, was the main profit earner for the corporation for many years because it was the approved production plant for the main product. It gained an importance in the organization in spite of being a branch. IRL Pharmaceuticals 1, being a small firm, cannot maintain simple compartmentalization of activities. The technical staff of NL Pharmaceuticals are noted for their commercial outlook. Finally, DK Pharmaceuticals is the main domestic production site of this Danish multi-national.

Environmental management

Where firms implement a formalized environmental management system, for example ISO 14000, EMAS, BS 7750, IS 310, they are likely to investigate their suppliers' performance as well. This has already been seen with companies that implement quality management systems, such as ISO 9000. Major purchasers are then able to influence the behaviour of other players within a production chain. The application of environmental management systems is at a relatively early stage, and little evidence has yet been found in this study of this chain effect. NL Pharmaceuticals supplies intermediates to other companies, and has been subject to audit by them, and had its environmental liability contractually defined. It therefore has been subject to regulatory, parent company and customer pressures.

However, many companies in this sector are very familiar with the quality management system approach, and have at least an internal environmental management system. DK Pharmaceuticals is seeking accreditation to BS 7750, and IRL Pharmaceuticals 1 to IS 310. IRL Pharmaceuticals 2 seems pre-occupied with the immediate concerns of satisfying their IPC licence, and are looking to achieve ISO 14000 within a five year horizon.

All of these companies already have a formal quality system in place. UK Pharmaceuticals has recently introduced this formal quality system, and is awaiting the clarification of the relative status of EMAS, ISO, BS etc, before embarking on another accreditation procedure.

Economics of environmental management

Takeovers, mergers, management buyouts, share issues and so on also expose the firm to the external pressure of the financial institutions. Pre-acquisition audits are common, and firms may plan for several years not only to get the firm into financial, but also environmental readiness. UK Pharmaceuticals was subject to a management buyout. This company has been concerned with getting its production affairs in good order, and preparing for the market flotation that followed. It reduced its water consumption and waste water production to minimize its costs. It also undertook a site soil survey. Conformity with required standards was the objective, rather than longer-term considerations.

Companies which adopt a strategic approach tend to anticipate ever-tightening regulation of waste and emissions. These are then more receptive to approaches which eliminate or minimize emissions. They believe they can thereby avoid future problems completely, which is seen to be beneficial to the long-term prosperity of the company, even though the immediate economic effects may be uncertain. Such companies welcome a clear direction for the 5–10 year future. IRL Pharmaceuticals 1, by choosing not to expand its treatment plant, and adopting self-imposed minimization constraints, may be seen to be taking this longer-term view. It has also had the benefit of an existing treatment plant which seems more than capable of passing existing standards.

Investment cycles must also be considered. Plant, once built, must be depreciated before additional capacity is provided. It may also be easier for a plant to obtain approval for a treatment project as part of a larger expansion project, as may have been the case for IRL Pharmaceuticals 2. Internal environmental costing can encourage minimization. DK Pharmaceuticals introduced an internal polluter pays system for its production plants. This resulted in a decrease in waste production. It also chose to distribute its sludge to farmers rather than to treat the sludge in a waste water plant on the basis of cost minimization. Internalization of environmental costs can bring significant improvements through low cost changes in operating and maintenance practices. These changes in practice were applied in both IRL Pharmaceuticals 1 and 2.

Communications: intra-firm

The usual corporate attitude is simply to conform to standards and minimize costs, and firms in this sector are strongly influenced by a team approach to management. While a champion may be recognized within a team, success is shared, thus reducing individual recognition. In UK Pharmaceuticals, the standards department has clearly expanded its operations to achieve greater authority within the firm. Its original responsibilities have been extended to the environmental arena. Furthermore, other departments consulted with it on projects, while there was no formal requirement to do so. These individual 'heroes' may function as product or project champions, or as information 'gate-keepers'. There is some evidence of such a 'gate-keeper' in IRL Pharmaceuticals 1. While it is difficult to generalize, there appears to be a trend that this hero or champion will emerge from the technical or quality function, though one might expect that the usual linkage of safety, health and environment would favour the safety function.

Communications: inter-firm

Many of the companies in this sector transfer product internally. Products from the primary manufacturers (eg IRL Pharmaceuticals 1 and 2) are active ingredients, which are diluted and packaged by secondary manufacturers, to be transferred to a marketing firm, all within the same company. A competitive internal market may exist, but this was not a significant issue among the firms studied. There can therefore be some distance between the firm and the eventual consumer. In only one of the firms studied (NL Pharmaceuticals), is there evidence of one firm cooperating with another (not in the same company), to improve environmental performance in the matter of the core business. NL Pharmaceuticals is a firm supplying intermediates to other companies. It developed water based chemistry, as described in the case study, and also provides a methanol-containing waste stream to an outside company, an example of industrial symbiosis. Others have cooperated on peripheral issues, for example moving to reusable bulk packaging with suppliers and customers, but only with this firm has this fundamental development been identified in the study.

There is a national sectoral organization in each of the regions: IPCMF in Ireland, VNCI in The Netherlands and so on. In turn, these organizations are affiliated to the CEFIC. These organizations have undertaken to follow the principles of 'Responsible Care', originally advocated in North America. While membership of the organization may be contingent on adherence to the principles, their application is the responsibility of the individual firm. The primary sanction that applies for non-application is peer pressure.

Communications: public and others

At an international level, the 'chemical' industry has been the subject of considerable media and public interest. The international nature of the business has meant that concerns in one country can be transmitted to the management of an associated operation in another. The concern of citizens for the environment in The Netherlands and Denmark may be said to be in the mature phase. High proportions of the populations in both countries are members of lobby groups. These environmental concerns are now part of the political establishment. In Denmark, the use by DK Pharmaceuticals of genetically modified organisms has been of concern, and the spreading of treatment sludge has also presented problems. DK Pharmaceuticals has been obliged to explain that the sludge issue has no bearing on the quality of their product.

In Ireland, there has been intense local concern in Cork, where there is a concentration of this sector. The firms maintain this has not had a significant effect upon their operations, but undoubtedly they are now much more conscious of public relations and communication than before. IRL Pharmaceuticals 2, who were the subject of pressure group criticism before, now engage in close dialogue with the same group. In addition, along with IRL Pharmaceuticals 1, they meet with representatives of community groups. Cork County Council has also initiated an Environment Forum to facilitate dialogue between all the parties interested in the region's environment. UK Pharmaceuticals has not been subject to any similar pressure.

Corporate environmental reports are issued by the headquarters of DK Pharmaceuticals and NL Pharmaceuticals. The former, in particular, has included detailed public reporting among its environmental policy objectives, and has been a leader in linking business and environmental matters through its support for the organizations European Partners for the Environment and the World Industrial Council for the Environment. Public emissions reporting remains an issue in countries such as Ireland and Scotland, in spite of the EU directive on freedom of access to information on the environment.

CONCLUSIONS

The particular features of this sector are as follows:

- Intensive regulation by medicine approval agencies. This inhibits, but does not prohibit change.
- The product, being low volume and high value, is the main focus, unlike the related fine chemicals sector which is also concerned about the process.
- The process methods are largely traditional, though overlain with high technology control and containment systems.

This sector has similarities with the fine chemicals sector, and reference should also be made to the conclusions and lessons drawn from that portion of the study. Regulation is the primary driving force for environmental performance.

Command and control

Some progress has been achieved by the introduction of the various integrated pollution control policies in the regions examined. NL Pharmaceuticals, for example, although tightly restricted, was aided by a cleaner production assessment. This suggests that demanding standards can expedite action, but also that industry must be given the flexibility to determine the best method to address these, possibly on a phased basis.

Self-assessment

Once a firm has decided to respond to regulatory pressures, cost-minimization appears to be the factor that predominantly influences the choice of response. Most of the IPC systems require the firms to develop an environmental management plan, with reduction targets set by the firms. This prompts firms to accurately quantify the magnitude and cost of their wastes and emissions. The putative VOC Directive would also demand a solvent management plan, or 'mass balance'. This would be helpful, as firms which are free to satisfy an overall ceiling emission value by adjusting their internal waste sources in an economically optimum manner appear to be more likely to adopt a cleaner technology approach.

While formal environmental management systems are common, the application of accredited standards such as EMAS is at an early stage. It is not possible to determine from the firms studied if production chain effects have yet been prompted by these standards, and no conclusion may be drawn with regard to their benefits.

Many of the cleaner technology improvements in this sector are incremental, and fall under the categories of improved operating and maintenance performance. As such, they are likely to originate from, and will certainly be implemented by, the general workforce. This suggests that training and education of the shop-floor staff could provide a cleaner technology 'push' as well as 'pull'.

Market pressure

For this sector, market pressures are a weak instrument. Of the firms examined, NL Pharmaceuticals is the only one which experienced market pressures resulting in its development of a new product. The eventual consumer is typically an ill patient, and the selection of medication is made by a medical practitioner. There is therefore a distance between production and consumption. To an extent, the drug regulatory agencies are the representatives of the consumers, and might play a part in influencing the environmental behaviour of companies. However, the US FDA, which did have a requirement for an environmental assessment, has now removed this requirement. Manufacturers of intermediates, which tend to bridge the sectors between fine chemicals and pharmaceuticals, are open to influence from their industrial customers. NL Pharmaceuticals is an example of this effect.

7 DAIRY SECTOR

Ian Thomson with Leo Baas, Noel Duffy and Brendan Ryan

Three companies were examined in this sector, one in Ireland, one in The Netherlands and one in the UK.

THE SECTORAL CONTEXT

Dairy processes

Daily milk is pasteurized and has a fat content variation of 0 to 3.5 per cent. Cheese can be made from raw milk (cheddar) or from skimmed milk (cottage cheese). Figure 7.1 outlines the processes.

Environmental issues

The sources of waste waters from dairy plants include:

- rinsing and washing of bulk tanks or cans in receiving stations, residual product remaining in or on the surface of all pipelines, pumps, tanks, vats and processing equipment;
- water–milk solid mixtures discharged during the start-up, product change-over and shutdown of pasteurizers, heat exchangers, separators, clarifiers and evaporators;
- sludge discharged from clarifiers;
- spills and leaks due to improper equipment operation and maintenance;
- unwanted by-products, like whey, or spoiled materials;
- loss in packaging operations through equipment breakdowns and broken/ disapproved packages;
- product returns.

The amount of water use and the BOD content in the effluent are the major environmental focal points for waste water management in the dairy sector.

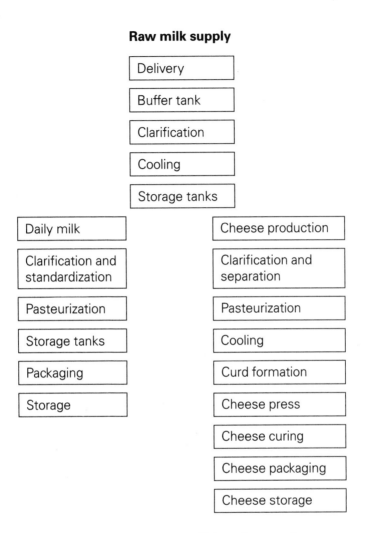

Figure 7.1 *The basic process of converting milk into cheese products*

Industrial structure and economic context

There are various similarities and differences in the primary features between the companies. The product range of the Irish and Scottish companies is in the same category of special milk products. The added value in this category is higher than in the category of daily milk and milk products, as in the Dutch dairy case.

The plants have annual production of 58 million litres (Scotland), 150 million litres (The Netherlands) and 320 million litres (Ireland). The total number of employees ranges from 75 to 190. Insofar as the number of employees is concerned, therefore, these cases are all medium-sized companies according to the EU definition, as they have less than 500 employees.[1]

The companies in Ireland and The Netherlands belong to cooperatives of farmer-members. The Scottish company is part of a Canadian multinational. The Irish company is oriented to export markets, while the markets of the Dutch and Scottish companies are regional.

Table 7.1 *Dairy sector cases*

Company	IRL Dairy	NL Dairy	UK Dairy
Products	Alcohol, cheese, butter, milk powder, food ingredients	Daily milk and milk products	Mozzarella cheese
Market	96% export	Regional market	Region and in-company
Number of employees in firm	165	190	75
in company	(165)	7350	(75)
Ownership/ relationship with parent	Farmer co-op membership/ Single site local firm	Farmer co-op membership/ site of Dutch dairy multinational	Site of Canadian multinational
Regional features		Dairy sector covenants	After two incidents pathway to waste reduction

CASE STUDIES

1   IRL Dairy

Company profile

The company was formed in 1965 by four local dairy cooperatives. It was reconstituted as a joint venture with a large British dairy (which held 80 per cent of the equity) in 1968. The British company was in turn taken over by a multinational conglomerate in 1970, giving the firm access to skills and technology from a diverse industrial base. The firm reverted to full ownership of the local cooperatives in 1992.

The company has grown from processing 27 million litres to in excess of 320 million litres per annum and an annual turnover of greater than IRL£70 million. There are 165 employees. The company's market is worldwide; 96 per cent of the production is for export, with 90 per cent going to Europe. An illustration of the worldwide market is the export of milk minerals to Japan with a very high added value of IRL£6 per kilogram. Effluents receive continuous attention because of the need to contain the milk minerals.

The firm produces skim milk powder, butter, cheddar and low fat cheese together with a range of innovative products. These include mozzarella cheese, with production commencing in 1994 (6000 tonnes per annum), high quality neutral spirit (alcohol) from the fermentation and distillation of lactose, and food ingredients.

The firm is technologically sophisticated. In 1978 it introduced the world's first commercial whey ultrafiltration and distillation plant to produce alcohol. It currently supplies 5 million litres annually to the Irish beverage industry and has recently developed the capacity to produce anhydrous alcohol for the pharmaceutical and food industry. It also claims to have pioneered Europe's first rapid cooling system in the cheese manufacturing process and was also involved in the early development of membrane technology. Ultrafiltration technology has been used to produce the varying whey protein concentrates demanded by the food ingredients market.

Its decision making procedure is relatively simple and flexible involving proposals from department head to the chief executive who in turn, where major investment is required, brings proposals to the board. As an independent firm, the board meets locally and therefore decisions are reached expeditiously.

Environmental profile

The firm is in receipt of air and water pollution licences from the local authority. It has no problems meeting its licence requirements. The firm did however appeal against the provisions of the air pollution licence initially granted by the local authority. As a result the SO_2 permit level was increased from 500 mg/m^3 to 1200 mg/m^3 (coal) and 1700 mg/m^3 (oil).

Aerobic waste water treatment plants were constructed in 1974 and 1978 and an anaerobic digester was installed in 1984. Sludge from the treatment plants is dried to 20 per cent solids and supplied free to local farmers as fertilizer. In addition, the firm has reduced (at source) BOD loading from production by 25 per cent since 1988. The firm has a generally proactive environmental policy. It is under no current environmental pressure, but expects environmental pressure to increase in future. It has a general commitment to waste reduction and avoidance, recycling and reuse, and to the conservation of energy and resources. The environmental impact of all new processes, plants and products are examined with these priorities in mind. It has undertaken programmes of waste minimization/recycling/reuse, and has employed external consultants to conduct an environmental audit independently of a similar audit carried out by the firm itself. It has also carried out environmental audits of suppliers. All staff have received environmental training, and it intends to comply with the IS 310 Environmental Management System in the near future. Amongst the additional environmental targets the firm set itself for 1995 were an overall 5 per cent reduction at source of all waste, together with reuse and recycling of 5 per cent of all waste generated. In addition the firm actively tries to influence the environmental performance of both suppliers and customers.

Project

The firm uses a variety of chemicals for plant washing and waste treatment. These include sodium hypochlorite, sodium hydroxide, sulphuric acid and nitric acid. Sulphuric acid and lime are used to precipitate minerals, in particular calcium and phosphorus, from the post-distillation alcohol plant effluent. This causes sludge problems, and the presence of residual sulphate radicals can result in the production of H_2S in the anaerobic digester. In addition both lime and sulphuric acid handling is, to some degree, hazardous.

The firm therefore investigated alternative mineral removal methods. This investigation was encouraged by the fact that milk minerals can sell for as much as IR£6000 per tonne in Japan. The chosen alternative involves installation of an ultrafiltration plant specifically designed to remove milk minerals. These are to be removed from the whey protein ultrafiltration permeate prior to fermentation. The separated minerals can then be sold.

Not all the minerals are removed, however, and therefore the distillation effluent still requires treatment. However residual mineral traces can be separated by dissolved air flotation, thus mitigating the need to use hazardous and environmentally threatening chemicals. The sludge problem is avoided, the odour problem is eliminated and a marketable product is obtained.

The idea for this project originated within the firm but the technology employed was bought in, the firm already having considerable experience of ultrafiltration. The direct air flotation technology was supplied by a UK firm. It was modified by the UK firm after earlier unsatisfactory tests.

The firm identified four sources of important information for the project. The first of these was the firm's own R&D team which identified the possibility of recovering milk minerals, while the second was their marketing and sales department which located a potential market and customer in Japan. The other two were the UK company and its associated consultancy.

2 NL Dairy

Company profile

The firm was founded in 1941. It was bought in 1974, and is now part of a multinational Dutch dairy products cooperative, owned by 9600 stock-breeders, but with subsidiaries in Belgium, Germany and the US. It is organized into divisions: Liquid Milk, Cheese, Industrial Ingredients, Dairy Products (butter, powder and condensed milk), and the foreign companies. Total group turnover is DFl 6670 million per annum. The products are sold in The Netherlands (42 per cent), where the group processes more than 99 per cent of the raw milk in commercial products, Europe (42 per cent) and the rest of the world (16 per cent). There are about 7350 employees, with 5000 in The Netherlands. The total milk processing capacity of the company in The Netherlands is 3315 million kilograms. The Liquid Milk division consists of six production facilities with a total milk processing capacity of 918 million kilograms per annum. Of the six facilities Maasdam, with around 190 employees, can produce 150 million kilograms per annum.

The Maasdam plant, 15 kilometres south of Rotterdam, is one of the two daily-milk dairies in the Zuid-Holland province. It is a primary dairy products facility, producing daily milk, sour milk, yoghurts and custards. The dairy was started by a Maasdam milk-trader in 1943. In the 1960s and 1970s all dairies in Rotterdam and surroundings were involved in mergers and takeovers. The Maasdam dairy was first taken over by a milk cooperative in the Rotterdam area and later by a cooperative operating in the provinces of Noord-Holland, Zuid-Holland and Zeeland. In the 1980s this cooperative merged with another, operating in the middle and south of The Netherlands.

The (added) value of raw milk is diminishing, partly because of EU quantum policy, and partly because of increasing logistical costs and discounts for big retailers. In 1994 the plant's turnover was some DFl 125 million. The plant has continuously improved and enlarged its process facilities, and now has 15 years experience with a Quality Management system.

Environmental profile

The firm's main focus is on waste water and packaging. The Maasdam dairy is regulated by a regional EPA and a regional Water Authority, because the water is emitted into the sewer. The regional Water Authority monitors the sewer disposal independently twice a year for BOD to determine the level of discharge (and fix it in terms of inhabitant equivalents [IEs]). The dairy industry maintains a Research and Development Institute (the Dutch Institute for Dairy Research, or NIZO), which has been involved in research to reduce the disposal of fat, enzymes and whey into the sewer. This research has led to reduced disposal and the development of a continuous monitoring system. NIZO analyses the disposal into the sewer every week.

During the 1970s and 1980s general pollution control approaches were developed, including containment floors for storage of chemical cleaners, and filters on drains. The focus on the continuous improvement and enlargement of the production, storage and other logistical facilities has also helped, however, to develop knowledge, both at both at the plant level and at the R&D level, about ways of reducing energy use and cleaner production issues. This approach is now increasingly driven by business improvement aims, although it continues to have positive environmental effects.

Projects

Waste water

In 1989–1990 the Maasdam plant joined the PRISMA project. An assessment of the cleaning procedure revealed the options for reducing water use through:

- reducing the number of cleaning water loops, and
- better product planning, in order to avoid the necessity of cleaning.

The firm has developed a computer guidance and monitoring system to control the production and cleaning processes. It is possible to control the timing of the processes precisely by carefully watching the turning point in the pH. The new system saved 110 IEs in the effluent out of a total of 3600 IEs in 1992.

Continuous improvement teams now analyse the IEs fluctuation as the basis for good housekeeping and continuous improvement measures, and have noted a 2:1 ratio between the value of the lost product and the cost of IEs.

The use of the computer system in this way was a radical innovation at operations level. Various participants were involved in this innovation at plant, division and R&D level within the corporation, and the computer system supplier played an important role.

Other elements of the project included:

- a circulation system to reuse water;
- the fine tuning of a heat power system;
- the installation of a continuous improvement team with representatives from several departments. This created a more effective response system. After the latest extension of production, for example, the level of IEs doubled to approximately 7000 IEs. The team were able to reduce the IE-load by 3000 IEs (cost saving DFl 210,000) by close weekly analysis, peak-shaving incidents and good housekeeping.

The target for the effluent level of 85 per cent of the average Dutch dairy level is now being met.

Packaging

Daily milk was originally sold without packaging. Later it was sold in glass bottles, then 'one way packaging' was introduced at the end of the 1960s. Milk products were eventually included in the 1991 Dutch Packaging Covenant (Ministry of Public Housing, Physical Planning and the Environment, 1991), with life cycle assessments being used for choices of one way or returnable packaging (Veld et al, 1992). New 200 gram glass bottles were also developed, just half the weight of the old 400 gram 1 litre bottles.

The substitution of polycarbonate bottles for glass bottles is an even more recent development. Polycarbonate bottles have certain logistical and economic advantages: they can be made square, so they can be packed more closely into crates and containers, they weigh less (only 10 grams), and they can be reused more frequently (approximately an average of 45 trips versus 30 trips for glass bottles). In the Maasdam production facility, filling in new glass was stopped in mid October 1995, and filling in polycarbonate bottles started in 1996.

3 UK Dairy

Company profile

UK Dairy started in 1978, was taken over in 1988, and is now a wholly owned subsidiary of a family controlled Canadian company. The group's main products are frozen convenience foods. The Loanhead plant is relatively small and employs approximately 75 staff. The main product is mozzarella cheese, although they also package blends of grated cheese such as mozzarella and cheddar. The cheese is sold within the group for the manufacture of frozen pizzas or to pizza restaurants.

An overview of the production process is shown in Figure 7.2 (the numbers refer to the main areas of waste minimization activity undertaken, see Table 7.2). The main effluents are whey, fats and grease and cleaning agents. Whey is the largest waste product as every kilo of cheese produces 9 litres of whey. Cleanliness is critical for cheese production and frequent cleaning of the plant is essential.

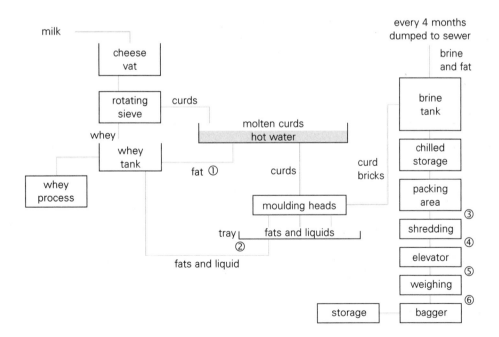

Figure 7.2 *Overview of the production process at UK dairy*

Environmental Profile

History

Until the late 1980s, environmental issues were not top priority, the main concern being the rapid expansion of production. The by-product whey was sold on to a local farmer for pig food. A solid waste/by-product was utilized as agricultural fertilizer, and the remaining effluents, with sour and fat compounds and cleaning agents, were emitted to the sewer.

The plant is located in an area of high unemployment which gave UK Dairy leverage in dealing with the regulator, Lothian Region Water and Drainage Department. However, a series of incidents led to a change in this relationship.

The local pig farmer went out of business and the limited storage facilities at the plant meant UK Dairy had to discharge the additional whey directly into the sewer. The regulator was informed and reluctantly accepted this as a temporary solution. This problem was eventually solved by finding a new pig farmer. Two years later a tanker reversed into a whey silo and ruptured the tank resulting in a large discharge of whey into the sewage system. During this period UK Dairy also had ongoing problems meeting the consent limits on acidity and free fat and grease.

Environmental responses

These incidents and increased pressure from regulators changed the attitude of management towards environmental issues. The firm's initial response to the need for further effluent reduction requirements was to call in consultants, who suggested end-of-pipe solutions such as a waste water treatment plant and automatic pH controls, then to ask the parent company for funds to build the waste water treatment plant. The parent company refused (on cost grounds) to fund this installation.

The rejection, combined with constructive advice from the regulator, led local plant managers to re-appraise their whole approach to waste from sewer disposal to waste minimization at source, which in turn led to a local waste minimization campaign which yielded considerable savings because of the reduction in lost product.

The solution involved a mixture of small capital investments and a range of procedural and process change. Some examples of these changes are illustrated in Table 7.2 (the numbers refer to Figure 7.2).

Managers designed a waste monitoring system and gather information on waste at all the critical production stages on a daily basis. The waste management programme has been integrated with a new Total Quality Management (TQM) System.

Decision making

The parent company operates a system of management which allows considerable operational autonomy, but within a strict set of financial controls. They do not have an environmental policy, but regard compliance with all regulations as

Table 7.2 *Examples of waste minimization initiatives at UK dairy*

1. Recovery of fat to the whey recovery process. Previously fat was discharged to the sewer.

2. A tray under the moulding heads was installed to recover fats and liquids to the whey tank. This was previously discharged to the sewer.

3. Recalibrated the shredding machines to reduce the amount of cheese loss, previously discharged to sewer.

4. New guards were installed which allows the cheese to be re-input into the process.

5. Filters fitted on all drains in this area to limit the amount of solids washed into the sewer. The waste is stored and sold as fertilizer.

6. Installed new automatic weighing machines and new bagging procedures to reduce spillage. Previously this spillage discharged to sewer.

an essential part of a manager's responsibility. In the past plant managers at UK Dairy and the UK board focused on minimum cost compliance. However, recent experience and knowledge of alternative strategies for dealing with waste has changed their approach to decision making in this area.

Waste issues are still evaluated on financial criteria, but the orientation has moved to a value-added approach, that is, waste minimization reduces costs. This helps to sell these plans to the board (increased profits) and to the workforce (help secure future employment). Plant managers have quantified the cost of waste and the consequent savings from waste minimization.

The introduction of TQM has resulted in decision making in waste minimization becoming an issue for all levels of employees.

Project

The project is the ongoing programme undertaken by UK Dairy and includes (in addition to the measures shown in Figure 7.2 and Table 7.2):

- quality circles established to deal with spillage in the packing area;
- waste measurement procedures introduced throughout the production process;
- feedback systems established to inform all levels of staff of the quantity and value of waste;
- a 'red bins' system, where all organic waste is collected and separated then sold as pig food;
- regular pre-planned cleaning of effluent balance tanks, recovered sludge used for fertilizer production;

- containment wall round silos and sewer outlets;
- probe installed in a remote whey silo to give notice when it was reaching full capacity;
- spillage recovery areas, recovering material to be used for fertilizer production;
- water use reduction and energy conservation measures;
- facilitating the recycling of indirect waste products, such as aluminium cans, paper and cardboard.

The combined effect of these and other measures has dramatically reduced the emissions from the site, giving, for example a 40 per cent reduction in suspended solids. There have been significant financial savings, currently estimated at £200,000 per annum, from an investment of just £10,000.

Summary of case

As a result of this radical change in management philosophy to waste and the ongoing waste minimization programme, UK Dairy is now regarded by the regulator as an exemplar for other plants in the region. UK Dairy, through a process of self-development and constructive interaction with the regulators, has significantly reduced its discharges into the environment. Their perception of environmental regulations as a cost and a threat, has changed; they now see the environment as an area which they can actively manage and potentially turn to their advantage.

COMPARATIVE ANALYSIS OF CASE STUDIES

Clean technology promotion

Despite the BATNEEC approach in the Irish EPA Act of 1992, the dissemination of information regarding cleaner technologies is not specifically seen by the EPA as one of their functions. The Department of Environment believe that there is insufficient experience anywhere in promoting relevant waste minimization plans to determine the optimal route at this stage. Cork County Council, however, are aware of the benefits associated with waste minimization and are actively seeking ways to promote it in the region. Two of the options available to the Council are to include waste minimization requirements in licences or to encourage voluntary uptake by industry. The Council also believe that there is an onus on industry groups to disseminate information on cleaner technology as they do not have the resources for such a task (EPA, 1994).

In the United Kingdom, several cleaner technology projects have been generated by the Department of Trade and Industry (DTI). No special programmes have been developed in Scotland.

Table 7.3 *Summary of environmental responses of firms*

Country	Ireland	The Netherlands	United Kingdom
Regulatory context	Recent transfer from Cork County Council to national EPA	Provincial EPA; Regional Water Authority	Lothian Regional Council (now as adviser for HMIPI)
	application to IPC system not yet requested	PRISMA project	
Environmental policy/ management	Formal	Formal	Formal
		Dairy covenant	
	ISO 9002 IS 310 in development Environmental Management system	Environmental Care in Total Quality Management	Total Quality Management
Environmental response/project	New product from waste – external recycling	Improved techniques/ working practices	Improved techniques/ working practices

Besides the general development of environmental management within Dutch companies as an integrated company management approach, cleaner technology approaches have been generated via different sources. For nearly two decades, cleaner technology promotion programmes have been developed by the Ministry of Environment. There are also tax write-offs available for certain environmental technologies, although these technologies are often still end-of-pipe. The activities of the Innovation Centres,[2] however, reveal a more integrated technology approach.

Role of the environmental regulator

All of the companies have a normal relationship with their regulators. As the dairy sector is not seen as hazardous, the regulations pertaining to discharges are not particularly strict.

The Irish legislation governing environmental regulation of industry has essentially been dictated by the obligatory compliance with the relevant EU Directives. The 1992 Environmental Protection Agency Act (EPA Act) established a new institutional framework for the control of environmental pollution in Ireland. Among other factors, the Act was motivated by concern about the lack of expertise in many local authorities for dealing with complex industrial facilities and the need for clear national standards.

The EPA Act of 1992 describes a BATNEEC approach (the best available technology not entailing excessive costs). A BATNEEC Guidance Note provides guidance to those applying for integrated pollution control licences under the EPA Act. BATNEEC will be used to prevent, eliminate, or where that is not practicable, limit, abate, or reduce an emission from an activity listed in the first schedule of the Act.

In the case study, Cork County Council was responsible for air and water emissions licences for the dairy. This Council tended to take a firm but cooperative approach. The dairy has now been now transferred to an integrated pollution control (IPC) licence, administered by the national EPA. This single licence will involve the regulation of all wastes and emissions.

The new integrated pollution control approach in Britain is based on a partnership model of regulation: guiding a firm's environmental performance over a number of years in the implementation of incremental waste minimization programmes. This approach requires firms to describe their plans for waste minimization and cleaner technology. It may also arise informally, based upon exhortation and advice rather than legislation. This was particularly notable in the UK Dairy case. After several incidents, the dairy came to see the Lothian Region Water and Drainage Department as sources of expert advice rather than as remote, strict regulators.

In the period 1970–1980 the development of environmental regulation and policies in The Netherlands involved media-specific approaches, starting with the 1970 Law on Surface Water Pollution. In the second part of the 1980s, however, more integrated approaches emerged. The relevant regulatory responsibilities are now divided between Environmental Protection (or Management) Agencies and Water Authorities. NL Dairy is regulated by a provincial EPA, while a local water board is responsible for the management of the waste water. Permits from these regulatory agencies have been recently renewed.

In the National Environmental Policy Plan (NEPP) (1989), and in the second version, NEPP+ (1990), the Ministry of Environment developed a target group policy for various sectors of industry. The aim of the 'target group policy' is to reach agreements with the (sub) target groups about the implementation of environmental targets as defined in the NEPPs. A covenant with the dairy industry has been agreed, with a pollution reduction target of 10 per cent. This Covenant explicitly recognizes the role of cleaner production. An earlier Covenant on Packaging played a role in the composition of 'one way packages' and the substitution of the traditional glass milk bottle by a lighter one, and after a further three years by the square polycarbonate bottle.

Clean technology and decision-making

The dairy industry is currently evolving quickly, diversifying into making new, higher value products in addition to processing traditional dairy products. Firms are now, for example, separating specific high value compounds, such as amino acids for the pharmaceutical sector. This also gives an incentive to adopt more advanced approaches to dairy processing. This is already reflected in the terminology; in The Netherlands, the process of separation of industrial proteins from whey is now described as 'milk refining'.

The Irish company has been an innovator in this direction. The company is very active in technological innovation and pioneering research. It has well-developed relationships with R&D facilities outside the company. They have focused, for example, on extracting proteins with special properties, in addition to the traditional practice of separating the 3.5 per cent of proteins (caseinates) and 4.5 per cent sugars (lactose) from the undermilk/whey mixture. Another research and development initiative, the project selected for this study, was concerned with development of new products from the recovery of milk minerals. The motivation for this project (the reduction of hydrogen sulphide generation and sludge production) was more economic than environmental. Environmental improvement was identified by the firm as only one of a number of incentives; there were also several business/economic incentives such as a reduction of materials use, the improvement of working conditions by reducing the usage of sulphuric acid and lime and the generation of hydrogen sulphide, and facilitating the development of a new market for recovered milk minerals.

In UK Dairy the project was general waste minimization by improved working practices and techniques. The development of their own capability for waste minimization can be seen as a process of 'organizational learning'. The original trigger was the pressure from the sewage authority to reduce fat and grease effluent discharge into the sewer. However the financial savings from reduced waste of valuable products/by-products stimulated a programme of continuous improvement in the firm.

NL Dairy has always had a very strong technological orientation, which is typical of the Dutch dairy sector. The project involved a general programme of continuous improvement in techniques and working practices. Originally this approach was stimulated by environmental issues, but it is increasingly driven by business improvement considerations, with positive environmental side effects, reflecting the 2:1 ratio between the value of the lost product and the costs of waste disposal (IEs).

Environmental management and objectives

In all cases the plant management is responsible for environmental performance. In NL Dairy one full time employee is responsible for environmental care. The Irish company has had an ISO 9002 system for some years. The company developed an Environmental Policy Statement and started awareness raising among its employees. The dairy has an IS 310 Environmental Management System in place, but it is not yet accredited.

UK Dairy develops its own policy; there are no corporate guidelines. In 1989, the company was operating at well over capacity, and discharging a lot of effluent. They initially responded to pressure from the regulators by involving consultants. The end-of-pipe solutions that the consultants suggested were too costly, however, and after a major spill in 1992, a dialogue with the Local Authority Water and Sewage department generated a shift to waste minimization. They developed their own capability for integrated solutions. In May 1995, a Total Quality Management system was started.

In the Dutch case, environmental care considerations are integrated at all management levels. There is a Director of Environmental Management on the board of the corporation. Environmental care is integrated in quality management, internal competitions, workers' participation meetings and continuous improvement teams. The company was involved in the PRISMA project in the period 1989–1990 (Dieleman et al, 1991).

All companies have moved towards a strategy of continuous improvement. The Irish company strives for a reduction of waste (in 1995 its target was 5 per cent reduction) by reuse, and by fostering both incident-specific and general learning to create the basis for further improvement. The company presumes that it will achieve 100 per cent compliance. The Scottish company strives for 75 per cent compliance, this being the agreed target between the company and the regulators. The Dutch company aims at a performance level of 85 per cent of the average pollution level in the dairy sector.

CONCLUSIONS

The public perceives the dairy sector, producers of primary food products, as strongly associated with health. In none of the cases, however, was any public pressure observed. The relation of all companies with the regulators is normal.

The amount of water use and the BOD content in the effluent are the major environmental focal points for waste water management in the dairy sector. The development of environmental performance differs in the three companies. The Irish company developed a technological and product development orientation, the Dutch company developed an energy saving and process technology orientation and participated in a cleaner production project. The Scottish company was stimulated by the local authority to consider a waste minimization plan after two incidents, and spurred by the refusal of the parent company to fund a waste water treatment plant. However, there are similarities in the approach adopted by the companies to environmental performance. The companies have all implemented a waste minimization programme, rather than a conventional end-of-pipe solution. Both the Dutch and Scottish companies have recently developed waste monitoring information systems, which have helped to improve the measurement and consequent 'visibility' of pollution, while the Irish company has had such a programme since 1988.

The waste minimization approaches show incremental steps which have synergistic impact for relatively small investments. More radical approaches in new investments can also be detected. Earlier obstacles to this development have been a lack of information, weak regulatory pressure and a reluctance to change (because of concerns over hygiene standards). More recently, however, key people in the companies were willing to transform the sector's traditional approach into a more responsive and proactive approach in order to maintain, over the long term, the public perception of the cleanliness of the dairy sector.

This suggests that incentives for process-integrated and innovative activities are the key to improving the environmental performance of the dairy sector. The environmental aspects already seem to be increasingly internalized, and to have stimulated the R&D departments and strategic management to use more compounds from the raw milk, giving increased profit margins and reducing pollution at the same time. Education of the workforce and technical innovations to improve efficiency have been the instruments for waste minimization, energy saving, product development and increased profits. Policy should therefore focus on reinforcing these positive trends.

8 BREWING SECTOR

Anthony Clayton and Ian Thomson with Leo Baas,
Noel Duffy and Brendan Ryan

Three companies were examined in this sector, one in Ireland, one in The Netherlands and one in the UK.

SECTORAL CONTEXT

The products and the essential biological processes and operations involved in the brewing industry have changed relatively little for centuries, although what started as a small-scale craft has become a large modern process industry. During the course of this change, the industry has become extensively automated, and scaled up production methods. The economies of scale also led to extensive rationalization, with a small number of large breweries and allied operations replacing a large number of small breweries. In Edinburgh, for example, there were about 200 breweries in 1840. These have now been replaced by one large industrial complex, the one in the study, which has greater capacity than all 200 combined.

The main industrial process

All firms in the brewing industry rely on the same basic fermentation process. This uses yeast, a fungus that grows and multiplies when it is supplied with sufficient energy in the form of digestible (called fermentable) sugars. The process creates more yeast, along with alcohol, CO_2 and heat.

The traditional source of fermentable sugar is malt, derived from barley. Barley is steeped in water, then aerated. This encourages the barley to germinate. Enzymes start converting the starch in the grain to sugar. After 4 or 5 days the grain is hot air dried, which stops germination but does not kill the enzymes.

The grain is then milled and crushed into small particles, called grist. The grist is mixed with hot water. The remaining starch dissolves, and the enzymes chop the long starch chains into short-chain sugars. Most of the sugars present at this stage are fermentable sugars. The hot liquid containing the sugar (called wort) is drained from the bottom of the mash, while fresh hot water is sprayed on from the top to wash out more of the sugars. The remaining solid material (spent grains or draff), from which all the fermentable sugars have been extracted, is traditionally sold on for cattle feed.[1]

Other cereals are sometimes added to the grist, and sugars from other sources (such as cane) are sometimes added to the wort, partly to utilize the most economic source of sugar, and partly because such additions can impart different characteristics to the beer. Coloured malts and roasted barley are also used to give colour to the beer.

The wort then goes to the wort kettle (also called the copper), where hops are added to give the beer its bitter taste and aroma. The liquid is then boiled for about 1 hour. This kills any organisms and stops all remaining enzyme activity, thereby leaving the liquid sterile, and evaporates some of the water, thereby reducing volume and increasing strength. It also causes remaining solid matter to flocculate. The wort is then sprayed into a vessel called a whirlpool, which spins out the flocculated solid matter.

This leaves a hot, clear, coloured and flavoured but sterile sugar solution, which then has to be cooled down before the yeast is added. The initial cooling is usually done with a heat exchanger, which transfers heat from the hot solution going out to the cold wort going in to the wort kettle.

The cooled wort is then injected with oxygen, and the yeast is added (or 'pitched') as the wort flows into the fermenting vessel. Sterile water is then added to adjust the volume and specific gravity of the beer. A sample of the mix is then taken, and its original gravity is measured and recorded (or 'declared'), as this is the basis for excise duty.

The yeast then grows and multiplies, using the sugars as a food source, and produces CO_2 and alcohol as waste products. Some of the CO_2 remains in the beer, but most has to be vented. Most of the heat produced during the fermentation also has to be removed. Fermentation is stopped after 30 to 180 hours by chilling the vessel, which makes the yeast settle out. The yeast is then removed by skimming and centrifuging. Surplus yeast is sold on to distillers (especially in Scotland), to food manufacturers for making yeast extract products, and for pig food.

Beer is produced with one set of yeasts, lager with another. The different yeast strains have to be handled quite differently. A wort with ale yeasts is pitched at 18°C and fermented at 22°C, and the fermentation can be stopped by cooling the vessel to 11°C. A wort with lager yeasts is pitched at 10°C and fermented at 13°C, and the fermentation is only stopped by cooling the vessel to 4°C. Thus lager yeasts prefer lower temperatures, and will be active at a temperature well below that which stops ale yeasts.

The liquid is then held for a while to allow it to mature, either in the same vessel, in a special maturation vessel, or in casks (when it is called cask conditioned). Ales only have to be held for a few days of cold conditioning, lagers usually have to be held for longer. Some yeast has to be left in lager during maturation. Finings are then added to settle out any remaining yeasts and residues. The matured product is then filtered. The filtered (or 'bright') beer is then ready for packaging, and goes from the bright beer tank to be canned, bottled, kegged or to fill tankers for bulk distribution to pubs. Filtration is mostly done with kiezelguhr, which is a kind of siliceous earth. After use, the kiezelguhr is pressed to extract any remaining beer before it is discarded. Used kiezelguhr generally goes to landfill.

CO_2 is injected into the beer before packaging to make it effervescent. Some brewers use the same CO_2 that was vented from the fermentation vessel to carbonate the beer, but those without CO_2 recovery facilities have to buy in CO_2.

Strict control and hygiene is required throughout the entire process. Contamination of the wort by other micro-organisms such as bacteria, 'wild' yeasts or just the wrong yeast from another process could result in a ruined batch. This means that constant cleaning is required. Steam, caustic soda, bleach and various acids are used to sterilize vessels, pipes and other equipment between batches.

Economic conditions for the sector

The total market for beer and related products, in any one country, cannot be indefinitely expanded, as there is a limit to the amount of beer that people will drink. UK beer consumption, for example, has declined since 1979, although there has been some modest growth recently. The total UK market is currently valued at £13bn, while the Irish market is valued at £1.5bn.

The market resembles a zero-sum game, which means that corporate growth and increased profits can only be sought by increasing exports, by capturing market share from competitors, by acquisition and takeover, by asset-swapping, by licensing deals, by diversification, or by capturing a larger share of the total drinks market from other beverages. In the last few decades much of the additional scaling up required for further cost reductions has been achieved via business acquisitions and takeovers. Thus there continues to be a great deal of competitive pressure in the industry. There are still more than 60 brewing companies manufacturing or selling in the UK market, for example, but these are of very different sizes. Four dominant companies control 80 per cent of the market, and further consolidation is anticipated.

The UK industry still has over capacity, but recent reductions in terms of capacity have outstripped the fall in consumption. The UK Brewery in the study recently rationalized operations after a major acquisition and closed two breweries, which removed 1.5 million barrels of annual beer production in a market of some 36 million barrels. The gap is being made up with increases in imports, particularly of premium lagers.

The process of economic rationalization has therefore continued, and all three of the companies in the study had been subject to recent corporate restructuring. The UK company disposed of its non-core businesses in 1988 in order to resist a predatory takeover, re-expanded in 1990 and acquired another brewing group in 1995. The Irish company went into receivership in 1983 and was bought by a large multinational operation based in The Netherlands. The company in The Netherlands was taken over by one multinational (based in the UK) in 1968, then sold on to another (based in Belgium) in 1995 as part of a larger corporate restructuring. All three appeared, at the time of the study, to be performing successfully relative to the general market. The process of acquisition and rationalization continued throughout the period of the study.

Regional identity, however, continues to be important to the industry. A significant number of beers are largely consumed locally. Many breweries are on sites where beer has been brewed continuously for many years, in some cases for centuries. This means that brewery companies tend to have a sense of local identity, a strong inclination to a 'good neighbours' policy, and a keen awareness of the importance of brands and the marketing of brands. As with foodstuffs generally, it is important that the product is seen as pure and uncontaminated.

Another factor that results from the maturity of the sector is that there are few core technical secrets, which means that the sector has a relatively free exchange of information. The environmental coordinators of the different Dutch breweries, for example, meet each other periodically and share information. There are also strong trade associations and a number of trade journals which disseminate information. Most breweries are also part of large corporations, and access information from within the larger group.

The combination of the maturity of the sector, the essential continuity of the basic processes and operations involved, the strong historical locus and regional identity, and the importance of brand name and image, inclines the sector as a whole to be rather conservative. Brewers are little inclined to unnecessarily radical change in products or processes. The industry is concerned about good public relations, environmental performance and a clean image, but it is not (and it is not perceived to be) a high environmental risk industry.

The effect of excise

A general feature of the sector is that excise duties form a high percentage of the product price. This has direct implications for the costs and benefits of improvements in environmental performance, as the excise duties dilute the effect of any improvements in the efficiency of production. Any reduction in production costs is unlikely to have a noticeable effect on the cost of the final product to the consumer, although it will improve profitability. Thus any reduction in production costs is unlikely to have much implication in terms of, for example, allowing the company to increase sales.

Long investment cycle

The industry has, by virtue of the common basic technology, a long investment cycle. There is therefore an economic incentive to defer environmental improvements until such time as plant has to be replaced. At that point, technological advances allow the operators to meet many of the higher environmental criteria, without any need for specific investment.

Environmental issues[2]

Each company has somewhat different environmental priorities, depending on the regulatory regime, their programme of equipment renewal and capital investment, and the prevailing economic conditions, but the basic similarity of the technical processes throughout the industry means that the core environmental issues are broadly similar. The issues of common concern throughout the industry are:

- the efficiency of water usage and energy efficiency;
- the disposal of waste water from washing and cleaning operations, and the associated discharges of cleaning chemicals such as caustic soda and various acids (the problem is usually with surges of highly alkali or acid wastes into the sewer, rather than with the average pH of the discharge);
- the environmental implications of the various packaging options;
- smell and noise;
- the disposal of by-products such as spent grains and excess yeast, kiezelguhr and other solid wastes, and CO_2 emissions.

Water use and effluent

Considerable progress has been made with water-use efficiency. Water consumption by the industry in the UK, for example, has declined by 40 per cent since 1976. This is partly accounted for by the decline in the consumption of beer and lager, but is also due to process improvements and efficiency gains. This has been driven by economic rather than environmental reasons; it costs money to buy and purify raw water and to dispose of waste water, so there is always an incentive for bulk users like breweries to increase efficiency.

The greater part of waste water effluent is from cleaning operations. Much of the plant and equipment requires frequent washing and sterilizing (a typical plant will run 150–200 cleaning operations per day) and kegs, cans and bottles have to be washed and pasteurized.[3] Some 60–70 per cent of the water used by the UK brewery in the study, for example, was used in cleaning operations (most of the rest came out as product, the remainder was evaporated through the ammonia coolers).

One of the major determinants of water emission is the type of container used to ship the beer, as each type requires a different cleaning process. Efficiency varies by size, so that bottles use the most water and tankers the least.[4] Thus any change in the way in which the output is packaged affects water usage. A move to ship more beer in cans and less in bottles, for example, will reduce the water usage relative to output, with no other improvement in production methods. The industry is therefore particularly sensitive to the recent EC directive on packaging, which will affect cost structures in brewing and retail operations.

CASE STUDIES

All three companies have a long history, and are strongly identified – in the public mind – with their regions, but ownership, size and market share varies between

Table 8.1 *Brewing sector cases*

Company	IRL brewery	NL brewery	UK brewery
Products and markets	1 stout, 1 lager, 1 beer. Largely domestic, some export	1 lager. Some 55% domestic, 45% export	Wide range beers and lagers, several stouts. Mostly domestic, some export
No employees (plant/company)	<500 / na	>500 / na	na / >30,000
Ownership/ relationship with parent company	Owned by a large multinational based in The Netherlands. Fairly high level of plant autonomy	Owned by a large multinational based in Belgium. High level of plant autonomy	Large independent company. The brewery has little autonomy

the three. IRL Brewery is a relatively small subsidiary of a large foreign multinational, with a dominant position in the Irish market for one of its main products but only a minor position for its other main product. NL Brewery is a relatively large subsidiary of a large foreign multinational, with a healthy export market. UK Brewery is a large independent company that recently acquired another smaller brewing chain, itself a large company, to take the biggest single share of the UK beer market.

1 IRL Brewery

Company profile

IRL Brewery was founded in 1856. Initially they brewed porter, but then switched to stout (for the local market only). In 1975 the company was licensed to produce a major international branded lager for the Irish market. In spite of the success of the lager, the brewery ran into difficulties and in 1983 was taken over by the lager brand owners, a major multinational. IR£35 million was invested in the plant, and the plant is now a modern state of the art brewery, producing stout for the home and export markets, lager for the home market and ale exclusively for the export market. They currently employ 300 people.

In 1994 total sales for this brewery in Ireland amounted to 63 million litres of lager and 11 million litres of their two other products. They estimate that they have some 36.5 per cent of the draught lager market in Ireland and 5 per cent of the stout market (this represents second place in the stout market, but the market leader has 80 per cent market share). Stout declined from 51.1 per cent to 47.8

per cent of the total Irish beer market in 1995/96, and ale declined to 10.1 per cent, while lager increased to 41.7 per cent. Allowing for the growth in packaged, rather than draught sales, this gives IRL Brewery about 15.4 per cent of the total Irish market. Overall sales for the brewery are given as IR£125 million for 1994.

Environmental profile

The brewery operates under a 1989 water pollution licence issued by the city council. It does not have an air pollution licence. Different standards apply to liquid emissions to the adjacent river and to the sewer. Considerably higher emissions are permitted into sewer than into waters, even though sewers ultimately discharge without treatment into the city's tidal estuary. The firm currently has a BOD to sewer permit of 2000 kg per day which is equivalent to domestic discharges from over 35,000 people (inhabitant equivalents [IEs]). The firm is currently preparing an IPC licence application to the EPA who have issued a BATNEEC standard for the brewing and related industries.

The firm has not been under any environmental pressure but recognizes that pressures may arise in the future. The parent company sees itself as an environmental leader, operates a formalized benchmarking programme, which regularly compares performance on a range of criteria including environmental issues, and the firm attempts to meet their objectives. Funding to improve environmental performance is readily available, but the equipment renewal cycle is still an important factor; the parent company have not yet installed the kind of advanced process control technology in their home plant in The Netherlands that they have commissioned for new plant under construction overseas.

The firm is accredited to ISO 9002. An environmental management plan was drafted in 1995. This focuses on a hierarchy of objectives, from load minimization through containment, recovery/recycle and emission reduction to waste treatment and disposal. Each has a specific target for a change in performance. The firm is also working towards an environmental management system, probably IS 310.

The firm began a detailed effluent survey in 1995, and has plans to institute daily monitoring of effluent. It foresees no financial problems in implementing its environmental strategy. Their most important source of information is the new owners. The second is the professional organizations; the firm is a member of the Brewers Guild and the Institute of Brewing, which represent important information networks. The third is other brewing firms. The regulatory body was not reported to be a significant source of information. The firm is also using consultants to assist them with their current developments.

Project

The parent company initiated a benchmarking exercise to compare water usage in each of the organization's breweries. Water is relatively cheap in Ireland

(IR£0.4/tonne), and the Irish brewery turned out to have a water usage well in excess of most other firms. Approximately 10 litres of water were used per litre of product. The firm set about reducing this, even though it was clear that the marginal cost savings based on water charges would not be immediately significant. A municipal waste water treatment plant is planned, however, which would result in the imposition of volume charges for sewer effluent. This will make any saving of water considerably more financially attractive. It was also noted that the water used for production purposes in brewing cost significantly more than the sum charged by the local authority. This is because product quality requirements necessitate filtration, UV sterilization and other pre-treatments. Reduced water usage, therefore, reduces the cost of these operations.

The anticipated local authority charges for waste water treatment did cause the firm to consider installing a waste water treatment plant, but this plan is currently checked by the fact that there is insufficient space on the site to construct an aerobic treatment plant.

Water recovery projects were undertaken in certain areas. Metering and monitoring were used to quantify water usage accurately. Simple technical changes helped further, such as the installation of triggers on all the hoses used in the plant. The result to date has been a reduction in water usage from 10 litres per litre of product to 4.8 litres per litre of product; one of the best ratios achieved anywhere in the group.

This project, while stimulated by the benchmarking exercise, was an entirely local operation, and involved no external sources of information.

2 NL Brewery

Company profile

The original Dutch brewery was founded in 1538. This original brewery and the three nearby breweries were taken over in 1968 by a UK corporation. Other Dutch brewers were integrated into the group, which was rationalized and subsequently sold to a Belgian International Brewing Corporation in 1995. The NL brewery has 900 employees, and now produces 2 million hectolitres of beer annually, about 50 per cent of which is sold (in returnable containers) within The Netherlands, and 45 per cent exported (in non-returnable containers). The beer is packed in glass bottles (50 per cent), vessels for draught beer (30 per cent) and tins (20 per cent). The rest of the production goes directly to selling points in 600 litre + tanks. The brewery is run on a largely independent basis, with its own brewing, bottling and distribution operations, marketing, sales, research and development and strategic management.

Environmental profile

NL Brewery appears to operate to the highest environmental standards of the three cases. This is because they operate in the toughest regulatory regime and expect standards to rise still further. As a result of regulations pertaining to BOD, for example, they are the only case in the sector to operate an aerobic water treatment plant. The brewery was the first one in The Netherlands with an ISO-9002 certificate for production, production facilities and distribution. The brewery has developed a Company Environmental Management System (CEAM) and is working towards BS7750, ISO 14000 and EMAS certification. They are also taking steps to eliminate the use of kieselguhr in response to rising disposal costs and the closure of disposal routes.

The company's attitudes and behaviour vary on different environmental issues. They are reactive on the issues of smell, noise and soil pollution, which are regulated in a rather traditional manner. They are more proactive on waste water and solid waste management issues. The main drivers for change are (a) economic incentives and (b) changes in the available waste treatment technologies. The company is currently focused on reduction of water use, reduction of effluents and the prevention of waste.

During the 1970s and 1980s a general pollution control approach dominated. Containment floors were installed throughout the factories, and an aerobic waste water facility and an external chemical waste treatment facility were developed. Environmental data is now collected from the separate locations: the brewery at Ceresstraat and the bottling and storage departments at Christiaan Huygenstraat. The brewery faces the general problem of public reaction and consequent restrictions on industrial activity in a residential area, and has a rather defensive attitude with regard to the perennial problems of smell and noise. These are important, as the brewery is located in the centre of the city.

In the late 1980s the emphasis shifted to a more preventive approach, for both economic and environmental reasons. The company started a programme of continuous improvement in production, storage and logistical operations, and began accumulating in-house expertise on energy efficiency and cleaner production, both at operational level and in its R&D.

The use of water for cleaning bottles and crates and for the pasteurization process has been very significantly reduced in recent years. Waste water data has been systematically collected since 1989. The firm appointed an environmental coordinator in 1991, who immediately developed a system for collecting and using key environmental data, with IEs as one of the key indicators. The data from the company's environmental monitoring system, originally developed to meet EPA requirements, are now used as a database for the management and saving of water and energy and as a generator for the incremental development of cleaner technologies. Thus the data are used both for external reporting (to several agencies) and for internal use (to show results and to promote continuous improvement).

The brewery is regulated both by a regional EPA and a regional Water Authority, because the effluent is emitted into the sewer. The regulator for the beer brewery, under the Law on Environment Management, is the Stadsgewest Breda (a regional EPA). The waste water, emitted to the sewer, is controlled by the Hoogheemraadschap West-Brabant (a regional Water Board). The Hoogheemraadschap monitors the BOD of the waste water periodically to ascertain the IEs.

Project

There was considerable financial pressure to improve the company's environmental performance. As of 1 January 1995, the weekly waste water effluent level was 1879 m^3 and 8475 IEs each day. The IE levy has increased by 10 to 15 per cent each year, from DFl 67 per IE in 1993 to DFl 93 in 1996. Total levy costs continue to ratchet upwards. Beer production in 1994 was 18 per cent higher than in 1993, and the total amount of IEs increased by 3 per cent, but the levy rose by 21 per cent over the same period. The company was also under pressure on the input side; the company's two locations used 758 m^3 and 9191 m^3 respectively of water per month over the period 1 July 1993–30 June 1994, while the law on ground water specifies a total maximum usage allowance of 1.04 million m^3 water per year.

The sharply increasing levies for waste water disposal stimulated a programme which included good housekeeping, computer monitoring, tighter control of processes and internal recycling. These measures enabled the company to significantly reduce the use of water for cleaning bottles and crates and for the pasteurization process in recent years, achieving a total reduction in water usage from 10 to 6 litres per litre of product.

In addition, some components of the waste water streams with economic value are now recovered. Waste prevention and reuse of tins, cracked and faulty glass, paper labels, old wooden pallets, and plastics are environmental targets, but the firm is currently focused on kiezelguhr use and disposal. This is because under The Netherlands National Environmental Policy Plan (NEPP) (1989), the Zevenbergen dump (where NL Brewery currently send their used kiezelguhr, via the Stadsgewest Breda regional waste management organization) is due to be closed in the near future. There are charges for dumping, which increased by more than 100 per cent – from DFl 52.50 per ton to DFl 115 per ton – over the period 1991–1994, and are set to increase further. NL Brewery's R&D department are therefore trying to develop a new technology, and are currently running a pilot project in cooperation with the branch organization. Used kiezelguhr can be used as fertilizer, but the current surplus of manure in The Netherlands makes this an economically unattractive option.

3 UK Brewery

Company profile

UK Brewery is part of a large group, with three main divisions, Retail (public houses), Beer (brewing operations) and Leisure (resorts, holiday camps, restaurants). The group had five breweries in the UK (the oldest was established in 1749), an acquisition gave them four more, but they then closed two of the nine in 1996 to rationalize the combined capacity. The acquisition gave them 25–31 per cent of the UK beer market. The Beer division makes a wide range of different beers and lagers. The brewery in the study makes both lager and ale.

Environmental profile

The company considers itself a good, responsible corporate citizen, and intends to meet its environmental obligations. It is largely responsive, however, and the breweries within the group adopt different strategies in the different regions of the UK in which they operate, according to differences in the local regulations. Corporate expenditure required to meet statutory requirements is given priority, but the company will still try and meet these obligations as efficiently and as cheaply as possible.

Project

This is a large brewery, a major employer in the city of Edinburgh, and the largest single user of the sewage system. The brewery uses a traditional brewing process, and has three main brands. Product is sent out in bottles, cans, kegs and tankers. The site has four main discharges: contaminated water (mostly from the washing processes), CO_2 from the fermentation process (released into the atmosphere), spent grains (sold for cattle fodder) and waste yeast (sold to distillers or for food production).

The brewery has undertaken a number of projects to reduce its energy and water consumption. The firm has introduced water recovery systems in wash cycles, installed monitoring and control equipment, and makes extensive use of energy recovery systems. A survey of the site resulted in a number of specific improvements in drainage and the development of spill control procedures.

As a result, the quantity of water used per litre of product has been reduced from 8.8 litres in 1979 to the current level of 5.5 litres per litre of product, largely for economic reasons, although the company was aware of the environmental benefits.

The brewery has had reasonably good compliance with its consent levels, and despite the occasional breach of consent has never been prosecuted. The main problem has been the occasional failure to comply with the pH range, due to surges of acid and alkali cleaning agents into the sewer. The brewery does not have a consent for BOD, so this high compliance rate does not imply a low level of environmental impact.

Consent levels have been tightened over the last few years, however, and the brewery has responded to these changes with the construction of a waste water treatment plant. This was designed in two phases. Phase 1 is a settlement, bulking and neutralization plant. This will settle out solid wastes and bulk acid and alkali wastes, so that they neutralize before discharge to sewer. The site was not under any regulatory pressure on the issue of solids, but their removal will have an impact on future sewage charges. Phase 2 will be an aeration and biological treatment plant, as the company expects that future constraints may well include a BOD consent level. This phase will not be built until the regulators have decided on the level of treatment required.

This was an end-of-pipe solution, generated in response to regulatory pressure. The treatment plant was designed by external consultants. Cleaner options were not fully explored; the company is relatively traditional, and radical change is unlikely to occur unless there is strong external pressure.

The company has a strong technical capacity (they developed the eco top end, or spring up tab, which replaced the detachable ring-pull on cans), and is aware of technology which could improve their environmental performance. They also have a subsidiary process control technology R&D company which develops and sells monitoring and control equipment. This subsidiary markets new instrumentation and process control technologies to the other divisions, as well as developing sales to other companies around the world. Some of these new process control technologies offer significant environmental improvements. Even though these technologies have been developed within the same group, however, the breweries are not pressured to adopt them unless they will help them to meet local requirements.

Table 8.2 *Summary of environmental responses of firms*

Company	IRL brewery	NL brewery	UK brewery
Regulatory context	Main regulator is Cork Corporation (for sewer and river discharge). Moving to the IPC system, which is administered by the EPA	Regulators are the Stadsgewest Breda (general EPA) and Hoogheemraadschap West-Brabant (sewer)	Regulators including HMIPI, NRA/local RPB and the local authority vary by site. The main current regulator for the Brewery is Lothian Regional Council (sewer)
Environmental policy	External formal ISO 9002 accredited; working towards IS 310	External formal ISO 9002 and working towards BS 7750, EMAS etc	Informal; formal policy being developed
Environmental response	Water recycling and water use benchmarking exercise change in working practice	Water recycling Internal recycling	Bulking and neutralization plant – prelude to waste treatment plant end-of-pipe

COMPARATIVE ANALYSIS OF CASE STUDIES

The sector is not perceived to be an environmental high-risk industry, and brewers are under no pressure to 'reconstruct' themselves, unlike the chemical companies.

The sector can be generally characterized as compliance-oriented, although there are some exceptions (which appear to be determined by the commitment of particular individuals). There is a generally positive attitude towards environmental performance, but the industry is currently inclined to be risk-averse. The sector is concerned with efficient resource utilization and waste minimization, but this tends to be seen as just good business practice.

All three firms are currently undertaking water reduction programmes as part of dealing with emissions, partly for economic reasons and partly in response to the local regulatory regime.

See Table 8.3 for specific case examples of water use improvements.

Table 8.3 *Water consumption ratio*

Brewery	Old level (water in:output)	Current level (water in:output)
IRL Brewery	10.0:1 (1983)	4.8:1
UK Brewery	8.8:1 (1979)	5.5:1
NL Brewery	10.0:1 (date unknown)	6.0:1

Reductions have been achieved by all three firms with a combination of operational changes and changes in the process technology. Table 8.3 does not represent a 'league table', as results vary in part by the packaging used, and the mix varies between the different sites (see Table 8.4).

Table 8.4 *Packaging*

Brewery	Bottles	Cans	Kegs	Tankers
UK Brewery	Y	Y	Y	Y
IRL Brewery	0%	0%	100%	0%
NL Brewery	50%	20%	30%	Y

Y = that route is used, but no quantitative data is available.

There were a number of fundamental similarities between the three companies, but there were also a number of significant differences between them in terms of their size, pattern of ownership, market share, economic environment, decision-making procedures, research and development, level of environmental commitment and proactivity, allocation of environmental responsibility, sources of information, and regulatory environment.

We thus have three firms, of different sizes and with different structures, doing essentially the same thing and with the same environmental problems, but with different environmental priorities. These priorities related largely to the *local regulatory context* (with regard to both current standards and anticipated change), the *length of the equipment renewal and capital investment cycles* (with environmental improvements being deferred until plant was renewed) and the *prevailing economic conditions* for the sector and economic circumstances for the firms. The environmental commitment of the firm was an important but secondary factor.

IRL Brewery operates to high standards because they have a new and modern plant. NL Brewery operates to even higher standards, because they face the toughest regulation and financial pressures. UK Brewery are concerned to be responsible citizens, but are actively risk-averse and will not move too far ahead of general standards for the industry. They will prioritize any expenditure required to meet regulatory requirements, but will try to get that result at lowest cost (they apply a cost minimization model, rather than cost-benefit), which will militate against more radical solutions.

The disposal of kiezelguhr is currently an important issue for NL Brewery, for example, but not for UK and IRL breweries. This is due to an impending change in the legislation surrounding landfill sites in The Netherlands. NL Brewery and IRL Brewery both have restrictions on the biological oxygen demand (BOD) of their effluent discharge, but NL Brewery is the only site with an aerobic treatment plant. This is because The Netherlands imposes a charge per inhabitant equivalent (IE) output, and this has risen from DFl 67 in 1993 to DFl93 in 1996, which makes IE reduction a priority for NL Brewery.

Economic factors – such as the market price for CO_2 – have also been significant determinants of corporate behaviour. UK Brewery, for example, has considered installing a CO_2 recovery plant. This would have enabled the plant to use its own CO_2 in carbonation operations instead of bought-in CO_2, but these plans have so far been rejected on cost grounds. The company calculated that the payback period would have been about 100 years, which is unusually long; the industry average is about 3.5 years (Coleman, 1993). The payback criterion depends largely on the existing layout of the brewery, which determines whether the recovery piping can be easily accommodated. This becomes less significant when a plant is to be replaced anyway, as the new plant can be designed to permit CO_2 recovery. IRL Brewery has installed a CO_2 recovery unit in their new plant, and is now 95 per cent self-sufficient in CO_2.

Similarly, the priority attached to improving process efficiency has tended to be largely determined by increases in the costs of inputs. The increase in energy costs, for example, has resulted in energy management programmes at all sites. Heat exchange and recovery systems are now in common use in order to reduce inefficiencies and wastage.

With the exception of NL Brewery, which operates in the toughest regulatory regime, the most significant changes in environmental performance occur when plant is renewed and replaced with modern and efficient equipment. IRL Brewery was operating a new and relatively clean brewery, as a result of an investment decision made in The Netherlands. UK Brewery would commit any environmental expenditure required on a 'stay in business' basis, but would commit no expenditure beyond that point. When plant was renewed, however, it would be replaced by equipment that would operate to higher standards, in line with general improvements in available technology.

CONCLUSIONS

The factors affecting the introduction of cleaner technology in the brewing sector, therefore, are as follows:

- Regulatory pressure. The industry is not, in general, under severe regulatory pressure. Where firms are placed under pressure, and obliged to upgrade existing plant, they tend to employ end-of-pipe solutions. This is mostly due to the second factor.
- The length of the equipment renewal and capital investment cycle. The relatively slow rate of replacement of outdated equipment and plant imposes a delay on the rate at which it would be possible to introduce radically new solutions. Firms do normally install more efficient equipment when outdated plant is replaced, largely for economic rather than environmental reasons.
- Economic incentives to reduce wastage or recover materials for re-selling.
- Lack of information or available cash are *not* significant obstacles to the large firms in this sector.

The equipment renewal and capital investment cycle creates relatively infrequent and therefore critically important windows of opportunity to encourage the adoption of cleaner technologies. There are various relevant technologies (such as process control technologies) which are both known and available, but are often not taken up until plant is replaced. Such opportunities, however, are rare, as some brewing plant can last for decades. A stainless steel vessel, for example, can have a 50 year life span.[5] This results in step-wise rather than continuous improvement in this sector.[6]

The most effective ways to promote greater energy and resource-use efficiency would therefore be:

- to gradually increase the regulatory pressure on firms, with such increases clearly signalled well in advance in order to encourage appropriate investment decisions when plant is replaced and upgraded;
- to increase the economic incentives for firms, with both negative incentives (higher charges for water and energy, for example) and positive incentives (developing markets for auxiliary products). This will also encourage appropriate investment decisions when plant is upgraded.

9 SUGAR SECTOR

*Søren Kerndrup with Leo Baas, Noel Duffy, Ole Erik Hansen
and Brendan Ryan*

Three companies were examined in this sector, one in The Netherlands, one in Ireland and one in Denmark.

THE SECTORAL CONTEXT

The European sugar industry is very homogeneous. It is dominated by large companies, typically with 2–5 sugar factories, which have diversified into areas that are more or less directly linked to sugar production. Investments in environmental R&D are largely corporate decisions, made in dialogue with the factories.

The main production processes

The basic physical and chemical principles of sugar refining have not changed during the last 50 years and are very similar at all sugar factories using sugar beets. Processes that will be familiar to chemical engineers are used to extract the sugar from the beets and to crystallize the white sugar. Technical development has focused on reducing the labour content by developing continuous rather than batch production, developing more effective machinery, economies of scale and process control, and reducing maintenance.

Sugar production is a continuous process that runs throughout the harvesting period (or 'campaign'), starting September/October and finishing in December/January. Because the sugar content of beet falls during storage, and there is a possibility of putrefaction, it is not economically efficient to lengthen the production period. It is therefore important to have a continuous flow in the production periods without breakdowns. The periods between the campaigns are used to maintain and upgrade the production facilities. These technical skills are an important part of the core competence of the sugar factories and they have a close collaboration with technical suppliers. Some sugar companies such as Danish Sugar have built up technical expertise and diversified into selling of know-how and process systems.

Harvesting the beet

The most important technological shift in harvesting has been the mechanization of the process. This has reduced the labour but substantially increased the soil content of beet deliveries (with impurities in sugar beet deliveries up from 4 to 20 per cent). To reduce the soil content, factories in The Netherlands and the UK have invested in cleaners in the field. This idea has been recently taken up in Denmark and Ireland.

The sugar refining process

Traditionally the production process consists of the following:

The preparatory stage: preparing the beets for processing
The incoming beets are weighed and stored. A sample is taken to determine the sugar percentage and the amount of 'tare' in the overall load. The tare consists of clay, stones, beet tops and so on, and is normally 10–20 per cent of the gross weight. Water is used as a medium for transportation and for washing and separating the beets from the tare, before the beets are cut into slices. It is important to remove stones because they will damage the beet washers and slicing machines.

Diffusion
The beets are cut into elongated slices to ensure an optimum diffusion of sugar. The sugar is then extracted from the beet by diffusion with hot water using a continuous counter current beet diffuser. Beet slices and hot water are fed in continuously; a solution of sugar emerges from one end and the exhausted beet slices from the other. The solution, 'the raw juice', has a sugar content of 14 per cent.

Waste 1: Sugar pulp
The exhausted slices are called 'sugar pulp'. The wet pulp is dried, mixed with molasses and sold as animal feed. In Denmark the pulp has traditionally been the property of the farmers, but with the reduction in cattle and pigs a greater share of the pulp is sold on the market.

Saturation
The raw juice is purified chemically using lime and carbon dioxide which cause non-sugars to precipitate.

Waste 2: Sludge
The precipitate is filtered off as sludge, which has a high calcium carbonate and water content. It used to be dried by vacuum filters to 40 per cent, then given away to farmers to use as a ground limestone substitute. Recent innovations, however, have made it a saleable product (see below).

Evaporation and crystallization

A two stage evaporation process then concentrates the sugar solution by boiling, taking it first to 60 per cent and then higher to facilitate crystallization. Syrup is fed through to vacuum pans in batches as the water is evaporated off, and the crystals of sugar begin to grow in the reduced temperature and pressure. The sugar is then separated from the syrup by centrifuge. The syrup from the centrifuges is put back through two more boiling stages in order to extract more sugar. The sugar is then dried, screened, cooled and sent to storage.

The process uses a lot of energy, and the increase in energy prices in the 1970s forced all the sugar factories to invest in the development of more energy efficient systems, including continuous innovative improvement of the evaporator system in order to minimize the energy consumed in the process.

Waste 3

It is not economic to crystallize the residual syrup to white sugar because of its high content of impurities. It contains both dissolved sugar and some non-sugars which were not earlier precipitated, and is called molasses. It is used for animal feed (blended with sugar pulp and pelletized), as industrial products (for the alcohol industry, for example), or as a raw material in the production of citric and gluconic acid.

One hundred tonnes of beet will give 12–14 tonnes of sugar and 3–4 tonnes of molasses.

Environmental regulations in DK, NL, UK and Ireland

The standards for waste water were relatively lax in Denmark, as a consequence of the factories' location in coastal areas, but stricter standards were established in the 1998 permits. The Irish factories were located inland and have more restrictive permits (except for phosphorus which is not limited). The sugar factories in The Netherlands, which discharge waste water into the Channel, are subject to standards which are almost as strict as the Irish. The restrictions on British sugar factories are relatively lax: only two factories have limits for nitrogen, and none have limits for phosphorus emissions.

The sugar factories facing the most restrictive regulations have invested heavily in developing waste water treatment plants. In The Netherlands and Ireland the waste water is cleaned in anaerobic plants followed by aerobic biological treatment plants. UK factories have aerobic treatment. In Denmark the limited regulation to date has resulted in only mechanical treatment, but the new permit requirements led to demands for cleaner technology for the two factories in Storstrøms County.

Taxes as incentives for environmental behaviour are more common in The Netherlands than in Denmark. Economic incentives for reducing the volume of soil delivered to factories are used in The Netherlands. In Denmark there is a bonus/penalty system which results in higher costs for the sugar factories. In the UK there is no penalty charge for delivering soil to the factories.

Table 9.1 *Industrial and regulatory profile*

	DK	NL	UK	IRL
Numbers of factories	4	6	10	2
Average size	9100	12,800	6800	
Waste water permit:				
BOD mg/l	3000	20	20–240	20
Nitrogen mg/l	100	50	20	40
Phosphorus mg/l	10	2	No	No
Waste water treatment %				
mechanical/biological	100	100	100	100
biological (aerobic)	0	100	90	100
anaerobic/aerobic	0	83	30	100
anaerobic/aerobic +N	0	83	0	Not known
% through beet cleaner	9	80	80	Not known
Soil recycled to farmers	No	No	No	Not known

Industrial context

Economic conditions for the sector

The competitive environment of the sugar industry is primarily determined by the EU's sugar regulation, which aims to subsidize European agribusiness. The subsidy is based on national quotas, with guaranteed minimum prices for growing sugar beet, and for the industrial production of white sugar. This sugar policy has a large influence on the competitive environment by creating barriers to entry. It is, therefore, not surprising that the industry has had high profits and has invested the accumulated profits in related sectors.

The regulation of quotas and fixed prices for input and output meant that the only way to increase profits was to increase efficiency in order to minimize cost of inputs like labour and energy or to increase the percentage of sugar extracted from the beets. The dominant strategy has been to develop economies of scale by moving to continuous processing (except for boiling and centrifugation), combined with automated production control.

Rationalization has meant that production has expanded on a subset of the old production sites, resulting in increasing environmental conflicts for factories located in towns. Up until the 1970s technical development was focused on substitution of labour by introducing continuous production and control systems. In the 1980s development was driven by increased energy prices and concentrated on substitution of energy and reducing the energy consumption in evaporation and boiling. There was also an increased focus on environmental investment.

The barriers to entry and keen bargaining between suppliers and customers limit the possibilities for expansion within the industry, so the companies have invested profits in expanding production into related areas: firstly supplying farmers with products and services for producing sugar, then into the use of by-products from sugar production as animal feed, and then into related products, involving industrial processing of farm products like vegetables and fruit.

IRL Sugar has reduced sugar production from four to two factories, scaling up to continuous production and automated control systems. Their diversification has taken them into the production of limestone for agricultural use, research centres for controlling beet disease, horticulture and food processing. The company is now one of the biggest food processors in Ireland.

NL Sugar has scaled up production and has the three biggest factories in the four countries. The company has diversified into a seeds group, a vegetables and fruit group, a spices group and a trade group which represent nearly half of the total turnover with DFl 2.1 million.

DK Sugar 1 had a similar diversification pattern in the period up to the takeover by DK Sugar Corporation. The company had diversified into seeds, vegetables and fruit, systems for grass and stone caches and environmental solutions. After the takeover the factory was integrated with DK Sugar Corporation, which in the early 1990s was transformed into an international business when all the old non-profitable businesses were sold off.

DK Sugar Corporation started as a privately owned sugar company with six factories, which was reduced to two before the takeover of DK Sugar 1. After the takeover the number of sugar factories were reduced by one and the other factories were scaled-up, especially DK Sugar 1. DK Sugar Corporation had diversified into many sectors: seeds, machining (producing technology for the sugar industry), general foods, and paper and packaging. After the merger the non-foods businesses (paper, machining and reverse osmosis) were sold off.

Management structure and style

All factories in the study are branch plants. The parent companies have introduced business units and central corporate management. The latter group controls the strategic functions, and makes the decisions about technological and environmental investments. They also control certain operational functions, including purchasing, and marketing and sales. The branches control logistics, production and maintenance.

Management focuses on two key issues: the political and regulatory conditions (negotiating with farmers on how to handle the sugar regulation issues, for example), and production economics and techniques to increase profitability within the quotas and prices fixed by the regulatory regime. The focus has therefore been on the technical efficiency of the factories and increasing efficiency through scaling-up and production automation.

Environmental management

In spite of, or maybe because of, strict regulation, NL Sugar has been very defensive in the past to the demands from the environmental authorities. It has been involved in conflicts over the location of its sediment fields with its neighbours, and resisted complying with the permits for smell and noise. This has changed, however, and the factory has now established a high specification waste water treatment plant after demands from the public authorities, and now produces the smallest emission into the sea of the four sugar factories.

After this major investment, NL Sugar shifted its environmental approach towards continuous improvement. The company has introduced continuous improvement through cleaner technology in the production process, thus reducing the costs of both production and waste water treatment. The company has also developed a continuous improvement approach to reducing energy use and associated costs.

In Ireland there are strict regulations governing waste water. IRL Sugar has an anaerobic/aerobic waste water treatment plant, which has reduced BOD emissions by 99 per cent since 1985. There are occasional breaches of the nitrogen limits, but the limit value is low by European standards. IRL Sugar developed many improvement projects in the 1980s, such as improved purification systems. They pressed the sludge from the saturation process and reduced the water content to 30 per cent, which was enough to convert the sludge to powder. The powder was easy to transport and apply to farmland. This made the waste saleable, thereby converting it to a product. A new decanter system has been installed, securing a more efficient sedimentation process and reducing the quantity of sludge sent into the sedimentation field. DK Sugar Corporation developed a similar automatic plate and frame filter press in the 1970s.

Production chain

Supplier relations

The EU regulation of agriculture has shaped the relationship between the sugar companies and the suppliers. There are two organizational structures in the industry: farmer owned cooperatives and private limited companies. It used to be difficult to accumulate capital for investment, but the stable and profitable market produced by quota regulation has allowed both cooperatives and companies to accumulate large amounts of capital for investing in related sectors.

Traditionally the factories were located close to the farms, but centralization has increased the average distance to the factory. This has favoured the big farmers, because they can manage the transport costs. This is potentially a positive development, as there is some evidence that increases in the scale and sophistication of beet farming can promote the adoption of cleaner production. In Denmark the sugar company has tried to develop incentives to stimulate scaling-up in the farming sector, but this has not been supported by the farmers' organization.

Suppliers of machinery and technical know-how

Technical know-how has been developed by the sugar factories and some main suppliers. Germany, with its tradition of machine industry, has played a central role in producing key parts of the equipment: diffusers, centrifuges, boiling apparatus and so on, but the Danish Sugar Corporation also has a strong position in designing and producing equipment for the sugar industry. They have developed diffusers, boiling apparatus and control systems, frame and filter presses for sludge and drying processes for pulp.

External suppliers have built strong links with the sugar industry and have a central role in the bigger projects. DK Sugar Corporation has strong technical competences; its R&D department is capable of developing and implementing large technical systems, often in collaboration with suppliers. The R&D department functions as an external consultant group to the factories, and is responsible for implementing projects. The R&D department developed, for example, the new concept for developing, handling, and receiving sugar beet (see below).

IRL Sugar have not built up this core competence, but have built up a close relationship with central equipment suppliers, such as Putsch in Germany. When IRL Sugar were asked to reduce environmental discharges in relation to storage and transport of the calcium carbonate-rich sludge, the firm used their 'partner' Putsch in the search for solutions. The search process was relatively uncomplicated because Putsch already had a solution. This solution was both economically and technically attractive because it reduced the water content in the sludge from 55 per cent to 30 per cent using conventional techniques, thus transforming the waste into a saleable product.

The Dutch company was in the same situation as the Irish, neither having built up core competencies in relation to the development of equipment. The environmental authorities demanded a reduction of the smell from pulp and suggested the building of a higher stack, but the company looked for alternatives and adopted a Danish steam drying process which cost DFl 2 million more, but gave a reduction in energy consumption.

Locality

The importance of locality is related to the supplier structure which, combined with the organizational structure, has created close local relations. Scaling-up has, in some regions, reduced these links but they remain important in the vicinity of the sugar factories. The local importance of the sugar factories is highest in Denmark, being located in areas with relatively few factories and high unemployment. In the other two areas – with higher industrialization – the sugar industry is less locally significant.

The case study from Denmark shows that this factor is important for understanding the levels of the permits and the dialogue between the environmental authorities and the companies, and the public perception of waste as a problem. Location is also important for understanding the possibilities for diluting the waste, the importance of the waste in relation to regional waste production, and the socio-economic consequences of factory closure.

CASE STUDIES

The structural characteristics of the sugar sector were addressed in the design of the case studies by combining one case study at corporate level, together with three case studies at factory level. These case studies focus on the environmental behaviour of the sugar factories in order to explain triggers and obstacles for implementing cleaner technology at this level. It is clear that regulation and the dialogue with the environmental authorities have influenced corporate investments in environmental techniques. The process has been investigated in relation to specific cleaner technology projects, one in each factory. The analyses highlight the importance of external relations in implementing the larger economic and technical changes.

The study of cleaner technology at factory level was supplemented by a study of corporate environmental behaviour at DK Sugar Corporation. This study focused on cleaner technology as R&D strategy, involving learning how to develop radically different solutions to existing practice. The corporate R&D programme, which was stimulated by public demands for much more restrictive environmental regulation, developed a number of projects in order to develop both knowledge and technology. The aim of the programme was to develop radical changes in sugar production methods to allow minimal use of water and generation of waste.

These projects led to practical environmental innovations in the factories, in new ways of receiving, distributing and washing the incoming sugar beets.

1 NL Sugar

The Sugar Cooperative is owned by 17,000 farmers with a turnover of DFl 1.1M. The Cooperative has diversified into seeds, vegetables and fruits, and formed a trading group. The traditional sugar production is primarily for the national market and the diversification is export oriented. About 45 per cent of the total turnover is exported. The public regulation of sugar factories in The Netherlands is one of the most restrictive in Europe. The regulation has forced the industry to build waste water treatment plants of the highest standard and the focus has therefore turned to waste and smell problems. The new government norms for smell and dust triggered the sugar factory to invest in a new steam-drying process for pulp. The steam drying process was a new technique developed in Denmark which allowed the pulp to be dried using much less energy. The trigger

Table 9.2 *Sugar sector cases*

Company	NL Sugar	IRL Sugar	DK Sugar 1
Product	White sugar	White sugar	White sugar
Market orientation	National	National	National
Number of employees in factory (nos during harvest)	270 (370)	150 (200)	na
Regional features	Minor importance for regional business	Minor importance for regional business except farming	Important for the regional business
	Local suppliers	Local suppliers	Local suppliers
	Environmentally significant	Not very environmentally significant	Environmentally significant
Ownership/ relationship with parent company	One of four sugar factories owned by Sugar Cooperative. Cooperative owned by farmers and diversified in agro-business	One of two sugar factories owned by recently privatized Irish agro-business	One of four sugar factories owned by a Danish international food company

was the environmental demand, but the technology also gave a direct economic benefit.

Company profile

Following the closure of small companies and the scaling-up of a number of sugar beet processing factories, there are now two big sugar corporations left in The Netherlands: the 'Centrale Suiker Maatschappij' (CSM) and NL Sugar.

NL Sugar is an agro-industrial corporation with headquarters in Breda, operating as a cooperative owned by 17,000 member-farmers. The Corporation has four sugar beet processing plants in Dinteloord, Groningen, Puttershoek and Roosendaal. Three of the four have optimal scale by European standards, processing over 1 million tonnes sugar beet per campaign. The annual sugar turnover is worth DFl 1.1M. There are also diversified operations, such as van Gilse, a Seeds group, a Vegetables and Fruits group, a Spices group and a Trade group with a total annual turnover of DFl 1M, of which about 45 per cent is exported.

The NL Sugar plant is located at the border of one of the delta streams (Oude Maas) of the river Rhine in the province of Zuid-Holland, 15 kilometres south of Rotterdam, producing 159,346 tonnes of white sugar per annum, plus pulp and pellets for feeding and calcium carbonate as limestone substitute.

NL Sugar was founded in 1906 and was independent until 1966. After a collaboration period (1966–1971), the plant became part of the NL Sugar Cooperative. There are 270 employees, with about 100 more who work seasonally. Employee numbers are decreasing because of mechanization and rationalization (two factories have closed in the last three years).

Environmental profile

The major environmental problems are waste water and odour. The odour issue is illustrative of the changing conditions for the sugar industry. The perception of odour during the campaign has gone from being 'normal practice' (a sign of wealth) via 'acceptance of annoyance' to 'reduction requirements' in the National Environmental Policy Plan +. The sugar industry representatives point to the subjective elements in the monitoring of the odour unit norms, and claim that this environmental policy is bureaucratic, not effective and a threat to the survival of the sugar industry. Though it is a homogeneous industry, no covenants have been concluded, because covenants are seen as pseudo-regulation. However, an energy covenant with a target of 20 per cent energy reduction in the period 1988–1998 was endorsed by the sugar industry.

At the technical level, general pollution control approaches were developed during the 1970s and 1980s. These included the use of containment floors for the storage of chemical cleaners and the waste materials left after washing the beet. Following the phase of pollution control, both at the plant level as well as R&D level, the focus shifted to efficiency through continuous improvement and enlargement of production, storage and logistics, and developing knowledge about reduction of energy use and cleaner production issues.

Each of the four operational sugar beet refineries of NL Sugar Cooperative bases its investments on the corporate production and business plans. Three types of investments are used:

- replacement investments with a lifetime of 30 years;
- renewal investments for better return on investment and a payback time less than four years;
- 'must do' investments, for environmental and labour condition issues and incidents.

The local plant management is responsible for environmental issues, but all factory environmental coordinators share information about environmental and energy issues. Waste water has been the primary issue for a large-scale initiative involving a waste water treatment facility to reduce the BOD content. In the past, water was taken out of the river. Until 1970, 2.5 million m³/year were extracted from the river, and 3 million m³/year were discharged to the river (the extra water arrives in the beet). Today the washing process needs 75 m³ water/hour, but the water is recirculated continuously. The use of cooling water has remained constant. Surplus water from the sugar beet (sugar beet is approximately 75 per cent water) is emitted to the river after treatment with the other waste water streams. High pollution effluent levies have forced the building and optimization of a large waste water treatment facility to treat 1.5 million m³ water each year. The factory monitors the waste water quantitatively and qualitatively every day during a campaign, and once a week during the rest of the year. The staff organization RIZA of the National Water Authority performs control samples. The analysis of the IEs is the basis for good housekeeping and continuous improvement measures.

Social and technical developments have played an important role in the environmental history of the NL Sugar factory. The factory has operated in agricultural surroundings since 1906. Criticism from neighbours was therefore a new phenomenon in the 1970s, and generated a rather defensive reaction. This can be illustrated with two examples:

1 The province controls the permit procedure for a sediment field for the sugar beet mud. These effluents had to be stored after a ban on direct emissions to the river. The desired sediment location in the neighbourhood of the sugar factory was agriculture. Since The Netherlands is a crowded country, physical planning of the destination of waste is very important; a change in destination needs a special procedure. Neighbours in the area resisted the change in the procedure, which resulted in a conflict lasting nearly 20 years.

2 Odour was a problem for many years. In 1981, five provincial EPAs approached ten sugar factories for a procedure for new permits. NL Sugar found that drafting the request required 2 man-years of work, so it was 1983 before they submitted their request. In 1985, a further request under the Air Pollution Law was also submitted. This request met many objections. Ultimately, it was referred to the State Council of The Netherlands.

It was 1989 before the definitive permit was given. Among the targets was an 80 per cent reduction of noise and odour compared with 1984. In 1994, the province reported that the requirement for the odour emission had not been met. According to the factory, however, a 1984 monitoring result was too low by a factor of four. In addition, the actual capacity was 70 per cent of the production capacity envisaged in the permit. The first results of the new pulp drying system in the NL Sugar factory were also unexpected. While the old system generated 30 odour units during the campaign, the new system was monitored at 15 odour units. Nevertheless, more complaints about the odour were registered, not less, because people seemed to feel that the remaining odour was somehow worse than before.

Project

These two experiences coloured the rather defensive approach to environmental issues. Management perceived the EPA as bureaucratic with sometimes unrealistic and threatening requirements (eg for odour). The firm's reluctance caused a delay, in which time the 5 year factory modernization plan created the conditions for a more sophisticated solution than the pollution control approach suggested informally by the EPA.

A great deal of replacement, including new as well as 'must do' investments, was then undertaken. The new drying process for the pulp was a combination of a replacement and 'must do' investment, based on two major considerations:

1 The new governmental norms for smell and dust. The EPA suggested to the sugar factories that they build a higher stack, some other sugar factories having acted on this proposition a few years ago. The costs for the Puttershoek factory were estimated at DFl 16 million.
2 Return on investment. A machining company subsidiary of the Danish Sugar Corporation had developed a new integrated steam drying process with 75 per cent energy reduction compared to the old system. The process, developed in 1987, had only been taken up on a handful of sites, and involved an outlay of DFl 18 million with no return on investment. The potential saving of DFl 1.5 million per annum in fuel costs, however, made this option more attractive. The old dryers from 1934 and 1935 were still functioning, but they were much less energy efficient and so less effective commercially.

The plant had some trouble with the new technology (wear and tear in the installation due to the pulp being forced through small tubes under a pressure of 3 bar), but these were solved in collaboration with a German engineering company, other French and German users, and the Danish manufacturer.

NL Sugar did not have the capacity to develop this technology themselves, but the plant management saw it as a good (commercially more attractive) alternative to the high stack solution for odour and dust reduction. Thus the modernization of the factory led them to progress from end-of-pipe to process-integrated solutions.

2 IRL Sugar

Company profile

This firm was one of three established by the state and combined with a fourth existing factory to facilitate the development of an Irish sugar beet industry. It was established in 1934, at which stage only 13,400 tonnes per annum of sugar were being produced within the state while 8500 were imported. By 1935 the four firms were producing 70,000 tonnes of sugar and by 1945 this figure had reached 89,000 with imports amounting to 156 tonnes. The company currently produces 220,000 tonnes of white sugar from 1.6 million tonnes of beet. This represents about 10 per cent more than the Irish sugar quota under EU rules. The company diversified over the years into limestone production, disease control research, horticulture, vegetable processing and machinery production. By 1984 the company was the second largest supplier of beet harvesters in the UK. In the 1980s two of the company's four factories were closed, although the remaining two are still small by European standards. In 1991 the majority share holding in the company was privatized. The company is highly profitable and international investment analysts have described it as among the best performing sugar producers in the EU.

Some 90 per cent of sugar production is for the domestic market, with the remainder being sold within the EU. The plant sends most of its production to two neighbouring confectionery manufacturers. The company's other factory, located nearer Dublin, supplies the general domestic market. The Cork firm has about 175 employees.

Environmental profile

The firm currently holds air and water pollution licences, with which it is in compliance. The permitted ammonia level in the treated water, which discharges into a salmonid river, is set at 40 ppm but may decrease further in the next five to ten years. The firm has, particularly since privatization, focused heavily on environmental performance. A combined heat and power plant is in operation generating approximately 11 MW. They have a five year energy use reduction plan involving a IRL£1.5 million expenditure, and have reduced BOD emissions by 99 per cent since 1987. In addition, a waste minimization programme has been undertaken to reduce liquid effluent flowrate and concentration. Staff operating the environmental control plant have had external training and a further 50 per cent of staff have been internally trained in environmental issues. An environmental audit has also been undertaken.

Water usage in the plant generally, particularly in the beet washing stage, is a concern in all beet sugar factories, involving as it does a mass of water up to 700 per cent of the beet mass. This concern was addressed by the installation in 1990 of a new decanter system costing IRL£1.2 million. The decanter facilitates separation of mud from the wash water, enabling a greater quantity of water to be reused.

There is a two stage treatment system involving the storage of waste water, mainly transport / wash water, in deep anaerobic lagoons. Autopurification occurs in this system with minimal usage of energy and virtually no sludge production. From September to January the effluent from the anaerobic lagoons of the previous year is treated in an aerobic activated sludge plant before discharge. The electrical power for this plant is generated efficiently on site. The anaerobic lagoons are a potential source of odour problems. These problems are largely eliminated by the addition of lime to the waste water before storage.

This lime has the added benefit of reacting with and eliminating any phosphate present.

The firm is accredited to ISO 9002, and intends to seek accreditation to an environmental management system after receipt of an IPC licence. Environmental legislation is the main external pressure, although the workforce, local community and company policy were also significant.

Project

In the mid 1980s the firm embarked on a major expansion in production subsequent to the closure of two of the company's four factories. This would have necessitated a significant expansion in the capacity to handle the sludge precipitated when the freshly extracted sugar juices were purified using lime followed by carbon dioxide. The firm did not own or have a realistic opportunity to purchase the land required and even if land were available it was estimated that additional lagoon capacity would cost IRL £300,000.

The sludge was rich in lime and had considerable potential as a substitute for ground limestone in the treatment of farmland. However at 55 per cent water it was so difficult to spread that farmers refused to use it. It also resulted in spillages during transportation and consequential complaints from the local authority. Even after water reduction via rotary vacuum filters, the water content of the sludge remained too high. The firm therefore decided to research the possibility of increasing the dry matter content to 70 per cent which would reduce spillages and facilitate spreading.

The original idea arose from visits to other European sugar facilities. The project was developed in collaboration with one of the sugar companies' traditional technical suppliers in Germany, who made a plate and frame filter press available free of charge for a trial period, an important consideration in the mid 1980s when the company was only marginally profitable. The plate and frame system, then used in many other European sugar factories, could dry the sludge to a dry matter content of 70 per cent. The trial proved a success and the firm invested IRL£1.2 million in five automatic plate and frame filter presses. The dried material is sold with 'no problem' at a price of IRL £ 3.50 per tonne generating about IRL £ 120,000 in revenue annually. This price compares favourably with ground limestone which currently sells for IRL£11–12 per tonne. An additional cost saving arises from the greater quantity of sugar-carrying water now recycled. Nevertheless, even if cost savings are incorporated, the payback time for the project on its own is close to ten years.

The project was still judged a success, as the environmental problem would have had to be dealt with in any case and it was likely that land would not have been available for additional lagoon space.

3 DK Sugar 1

Company profile

This firm was established as a cooperative by the local farmers in 1885 in order to produce and sell sugar made from the locally grown sugar beet. In 1989 the firm was taken over by DK Sugar Corporation, a business unit of Danish Food Corporation, which owns all the other Danish sugar factories. With the takeover DK Sugar Corporation owned four sugar factories in Storstrøms County less than 100 km apart. DK Sugar Corporation decided to close two of these factories in 1989, and in 1992 to increase sugar production in DK Sugar 1. DK Sugar Corporation expanded the daily capacity from 6800 tonnes of sugar beet to 8000 tonnes. In 1994/95 the factory produced 97,500 tonnes of white sugar, the standard by-products of molasses (26,500 tonnes) and sugar-pulp pellets (12,200 tonnes), plus non-standard by-products (the drying plant is also used for producing dried lucerne and grass pellets, and the factory produces energy for the town of Nykøbing). The increase in production volume, in conjunction with concern about the waste water and ongoing negotiations about renewing the licence limits, necessitated investments in new facilities and environmental technology.

Environmental profile

Up to 1989 the environmental performance of DK Sugar 1 was below best practice of DK Sugar Corporation in relation to use and emission of water. DK Sugar 1 only achieved 50 per cent recirculation of the flume water. As a result, the mass of water input was between 350 and 450 per cent of the sliced beet mass, and the discharge of water fluctuated between 400 and 465 per cent of the sliced beet (compared with 50–70 per cent at the other factories). The discharge to sea included organic materials, nitrogen and phosphorus (2100 tonnes COD, 1434 tonnes BOD, 65 tonnes nitrogen and 4.1 tonnes phosphorus).

After the takeover, DK Sugar 1 was integrated into DK Sugar Corporation. The latter had a proactive corporate environmental policy with a strong focus on continued improvement in environmental performance. DK Sugar Corporation also had a corporate environmental department to coordinate environmental activities and to manage the factories' relations with the local environmental authorities. DK Sugar Corporation provided additional expertise through consultancy relations with its factories.

The proactive element in the corporate environmental policy of Danish Food led to policy statements demanding that 'environmental effects have to be evaluated before a new capacity or new projects start...' and stating that 'it is the responsibility of the leadership to educate and motivate all employees to a positive participation in environment...' and ensure that the environment 'is actively discussed with employees, authorities and relevant neighbours'.

In the mid 1980s, Danish Sugar had started researching cleaner technology in order to reduce the impurities delivered to the factories and to develop new and more water-efficient sugar production systems. The projects were developed in collaboration with the factories, and projects were set up in factories in Assens and Saxkøbing, areas where the recipient waterways were seen as most sensitive to pollution. The regulatory framework imposed different restrictions on the two factories.

Assens had the tightest restrictions. These restrictions were imposed in a short timescale, and only really allowed the adoption of traditional approaches involving waste water treatment plants and settlement facilities.

At Saxkøbing the environmental authorities had established a medium term demand (to 1995) for the reduction of organic materials and nitrogen via better management of the beet preparation process and the use of a new beet washer, which allowed a reduction in water consumption.

This can be contrasted with the regulatory framework in Storstrøms County, which involved a dialogue between regulator and firm, directed towards long-term environmental targets and the accumulation of knowledge inside the company based on a search and learning process, thus creating a 'social space' for environmental innovations.

The expansion of capacity in DK Sugar 1 in the 1990s necessitated the development of new ways of preparing the beet, including a new beet washer, a transport system and a water system, all of which were shaped by the new proactive policy framework.

The dialogue between the firm, the corporate company and the environmental authorities in Storstrøms was also a crucial factor, especially with the renewal in 1990 of the environmental permits for the discharge of waste water and the emission of smell. The proactive environmental behaviour of the company helped to develop trust between the firm and the environmental authorities. Both the firm and the environmental authorities saw the new permits as a step in the direction of pollution prevention in the regulation of sugar production.

This relationship made it possible to create a new form of permit: the frame-permit. The core element in the permit was that it linked short-term environmental demands for reducing the discharges of nitrogen, phosphorus, organic substances, waste water, odour, and other air and solid waste emissions, with more long-term demands for the use of best available technology and for the development of integrated cleaner technology beyond the best available technology. The regulatory initiative tried to capitalize on the accumulation of knowledge and technology inside the company by giving the company time to evaluate initiatives set up in more environmentally advanced sugar factories. DK Sugar 1 was required to evaluate the economic and technical possibilities of reductions, including an 80–90 per cent reduction in organic materials, and a 40–50 per cent reduction in nitrogen before 1995. There was also a proposal to restructure the company's water system, implying a reduction in the level of pollution comparable with the best available technology in 1995.

The company assessed the options and developed proposals. In 1994 the collaboration with the local authorities bore fruit with the company's investment in a cleaner production concept based on new technological solutions for handling, depositing and cleaning sugar beets. This involved dry cleaning the sugar beet. The new plant is the first facility of its kind in Denmark. It has greatly reduced the use and discharge of water, discharges of organic materials and nitrogen, and significantly reduced odour, dust, noise and air pollution. It was seen as the first step in reaching the objective of developing a sugar production process generating minimal waste water.

Project

In 1992, a year after the new permissions, the environmental authorities sanctioned a new flat depot, a new beet washer and the renewing of the water system.

The new process, based partly on experience from the development of cleaner technologies in the Anklam factory, involved the use of 'flat depots', mechanical transport of beet and stone-sorting, and washing the beet with minimum water. The 'flat depot' is constructed to minimize damage to the sugar beet when delivered from the tipper. The use of back-tipping trucks also helps to reduce damage to the beet. The sugar beet is then transported to the washing process on a conveyor belt. The washing and rubbing process removes the soil and the beet is distributed to a 'catch stone', before passing a steel scraper. The dirty water is shaken off and the beet goes on to further processing.

The new process was designed to reduce water use and to reduce the discharge of organic materials by 25–50 per cent. In the 1994 campaign there were problems with the run-in of the new plant, and the result was a reduction of:

- Water consumption: 15,000 m^3/24 hours to 5000 m^3/24 hours
- Organic materials: 18 tonnes BOD/24 hours to 16.6 tonnes/24 hours

4 DK Sugar Corporation

Company profile

This company is a business unit in Danish Food Co. Following the acquisition of DK Sugar 1 in 1989, DK Sugar Corporation controls all Danish sugar production. The factories are in the towns of Nakskov, Nykøbing, Görlev and Assens. The holding company, Danish Food, is one of the largest Danish companies with four business units: Sugar, Food & Beverage, Ingredients and Packaging. The sugar sector is the largest business unit and has been expanded by acquisition both inside and outside the country, the latter via the acquisition of the Swedish sugar industry and eight factories in the former German Democratic Republic. The DK Sugar Corporation is now the third largest sugar producer in Europe with a total production of 885,000 tonnes: 448,000 tonnes in Denmark, 339,000 tonnes in Sweden, and 98,000 tonnes in Germany.

DK Sugar Corporation is one of the most efficient sugar producers in Europe and is very profitable. Its competitive position is based on its technological core competencies. These are developed in a large corporate R&D department, in collaboration with the detailed production knowledge in the factories. DK Sugar Corporation's innovative capability is well known in the sugar industry, and it holds many patents on equipment used throughout the industry. Some of the most important innovations have been the DDS-diffuser and equipment such as vacuum pans and control systems, maische and plate and filter presses for calcium carbonate-rich sludge.

Environmental profile

The environmental problems are primarily related to the deliveries of impurities with the sugar beet to the factories. Each year the sugar factories receive 500,000 tonnes of stones, soil and grass along with the 3,500,000 tonnes of sugar beet. To remove this waste, it is necessary to use approximately 2,000,000 m³ of water.

The discharges of waste water contain a high value of BOD, nitrogen, phosphorus, and a large amount of solid waste as soil and stone. Traditionally, the discharges have been reduced by end-of-pipe technologies that combine mechanical waste water treatment with a long pipe line into the sea to dilute the waste water and to deposit the soil. These solutions are developed in close dialogue with the public authorities and reflect a common understanding of the environmental effects of sugar production.

The company operated under limited environmental pressure until the permissions were due for renewal in 1991. Conflicts (with local anglers) over the permissions in the 1980s, in conjunction with increasing awareness of the effects of nitrogen and phosphorus in the sea, and tighter licence limits and restrictions, caused corporate policy to change from an end-of-pipe approach to a cleaner technology approach, with a special focus on ways to minimize the discharge of waste water and reduce its content of nitrogen, phosphorus and BOD. The new permits specified large reductions in line with the best available technology in the discharge of nitrogen, phosphorus and organic substances before 1998. The time frame, combined with a demand for an action programme, stimulated action beyond the traditional waste water treatment plants (which would have cost nearly DKr 90 million per factory).

The new corporate strategy was one of continuous improvement, diminishing the soil content in the sugar beet deliveries to 1 per cent and minimizing the use of water. In 1986 two research groups were established to consider the internal (factory) and external (beet delivery) possibilities for cleaner technology.

Waste minimization in the production chain was introduced by the development of a best practice procedure for harvesting, storing and distributing the beet to the factories. A very intensive information campaign was used to promote best practice. At the same time the company researched new beet load techniques to reduce the amounts of soil taken up with the beet, and identified a possible solution, but this was never taken up by the machining industry. Waste minimization at the factories focused on the water use and its importance for the discharges of BOD and nitrogen. One way to reduce the amount of BOD was to minimize the time the beet was in contact with water, as research showed that high BOD was caused by even very short contact times between beet and water. The way to reduce water use in the factories was to develop a new way to wash and transport the beets in the pre-processing stage.

Improvements in the environmental performance were limited up to 1993/94, at which time another initiative from the sugar factory made some impact. At the end of the 1980s, Danish Sugar Corporation and the farmers had agreed on a system that gave farmers a higher price for beet delivered with fewer impurities. Initially, the only effect was to reduce the number of farmers delivering with a high content of impurities. In the 1990s the limits and payments were increased and now give farmers and distributors an additional incentive to invest in technology that cleans the beet at the fields, thus leaving the stones and soil at the site.

Project

In 1993 Danish Sugar Corporation launched an ambitious programme for developing cleaner technology beyond the existing best practice, with the cleaner sugar beet project. The main objective was to see whether cleaning the beet at the fields was a better solution than cleaning the beet at the factory, and to identify the technical options. The project contained two sub-projects:

1   Cleaning at the fields.
2   The effect of impurities in the sugar processing.

The projects, organized in collaboration between the Research & Development department and the sugar factories, and supported by a small grant from the National Environmental Authorities (with public relations rather than financial value) studied the consequences for the environment, the farmers and the sugar company and assessed the technological options. The project showed that cleaning the beet at the field is a better solution than cleaning at the factory because it ensures that:

- soil and nutrients stay on the fields;
- there is no transport of soil;
- minimizing soil and water reduces the necessary level of environmental investment at the factories.

The project showed that it is necessary to choose between different trajectories for the cleaning of the beet at the field. They chose to develop end cleaning, and developed a new concept for flexible loading cleaners. More research has to be done, however, to develop a technical and economically optimal solution. In conjunction with the new concept for the preparation of sugar beet for processing developed by DK Sugar 1 in 1994, it represents another step towards water-free sugar production.

In order to further reduce water use, it is important to analyse the options for processing the sugar beet that arrives with a higher content of impurities. The second part of the project's objective, therefore, was to analyse the possibility of adapting the process to sugar beet with impurity levels of 1–3 per cent.

Table 9.3 *Summary of environmental responses of firms*

Company	NL Sugar	IRL Sugar	DK Sugar 1	DK Sugar Corporation
Regulatory environment	National Water Authority and Regional EPAs (air)	Regulated by Cork County Council To be licensed under IPC	Classified as environmentally important factory regulated by the county	Factories regulated by the county
Environmental policy	Informal (reluctant)	External formal ISO 9002 move to EMAS expected with IPC	Formal internal	Formal internal
Environmental response	Radical process change Steam-drying of pulp	Internal recycling Water recovery from waste sludge (plus external recycling of dried sludge)	Incremental process change. Beet handling and washing to reduce water use and waste	Product chain management; radical process change. Beet cleaning in fields; search for water free sugar processing

COMPARATIVE ANALYSIS OF CASE STUDIES

Environmental policy and regulation

Environmental regulation has focused on the discharge of large volumes of waste water contaminated with organic materials, nitrogen and phosphorus, deposits of solid waste, and increasingly on odour and noise. The regulatory demands for limiting waste water vary greatly between the countries, and there is a tendency for the most restrictive demands to be in areas with the lowest ecological capacity. These variations in environmental demands have a significant influence on the development of environmental technology.

The demands for discharge waste water treatment have forced the sugar industry in The Netherlands and Ireland to invest in costly end-of-pipe technology, such as anaerobic and aerobic biological treatment plants. In Denmark the sugar factories are located in the coastal zones and the demands have focused on end-of-pipe solutions, such as sea-pipes, to disperse the waste water. Consequently, these factories had only invested in mechanical treatment of the waste water. The renewed permits in 1991 set up restrictive demands for the reduction of discharges of nitrogen, phosphorus, and organic substances to the level of best available technology. As BOD, nitrogen, and phosphorus levels in the waste water declined, the focus shifted towards odour and noise problems. These demands have been increasing in both Denmark and The Netherlands.

Management structure and style

The three firms in the study were farmer-owned or state-owned companies up to 1989. The Dutch sugar firm is still a farmer-owned company, but ownership of DK Sugar 1 and Irish firms have changed. DK Sugar 1 was taken over by the Danish Sugar Corporation, and the Irish firm was privatized in 1991. For both firms the change in ownership has led to a more proactive and dynamic management culture.

The competitive environment is changing, and changes of ownership are encouraging a shift from the traditional management style (with the focus on technical aspects), towards a more market-oriented management style. The typical branch plant management focuses on economic and technical control of the operations, but has no influence on the strategic positioning of the company. Most aspects of strategic importance, such as investments, R&D, marketing, and environmental policy, are controlled by the corporate management of the business units.

Strategic investment and environmental decisions in DK Sugar Corporation are taken at corporate level. Many of the projects set up at plant level are part of a broader research and development programme and it is necessary to assess the projects in this context to understand the wider context of the project. The Danish firm's investment in new technologies for the preparation of beet for processing can be seen as an investment in a technology to minimize the environmental effects of the expansion of the capacity of the factory. Thus the change of beet handling is part of an ongoing research and development programme for cleaner technology, with the objective of creating a fundamentally new concept of sugar production.

Environmental management

Management structure and style has a significant influence on the environmental management of the branch plants. After the change of ownership the firms initiated a more proactive approach to environmental management. Dk Sugar 1 was integrated into a corporate sugar business that over the years has developed a focus on pollution prevention and R&D expertise in cleaner technology. This cleaner technology expertise allowed the firm the possibility to expand capacity without increasing their environmental impact, by developing a fundamentally new approach to preparing the beet for processing.

In the Irish firm the new management following privatization opened up a more proactive environmental management style. The firm has set up a plan for the reduction of energy use and has claimed to have reduced BOD emissions by 99 per cent since 1985.

The Dutch firm did not change ownership but has also changed environmental management from a defensive to a proactive approach, with continuous improvements in the reduction of energy and waste water.

In general, factory management is mostly focused on continuous improvement. The Danish Sugar Corporation study, however, shows that corporate environmental management can be integrated in the strategy of the company.

Economics of environmental management

Environmental cost has been an important motive for the firms to shift from traditional end-of-pipe technology to pollution prevention. The sugar industry has a long tradition of reducing environmental cost by converting waste to saleable products. Up to the 1990s, the Danish sugar industry had the lowest limits. Their new permits demanded that water effluents be reduced to the level of the best available technology, including the maximum effects by end-of pipe technology. The traditional waste water treatment plant costs nearly DKr 90 million, so the company established an R&D programme in order to reduce the water use and the impurities delivered to the factories.

As a first step to reducing water effluent, Danish Sugar Corporation tried to minimize the cost by developing new technologies for preparing beet for processing. The Dutch firm saw environmental regulation as a cost, and invested in a new drying process for pulp which both met the new environmental norms and provided a return on investment (via savings in the fuel needed to dry the pulp). The Irish firm introduced a new process (one that had already been adopted in continental Europe) that made it possible to convert the lime-rich sludge to saleable products, thereby minimizing the cost of the investment.

Danish Sugar Corporation set up an R&D programme for developing cleaner technology as a way of minimizing the environmental cost; the objective being to find an alternative to investing DKr 270 million in waste water treatment plants. The company also reduced their environmental cost by developing cleaner technology for converting waste to saleable products, such as a drying process for sugar pulp; a press for lime rich sludge; and technology for reducing the cost of energy in the evaporation and boiling process.

Internal innovative expertise

Technical expertise is very important in continuous sugar production, and the need to maintain and renew plant between the production campaigns has fostered this competence.

The engineers and the workforce are able to develop and implement technological projects in collaboration with the technical suppliers. IRL Sugar is an example of the importance of internal competence in the implementation of new techniques for drying the sludge. The new technique was bought from their technical supplier in Germany, but the project was developed locally with the involvement of the company's chief engineer. Expertise played the same important role in NL Sugar's implementation of new drying processes. The importance of internal competence at factory level could also be seen when the new process ran into difficulties, as factory staff made a significant contribution to the development of a technical solution.

Besides putting great emphasis on internal competence in the sugar *plants*, the study of DK Sugar 1 and DK Sugar Corporation also shows the importance of strategic competence in the sugar *companies*. In DK Sugar Corporation the internal expertise has been developed into a business area. DK Sugar Corporation are now selling know-how and technology for sugar production. Before the merger, DK Sugar Corporation had used its internal competence to build up a diversification strategy selling different forms of equipment. Today its competitive edge is mainly know-how. Many techniques used throughout the European sugar industry were developed by the Danish sugar industry.

External innovative expertise

The technical environmental innovations are mostly developed in collaboration with external partners. Innovation is a searching and learning process, with many uncertainties, and the companies try to minimize these by using existing technical or knowledge suppliers. IRL Sugar's problems of production and space restrictions made it impossible to increase the capacity of waste treatment facilities and the firm was able to use its close contact with Putsch to search for and find solutions to its problems of transport and distribution of calcium carbonate-rich sludge.

It is not always possible, however, to use existing suppliers. NL Sugar implemented a technical innovation that had only been introduced at perhaps six factories. The implementation failed at first, but NL Sugar were able to work with a group of collaborating firms to find a technical solution. As this example suggests, there is a relatively high degree of collaboration and flow of technical information between companies in the sugar sector.

CONCLUSIONS

The particular features of this sector are as follows:

- The competitive environment is regulated by EU sugar policy, which limits entry and shapes the form of competition within the industry. This has created very profitable conditions.

- The fixed prices of inputs (sugar beet) and outputs (sugar) shape competition inside the industry to focus on the reduction of the cost of capacity, and the reduction of the cost of variable inputs such as energy and wages.
- Production is very capital intensive, and the technology is relatively traditional, so the main focus is on the reduction of capacity cost.
- The sugar factories have a dominant economic position in the production chain.
- Waste water emissions are primarily caused by the need to wash out the soil, stones and grass arriving at the factories.

Regulations are the primary driving forces for environmental performance and have forced the industry to introduce end of line technology. Environmental innovations in the sugar industry are shaped by a complex of factors: increasing production capacity at the factories; concern about water and energy use; tighter licence limits and restrictions on space available. These factors necessitated improvements in environmental behaviour in the sugar industry. The improvements have followed different technological trajectories of environmental innovation in the three regions, reflecting the differences in forms of regulation and in the systems of innovation.

Regulation

Traditionally, studies of environmental regulation have focused on the question of whether strict or relaxed regulation enhance environmental innovation. This study indicates that neither view is correct, by showing that:

- Tight limits and restrictions have forced the sugar industry to improve their environmental behaviour via investment in expensive waste water treatment plants in Ireland and The Netherlands. Strict regulation alone, therefore, cannot force the industry to invest in cleaner technology. On the contrary, strict regulation can restrain their investment in cleaner technologies, because the firms do not want to invest in cleaner technology when they have already reduced their emissions.
- Loose licence limits and restrictions have not encouraged the industry to develop environmental improvements to a level comparable with strictly regulated industries, or to use, for example, waste minimization strategies.

The Danish case, however, shows that intelligent regulation can stimulate processes of learning, and searches for new technological options that may not yet exist. This option is, of course, inherently uncertain and complex, and demands collaboration between the firm, its suppliers and research institutions, and a dialogue between the environmental authorities, the firms and their networks.

Environmental innovation

The case studies demonstrate that the firms have developed continuous improvements in their environmental performance by developing new processes to convert waste to saleable products, or by making improvements in their existing processes via changes in the evaporators and vacuum pans to reduce the use of energy. It is important, therefore, that regulation gives companies the opportunity to use and develop the necessary expertise, both internally and with external networks.

Innovation along the production chain

Discharges of waste water from the factories with a high content of nitrogen, phosphorus, and BOD are a consequence of activities upstream in the supply chain: the methods of farming and of harvesting beet, which cause large quantities of contaminants to enter the chain. This highlights the importance of assessing the whole supply chain, and identifying the possibilities for collaboration between the different actors in the chain.

10 PAPER MILLS SECTOR

Graham Spinardi with Inger Stauning, Birgitte Larsen and Robin Williams

Three companies were examined in this sector, one in Denmark and two in the UK.

SECTORAL CONTEXT

Main industrial processes

The basic building block of all paper and paper board is cellulose. Cellulose fibres are typically obtained from wood, although straw, hemp, grass, cotton or other cellulose-based materials can be used. Paper is made from a pulp in which the raw material has been broken down into its individual cellulose fibres. The final product may also comprise up to 45 per cent of its weight in fillers, coatings and other substances.

Paper products include newsprint, both coated and uncoated writing and printing papers, packaging papers, packaging board and tissue. The nature of the final product affects the choice of production process, including the way the pulp is sourced, and this in turn affects the potential pollutants.

Pulp production

Pulping is done to break down virgin fibre material into cellulose fibres. The cellulose is bound up by lignin, and can be freed either chemically or mechanically. Chemical pulping not only involves the use of chemicals, but also works by dissolving the lignin, and thus produces a potential pollutant containing many dissolved substances. Mechanical pulping works by simply breaking up the fibres physically, leaving the lignin with the fibres, although some organic substances are still dissolved. Bleaching of pulp may be done either as the final stage of pulp production or as the first stage of paper making.

The most common chemical pulping method remains the traditional *Kraft* process, which uses sulphate. Almost half of EU pulp is produced in this way, and about 65 per cent of pulp production worldwide. Other methods use sulphite, either alone or in combination with mechanical separation. The potential effluent problem is considerable with these processes, but most modern chemical pulping mills use a recovery boiler to recycle the chemicals and dissolved wood organics;

the latter can be used in by-products or, more typically, as fuel for the mill. However, in the late 1980s it was discovered that relatively high levels of dioxins were being formed in the bleaching processes, leading to process modifications (Bonifant and Ratcliffe, 1994, pp33–34). Bleaching of chemical pulp is done to achieve the desired brightness, traditionally using chlorine-based processes to remove the residual lignin. Another consequence of chlorine use has been high BOD levels in the discharge because the chlorine prevents recycling into a recovery boiler. Substitution of chorine dioxide for chlorine was the widespread solution adopted to reduce dioxin levels. However, continuing concern over harmful properties of effluents has also led to the use of alternative processes based on oxidation by peroxides, ozone or oxygen, and investigation of the potential of enzymes.

Mechanical pulping produces less potential pollutants, but results in a pulp which is only suitable for certain products. The mechanical process results in shorter fibres than those produced by chemical pulping, which means a lower strength product, and the high residual lignin content impairs bleaching, which makes the pulp unsuitable for high brightness products. Temporary bleaching (as in newsprint which yellows with age) is achieved by the use of chemicals such as hydrogen peroxide, sodium hydrosulphite or formamidine sulphinic acid. Some mechanical pulp mills are integrated with paper making, which means that most of the water requirements of pulp making can come from the output of the paper making machine. Apart from water, mechanical pulp making need only use timber and energy, although in some cases chemicals are used to pre-soften the wood.

Finally, pulp can be obtained from recycled fibre (RCF) – done by DK Paper Mill. Waste paper or packaging is repulped in a hydropulper, followed by various stages of screening and cleaning to remove staples, adhesives, and so on. This might then be followed by de-inking where required. Typically, RCF used for newsprint and writing/printing paper will be de-inked, but RCF used for packaging will not (this latter being the practice used by UK Paper Mill 2).

De-inking can be done by one or a combination of two basic processes. Smaller ink particles can be removed by wash de-inking in which the ink is washed out in the water used to create the pulp suspension. This is enhanced by the use of chemical surfactants. Larger ink particles can be removed by flotation de-inking in which chemicals – such as fatty acid soaps – bind with the particles and form a scum which can be floated off. De-inking typically produces waste water containing more contaminants than any other paper making activity apart from pulping.

In summary, pulp production is a major potential source of pollution. A wide range of processes are used, depending on the raw material used and the intended use for the pulp produced, and this means that a wide range of abatement and treatment techniques are available. However, at a local level paper mills can simply 'outsource' this problem by buying in already treated pulp or by using recycled paper. For example, the use of elemental chlorine free (ECF) pulp greatly reduces the levels of chlorinated organics that will be released into the process water.

From pulp to paper

Although there are many variations, the typical paper-making process uses a Fourdrinier machine. This involves pouring a suspension of fibres (along with fillers, dyes, and other chemicals depending on the particular process) onto a moving mesh or 'wire'. Typically, the suspension will be between 0.2 and 1 per cent solids when deposited and will form a self-supporting web after draining to about 10–15 per cent solids. Multi-ply paper or board is made on machines with a number of wires.

Further water is removed from the web as it is compressed through a system of rollers, often with vacuum sections, followed by heated rollers. At this stage, or sometimes in a separate machine, various coatings may also be applied to improve the surface properties, for example for printability or other specialist applications. 'Broke' – produced both from trimmings of the edge of the web and from breakages or process changes and start-ups – is returned to the start of the process for repulping. Where this broke is starch-coated, as in the production of writing and fine paper, this can be a major cause of BOD in the paper mill's waste water.

Water is a highly used resource for paper-making, and some recycling is found in all mills. Two main recycling loops are typical of the paper-making process. The primary loop recycles water which has drained through the wire into the wire pit, returning some of it back to dilute the incoming stock. The excess passes into the secondary loop which also recycles water from the couch pit (which is where trimmings and other broke is collected at the end of the wire) and from the showers used to keep the wire and rollers clean. A key feature of the secondary loop is the save-all, which is normally either a filtration or flotation unit designed to recover fibre from the water, but which also thus produces clarified water that can be reused.

Water which is considered too contaminated for reuse constitutes a waste stream which will usually (nowadays) go to a waste treatment plant. In some cases effective biological second stage treatment has led mills to introduce a third recycling loop, reusing treated water.

Environmental issues

Paper mills have historically been a source of liquid pollution of waterways, particularly affecting small rivers. The environmentally damaging properties of paper mill effluent stem mainly from two aspects of the paper-making process.[1] First, there is the pulping in which chemicals may be used to break down and bleach the wood. As well as using large quantities of energy and water this process also leaves a chemical residue in the effluent, and in the case of chlorine bleaching has been associated with the production of dioxins. Second, even where paper fibres can be obtained without this chemical residue (through recycling or through the use of alternative ways of breaking down wood pulp) effluent contamination with the fibres themselves, and substances used in papermaking – such as clay, chalk and starch – can cause local environmental degradation.

Potential for cleaner technology

Apart from general reductions in energy usage there are four main options available for cleaner technology in paper mills. First, there is the possibility of increasing water recycling to achieve a greater degree of closure. Second, there may be potential for reducing the amounts of fibre lost to the effluent stream. Third, there may be scope for changing the use of chemicals in the process which currently contribute to effluent problems. Finally, anaerobic rather than aerobic waste treatment can be implemented.

The most obvious potential for reducing or eliminating aqueous emissions from paper mills lies in increased water recycling within the plant. In some cases it is possible to achieve 'effluent-free' operations with closed water systems. This may be more difficult to retrofit to existing plant, which 'may be constrained in closing up water circuits by the historical lay-out of the site and the way that it has developed in a probably less-than-systematic manner' (Webb, 1993, pp4–42). Concern over product quality is also a significant barrier to increased water recycling in fine paper mills (as in UK Paper Mill 1). Similarly, DK Paper Mill found that bacteria growth and quality problems limited the extent of water recycling that could be used in the de-inking process.

Second, increased water recycling typically goes hand-in-hand with mechanisms for fibre retention. At present the extent to which save-alls are used varies considerably from mill to mill. In some cases – such as integrated newsprint mills – wire retention is so low (55–60 per cent) that save-alls are necessary simply on economic grounds, to recycle fibre. On the other hand, at mills making small batches of high quality paper – such as UK Paper Mill 1 – it is the practice simply to discharge unused prepared pulp into the waste stream as it is not considered practical to reuse it. In DK Paper Mill, the process is specifically designed to remove fibres that are considered too small to meet the strength requirements of the high quality paper pulp produced, with these short fibres comprising the bulk of a sludge waste stream that now goes to be recycled in cement production.

Third, a variety of substances used in paper making – especially fillers and coatings – will enter the aqueous waste stream. Much of this is caused by the repulping of broke and can therefore be reduced by minimization of the amount of broke produced. Further improvements can also be made by careful choice of the substances added. In particular, better retention can be achieved by using cationic chemicals which are attracted to the anionic fibres in the web. High levels of BOD in paper mill effluent are usually due to the release of starch in the repulping of broke, and this can be reduced by the use of cationic starch.

Finally, a 'cleaner' end-of-pipe approach is possible by using anaerobic rather than aerobic biological digestion in the waste treatment plant. Anaerobic treatment is cleaner because, in essence, it converts some of the biomass into usable energy which also results in less sludge for disposal. In many cases, anaerobic treatment would complement greater closure of water systems because this results in a more concentrated effluent which suits anaerobic micro-organisms.

Industrial context

Despite some common processes, the paper industry is extremely diverse both in terms of firm size and as regards the particular processes and products found in any one mill. The three firms (plants) investigated here are all small and represent three differing aspects of the industry. DK Paper Mill de-inks waste paper to produce pulp, UK Paper Mill 1 buys pulp to make high quality papers, and UK Paper Mill 2 produces low quality paperboard from recycled paper products. A particular characteristic of the industry is that international trade in pulp provides a way of 'out-sourcing' the most potentially polluting part of the production cycle. The UK, for example, now produces little virgin pulp, instead relying on imports or on wastepaper recycling. Indeed shifting patterns in the relative use and source of virgin and recycled paper have been driven in the UK mainly by environmental concerns. In Denmark, on the other hand, where there is no virgin pulp production, paper recycling has been seen since the 1970s as an important way of supporting the national industry by using national resources and manpower.

The literature indicates that the paper sector is well served by scientific/ technical understanding of environmental issues, and that the industry as a whole takes these issues seriously. The ability of individual firms, especially small firms, to access this information in the UK – as well as their motivation to do so – is less clear. In Denmark, however, two factors have enabled greater access to knowledge of cleaner technology expertise. First, there is a long history of tight relationships between different plants because of common ownership, with, for example, DK Paper Mill having been a member of the 'united paper factories' for a century. Second, the Danish emphasis on waste paper as a national resource has meant a high degree of state involvement in all aspects of the product cycle: from paper collection to new plant start-up subsidies or joint ownership, and dissemination of information.

Table 10.1 *Summary of paper mills sector cases*

Company	DK Paper Mill	UK Paper Mill 1	UK Paper Mill 2
Products	De-inked pulp	High quality paper	Low quality paperboard
Employees	66	165	25
Ownership	Branch site of Swedish company	Branch site of US corporation	Family-owned

CASE STUDIES

1 DK Paper Mill

Company profile

This paper mill in Maglemølle is owned by Stora Papyrus Dalum Ltd, which is part of the Swedish concern Stora. Before 1988, it was partly owned by the Danish concern Danisco. The paper mill was established in 1874 and produced paper until 1992. It now produces de-inked pulp from waste paper (paper production was moved elsewhere in 1991). The pulp is delivered to another firm in the concern in Odense, which produces 100 per cent recycled, fine paper for print and office use.

The joint factories Stora Dalum had a turnover of Dkr 500 million and 420 employees in 1993. The plant at Maglemølle had 66 employees. The joint factories in Maglemølle and Odense have a total capacity of 130,000 tonnes of paper, including 75,000 tonnes of recycled paper from 100,000 tonnes of waste paper.

The firm has an environmental manager and a laboratory section, and makes extensive use of consultants, research institutes and the local authorities. The capacity to develop new technology, however, lies with the machine and chemical suppliers and with the parent company.

Environmental profile

The company installed a waste water treatment plant in the 1960s, which was enlarged in the 1970s. In the 1980s several measures were taken to reduce waste water discharge, such as internal recycling, energy saving and some chemical substitutions.

The firm had many contacts with the regulatory authorities in the mid-1980s, caused partly by complaints from citizens and organizations about water quality and smell. At the same time, the firm opted to produce high quality paper out of waste paper by designing and installing a de-inking plant, in a project supported by the Environmental Protection Agency.

The firm had to apply for a new waste water discharge approval, and chose to apply for a voluntary approval of the production site as a whole, including the proposed new de-inking plant. This approval was given in 1989, and contained a strengthening of limit values. The company therefore had to install a new waste water treatment plant with biological cleaning.

In 1991 the de-inking plant was installed, together with the new treatment plant. The treatment did not work satisfactorily until 1994, which resulted in many complaints and a fine from the authorities. In 1992 the company obtained a new approval, which specified progressive decreases of limit values over the subsequent four years.

Project

Little regard was given to the management of the waste water and sludge when the de-inking plant was being planned. A waste water treatment plant and an incineration plant were regarded as sufficient. After the plant was built, however, it became clear that this oversight had resulted in a lack of process control. The firm had to use a lot of time and external consultants to make the biological processes function over the subsequent 3–4 years.

The incineration plant was never built, and the municipality did not want to deal with the sludge, so the company then had to investigate external recycling. They looked at building materials and agricultural use. Eventually, they found a cement factory that could combine fibres (as fuel) with material (chalk, kaolin etc). Had this outlet not been found, the benefits of recycling would have been brought into question by the amounts of waste sludge produced.

The firm still tried to get approval to spread sludge on soil, to get rid of their backlog, but analysis indicated that there would be some environmental impact from the chlorinated organics and toxins from the bleaching and printing processes, so the county refused permission.

Thus the firm has gone through a learning process, from regarding the waste streams as incidental to regarding waste handling as an integral part of the production processes. It was, in part, responding to external pressure. The regulatory authorities provided flexible regulation in providing a series of goals for the company, recommending cleaner solutions, and allowing time for the company to adjust their waste handling. During the 1990s, the parent company also adopted a policy of waste recycling and minimization of environmental damage, and asked the firm to achieve EMAS certification. This pressure encouraged the firm to adopt a proactive and open environmental strategy, and to implement many cleaner solutions (such as water recycling and energy saving) as well as end-of-pipe solutions.

This case highlights the need for a life cycle perspective. The main causes of environmental impact from waste water or sludge lie in paper production, especially the bleaching and the printing processes, but the solutions may lie in external options such as external recycling.

2 UK Paper Mill 1

Company profile

UK Paper Mill 1 is a small, specialist paper mill, located at Dalmore on the North Esk river in Midlothian. It was acquired in 1989 by the American James River Corporation, and together with GB Papers of Guardbridge, St Andrews in Fife (acquired in 1984), UK Paper Mill 1 constitutes James River Fine Papers Ltd (JRFP). Currently, UK Paper Mill 1 has a turnover of about £12 million, around 165 employees, and production of about 10–11,000 tonnes of paper per annum.

The product is high quality printing and writing paper, aimed at a specialist position in the market based on the ability to make small quantities to order.

The paper is produced mainly from wood pulp which is bought in already bleached and digested. This is processed into paper which differs in four main respects: colour, weight (or grade), texture and size. A further product variation is the level of recycled pulp used, which forms a selling point for some of the mill's products, including an own-brand 'conservation' range.

The niche bespoke market which UK Paper Mill 1 supplies requires very flexible production. Whereas a bulk paper manufacturer could run the same process continuously, UK Paper Mill 1 must frequently switch between paper grades, colour and so on, to meet the relatively small orders placed by customers. Thus, paper grade is changed about 40 times in a week, and the average run length is only about 4 hours. Each batch requires the preparation of the pulp in a particular way as regards fibre length and quality, and the addition of various substances. Frequent and small batches of high quality paper production mean that there will inevitably be leftover pulp and this simply goes into the effluent.

The effluent contains suspended solids (mainly fibre, chalk and clay) and starch in solution. Because of the many changes between short production runs, the firm discards quantities of unused pulp mixture prepared for specific jobs, making the effluent more contaminated than typical for a paper mill. The production process thus involves a higher degree of unavoidable waste compared to more continuous or lower quality paper making.

Environmental profile

Until recently UK Paper Mill 1's environmental policy was reactive in nature, and mainly driven by the local regulatory system. UK Paper Mill 1 discharges into a river (the North Esk) and is thus regulated by the Forth River Purification Board. Tightening of regulatory standards by the FRPB since 1975 (and its predecessors before then) has led to great improvements in water quality.

In 1989 the consent for UK Paper Mill 1 was changed to limit the permissible BOD in the discharge to 30mg/l. This regulatory pressure led to the decision to install a two-stage treatment plant, with a biological second stage using oxidation. After the construction of this treatment plant, and the roughly contemporaneous takeover of the company by James River Corporation, the firm became increasingly environmentally conscious, and policy became more proactive.

The firm published an environmental report in 1993. A member of the management board of James River Fine Papers (the managing director of UK Paper Mill 1) was also designated Director of Environmental Affairs. Both UK Paper Mill 1 and the other JRFP mill, GB Papers, have achieved accreditation to BS5750 (ISO 9002) for Quality Management, and JRFP took part in a pilot programme for BS7750 which will result in a standard for environmental management. JRFP has won the 'Scottish Environment Awards for Business' competition.

Project: the effluent treatment plant

The effluent treatment plant was built in 1989, about two years after the FRPB had warned UK Paper Mill 1 of its intention to tighten the consent to include a BOD limit. It was designed to reduce suspended solids and biological oxygen demand levels to meet the Royal Commission standards. It is, in essence, a small sewage plant of circular design in which the solids (fibres and minerals) are settled out, and dissolved starch (the cause of the biological oxygen demand) is digested by micro-organisms.

The companies chosen to tender for the treatment plant were furnished with data on the paper mill effluent as regards volumes and concentrations of materials, including potential peak values. The physical constraints for construction of the plant were also a major consideration due to the nature of the site and very limited area available between the mill and the river.

The contractor chosen, Biwater, had been applying its effluent treatment approach to paper mills since the mid-1980s. Because the company's own technical expertise lay in mixing rotors this approach was based on the use of oxidation ditches for biological treatment. Throughout the UK regulatory pressure was leading many paper mills to replace their existing settling tanks with biological treatment plants.

As suppliers of waste treatment plants, Biwater (which has since reduced its involvement in this field) bid for and won the tender to build a treatment plant based on UK Paper Mill 1's effluent characteristics. Treatment plant suppliers like Biwater do not typically see their role as advising on waste minimization. In some cases, companies will carry out waste minimization programmes, either by themselves or with the help of consultants. In UK Paper Mill 1's case the treatment plant was built to deal with the existing effluent profile, with no waste minimization carried out during the process of design and construction.

Given the availability of capital, the end-of-pipe approach can improve emission quality without interfering with the traditional working practices of the company. Further waste minimization efforts could have been explored before the large capital investment in a treatment plant, but there were two limiting factors. One was that the contractor had no particular expertise, or incentive, to advise on waste minimization. The other was that waste minimization offered only marginal benefits to UK Paper Mill 1 because it specializes in producing short runs of high quality paper.

Although the chosen solution was an end-of-pipe treatment plant, this does not involve the typical problem of transferring the waste from one medium to another. The plant 'recycles' the waste, in the sense that BOD-producing starch (which does pose a potentially serious environmental threat to the river ecosystem) is converted into a marginally useful sludge (a mixture of the settled solids and micro-organism biomass). This can be applied to agricultural land in appropriate concentrations. It is not a financially viable by-product, but spreading it on agricultural land costs less (about a tenth) than sending it to landfill. This would not typically be considered as cleaner technology, but this transformation of harmful waste into a non-harmful by-product need not necessarily be seen as an inferior approach (except for the proviso that fluctuations in the performance of the treatment plant detract from its effectiveness in environmental protection).

3 UK Paper Mill 2

Company profile

UK Paper Mill 2 is a very small family-run paper mill situated at Mid-Calder beside the River Almond. The company has a turnover of about £1 million and about 25 employees. Annual production is about 3000 metric tons of low-quality paperboard made from waste paper and corrugated cardboard. This is mixed with water to form a slurry which then goes through three separation stages to remove 'contraries' before it enters the paper-making machine. The slurry is fed onto the moving nylon wire through which water can drain away leaving a layer of paper behind. Water is removed first simply by gravity, and then by vacuum, after which the soft paper is compressed between rollers. This compressed paperboard is then passed through more compression rollers and over a series of steam-heated drums. Surfaces are smoothed and then the roll of paperboard is trimmed and cut to the desired sizes by another machine.

Environmental profile

The mill is situated beside the River Almond and historically the river was both the source of water for use in the mill and the means of disposing of effluent. This effluent was rich in paper fibres, with levels of suspended solids and biological oxygen demand likely to exceed the consents agreed with the regulatory body, the Forth River Purification Board (FRPB). In 1990 the company was taken to court by the FRPB because of persistent pollution of the river in contravention of the 1974 Control of Pollution Act.

Following this episode the company agreed instead to discharge its effluent into the sewer system. In effect, this meant that the company paid Lothian Regional Council to take the effluent, and the council then had the responsibility to treat it to the satisfaction of the FRPB (which monitors the discharge of sewage works). This, however, was expensive, with charges from the council of as much as UK£4000 per quarter. Moreover, there was every indication that these charges were likely to increase as the 'polluter pays principle' was emphasized by the council.

UK Paper Mill 2 had a preliminary environmental review carried out, funded by Lothian Regional Council. Although the recommendations were generally considered 'reasonable' within the company, they did not stimulate any changes. Decision-making within this family-run company does not seem to have environmental concerns integrated into it in any formal way. There appears to be little spare capital, and a completely reactive position on environmental issues.

Project: water recycling

The sudden imposition of large charges for discharging effluent to the sewer system, when UK Paper Mill 2 was forced to switch from discharging into the river, caused immediate concern. Discussions with LRC Water and Drainage Department staff made it clear that the charges could be considerably reduced if the effluent was treated before entering the sewer to lower its levels of suspended solids and BOD, or to reduce the volume discharged.

Treatment of paper mill waste water would typically involve two stages: primary settling and removal (and perhaps recycling) of solids, followed by some form of biological treatment to reduce BOD. However, for a company as small as UK Paper Mill 2 most of these forms of treatment would involve capital investment which would be hard to justify in terms of savings from reduced sewer charges. An alternative 'cleaner' approach was to increase waste water recycling, an idea which grew out of the discussions with LRC and a student from a local technical college (introduced to the company by LRC). The consequent reductions in effluent would mean reductions in sewage charges.

In August 1991 the company installed a 'float-wash', a filter which screens out large fibres which would otherwise block the pumps. This allowed recycling of water for the first time, and major reductions in effluent charges ensued. In July 1992 an old pond was dredged and converted for use as a balancing tank. A system of pipes and a pump is used to recycle all the waste water, either into this tank, which then, because of its height relative to the rest of the mill, feeds into the start of the process, or directly into the pulping stage. The mill has thus become virtually a closed loop, with no regular discharge. Water loss due to the paper drying process is replaced with fresh water from the river when required. Only occasionally will the balancing tank not be able to accommodate excess recycled water, and little, if any, discharge now goes into the sewer system. Thus for quite limited capital outlay (about UK£2000 for the piping, about the same to prepare the balancing tank) UK Paper Mill 2 has cut its sewage charges substantially. Maintenance of the approach requires the balancing tank to be drained twice a year because of the build-up of sludge and of the effects of biological activity in this sludge.

It was the low quality of the product that made virtually total closure of the system possible. A necessary concomitant of closing up the system was that white recycled paperboard could no longer be made as the recycled water would make it too grey. This would have been a serious impediment for other firms.

The triggers, in this case, were the threat of legal action followed by the charges for sewer usage, a form of the polluter pays principle. This made the costs of creating waste very visible, especially to a small company. At the same time, the authority offered informal advice to the company as to how these charges could be reduced. It was the lack of capital that favoured a cleaner approach, as a treatment plant would have been more expensive. The solution adopted was 'low-tech', but typical of a trend throughout the paper industry to closing up mills and pulping plants to reduce the water usage and volume of discharge.

Table 10.2 *Summary of environmental responses of firms*

Company	DK Paper Mill	UK Paper Mill 1	UK Paper Mill 2
Regulatory context	Storströms County	Forth River Purification Board	Lothian Regional Council
Environmental policy	Environmental manager. Plan to have EMAS by end of 1996	TQM (ISO 9002), BS7750 pilot	None
Environmental response	End-of-pipe, waste minimization and external recycling	End-of-pipe plus sludge re-use (external recycling)	Internal recycling

COMPARATIVE ANALYSIS OF CASE STUDIES

Each of the three cases has a different outcome. UK Paper Mill 2 has adopted a cleaner technology approach through internal recycling of its water. UK Paper Mill 1 has built a waste treatment plant without special waste minimization efforts, though the potential agricultural use of the biosludge may allow external recycling. DK Paper Mill has implemented both end-of-pipe treatment and waste minimization, and is seeking to find uses for all its waste products, which go to incineration, to cement making and to agricultural use.

Regulatory mechanisms

All of the firms have responded to action by regulators, but the particular nature of the regulation and their corresponding reactions to it, have differed. UK Paper Mill 1's end-of-pipe response came in the face of an impending tightening of the consent by the FRPB which has a statutory legislative obligation to protect waterways. During the 1980s DK Paper Mill also upgraded its end-of-pipe treatment (from simply mechanical to biological) in response to regulation, but also sought to implement cleaner approaches – energy saving, water recycling, chemical substitution – where possible. In this Danish case, there seems to have been more information exchanged between firm and regulators than in the UK situation of UK Paper Mill 1. Regulation has been permissive, with the regulator open to the plans and suggestions of the firm, and amenable to allowing time for these plans to be realized. UK Paper Mill 2, however, came under a different UK regulatory framework when it discharged to the sewer, in which sewer charges embodied the polluter pays principle and advice was given by the regulator as to how these charges might be reduced.

In general, these cases support the view that strict emission regulation can push firms to end-of-pipe solutions whereas more permissive regulation may both allow firms more time to envisage radical solutions, as well as making explicit the financial benefits of waste minimization rather than treatment. This accords with another recent study (Bonifant and Ratcliffe, 1994), which shows that US paper mills that had installed secondary treatment plants as a result of strict regulation of BOD in the 1970s were then faced with a sudden need to make internal changes because of the dioxin concerns of the late 1980s. In contrast, Swedish paper mills, which typically discharge to large water bodies, did not face such strict BOD limits and so were able to focus their environmental improvements on more gradual changes in internal processes. BOD levels could also be reduced (though not as quickly or as much as by end-of-pipe treatment) by using oxygen and not chlorine for the delignification process. Having already incorporated this technology, Swedish paper mills were thus much better placed to achieve reduced dioxin levels, which is another consequence of reducing or eliminating the use of chlorine.

Sources of expertise

The role of the regulator in discussing environmental solutions with firms highlights the importance of external sources of expertise. UK Paper Mill 1 did not receive any advice from the FRPB as to how it should meet its discharge consent; that would have been seen as inappropriate by the FRPB, given their legal position as regulators. The only source of external expertise used by UK Paper Mill 1 was a waste treatment plant contractor and waste minimization issues were thus not raised. Specifications for this treatment plant were put out to tender to contractors with experience of building paper mill effluent treatment plants. The chosen contractor (like all such contractors) did not perceive its role as encompassing internal mill waste minimization. In practice, some cleaner techniques – such as the use of cationic starch and further closure of the water system – could have been implemented, whereas others would have involved significant rebuilding of the mill. UK Paper Mill 1 thus built a larger treatment plant than would have been needed if cleaner technology had been implemented. This has been a typical experience for UK paper mills responding to environmental pressures during the last decade or so.[2] This has, in a sense, provided room for growth. Although the size of the treatment plant limited the capacity for handling effluent, it was possible to increase mill production by incremental introduction of waste prevention measures.

DK Paper Mill, on the other hand, did access external expertise. In 1987 they used a research institute to carry out an environmental assessment with which to contest the limits set by the county regulator. This process involved both the company and environmental organizations (which thought the limits too lax) presenting their cases to the EPA. After the installation of the de-inking plant, DK Paper Mill used other consultants and research institutes, both to address problems with the working of the treatment plant and to find uses for the sludge.

External expertise was also important to UK Paper Mill 2 in that the council, and an academic contact suggested by the council, triggered the water recycling project. It is worth noting that no great innovation in technology was involved, but rather an innovation in thinking about the way the mill was operated and how effluent might be reduced.

Availability of capital

It may also not be a coincidence that the firm which implemented a cleaner solution (UK Paper Mill 2) had the least available finance and was subject to sewage charges which made the polluter pays principle extremely explicit. The question of 'how will you do less damage to the environment?' thus became instead 'how will you save yourself some money?' In DK Paper Mill and UK Paper Mill 1, on the other hand, the financial restraints were not so great and both the ownership by large companies and the emphasis on an environmental image meant that environmental costs were seen as worth paying. Indeed, the desire for a good environmental image may favour the choice of an end-of-pipe treatment plant rather than cleaner technology because of the high visibility of such a project. Not only is the firm protecting the environment, but it is *seen* to be protecting the environment (end-of-pipe treatment has been commonplace in Denmark for decades, however, so the public perception of environmentally friendly industry there seems more attuned to cleaner approaches such as recycling and renewable energy).

Life cycle analysis

The paper sector provides a very clear instance of the potentially arbitrary nature of definitions of cleaner technology and of the need for environmental benefits to be judged through life cycle analysis. Defining cleaner technology in terms of waste minimization and resource use reduction *within* a particular firm or segment of the production chain can give a misleading impression of the overall environmental impact.

All of the mills play some part in recycling waste paper. UK Paper Mill 2's only product is made from waste paper, but the low quality of this product makes closed loop water recycling possible. UK Paper Mill 1 uses pulp from recycled sources for some of its products, but this pulp is produced elsewhere (along with any associated environmental problems). These problems are highlighted in the case of DK Paper Mill, which is now solely devoted to de-inking waste paper to produce good quality pulp.

DK Paper Mill's de-inking plant project was developed in conjunction with the Danish EPA (including support of DKR 50 million or about one fifth of the total investment) because it was seen as environmentally desirable. However, the extent of the environmental impact of the de-inking process was not specifically addressed in this process. It was assumed that the mill's waste water treatment plant could be expanded and that extra sludge could be burned as an energy source. This extra sludge, due mainly to rejection of short fibres and fillers, amounts in total dry weight to about half as much as the pulp produced.

Another problem DK Paper Mill found with such recycling is that the highly heterogeneous character of the waste paper causes difficulties in assessing potential causes of toxicity, and can make it difficult to control any effects on the biological treatment process. This raises the obvious point that effective recycling requires that products are designed to be recycled.

As well as raising the issue of the cost/benefit of recycling, life cycle analysis also calls into question the utility of the cleaner technology/end-of-pipe distinction. Process changes using cleaner technology may not be able to eliminate all waste streams, especially when applied to existing plant. Many of the potential pollutants are product or raw materials that are being lost from the process, so preventing this loss could be financially beneficial, but it may not be possible or cost-effective to ensure 100 per cent retention. UK Paper Mill 1, for example, produces short runs of high quality paper of differing grades, colour and surface. A small percentage of 'broke' from each batch is simply discarded into the effluent stream because it is not considered worthwhile to recycle it. UK Paper Mill 2, on the other hand, making one, much lower quality, product, found it relatively easy to implement a closed loop system.

For mills where it is considered impractical to recycle all the paper/pulp bearing waste stream, biological treatment plants (whether aerobic or anaerobic) provide a catch-all means of treatment which removes the locally damaging effects of high BOD. The resulting sludge, moreover, may have use in agricultural production systems, even if it has no significant value. It may not necessarily be the case that absolute adherence to the cleaner technology approach is environmentally preferable to the use of a treatment plant. Ignoring the potential for *some* cleaner technology will most likely be financially unwise for the firm, but equally attempting to eliminate all waste streams within the firm may entail higher environmental costs than enabling external recycling. However, it is clear that such recycling throughout a product chain can be enhanced, notably by ensuring that the original paper products are manufactured in such a way that they do not contain toxic substances.

Public pressure and the role of environmental groups

A life cycle perspective also highlights the potential for public concern over the environment to be effected through consumer pressure. The paper industry produces products which are traded globally and which are typically available to a uniform or very similar specification from many manufacturers. There is thus considerable scope for consumers to select on the basis of environmental concerns and for pressure groups to shape such behaviour, especially since the environmental association with paper has already been made in many societies through waste paper recycling.

A dramatic example of this occurred in Germany in 1991, when Greenpeace issued a magazine titled *Das Plagiat* (the Plagiarist) which mimicked the appearance of the popular magazine *Der Spiegel*. The Greenpeace magazine used Swedish chlorine-free paper and urged German readers to demand that publishers switch to use of chlorine-free papers. By the end of the following year, *Der Spiegel* had switched, as had others, including IKEA, whose catalogue alone constituted a shift to chlorine-free paper of 40,000 metric tons (Bonifant and Ratcliffe, 1994, pp57–58).

It is clear, then, that in some circumstances consumer pressure can influence the development of cleaner production systems. All of the case study firms have been influenced to some degree by the high public profile of paper recycling. DK Paper Mill's de-inking plant has received substantial government financial support because of the perceived virtues of paper recycling in Denmark. UK Paper Mill 1 now promotes its own range of 'conservation concept' recycled products as part of promoting its environmental image. UK Paper Mill 2 encourages the local populace to use its site as a recycling deposit.

Implementing cleaner technology in practice: technological possibilities and firm decision-making

A survey of cleaner technology possibilities for paper making reveals a range of techniques that may be applicable. In practice, the actual 'best available technology' will be specific to the type and age of mill and its product range. This in turn may limit the possibilities as far as choice of raw materials. In general, however, there are many cleaner techniques which are already tried and tested, along with a few – such as enzyme bleaching or recovery of coating materials by ultrafiltration – which have been recently implemented at a few sites. Apart, perhaps, from improving the alternatives to chlorine-based bleaching, there do not seem to be any problems which require radical new solutions; much more could be done with the existing solutions.

What can be done in practice will vary greatly according to the specifics of the mill and its product. The cases of UK Paper Mill 1 and UK Paper Mill 2 constitute the extreme ends of the spectrum in terms of product quality. The latter's production of low quality paperboard made from waste paper means that the process at that mill is amenable to complete closing up, whereas the short run production of high quality paper at UK Paper Mill 1 is seen to militate against water recycling, as well as leading to the deliberate discharge of unused prepared pulp when each run is complete.

Since much of the waste from mills producing paper is effectively lost product – indeed the unused pulp discharged by UK Paper Mill 1 is deliberately lost – it seems that there may be some potential for reducing these losses, giving a double saving both in product not lost and in waste not needing treatment. It may be, as is often the case, that a culture of accepting 'reasonable' waste levels has developed, whereas small, but significant reductions in these losses could be readily achieved with innovative thinking.

In summary, the paper-making industry does not appear to need scientific breakthroughs or new high technology developments in cleaner technology.

There are many existing techniques, but their uptake is uneven. The main barriers to wider implementation of cleaner technology appear to be limited dissemination of expertise, along with the difficulties of retrofitting new developments into old plant. This is not helped by organizational inertia in mills whose plant *and* management have changed little over the years.

CONCLUSIONS

1   The uptake of cleaner technology is not limited by lack of scientific/technical possibilities. Further research should be encouraged, of course, especially in cleaner life-cycle solutions (see point 6 below), but whether this leads to actual industrial innovation will depend on the extent to which new knowledge can be accessed by firms and adapted to their specific needs.

2   The uptake of cleaner technology is not limited by lack of financial resources; indeed, there is evidence that lack of finance may promote innovative thinking geared towards cleaner/waste prevention approaches, whereas availability of capital may favour the construction of end-of-pipe treatment plants.

3   For small firms, access to expertise is important if innovative cleaner technology is to implemented. Reliance on traditional contractors (whose business is building treatment plants) means little exposure to cleaner approaches.

4   Government agencies are an important potential source of cleaner expertise, but will probably be ignored unless this expertise is linked to regulation. Small firms typically lack the time/personnel to be concerned unless there is a potential threat or very clear financial gain at stake.

5   Regulation can lead firms to take environmental action. If geared towards short-term enforcement of emission levels, however, this will usually encourage the implementation of proven, end-of-pipe treatment technology. Regulatory mechanisms which incorporate the polluter pays approach, and thus make visible the environmental costs which were previously externalized and the potential financial benefits of waste reduction, may allow more time to develop innovative, cleaner solutions. Such an approach can be implemented through permits or allowances with stepwise strengthening of effluent limit values which allow time for the firm to incorporate innovations without interfering with production.

6   Cleaner technology must not be considered simply as a matter of *internal* firm innovation. External recycling and product chain restructuring are necessary for cleaner production systems, but are unlikely to be achieved through measures which focus entirely at the firm level. For example, paper recycling is much easier and cleaner if the original paper does not contain certain potential pollutants (which may stem from upstream production, as some pollutants arrive in the raw material).

There is a need for further research on innovative life cycle perspectives which minimize waste and resource use, and investigate fully the potential for developing by-products and external recycling. There is also a need for public policy measures which encourage approaches that take a cleaner life cycle perspective. The evidence of DK Paper Mill suggests that taxes on waste, for example, can encourage external recycling.

11 ELECTROPLATING

Søren Kerndrup with Leo Baas, Ulf Nielsen and
Jacob Haas Svendsen

Two companies were examined in this sector, one in The Netherlands and one in Denmark.

SECTORAL CONTEXT

Main industrial processes

The products and processes in this sector are very wide ranging but the companies in the study have identical processes and products. The activities are performed in three phases:

- pre-treatment: where the work pieces get cleaned and activated;
- plating process, where work pieces are coated electrolytically with metal;
- post-treatment, that is, protecting against corrosion.

In *pre-treatment* rust and scale is first removed in an acid-pickle bath or alkaline cleaner. Second, oil and impurities are removed in electro-cleaning (degreasing), and finally the thin coat of oxide (from electric degreasing) is removed in a diluted acid bath (acid-dip).

In the *plating process* the work pieces function as the cathode, and the anode is made of the metal to be deposited (zinc or nickel). The electrolyte is a solution containing the metal to be deposited, weak acids to make the solution conductive and additives like brighteners (which give a smoother coating). As the current increases from the power supply, the metal plating begins to take place on the cathode (the work pieces).

In *post-treatment* – zinc plating chromate conversion coatings is the most popular – a thin coating of passivation is deposited. This improves the corrosion resistance of the zinc, and partly gives its colour (usually bluish or yellow).

Between every process the work pieces must be rinsed in water. As a final treatment the work pieces dry by simple drip-dry or by air-drying. In automated lines the work pieces (on racks or barrels) are moved between the tanks by automated equipment. Delay, temperature, and eventually stirring are operated by electronics. Both of the companies studied in this sector focus on low cost and large production runs. They have invested in production automation and in cyanide-free production as part of this process.

Environmental issues

The most important environmental impact from the plating process is the discharge of waste water containing heavy metals, organic solvent and chemical waste in the form of sludge containing metal hydroxides. Environmental regulation has focused on the use of toxic compounds and organic solvents since the 1970s, and has largely been aimed at forcing firms to invest in end-of-pipe technology. In the 1990s, the best available technology approach dominates the implementation of the IPPC (integrated pollution prevention and control) in national regulations. In Denmark regulation in this sector has combined both technology-based and recipient-based regulation, but the latter seems to dominate in local environmental regulation.

A deteriorating environmental reputation has been an increasing problem for the industry, forcing the industry to change its environmental behaviour. In Denmark, the plating industry association has been particularly active in the process of change by coordinating information on cleaner technology and encouraging companies to get involved in cleaner technology projects supported by the national environmental authorities.

Industrial context

The electroplating industry is still dominated by very small companies in both countries, though it is gradually consolidating and a few small non-specialized companies have closed. There are different structural changes in the industrial context that enhance this development: the changed supplier–customer relation (especially in relation to subcontracting), the location of the electroplating process in the production chain, and environmental demands.

Table 11.1 *Size distribution of plating firms in Denmark and The Netherlands*

Size	1–10	11–50	>50	Companies
Denmark	46%	22%	26%	146
The Netherlands	80%	18%	2%	350

Product range

The plating companies are subcontractors delivering a surface coating to the customer's product. The product range can therefore be described in relation to the end-use of the product and to the coating specifications.

Short and stable lead times

The surface treatment is typically the last link in the production chain before the product is sent to the market. Delays through the whole chain often result in increased delivery pressures on surface treatment companies.

Quality

The function of the surface coating is to draw attention to the quality of the finish and its resistance in use. The finish is often a factor that appeals to the conservative purchasing policy of customers, and help to enhance the position of the product.

Partnership

The electroplating industry has been moving away from a subcontractor role, reflecting a shift in the manufacturing industries' attitude towards subcontractors, from arms-length contracts to partnerships, involving fewer subcontractors but working more closely with them. Another change in the subcontracting policy of major manufacturers is their integration of suppliers in technical development that in the coming years will include environmental parameters as well.

The plating companies are small companies without formalized research and development activities. The managers and employees often have practical, but little or no theoretical knowledge of the processes. Most of the innovations are developed in collaboration with the suppliers of equipment and raw materials. The strong focus on the relationship with the suppliers can be seen in relation to the internal development and knowledge resources of the firms, the process characteristics and the position in the production chain.

The innovative resources of the small plating companies mainly reside in the owner-manager. This is the only person in the production with 'plating' skills. This pattern is the reason for the low innovation orientation in the production because the work is low-paid, with unattractive working conditions. The owner managers' lack of theoretical knowledge results in innovations based on incremental changes. Knowledge from outside is therefore important, and in this respect the suppliers play a very important role. Plating firms are very dependent on good collaboration with suppliers as a way of getting information to develop new processes, or to optimize the existing processes. Both of the companies studied in this sector use their existing suppliers, both as sources of knowledge and as partners in the development of new processes.

CASE STUDIES

Table 11.2 *Summary of electroplating sector cases*

Company	DK Plating	NL Plating
Product	Zinc-electroplating Nickel-electroplating Mass production hanging-goods (chair-legs and post containers) Barrel-goods (screws, nut and rings)	Zinc and nickel plating Full automatic hanging-line capacity 5000 kg/hour – small objects Two semiautomatic barrels zincing capacity 2500 kg/hour – small objects Nickelling installation for objects up to 6 metres
Market	Zealand, Denmark Big series, big customers	The Netherlands Big series and small objects
Employees	12	30
Industrial setting	The sector consists of small companies. 56% of the companies have less than 10 employees. Compete on cost and service. Customers are located in Zealand. Close links with suppliers are important for technical developments. Collaboration with companies in other market segments of the industry	The sector consists of 350 plating companies with approximately 3500 employees. 80% of the companies have less than 10 employees. Competitive situation: low cost competition by East German competitors
Regional features	Small firm located in a little town with 4000 inhabitants and 10 companies. The firm has minor economic and employment effects on the local area. The waste water causes adversarial relations between the firm and the municipality	Small firm located in an industrialized harbour area in Zuid-Holland with minor effects on development of economy and employment in the area. The environmental effects are also limited in relation to the total environmental impact of industry in the area

Table 11.2 *Summary of electroplating sector cases (continued)*

Company	DK Plating	NL Plating
Regulatory environment	Regulated by the municipalities that focus on emissions to the municipally owned waste water treatment plant. This pushed the firm to invest in end-of-pipe solutions	Regulated by Directorate of the National Water Authorities and the regional EPA. The regulation focuses on using end-of-pipe technology and the company also focuses on end-of-pipe
Ownership	Limited company. Owned by the son of the founder	Family owned
Cleaner technology programmes	The investment in cleaner technology is triggered by the collaboration with the suppliers of raw materials and technology. A new project got a subsidy from the national Cleaner Technology scheme	Involvement in the PRISMA programme 1989–90 inspired the company to introduce cleaner technology. The incentive was cost price reduction but the investment also contributed to the onset of the firm's financial difficulties

1 DK Plating

Company profile

DK Plating was founded in 1959 in Roskilde as a family company. It moved to Stenlille in West Zealand in 1979. In 1983, the son of the founder took over, and in 1994 it became a limited company. It is located in a small community, with 5000 inhabitants and perhaps 10 companies.

DK Plating carries out traditional electroplating: nickel electroplating, chromium plating, and zinc electroplating with post-plating treatment of chemical chromate conversion. DK Plating makes both 'hanging goods' (see below) such as chair legs and post-containers and 'barrel-goods' such as screws, nuts and rings.

DK Plating has five production lines: two nickel/chromium lines and three zinc lines:

- The nickel hanging goods line has 2500 litre tanks.
- The nickel barrel line has 400 litre tanks.
- The zinc barrel line one has 500 litre tanks, and works with acid ammonium based zinc.

- The zinc barrel line two works with warm acid zinc, potassium rather than ammonium based.
- The zinc hanging goods line has 4000 litre tanks, and works with ammonium based zinc.

The customers comprise a few large companies, buying DKr 1–2 million per year, some medium sized customers buying nearly DKr 500,000 per year, and many small customers buying DKr 50,000–200,000 per year. DK Plating is a mass producer and it competes on price, quality and short lead times. This is possible because they have their own distribution system.

Through the last few years DK Plating has grown, in turnover and in profit. This positive development has given the firm the resources to focus more on its environmental problems.

Environmental profile

The most important environmental impact comes from the emission of heavy metals in the waste water, and the production of sludge with metal hydroxide. The firm has installed a traditional internal waste water treatment plant, and implemented a range of cleaner technology solutions.

DK Plating discharges waste water to a small publicly owned waste water treatment plant that has its outlet in the stream of Sandlyng, which flows into the stream of Aamose, and later into the sea of Storebelt. The municipality cannot deposit the sludge from the treatment on farming land because of the high nickel concentration, among other things. The municipality is convinced that the high level of nickel is caused by the waste water of DK Plating, but there is no reliable data from either the company or the municipality. There is disagreement about the quantity of the discharged waste water, as well as the concentrations.

DK Plating has installed extraction ventilation on part of the process. The company used to produce about 31,000 tonnes of metal hydroxide sludge per year. After installing equipment to dry the sludge into filter cakes, this sludge has been reduced to one fourth. The dried filter cakes are delivered to Kommune-kemi as chemical waste. DK Plating has implemented a range of traditional cleaner technologies and was one of the first companies in the plating industry to use cyanide-free electroplating for mass production.

Project

DK Plating chose to introduce cyanide free electroplating at the time when they decided to shift from manual to automated production. At the time of the shift there were only a few examples of alkaline cyanide-free zinc electroplating.

Hydrogen cyanide is a very toxic substance. Cyanide has received much attention, therefore, from the regulatory authorities, and there is a long history of attempts to find substitutes. It is relatively easy to detoxify cyanide, however, or to build closed systems with selective ion exchange. There are several cleaner solutions, therefore, such as alkaline and acid cyanide-free baths, which can reduce environmental impact.

The alkaline bath method has encountered some problems with dispersing the metal. The focus has therefore been primarily on the ammonium chloride-based bath method, as this allowed better metal precipitation and a quicker dispersion.

At a later stage the company discovered that this process had an important disadvantage in terms of levels of heavy metals in the waste water treatment process. The focus today, therefore, is mostly on warm potassium chloride-based acid zinc. The warm process also gives the advantage of better surface quality plating. It is also possible, with this method, to reuse the chemicals discharged into the rinse water, as well as reducing losses through evaporation from the process bath. In this way the use of rinse water can be minimized and the system can be closed.

There were various reasons why DK Plating wanted to get rid of the cyanide in the production process:

- A big new contract meant that the company had to expand. This, in conjunction with the change in leadership, was a trigger for the decision to invest in new technologies.
- Cyanide-based production has several disadvantages. The cyanide bath works slowly and needs frequent correction. This costs time and money, especially in relation to automated production.
- The company's health and safety problems were largely due to the toxic baths.
- The company was under pressure from the local environmental authorities to invest in end-of-pipe solutions to reduce the nickel emissions because of its impact on the waste water treatment plant. This pressure was expected to increase, with increasingly restrictive regulation.
- The company's alternative to change (to rebuild the waste water treatment plant and install detoxification technology) would have been expensive both in terms of the investment and the cost of operation.

A cyanide-free process was attractive because it offered the company a way to reduce their costs, health and safety and regulatory problems. It therefore made sense to change the process. It was also feasible; the firm was able to get advice from some of its suppliers of raw materials and equipment on new technological options, and this close collaboration with the suppliers minimized the risks associated with being a frontrunner.

Clearly the substitution of cyanide means the total avoidance of a toxic chemical, in both waste water and the working environment. From the local authority's point of view, however, the problematic substance was nickel, because of their problems with the sludge from the local waste water treatment plant. The difference in priorities may have caused, or at least reinforced, poor relations between the company and the local authorities.

From the company's point of view the trial concerning the exceeding of the limit values seemed like a provocation, coming immediately after the company had shown willingness to invest in cyanide-free production and other cleaner technology solutions; solutions many other electroplating companies were not ready to consider at that time.

At the same time, it is important to remember that it was economic rather than environmental arguments that led the company to make the substitution. Viewed in a broader perspective, this combination of environmental and economic considerations has delivered an environmental advantage. The relatively quick financial returns then made it possible to continue with other environmental solutions, such as new rinse processes, ion exchange systems and ultrafiltration.

2 NL Plating

Company profile

NL Plating is a second-generation family owned company with 30 employees, located in the harbour jetty of the Waalhaven in Rotterdam. It is a medium-sized company, specializing in large volumes of big and small objects and the nickelling of very long objects, and serving market segments where the required finishing is limited.

The company has installations for electrolytic zinc and nickel batch processing. The processes are performed by three departments.

- a fully automated hanging zincing installation with a capacity of 5000 kg per hour;
- two semi-automated barrel zincing installations with a capacity of 2500 kg per hour;
- a nickelling installation for objects up to 6 metres long.

The company has a typical organization for small firms, with a simple organization and an informal culture, though there is a strict hierarchy. The directors decide the activities in the whole company and take decisions without much consultation. Contact with the workers is limited, because many workers are recent immigrants with limited Dutch language skills.

Environmental profile

The environmental activities of the firm are in accordance with national environmental policy. Water pollution is the main issue. Containment floors were constructed under all the process baths. The company had to meet the new strict regulation for the plating sector, by increasing the quality of the effluent. After treatment in an ONO installation, 3500 m³ of treated water is emitted. Some components are still in the treated water, but the emissions comply with the regulatory requirements. The ONO installation produced 140,000 tonnes of sludge in 1994. The sludge is stored in a special landfill, because of its chemical waste content.

Project

As noted earlier, hydrogen cyanide is a very toxic substance. Environmental policy, supported by subsidy, has focused on the installation of end-of-pipe treatment techniques, especially ONO installation.

Cyanide and chromate-6 are detoxified in the ONO installation by oxidation of the cyanide and the reduction of chromate-6. In the next step the cyanide is precipitated by pH adjustment. After a percolation phase, the waste water is emitted to the sewer and the galvano sludge is transported to a landfill storage.

In 1989–90 the company joined the 'PRISMA' public financed cleaner technology project. For more than a year, the researchers tried to convince the firm of the benefits of cyanide-free electroplating processes, but the managers did not want to take the risk of moving to a process that was not used by anyone else in the country at that time. The firm then joined a study trip to the UK organized by the union of the national plating industry, and visited a company using the cyanide-free process. This demonstrated that the process was economically attractive. The firm then implemented the process in 1992, one of the first firms in The Netherlands to do so.

The company had to expand its capacity, and saw the new cyanide-free process as a way of saving time and reducing the costly deposit of toxic waste from the ONO process.

Unfortunately, the company used its existing canister supplier to build the new line. This supplier did not have the necessary experience, but wanted to use the order as a chance to build up its competence in this promising area, and so did not want to use subcontractors. The supplier's lack of experience caused a number of problems; the installation was finished half a year behind schedule, with many remaining technical problems. This, in conjunction with new, low cost competition from former East Germany, caused a crisis for the company. The delay gave the new entrants time to seize market share, so the new installation had excess capacity from day one, and the company ran into financial difficulties. Today, the company survives under a bank guaranty.

Table 11.3 *Summary of environmental responses of firms*

Company	DK Plating	NL Plating
Regulatory context	Stenlille municipal authority	Regulation plus government subsidy for environmental investments
Environmental policy	Informal	Informal
Environmental response	Cyanide-free plating process radical process change	Cyanide-free plating process radical process change

COMPARATIVE ANALYSIS OF CASE STUDIES

Environmental policy and regulation

Environmental regulatory authorities have paid special attention to the industry since the 1970s because of the industry's waste production.

The Dutch environmental protection body focuses on the use of toxic compounds and organic solvents, and on air and soil pollution. Since 1981 there has been a special subsidy to encourage environmental investment, mainly for the installation of end-of-pipe technology (especially ONO, a form of processing that removes most of the heavy metals from the waste water, leaving a concentrated chemical waste that can go to special landfill). The subsidy has rarely been used to support cleaner technologies, like ion exchanges and the use of substitutes for chromium-6 and cyanide. The focus on end-of-pipe is also embedded in the limit value of heavy metals in the waste water effluent. Indeed the limit levels have strongly encouraged the use of end-of- pipe technology, and the environmental authorities have strongly recommended the use of ONO installation in the whole sector. NL Plating has met the regulatory requirements for the galvano sector by the construction of containment floors under all process baths and by investing in an ONO installation.

Danish regulation of the electroplating industry is governed by local environmental authorities. The focus has been on the heavy metals in the water effluent.

There have been two regulatory approaches:

- A recipient based regulation of waste water with standards set in terms of the capacity of the recipients to absorb concentrations of pollutants eg in waste water emissions; and
- Technology oriented regulation based on the principle of best available technology. This approach is based on the EPA's 'Industry orienting for Electroplating industry.'

In practice, the regulation of DK Plating has been based on the recipient oriented approach, with special emphasis on the possibility of depositing the sludge from the municipality owned treatment plant onto farming land.

DK Plating is regulated by the environmental authorities of a small municipality. The firm received an approval in 1979, but relations between the authorities and the company have been marked by a reciprocal loss of confidence between the parties. The local authority has in several cases indirectly forced DK Plating to invest in filter technology instead of cleaner technology. This was a consequence of a one-sided focus on emissions of waste water without any dialogue with the firm. With dialogue, and a little encouragement, the firm might well have preferred best technology standards.

Management structure and style

The companies in the study are very small family owned companies managed by the owners. It is the owner-manager who takes all the strategic decisions about investments and business relations with customers and suppliers. In the Dutch company the lack of marketing skills had made it necessary to hire professional marketing expertise.

Company culture tends to be determined by the founder's management style, and generational change can mean cultural change. This cultural change has been most pronounced in the Danish company where the sons, as the new manager-owners, introduced a period of expansion, continuous improvement of production, and the development of cleaner production.

The Dutch workforce consists primarily of unskilled workers without much knowledge of the plating industry, whereas the Danish company recruited a flexible, stable workforce. The Dutch company had difficulties hiring its workforce (because it is located in an industrialized area), and it consists mostly of foreign nationals, which causes communication difficulties.

Environmental management

The environmental management of the companies has focused on compliance, resulting from the attention of the environment agencies to this sector. The pressure to comply has also caused a focus on end-of-pipe technology as the way to reduce emissions. The companies have therefore invested in different waste water treatments to reduce their emissions.

In both cases, the companies came to focus on cleaner production because they had an opportunity to expand production, which required them to invest in new technologies. From a management point of view, cyanide-free production was the most profitable solution but also the most risky because it was a new technology, so there was little practical experience to draw on. Both companies minimized the risk thorough collaboration with external partners. Although financial considerations were the main driver of the introduction of cyanide-free production, the combination of environmental and economic reasons produced a significant environmental advantage.

At the Danish company, this initiative opened up a floodgate of environmental initiatives. The quick profits made by the change to cyanide-free processes made it possible for the company to continue with other environmental solutions, such as new cleaning processes, ion exchange systems and ultrafiltration. Unfortunately the process at the Dutch company was terminated because the company ran into financial difficulties in a context of cut price competition from former East Germany, which made it impossible for the company to use its expanded capacity to reduce costs.

The competitive situation

Both companies focus on cost minimization, quality and service, in market segments where product finish is of limited importance. The driving force for introducing cleaner technology has been the search for ways of reducing cost. DK Plating invested in new installations on the basis of customer forecasts of increasing orders.

The companies have not used the cyanide-free production in marketing their products, because it is not valued per se by their customers.

Internal relations

The organizational structure of the company is a very important factor in developing technological projects, because the generation and implementation of ideas are social processes. Technological projects often collapse because of organizational problems. The Danish firm is a dynamic organization with flexible workers who have the skills and capabilities to install and build a new production line. This capability was efficiently used by the firm to build the new production line in the holiday period, without any delay or use of external firms, apart from some advice from the suppliers.

The Dutch company has a hierarchical structure and unskilled workers without capabilities for building new production lines, and the implementation of new technology was dependent on the knowledge and expertise of their suppliers.

External relations

Both companies have cooperated with other companies to develop their technological projects; collaboration with suppliers has been especially important for the success of their projects. If we look at the process in two stages we can see the following.

Idea generation

Both companies focus on developing technologies from a strategic point of view. Their investment was prompted and supported by new orders. Communication with external partners influenced the search for technological alternatives, and also helped to minimize the risk of implementing new non-proven technology.

At the Danish company it was the dialogue with suppliers that helped them choose between technological alternatives and minimize the technical and organizational risk. At the Dutch company it was the dialogue with partners in the PRISMA project and a journey to the UK that convinced the company that cyanide-free technology looked promising.

Implementation

Implementation is a risky process with many technical and organizational difficulties. It is important for the companies, therefore, that they minimize these risks by collaboration with suppliers, customers and consultants. The suppliers to the Danish firm had knowledge and practical experience with the implementation of cyanide-free technology, so the technology was implemented successfully. These close links with the suppliers also solved some unexpected problems with the technology, by introducing warm acid-zinc as a better method.

The Dutch company also chose to use an existing supplier. However, the suppliers' limited expertise and unwillingness to work with other contractors critically undermined the whole project. The implementation was delayed half a year, which precipitated a financial crisis for the firm.

CONCLUSIONS

The particular features of this sector are:

- small and medium sized subcontractors managed by the owners;
- competition on price, quality, fast deliveries;
- strict regulation by the environmental authorities, involving the use of both recipient standards and best-technology standards;
- an industry organization active in changing the image of a heavily polluting industry.

Regulation

Regulation is often a driving force for environmental performance, but the way it affects performance is still not understood in detail. In this sector environmental regulation has clearly been important in convincing the industry that it needs to manage its impact on the environment. At the same time, regulatory pressure to deal with emissions has tended to force solutions based on end-of-pipe technology, and thus has been a major obstacle to introducing cleaner technology solutions. This has in some cases created a tension between the companies' interest in cleaner technology as a way to integrate economic and environmental demands and the public authorities' demands for emission reduction.

Our cases show that regulatory pressure has forced, directly or indirectly, the companies to invest in expensive end-of-line technology, creating conflicts between the companies and municipal authorities because they have different goals. The Danish case is an example of this tension between a company investing in one area of pollution control (one of the first in the country to implement cyanide-free production), yet at the same time coming into conflict with the municipalities in another area of pollution management (emissions of nickel to the municipality's waste water treatment plant). The case from The Netherlands shows that the limit values are constructed with a focus on the use of end-of-pipe technology, and this technology is also supported by the EA.

Business network of suppliers, customers and consultants

The internal and external dynamics of firms and their relations with suppliers, customers and other institutions is very important for environmental innovation. In this sector suppliers have been most important for developing and implementing cleaner production. The firms used their usual suppliers to develop the new technology. By using familiar suppliers the firms were exploiting the activity links, resource bonds, and actor bonds, built up over many years. This is important, particularly for small companies, but it is also important that the supplier structure has the necessary skills. In the Danish case we see familiar relations enhancing the process, while in the Dutch case they were an obstacle because of the lack of competence.

The Danish case indicates that, with the right partnerships, it is possible for even very small companies to develop activities and resources that create a virtuous cycle of environmental activities, breaking with the institutional limits of an end-of-pipe, emission-oriented environmental regulatory approach.

Customers have played a largely passive role in the process, which is reflected in the strategies of the firms. The firms did not, for example, feel it worthwhile to use their cleaner technology in their marketing strategies. This does not mean that customers are unimportant, but until now they have played a minor role in encouraging progress in this sector.

The public authorities can use these existing networks of relationships, however, to build up competence in managing environmental performance. One good example is the cleaner technology projects that themselves create an important network for communicating cleaner production concepts. However, it is also important to ensure that the network is capable of implementing such concepts. In Denmark the cleaner technology programme had an indirect effect by increasing the expertise of suppliers (but we should note that the real goal must be to stimulate a group of suppliers, rather than single firms).

Business strategy and environment

Business strategy is the prime driver of the company's environmental behaviour. The small and medium companies in this sector compete on price, quality, and fast order times, and their competitive strategy is largely based on cost minimization. Both the companies in the study chose cleaner technology because that particular approach represented a way of reducing their costs.

12 WHAT SHAPES THE IMPLEMENTATION OF CLEANER TECHNOLOGY? CONCLUSIONS AND RECOMMENDATIONS

Anthony Clayton, Graham Spinardi and Robin Williams

We are now in a position to examine the key factors that may promote or impede the adoption of cleaner technologies. This chapter pulls together the main research findings from our studies of 31 cases across nine industrial sectors. It reviews the different factors shaping the behaviour of the firms studied and the interaction between them.

The first section reviews the main drivers of change. Foremost are the direct effects of regulation, coupled with the indirect effects of regulation (and consumer and public pressure) on corporate policy. However regulation does not necessarily lead to the adoption of particular approaches (for example cleaner technologies as opposed to end-of-pipe solutions). Other factors play an important intervening role here, notably process economics and the organizational context. The main part of this chapter explores these in turn: with separate sections addressing regulation and economic factors, and a section on the interaction between them in shaping production processes and environmental responses. We then consider the organizational setting. Finally we present a model of decision-making in the firm which pulls together some of these observations about factors shaping the behaviour of firms. This brings us on to the final section which offers a number of conclusions and makes some policy recommendations.

THE MAIN DRIVERS AND SHAPERS OF CORPORATE ENVIRONMENTAL PERFORMANCE

Our case studies show environmental regulation to be the sine qua non of corporate environmental performance. It is clearly the most significant reason why firms initiate improvements. Regulation influenced firm behaviour both directly and indirectly. Corporate policy was also an important direct influence on organizational behaviour, though this can be seen to result mainly from the firms' perceptions of both actual and potential regulatory impacts on business, as well as from their desire for a favourable public image.

Consumer pressure was not cited by firms as being a major factor, a finding which can be related to the fact that most firms in the sample did not sell directly to the public. However some firms with strong brand identities or high public profiles showed particular sensitivity about their public image, especially in product areas seen as potentially hazardous. Similarly, though public pressures did not in general appear to drive environmental improvements, they had greater salience in firms in which environmental and related accidents had attracted public attention. Public perceptions also shape the wider political setting, affecting the structure and institutional framework of the formal regulatory system, and also the way that the regulatory system operates and regulations are interpreted and applied. For example the environmental movement had been influential in the Danish and Dutch regions over several decades, and there had been recent intense public pressure about industrial activities around Cork.

Regulatory pressures were found to be important in every case. However regulation per se did not necessarily lead to particular kinds of environmental response; a range of outcomes was observed, ranging from the installation of end-of-pipe solutions to more or less far-reaching searches for cleaner approaches. This range of responses could be related to:

- differences in the form and content of regulatory pressures;
- differences between sectors in the kinds of technology and expertise deployed;
- differences in product markets and cost structures, and in particular the *(perceived) value in waste streams*. This in turn is related to the characteristics of the product market, which is considered further in the section on economic factors.

The influence of regulation varied, depending upon the particular circumstances. For example, as we see below, the inflexible and rapid implementation of strict emission standards tended towards the certainty of 'end-of-pipe' solutions; but such standards could also stimulate the search for cleaner solutions where they were seen as a longer-term constraint that had to be overcome in order to develop new production facilities. Some of the most effective outcomes emerged where environmental concerns reinforced existing technological and economic trends within the firm/sector. This raises issues about how public policy might best be fitted to industrial dynamics. Conversely, inappropriate policy, and a misguided use of either regulatory or economic levers, could have undesirable consequences, for example by further embedding short-term end-of-pipe solutions.

The actual environmental solutions adopted in particular cases were thus shaped by a number of factors – legal, political, economic, technological – and the interactions between them. To address the interaction between these variables, we need to consider the findings at the detailed level of individual firms as well as the sectoral level.

Table 12.1 therefore seeks to capture the diversity of firms' environmental response, and the factors underpinning this for the complete set of 31 detailed case studies.[1] The key features of each case study have been summarized for ease of presentation. We have categorized the types of environmental responses embodied in the particular *projects* selected for detailed study.[2] This categorization allows us to examine groups of cases adopting broadly similar kinds of response,

Table 12.1 *Summary of case study findings*

Environmental response	Project description	Case study	Products/markets
End-of-pipe	Bulking and neutralization plant – in preparation for waste waster treatment plant	UK Brewery	Wide range of beers – mostly domestic some export Medium value product
End-of-pipe	Extraction of solvent from aqueous waste stream	UK Pharmaceuticals	Extraction of opiates and other licensed drugs Very high value
End-of-pipe	Removal of nitrogen	DK Refinery 1	Petrol, diesel, LPG Medium value product
End-of-pipe	Chemical treatment of spent caustic soda	IRL Refinery	Petrol, diesel, LPG Medium value product
End-of-pipe	State-of-the-art waste water treatment facility	UK Refinery	Petrol, diesel, LPG Medium value product
End-of-pipe plus sludge reuse	Waste waster treatment plant	UK Paper Mill 1	Speciality paper medium value product
End-of-pipe plus sludge reuse	External recycling of sludge from wwtp for de-inking plant	DK Paper Mill	Paper pulp low value product
Improved techniques/working practices	Waste monitoring and continuous improvement (eg reduction in water use)	NL Dairy	Daily milk and primary milk products (eg yoghurt) high value product
Improved techniques/working practices	Water recycling and 'water use benchmarking exercise'	IRL Brewery	3 types of beer, mainly domestic market; some export. Medium value product
Improved techniques/working practices	Waste monitoring and continuous improvement (eg reduction in waste product)	UK Dairy	Mozzarella cheese – high value product

Trigger to change	Regulatory context	Environmental policy	Size, ownership
Expectation of tighter consents, when local authority sewage works has to meet stricter discharge standards	Local council water/ sewage authority – which in turn is regulated by the river board	Informal Formal company environment policy being developed	Operating plant of large UK corporation 30,000+
Pressure from sewage authority	Sewage authority limits on discharges to sewer	Informal	SME 200 (management buyout from MNC)
Legal etc. pressure from county council over N discharge to shallow waters	Application for new licence from West Zealand County Council	Formal	Branch site (250) of a MNC
Search for secure method of disposing caustic soda waste from treatment of mercaptan/H2S to reduce smells – following local community pressure.	Cork County Council	Formal	State owned firm (200–150 on this site)
Green Corporate image	Integrated pollution control and anticipated application of European discharge standards by river board	Formal	Branch site of UK MNC
More stringent emission standards	River Board	External formal BS7750 ISO 9002	Branch 165 of US Company
Stricter emission standards; EPA collaboration	County (Størstroms)	External formal EMAS by 1996	Branch 66 of Swedish Company
Search for environmental improvement stimulated commercially motivated programme	Regional EPA and Water Authority	Formal internal plus external (environmental care in TQM), ISO 9002 Plus dairy sector covenant	Branch 190 of amalgamated Dutch farmers cooperative 7350
Anticipated local authority charges for waste water treatment	City council application to EPA for IPC being prepared	External formal ISO 9000 and draft environmental management plan	Branch c 500 of Dutch MNC
Search for environmental improvement stimulated commercially motivated programme	Pressure from sewage authority after incidents (and encouragement)	Informal	Plant 75 owned by Canadian MNC

Table 12.1 *Summary of case study findings (continued)*

Environmental response	Project description	Case study	Products/markets
Internal recycling/ end-of-pipe	Membrane technology to extract organic solvent from waste water	DK Fine Chemicals	Membrane filtration devices High value product
Internal recycling	Condensate storage and recovery	IRL Chemicals	Ammonia Medium value product
Internal recycling	Capture/regeneration of lost volatiles	DK Refinery 2	Petrol, diesel, LPG medium value product
Internal recycling	Water recycling	NL Brewery	One beer: 55% export, 45% local medium value product
Internal recycling	Water recovery from waste sludge (plus external recycling of dried sludge)	IRL Sugar	Sugar for national market Medium value product
Internal recycling	Water recycling	UK Paper Mill 2	Paperboard Low value product
External recycling	Waste biomass distributed as fertilizer	DK Pharmaceuticals	Insulin and other enzymes very high value product
External recycling	Recovery and sale of waste acetic acid (+ reduced water usage)	IRL Fine Chemicals	Ion exchange etc reagents high value product
Incremental change in process technology	New plant design incorporates waste minimizing features	UK Chemicals	Polyethylene Medium value product
Incremental change in process technology	Change of cleaning agent (acetic acid in place of organic solvent)	IRL Pharmaceuticals 1	Range of drugs and intermediates (60% to affiliate) very high value product
Incremental change in process technology	Waste waster treatment plant plus waste minimization	IRL Pharmaceuticals 2	Range of drugs and intermediates for affiliate companies Very high value

Trigger to change	Regulatory context	Environmental policy	Size, ownership
New owners changed firm's response to regulatory pressures from resisting environmental improvement to searching for economically sound solutions	Størstroms County Council: Clean Technology project	Formal internal Responsible care	Following takeover became branch 177 of US MNC 60,000
Waste minimization discussed with Cork Council (regulator), plus economic motive	Transfer from Council to EPA – stricter; IPC, waste minimization encouraged	External formal IS 310 Responsible care	Branch 200 Joint venture with UK company
Legal etc pressure from county council over N discharge to shallow waters	Application for new licence from West Zealand County Council	Formal	Branch site (250) of a MNC
Financial pressures to improve environmental performance with sharply increasing sewage treatment levies	Regional EPA and Regional Water Authority; informal community pressure	External formal ISO 9002 and working on BS7750, EMAS etc	Branch c 500 of Dutch MNC
Increased production, coupled with environmental pressures (limited capacity of, and problems with, existing waste water treatment)	Regulated by Cork County Council To be licensed under IPC	External formal ISO 9002 move to EMAS expected with IPC	One of two sugar factories owned by recently privatized Irish agro-business
Sewage authority: prosecution, charges and encouragement	Sewage authority (local authority) - implementing stricter standards	None	Small family owned company with 25 staff
Firm policy – seeks to pursue environmental image	Different responses to spreading waste biomass from different regional authorities	Formal external; working towards BS 7750 Signatory to ICC-BCSD, member EPE, WICE	Main site of Danish MNC 12,800
Expansion increased acetic acid discharge, legislation would require new wwtp; recovery and resale was a cheaper alternative	Shift from Cork County Council to EPA	Formal external ICC - BCSD ISO 9002 IS 310 soon Responsible care	Plant 150, of European MNC 40,000
Proactive company environmental policy, with cracker upgrade	Shift of regulator from FRPB to HMIPI (IPC)	Formal internal Responsible care	Branch 1450 of UK MNC 56,000
Environmental concerns and savings from reduced material usage	Recent transfer from county council to national EPA. IPC licence received US-FDA approved	Formal external; working towards IS 310; ISO 9002 Responsible care	Branch 135 of US MNC 81,000
Company policy, following IPC and earlier community pressure	Recent transfer from county council to national EPA. IPC licence received US-FDA approved	Formal external; working towards ISO 14001 Environmental Management Programme submitted Responsible care	Branch 180 of UK (formerly US) MNC 57,000

Table 12.1 *Summary of case study findings (continued)*

Environmental response	Project description	Case study	Products/markets
Incremental change in process technology	Optimization of fluorine recovery process	UK Fine Chemicals	Dyestuffs, biocides and other fine chemical high value product
Incremental change in process technology	Beet handling and washing to reduce water use and waste	DK Sugar 1	Sugar for national market Medium value product
Radical change in process technology	Cyanide-free plating process	DK Plating	Plating mass production goods
Radical change in process technology	Cyanide-free plating process	NL Plating	Plating large and small objects in large batches
Radical change in process technology	New catalyst	NL Chemicals 1	Plasticizer High value product
Radical change in process technology	Process simplification (w. catalyst) not fully successful	NL Chemicals 2	Phenol High value product
Radical change in process technology	Steam-drying of pulp	NL Sugar	Sugar for national market Medium value product
Radical change in process technology	Developed aqueous based chemistry to substitute for organic solvent based one	NL Pharmaceuticals	Intermediates for antibiotics and cardio-vascular medicines Very high value
Product change; specifically new product developed	Milk mineral separated and sold (IRL£6k/tonne)	IRL Dairy	Cheese, butter and other milk derived products High value product
product chain management	Beet cleaning in fields	DK Sugar Corporation	sugar for national market Medium value product

Trigger to change	Regulatory context	Environmental policy	Size, ownership
To reduce cost of planned waste water treatment plant	Shift of primary regulator from River Authority to HMIPI	Formal internal Responsible care	Branch 600 of UK MNC 31,500
Dialogue with regulators about renewal of licence and concern about waste water, in context of expansion of plant	Regulated by (Størstroms) county (classified as environmentally important factory)	Formal internal (from parent company)	Production plant (one of four) of Danish Sugar Corporation
Expansion and shift to automated production; traditional cyanide process slow and variable and new wwtp would be required	Municipal council – as operator of sewage treatment plant (which stimulates investment in end-of-pipe solutions)	Informal	SME (12 employees) family owned
Grant from DK Clean Technology scheme; Collaboration with suppliers			
Involvement in PRISMA (1989/90) stimulated awareness of cleaner technology; change motivated by cost-saving potential	National water Authorities and regional EPA. Regulation focuses on end-of-pipe technology	Informal	SME (30 employees) family owned
Market driven – better quality; environmental improvement helped decision	Regional EPA and Water Authority covenants Environmental Action Plan	External formal ISO 9002 Industry covenant Responsible Care	Branch 430 of US MNC (over 10,000)
Cost reduction – in context that emphasized environmental improvement	Regional EPA and Water Authority covenants Environmental Action Plan	External formal ISO 9002 Industry covenant Responsible Care	Branch 230 of Dutch MNC (over 10,000)
Energy and cost-saving investment also provided solution to long-standing environmental (odour) problem	National Water Authority and Regional EPAs (air)	Informal (reluctant)	Factory (one of four) owned by diversified Sugar Cooperative (owned by farmers)
Growth in production, doubts about getting permission for greater discharges, plus environmental ethos of firm	Strict limits on water emissions by National Water Authority	Formal external, ISO 9001 Responsible Care	3 site subsidiary 695 of Dutch MNC 19,000
Market opportunity identified for current, problematic, waste	Shift from Cork County Council to EPA	Formal external ISO 9002, IS 310 in development	165 SME now owned by farmer cooperative
Stricter regulatory requirements over long (10 yr) time scale, coupled with costs of waste treatment	Various local authorities (county)	Formal internal	Sugar business unit of large multi-divisional food manufacturer

and thus gain access to particular factors that may underpin certain types of change. Many of the other key features of the cases have also been presented in summary form, including the environmental response adopted, the firm, sector and nation, the firm's products and markets, the trigger for change, the regulatory context, the environmental policy and firm size and pattern of ownership. As explained in Chapter 1, each case study focused on a project that had a significant impact on a firm's environmental performance. This was not necessarily 'cleaner technology', and it was not necessarily adopted for environmental reasons per se. We are able to categorize these responses. The first distinction is between those which operate within existing production parameters (ie end-of-pipe solutions), and those that seek a more integrated approach to environmental improvements. We can differentiate the latter in terms of the extent to which they represent more innovative approaches to production processes and products.[3] The range of responses found comprise:

- *end-of-pipe solutions* (typically waste water treatment plants), sometimes combined with internal recycling or sludge reuse;
- *improved techniques/working practices;*
- *internal recycling* (where waste materials are reintroduced into a production process);
- *external recycling* (where waste materials are sold to another party);
- *incremental change in process technology;*
- *radical change in process technology;*
- *changes in products;*
- *product chain management* (where environmentally oriented change takes place across a supply chain).

Our survey included only one example each of the last two categories. These, respectively, involved the development of a new product to use waste milk minerals in Irish Dairy, and the initiation by Danish Sugar Corporation of a collaborative attempt to get farms to provide cleaner beet to reduce pollution in sugar refining. These kinds of cleaner approach seem to be very difficult to achieve, at least in the short term, as they involve coordination between a wider range of players (suppliers and consumers). There seem to be particular difficulties in those cases where the changes need to be accepted by large numbers of customers, over whom the firm has little direct influence. There is much more evidence that firms have been able to implement those kinds of change that have mainly involved players within a single firm.

Overall we emphasize the diversity of outcomes in individual cases, which can be related to the interaction between an array of economic, technical, political and cultural factors. However, we can group the main influences under three broad headings: regulation, economic factors and organizational factors.

Regulation is one of the key elements which varies according to the regional and sectoral context of the firm. It includes both regulatory requirements (broadly conceived, for example, to include waste disposal charges and other policy instruments) and the manner of their implementation, themselves shaped by the broader political economy in that region and sector.

Economic factors include cost considerations and the competitive dynamics of a firm/sector (shaped in turn by the particular industrial processes and product markets in the firm/sector) and are particularly relevant in terms of pressures for resource efficiency.

Organization level factors relate mainly to decision-making processes in the choice of production processes and environmental responses, which in turn are shaped by divisions of labour and knowledge and flows of knowledge and information within and beyond the firm.

This chapter discusses each of these influences in turn, and considers the interaction between them.

REGULATION

Regulation was the main factor stimulating firms to respond to environmental issues. The strength and nature of regulatory pressures was not uniform, however, but varied between sectors and regions, depending upon perceptions of risk and particular historical circumstances. It was also clear that firms responded in a variety of ways to regulatory pressures. Strict regulation did not necessarily favour the adoption of cleaner approaches. There was some evidence that emission standards could encourage firms to adopt 'tried and tested' end-of-pipe solutions, particularly if rapid improvements in performance were required or if the perceived consequences of non-compliance were high. This underlines the importance of *the content of regulation*. The way in which *regulation is implemented*, and especially the role of the regulator, were also significant factors: the search for cleaner innovation could be facilitated where the regulator had adopted a *mission* to promote cleaner approaches, involving collaboration and joint learning between the regulator and regulated.

Sectoral differences

The sectors show marked historical differences in terms of the stringency of the regulatory regime, the perceived environmental risk and approaches to hazard control in relation to industrial processes and products. The chemical industry, for example, has been relatively strictly regulated in every country in the study, while this has not historically been the case in dairying, which has not generally been seen as a hazardous industry. This pattern is, however, partly masked by various national differences, which tend to reflect different historical contingencies. Brewing, for example, is relatively lightly regulated in the UK, but has come under more severe pressure in The Netherlands because food-processing was one of the three industrial sectors selected at the start of the Dutch target group environmental policy framework in the 1980s. There may also be differences in the implementation of regulation; the standards applied to the plating industry in the UK and The Netherlands were not dissimilar, but the mode of implementation varied. In recent years there have been pressures towards the harmonization of regulatory standards, between sectors and between different European member states (though, as we have seen, differences continue in the implementation of regulation). Current regulatory requirements operate, and have differing significance, within different historically specific contexts.

The sectors can be split into four main groups in terms of the extent to which regulatory requirements have been institutionalized over time, which in turn reflects the underlying character and intensity of regulatory pressures in each case. These groups range from the relatively lightly regulated to the relatively strictly regulated.

Dairy, Brewing and Sugar. These products have not been seen as hazardous, and in general regulation has not been particularly strict (except with regard to hygiene), with the exception of The Netherlands where brewing and sugar are under somewhat more pressure.

Plating and Paper Manufacture. These industries are now strictly regulated as a result of a history of poor environmental performance. These sectors have, historically, been dominated by relatively small firms, with limited internal resources. The level of environmental expertise in the plating sector in The Netherlands was found to be so low, compared to the chemical sector, that a far more prescriptive approach was adopted. Thus, where the standards applied to the chemical sector were extensively debated with the firms in the sector, the standards applied to the plating sector were simply imposed with little consultation.

Pharmaceuticals. Stringent regulations apply to product quality (US Food and Drug Administration (FDA) standards are extremely influential) and worker hygiene. The sector is subject to similar environmental regulatory requirements as other parts of the chemical industry, but pressures tend to be moderated by the fact that operations, and thus environmental hazards, are typically on a smaller scale than other chemical sectors.[4]

Fine and Petro-chemicals, Refining. These sectors have long been subject to stringent regulation on the grounds of the intrinsically hazardous and aggressive nature of the materials, and the associated toxicity and flammability hazards. More recent product regulations (eg regarding sulphur content or eliminating lead additives) have also had an important influence on refining operations.

Regional differences

There were important differences between the regulatory systems in the study in terms of their approach, structure, content and ethos. In Chapter 2 we focused on the differences in approach, and outlined the two main ways that regulatory systems operate. Regulatory change and experimentation was a feature of all our regions, though regions were perhaps at different stages of development. In particular, the UK region studied was a coastal region; regulators had until recently allowed considerable leeway in discharges to coastal waters, like the Forth estuary, which offered enormous potential for dilution of aqueous wastes. As a result of recent increases in environmental awareness, and in particular, EU standards, many firms in this region were introducing waste water treatment plants for the first time. This was two decades later than their counterparts in The Netherlands and Denmark, which had been operating in a context in which environmental concern had developed rather more strongly and at an earlier stage, particularly where their aqueous wastes were being discharged to inland and shallow waters. It could be argued that Denmark and The Netherlands are further down the 'clean technology' learning curve, though the regional variation observed cannot be reduced to a simple time lag in the development of environmental concern between the countries. The continuing development of international standards and approaches does seem to herald a period of harmonization of regulatory frameworks and standards.

The content of regulation

Today we find two main approaches to environmental regulation. The first is to set *emission limits* for the levels of effluent which a firm is permitted to discharge. The environmental consequences of the firm's activities are controlled and limited, but the regulator does not seek to directly control the means by which the firm achieves this. As we saw in Chapter 2, much environmental regulation has traditionally followed this model, particularly in relation to aqueous discharges. The main alternative regulatory approach seeks direct influence over the firm's choice of technology and procedures. Today this usually involves requirements that the firm use what is considered in environmental terms to be the best available technology (BAT).

Emission limits

The evidence, from this and other studies, suggests that implementing emission limits in a rigid manner may encourage an end-of-pipe response from firms. Regulation in some instances *institutionalized* end-of-pipe solutions, as we saw in the Dutch Plating case where the values of emission limits applied were constructed around what could be achieved by end-of-pipe technology. This was particularly marked where a significant improvement was required in a short period. Such an outcome can divert resources from the search for cleaner responses, both through the opportunity costs of investing in end-of-pipe facilities, as well as by offsetting pressures for environmental improvement, as we saw in UK Fine Chemicals and Danish Plating.

Where waste minimization approaches remained unproven, and where the costs of failure to comply were perceived as high by a firm (eg prosecution, loss of reputation, or head office censure), 'end-of-pipe' solutions were often seen as a more reliable way to meet requirements. Conversely, it was not easy to guarantee in advance that the search for process improvements implied by 'cleaner technology' would deliver significant reductions in discharges within a limited timescale. This has a policy implication: *if stricter emission limits are to be applied in contexts where the scope for cleaner technologies remains unproven, it may help promote more innovative 'cleaner' approaches if relatively long timeframes are allowed, with the flexibility to delay enforcement if initial attempts do not prove successful.* Such an approach was explicitly adopted by Størstroms County (Denmark) in encouraging cleaner production in the sugar processing industry. We return to this in relation to the role of the regulator.

Paradoxically, there were circumstances under which strict emission limits stimulated the search for cleaner solutions. This was noted in several cases where firms were seeking to expand production facilities which were already subject to existing strict discharge limits. Thus in both Irish Fine Chemicals and Netherlands Pharmaceuticals, there were doubts about getting the regulator's permission to increase discharges with the proposed expansion of production. Where strict limits create an obstacle which must be resolved for a project to proceed, the search for cleaner approaches can be incorporated within the technical and commercial parameters of the new development. This is facilitated by the fact that such improvements are integrated with the equipment renewal cycle and the timeframes of company planning.

Promoting best available technology

The regulatory strategy known as 'best available technology' (BAT), requiring firms to adopt best practice in their choice of technologies and processes, has been pursued for some time in Denmark and The Netherlands, and has been introduced more recently in Ireland and the UK, with integrated pollution control (IPC) which requires the use of BATNEEC (best available technology not entailing excessive cost).

Historically, the term BAT was associated with the application of established 'end-of-pipe' treatment technologies – with which it is still equated by some (see, for example, the discussion in Baas et al, 1990, pp7–8). Broader approaches to BAT have been proposed that would support R&D and innovative solutions. However, BAT does not necessarily mean cleaner technology; BAT is often interpreted to mean the best available *proven* technology, which can discourage the taking of risks with more innovative solutions. This depends, in practice, on the attitude of regulatory bodies. If their priority is an immediate reduction of discharges, BAT will often mean an end-of-pipe solution; if they are willing to adopt a longer-term perspective, innovative and beneficial solutions based on waste minimization might emerge.

Another problem is that BAT implies some comparison about what technologies are available and which is best. If regulators are to be involved in such judgements they may need expertise on the technological principles of the industry and its processes. Problems may arise because of 'asymmetries' between the expertise of the regulator and the firm. Though varying between sectors, these are likely to be particularly marked in high-technology sectors. We return to this point later.

However, procedures for establishing what constitutes BAT can be defined to support cleaner technologies. In particular, under the Irish IPC system, BAT stipulates a hierarchical search amongst options that gives priority to waste reduction.

Sewage and water charges and other fiscal measures

The other form of regulatory pressure associated with the search for cleaner technologies comprised increased charges for waste disposal and water use. Thus in a series of cases – NL Brewery, UK Dairy, UK Paper Mill 2 – firms were confronted with increasing charges (in the first case, increasing sharply over a number of years). A similar outcome arose in the Irish Brewery in a context of anticipated discharge charges to a planned local authority sewage treatment plant and following a company-wide water-use benchmarking exercise. In the UK cases, the 'carrot' of reduced costs was supplemented by the threat of prosecution by the sewage authority. These all stimulated a search for economies in water use and discharges (notably by waste water recycling). Interestingly, in these two UK cases, waste charges had a further catalytic effect of drawing attention to the costs of waste that had hitherto gone overlooked. Advance warning of future changes in charges (as with standards) also enabled waste minimization to be 'built-in' to future plans and encouraged the search for cleaner approaches.

These findings suggest that various kinds of 'green tax' may be effective in promoting resource efficiency. The study additionally provided some evidence that negative taxation, that is, subsidies, may also have a role, even though recent trends in industrial policy are towards neo-liberal approaches and strongly against subsidies. We saw this in Danish Plating, where subsidies, designed to assist small and weaker firms with the high costs of end-of-pipe waste treatment plant, were used to support the development of cleaner processes. Equally, NL Chemicals 1 utilized a public subsidy in its search for a radical change in process technology. These cases indicate that subsidies can help stimulate the search for cleaner solutions (though they need to be designed with care since they can also be used to support end-of-pipe solutions).

The implementation of regulation

The influence of regulation cannot be reduced to formal legislative or policy requirements but depends significantly on the way in which regulation is implemented, interpreted and buttressed by informal regulatory pressures. Many of the cases involving cleaner approaches (particularly where there was a search for longer-term and more innovative solutions) were associated with a shift away from the traditional 'arms length' policing concept of the regulator's role as simply monitoring compliance with standards. The regulator might, for example, give some flexibility in the *implementation* of standards where cleaner approaches were unproven (and thus might be slower or even might fail to deliver improvements), as we saw in the agreement between Størstroms County and Danish Sugar.[5] This points to the development of a more *collaborative relationship* between the regulator and the regulated firm. This seemed to arise where the regulator had adopted a positive mission to support cleaner technology and waste minimization. We note the lead taken by Størstroms council in Denmark (a move that was not always followed by nearby local authorities). In The Netherlands similar kinds of collaboration and approach had emerged, notably through the sectoral covenants in the Dutch chemical industry, involving inter-firm collaboration under The Netherlands Environmental Action Plan.

In the UK, there has been an important difference between the statutory regulation by the Scottish river boards and the more permissive approach of local councils dealing with firms that discharge to their sewer system. In the latter case, two UK firms – UK Paper Mill 2 and UK Dairy – were encouraged by the sewage authorities to reduce their sewage charges through the use of internal recycling and waste minimization respectively (although some firms in the same jurisdiction opted for end-of-pipe waste water treatment plants). In addition, the sewage authority provided important technical support for water recycling and waste minimization, two areas in which it had expertise. Both these cases were small establishments, and the paper mill in particular had limited internal resources. In other sectors, however, the balance of expertise will often be heavily weighted in favour of the regulated firm, which may be less favourable to such a collaborative approach. We return to this point in the following section.

These cases highlight the scope for regulatory agencies to actively foster cleaner approaches by encouraging awareness of its potential, rather than by legislative stipulation. The provision within recently adopted IPC systems for firms to set out programmes and timetables and monitor their progress towards waste minimization is likely to exert growing influence in future. Similarly, Dutch firms (in certain designated sectors with a high pollution potential) must produce and publish their four-year environmental care plans as well as annual reports on progress in implementing these, which is likely to provide a powerful informal incentive to improve performance.[6] Various kinds of public environmental initiative seemed to be important, such as the PRISMA and SPURT Clean Technology initiatives in Denmark and The Netherlands, and the Dutch sectoral covenants. These points are discussed in more detail in Chapter 13.

Quality and balance of expertise

There is often an uneven distribution of expertise between regulated firm and regulator, though this will vary between firms, sectors and regions. For example, firms in the petro chemical or refinery sectors, at one extreme, are typically large corporations, and possess a breadth and depth of technical expertise in their own particular production processes and operations that will not be matched by regulators, whose technical expertise has traditionally been in the area of hazard assessment and control. This sharp imbalance of expertise may make it difficult for the regulator to discover what the technological state-of-the-art is, and to promote particular solutions as best available technology. The fact that such firms are more likely to have a greater depth of in-house expertise also potentially helps them legitimate their decisions and puts them in a more powerful position in negotiations. At the other extreme, for example in the paper-making and plating sectors, which are less dynamic and often involve smaller firms, firms are likely to have more limited technical capacity and thus be both more in need of and potentially more open to flows of expertise and advice from the regulator (as we saw for example in UK Paper Mill 2).

There are also regional differences in the relative size and thus scope for specialization of regulatory agencies. Though precise comparisons may be misleading, the Danish regulatory bodies, taken across all regulatory and educational functions, have several times as many personnel as their UK counterparts per unit of population. This may reflect the fact that in Denmark local government plays a comprehensive role in industrial regulation and promotion, including the provision of information to local firms. Thus the UK regulators are not in a position to provide the same extensive range of local functions provided in Denmark. Conversely, in a larger economy like the UK, there is greater scope for regulators to centralize their activities and develop a greater depth of technical specialization.

The level and types of expertise available to the regulator may have important implications for the search for cleaner technology. Extensive expertise can both underpin and legitimize a stronger, more active and interventionist role for the regulator, providing the basis for a broader hegemonic role rather than a narrow policing function. In Denmark and The Netherlands, regulators provide an effective conduit to channel information about best practice to firms.

On the other hand, one of the most significant features of The Netherlands model is the emphasis on the provision of information by the firm. In this system, the regulator relies explicitly on the expertise available within the firm, thus creating an opportunity for a more sophisticated dialogue about goals and means. In The Netherlands, therefore, the regulator is able to play a strong role in facilitating or mediating approaches to other companies in the same or other sectors, and establishing performance benchmarks, even in those cases where the balance of expertise may be with the firms concerned. Disclosure of information coupled with scrutiny by regulator and public alike may be as effective in achieving influence as the regulator's level of technical expertise per se.

The political economy of regulation

The role and influence of the regulator are also subject to broader influences, which vary between sectors and regions depending, for example, upon the political context, and the economic importance of the regulated sector/firm.

Different firms and sectors exercise very different levels of political leverage. The petro-chemical and refinery sector is generally regarded as being of strategic importance, and is dominated by a small number of large and powerful companies whose interests are well represented in the political decision-making process. Such firms are in a position to have relatively high levels of influence over public policies and regulations affecting them. Sectors which perhaps command less economic or strategic importance, and which are made up of large numbers of small, disparate companies that are less able to express a common view tend to have much less political influence, and thus have less control over public policy. Similarly, firms that are major employers in their local economy are in a much more powerful position – especially in economically depressed areas – to articulate their concerns to a local authority.

However, it would be misleading to presume that firms simply seek to resist regulatory pressures. The spectrum of responses ranged from some cases (not reported here) where firms decided to ignore or do the minimum needed to comply with regulatory requirements, to firms, such as UK Refinery, which had adopted a policy of 'conspicuous compliance'. It saw public relations benefits from its acquisition of an expensive 'state-of-the-art' waste water treatment plant, using what it claimed was the best available technology in the world. Such 'proactive compliance' may make sense in an industry which plans its activities and investments on a long-term basis, and which may fear the consequences of environmental mishaps. The company's stated strategy – of setting environmental performance standards rather than simply responding to regulatory requirements – reminds us that regulation can moreover be a competitive tool. If companies can achieve stricter environmental standards and then get these adopted as the new norm for their sector, nationally or internationally, they can put pressure on weaker competitors. In so doing, they also achieve a modicum of certainty and control over their own regulatory context.

The development and implementation of regulation is not reducible to relations between the state and industry, but is also influenced by broader civil society. Public perceptions are also important in relation to both how the risk of the process and the necessity and desirability of the product are perceived. Thus the activities of the chemical industry are regarded with more suspicion than, say, the food or brewing sectors. The principles of its operations are not well understood by a public that in recent years has come to see 'chemicals' as 'unnatural', imposing potentially large hazards and dubious benefits. The industry fears that the public have little awareness of its products (which are mainly incorporated into other products) and their contribution to many other manufacturing operations, and the extent to which current lifestyles depend on the sector. Beer, on the other hand, is a familiar product which is retailed directly to the public, and is seen as natural and relatively harmless. Thus UK Brewery could afford to be far less concerned about minor breaches of environmental regulations, partly because the public regard the brewing industry in a relatively benign light. The desirability of the product tends to be weighed off against the perceived riskiness of the process: refineries tend to be regarded with much more suspicion than breweries, even though the public probably want petrol at least as much as they want beer.

The sense of public accountability and responsibility of firms seemed also to differ according to their size and technological/commercial salience and whether this was local, national or international. Large firms that hold a dominant position in a given sector tend to provide a benchmark for corporate behaviour for the other firms in that sector. Such firms are more likely to judge their performance in relation to their peers at international level rather than by reference to other, smaller, local firms. Small firms, by contrast, tend to be self-referential, and are more likely to compare their current performance with their past performance than with the performance of other firms in their sector. The scale and degree of concentration of industrial activities is also relevant here. Large-scale, centralized chemical plants are highly visible and attract considerable public attention in comparison with, for example, domestic sewage works or the many small plating plants.

Although firms did not in general see consumers or pressure groups as directly influencing their behaviour, reputational issues did have an important indirect role, as part of this informal political economy of regulation. The significance of reputational issues varied depending upon the firm's markets (whether it sold to intermediate or to final consumers, and in the latter case whether it marketed products under its own brand name). Thus it is not surprising that UK Refinery, which markets a wide range of products under its own brand name, wanted to implement a highly visible environmental improvement. The company as a whole is very sensitive about even minor transgressions and breaches, because such incidents reflect on the corporate image and thus affect the group as a whole. Similarly, DK Pharmaceuticals developed an expensive system to distribute waste biomass as an agricultural conditioner. It is hardly a coincidence that this biotechnology-based firm should be particularly concerned to promote a greener image, as biotechnology products have to contend with a high level of public concern and suspicion of genetic engineering (Green, 1992; Walsh, 1993). Concern about environmental and other hazards, however, does not necessarily promote cleaner responses. Where it is seen as critical to demonstrate human and environmental safety, firms may be drawn to opt for known and tested solutions, which may well be end-of-pipe solutions, rather than to take risks with innovation.

ECONOMIC FACTORS

The role of economics and its interaction with other factors

Whilst regulation was the major stimulus for firms to improve their environmental performance, it did not necessarily lead to particular kinds of environmental outcome per se. Instead, a range of responses were visible including traditional end-of-pipe and more innovative cleaner technology responses. Which responses were adopted depended upon the interaction between regulatory and a range of other social and technical factors, with economic pressures perhaps the most notable.

.. ressures to reduce costs provide a direct incentive for firms to improve their resource efficiency and reduce wastage, and in this way encourage firms to adopt cleaner solutions for financial reasons as well as a way to respond to environmental pressures. However the strength of these incentives, and the consequent readiness of firms to implement cleaner technology as a solution, were not uniform but appeared to vary between sectors in terms of their product markets, and the nature of their processes. This was partly a question of the relative prices of raw materials, products and waste streams, but also reflected the extent to which resource efficiency had become institutionalized within the sector (partly a function of the maturity of the sector). For example, industrial sectors, such as the chemical industry, in which competition is heavily focused on production costs, will be more open to the improvements in resource efficiency which also underpin ideas of waste minimization and cleaner technology. In contrast, it would take a relatively high level of market pressure before the benefits of process change would outweigh the risks of product change for a typical firm in the pharmaceutical sector. This is because pharmaceutical manufacturers compete mainly on product innovation, with a large proportion of their costs devoted to the development and testing of new drugs. Once established, these drugs are sold in a market place that is effectively not price-competitive (at least until patent rights expire) and the benefits of small increases in process efficiency, though potentially worthwhile, remain relatively modest and are outweighed by the potential dangers of changing the production process (especially when FDA approval has been gained). UK Pharmaceuticals company constitutes an extreme example of this particular trade-off, since its status as one of the few legal manufacturers of narcotics in the world largely guarantees its dominant position in that market. This means there has been relatively little incentive to reduce production inefficiencies (compared, for example, to concerns to maintain the level of security required for this particular product range).

Such market factors were not simple determinants of firm behaviour; the role of economic pressures remains complex, and is mediated by other factors. We discuss a number of aspects in the next section on 'organizational factors'. For example, the availability of capital within the firm was an important economic influence over the choice of production processes and environmental control strategies. However we found that this, in turn, was shaped by company decision-making structures and accounting practices. Much depends upon the decision-making criteria, culture and expertise structures within the firm which shaped how economic pressures were *perceived*. Cost considerations *can* stimulate improvements in internal efficiency leading to reduced environmental impacts. However this is *by no means automatic*. Firms do not always have complete information about the costs of different activities, especially smaller firms with low levels of specialist expertise. The competitive dynamics of the sector/product market constitutes an important intervening factor here. Firms operating in dynamic and competitive markets recognize the need to maintain high levels of internal expertise and links with external sources of knowledge about developments, which in turn improves their awareness of opportunities to improve resource efficiency. Another factor concerns the role of taxes and charges for waste disposal. In our discussion of regulation, we argued that such charges could encourage firms to incorporate waste reduction into their commercial planning. Cases such as UK Dairy and UK Paper Mill 2 showed that such charges, or the threat of their imposition, could have a catalytic effect, and draw the attention of management to the cost of waste which had hitherto been overlooked (especially when coupled with advice on ways of reducing these charges). In UK Dairy this stimulated a longer-term programme and culture of waste minimization driven by cost savings as much as environmental concerns. Such fiscal measures may encourage better integration of environmental and commercial planning, promoting more innovative approaches than might result from conventional regulatory mechanisms. Thus NL Brewery responded to a proposed rise in landfill taxes by initiating a research programme into alternative uses or disposal routes for used kieselguhr. The adoption of cleaner technology approaches thus depends upon the way that firms perceive external environmental pressures, and cost structures, and integrate them into their internal decision-making.

Overall we find a complex interplay between economic and other factors, which precludes a reduction to any single determinant. Many decisions are made on the basis on multiple rather than single criteria. NL Pharmaceuticals, for example, engaged in a search for aqueous-based chemistry in place of the use of organic solvents as part of its long-term process of change, which was shaped by a complex interaction of environmental pressures and positive market opportunities. Despite this complexity, the most striking feature in our cases is *the interaction between environmental regulation and the economic and commercial situation of the firm*. This is evident from the overview of all the case studies provided by Table 12.1, which summarizes the factors that were perceived as the important triggers for the specific projects studied. These typically involved an interaction between cost and commercial considerations and regulatory and other public pressures on the firm's environmental performance, particularly in relation to the more innovative solutions at the bottom of the table, such as incremental and radical changes in process technology.

This interaction is particularly evident when we consider the different types of environmental response adopted by firms. By categorizing the kind of environmental response of the project studied in each case, Table 12.1 demonstrates how particular approaches are closely related to the characteristics of the product market, and in particular product/raw material value and the latent value of wastes. This highlights some distinctive features of groups of sectors and cases. For example, there was little incentive to introduce waste minimization where waste products have little intrinsic value and waste disposal charges are low (eg in the brewing and paper sectors). In these cases, environmental improvements are largely reactive to regulation, and are likely to be end-of-pipe. This is in contrast to the chemical sectors, where raw materials are expensive and efficient resource utilization is both key to the competitive dynamics and strongly institutionalized, forming part of the criteria by which production processes are assessed. In this context, waste minimization is intrinsic, and environmental concerns may only play a secondary role.

Relative value and resource efficiency

Figure 12.1 summarizes the distribution of cases and sectors in terms of the *value* of their products, feedstocks and waste streams, and *resource efficiency pressures* which might foster cleaner technology. It reveals a broadly U-shaped curve with little weight given to efficient resource utilization in relation to low value products/wastes. As the value of raw materials (and wastes) increases, the propensity to use cleaner technologies for simple commercial reasons also increases. However this tails off in relation to the highest value products covered in our survey, which were found in the pharmaceutical sector. Although these products have very high value, process costs and waste costs are relatively low compared to product price, and are not major determinants of profitability. Product quality, rather than process efficiency, is the key to competitiveness. In this sector, therefore, we find a range of responses which are mainly influenced by the firm's particular regulatory and political context.

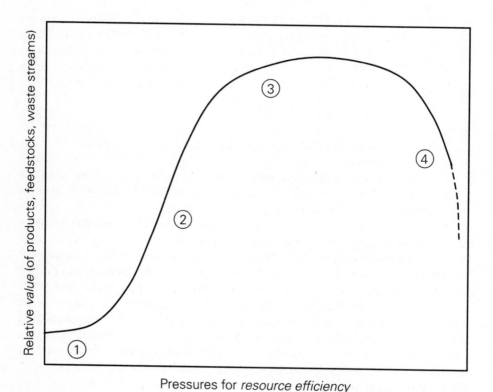

Figure 12.1 *Schematic representation of the relationship between relative value and resource efficiency*

We can thus distinguish between four basic categories of corporate behaviour in terms of the value in waste streams, products and feedstock, each of which is associated with different approaches to environmental issues. These were:

1 Activities such as brewing and paper with products or feedstocks with low per unit value, where wastes consequently had little market value, and where any attempts to minimize waste streams tended to be a result of regulatory rather than market pressure.
2 Activities with moderate or high value products or feedstocks, but where resource efficiency has not been a necessary competitive feature to date, such as the dairy sector, in which the attempts to retain the value currently being lost in waste streams had hitherto been sporadic.
3 Activities with high value products or feedstocks, such as petro-chemicals, in which resource efficiency is already a key competitive feature. This is characteristic of a technologically advanced, mature international market.
4 Activities with very high value products, such as pharmaceuticals, in which resource efficiency is a less important competitive factor than product quality.

This categorization allows us to understand the different kinds of environmental response adopted. The finding that the relative importance of regulatory and economic considerations varies between these groups also suggests that different types of intervention might be most effective in particular circumstances and in bringing about particular kinds of clean technology response. We consider each in turn:

1 Cases involving waste streams with low per unit value

Cases in the brewing, paper, sugar and plating sectors generally fall into this category. In these cases any environmental change was stimulated primarily by regulatory requirements (including public charges for the use of water and for waste water treatment). The main motive was to comply with limits on emissions (or reduce disposal charges) rather than to *recover* the value in the waste stream.

Responses to new environmental requirements typically involved end-of-pipe treatment (eg UK Paper Mill 1). We can also consider with this group initiatives to extract waste from waste waters (eg in DK Fine Chemicals) which were closer to end-of-pipe controls than cleaner technology. In this group we also find some cases of recycling waste and recycling water and sludges within the production process (as in the case of UK Paper Mill 2) where this was done in order to reduce waste disposal volumes. If there was an economic motive, it was to reduce disposal charges or water costs (or anticipated costs as in the Irish Brewery), rather than to recover value in the waste stream.

We can also consider with this group cases involving external recycling of zero value and low value products, such as biomass from biological waste water treatment plants (eg UK Paper Mill 1) and biotechnology processes (eg DK Pharmaceuticals). This was partly undertaken to improve the public image of the firm, although it did also reduce waste treatment and disposal costs; DK Pharmaceuticals generated relatively large volumes of waste biomass and found it cheaper to give this away than to treat or send it for disposal. Such behaviour could therefore be promoted by increasing the charges for landfill and the loading of liquid wastes.[7]

2 Initiatives to retrieve value from waste streams: cases involving moderate or high value products or feedstocks, where resource efficiency has not hitherto been a key competitive feature

This is an intermediate and transitional group, in which resource efficiency has not been fully institutionalized. This could arise as a result of a number of factors:

- where cost pressures had been moderate; or
- where the sector had been protected from competition and was not mature.

Several cases from the dairy sector fell into this category. This included an instance involving the development of a new product (IRL Dairy) in which a high value product (milk minerals) was derived from what had formerly been a low value waste stream, together with two cases where improved techniques were adopted, leading to reduction in the loss of a high value product (UK Dairy and NL Dairy). In these cases, there were powerful cost incentives to stimulate action to retain the value that was being lost in waste streams. The interesting question, of course, is why such changes had only recently been introduced. This highlights the fact that we cannot assume that the value in waste streams is always recognized. It is perhaps no coincidence that these cases were in the dairy industry; an industry with a traditionally established product range, which in the past has had a largely local focus and relatively low levels of market and technical sophistication. However recent trends in the sector have been geared towards cost-cutting through economies of scale and rationalization and attempts to improve value-added through product diversification.[8] It was also clear that changes in the culture and management practices of the firms were an important feature in every case. Earlier product diversification in the Irish case had established a successful business model which could then be further applied in search for new markets for otherwise wasted materials. In contrast, the UK dairy had simply been working to satisfy the growing market for mozzarella cheese; here the stimulus to change was the action of the sewage treatment authority in prosecuting infringements and suggesting opportunities for waste minimization, which had stimulated awareness within the firm about the value of materials that were being wasted. This eventually developed into a change of culture and a larger programme of waste minimization. We can see these cases as being in transition towards resource and environmental awareness, though perhaps at different stages in this process.[9]

Such developments could be facilitated by education and awareness initiatives. These could include, for example, better management training, demonstrator programmes and help with the assessments of mass-balance and 'value-balance' within the firm. Regulators could play an important role here, particularly in relation to smaller firms with lower levels of technical and managerial expertise. Waste disposal charges, too, clearly have potential value as catalysts of change amongst firms with little environmental awareness.

Dairying has been a relatively traditional industry, which has been going through a process of diversification and rationalization. It would seem that, as the sector matures and competitive pressures intensify, resource efficiency could become more institutionalized. Similar kinds of industrial concentration and rationalization can be seen to have provided the basis for commercially driven improvements in resource efficiency in DK Sugar (and other cases from the sugar and brewing sectors).

3 Cases involving high value products or feedstocks, in which resource efficiency is already a key competitive feature

Cases in this group involved technologically sophisticated firms, operating within globally competitive markets, synthesizing high value products from high value feedstocks. They represent mature sectors, in which continuing product and process improvement is pursued through a sustained research and development effort. In our sample these were represented by cases from the fine chemicals and petro-chemicals sector. They had undertaken incremental (eg IRL Fine Chemicals, UK Fine Chemicals), and more radical (eg NL Chemicals 1, NL Chemicals 2) changes in process technology. The last two involved process simplification, a relatively long-term response that was driven by a combination of environmental and economic reasons and involving a more sustained level of R&D, while the UK Fine Chemical case was a simpler process optimization, based on a lower level of initial development, and motivated by the need for immediate savings.

These are mature, highly competitive sectors, and the effective utilization of resources and energy plays a key part in the competitive dynamic driving these sectors. In these contexts 'good' technology is 'clean' technology; indeed it is not always clear how cleaner technology might differ from conventional technology. Efficient resource utilization is strongly institutionalized, within chemical engineering expertise and the highly formalized planning of production in these sectors.

Some of the projects studied were initiated for commercial reasons (NL Chemicals 1, NL Chemicals 2, UK Chemicals), and were not necessarily seen as environmental initiatives. The key differences within this grouping are less related to sectoral boundaries (there are few clear distinctions between 'petro-chemicals' and 'fine chemicals') than to the scale of production. The important distinction lies between smaller-scale batch and larger-scale continuous process production. The latter is characterized by substantial levels of fixed capital investment design. The configuration of plant is also relatively fixed, and expensive to change except during periodic plant replacements (technological inseparability). Batch production, in contrast, may involve more flexible combinations of devices (which are often generic). This allows greater flexibility in changing processes.

The conclusion is that the industry may well be utilizing resources very efficiently, for competitive as much as environmental reasons, and environmental considerations are already being taken on board increasingly in the design of future production processes. Measures may be needed to link environmental and economic concerns more closely in corporate decision-making. There is an important implication for public policy, which is that regulators should recognize and seek to reinforce these useful trends that are already under way.

4 Cases involving very high value products, in which resource efficiency is a less important competitive factor than product quality

This category relates to the cases in this study from the pharmaceuticals sector. This sector exhibited a wide range of case types and outcomes. The distinguishing feature of this category is that the value in waste streams (or even raw materials) is not critical to competition. The main competitive feature is the efficacy of the product, which has a high value (relative to the costs of raw materials and wastes) sustained by patent protection. For the manufacturing plants studied, therefore, the key issue was to guarantee the quality of the product. Process efficiency was not necessarily such a priority, and environmental pressures were not generally critical (partly because the production and waste volumes were moderate compared to the larger-scale activities of other chemical manufacture). There were cases where firms sought to improve their performance, for reasons which appeared to be closely tied up with the development and maintenance of a green image. NL Pharmaceuticals, for example, engaged in a search for aqueous-based chemistry in place of the use of organic solvents. At the other extreme, UK Pharmaceuticals gave little evidence of any motive to change their processes. Their primary consideration, as one of the largest suppliers of legal narcotics in the world, was the security of their products and premises against theft and intrusion.

THE INTERACTION OF ECONOMIC AND REGULATORY FACTORS

We now explore the interaction between economic and regulatory factors in shaping industry behaviour and responses to environmental pressures. We can broadly characterize sectors in terms of the level of institutionalization of regulatory pressures (notwithstanding differences between countries, resulting from their particular histories and circumstances). Thus we can distinguish sectors in which regulatory pressures are generally low (Brewing, Sugar, Dairy), weakly institutionalized (Paper, Plating), and strongly institutionalized (Fine Chemicals, Petro-chemicals, Refining and Pharmaceuticals).[10] We can map this against the differing extent to which competition is based on resource efficiency (largely a function of the ratio of (perceived) value of products versus waste streams/ feedstocks), which we laid out earlier. The result, summarized in Figure 12.2, shows something of the interaction between regulatory pressures and resource efficiency pressures.

REGULATORY PRESSURES

RESOURCE EFFICIENCY	Low	Weakly Institutionalized	Strongly Institutionalized
Low	*Reluctant* Brewing	*Reactive* Paper-making Plating	
Increasingly recognized	Dairy	Sugar	Pharmaceuticals
High			*Proactive* Fine chemicals Petrochemicals Refining

Figure 12.2 *The interaction between regulatory pressures and resource efficiency pressures*

This shows a group of chemical industry sectors (fine chemicals, petro-chemicals, refining) with very similar features in so far as regulatory pressures and commercial pressures combine to encourage a proactive response to environmental concerns, and the adoption of resource efficient solutions. The pharmaceuticals sector was similar in terms of regulatory pressures, but had less economic incentive to adopt 'cleaner' solutions, and there was no clear pattern to the environmental responses adopted. This does not mean that pharmaceuticals cannot move towards cleaner production, as we saw in the case of NL Pharmaceuticals, which began to focus on its economic benefits after adopting a cleaner production initiative.

At the other extreme, in the brewing sector, relatively low regulatory pressures and the low value of waste streams provided little incentive for environmental improvement, let alone the adoption of cleaner approaches. The sugar sector, was intermediate between these groups, facing somewhat greater regulatory pressures and with an established dynamic of efficiency improvement.

In the dairy sector, though regulation was not generally an important pressure for change, a competitive dynamic was being established around product and process innovation, that was stimulating moves towards resource efficiency, though lack of awareness of the scope for such developments was a potential obstacle.

In the plating and paper-making industries, regulatory pressures have been increasing (though are still as yet only weakly institutionalized within the sector), while the low value of wastes provided little incentive to change. The result was a 'reactive' response to regulation – of complying with regulations – mainly through the adoption of end-of-pipe treatment.

This mapping exercise, in addressing regulatory and resource efficiency incentives, and the extent to which these were institutionalized, also has a bearing upon how organizations responded to these exigencies, and especially the types of specialist knowledge they needed to deploy. This throws light on how access to expertise emerged as an important secondary factor according to the particular circumstances of the firm/sector. It did not seem to be a problem, for example, in the chemical industry, where relatively large establishments, often part of global corporations, had substantial internal R&D and other specialized facilities. However it did emerge as a potentially important constraint in relation to SMEs, and thus figured in sectors such as plating, paper and dairies in which small firms prevailed. Expertise issues were most noted in those sectors (and parts of sectors) in which a lack of market and technological dynamism had provided little incentive for firms to develop in house capabilities. However, not all small firms suffered from lack of expertise; the effects of lack of internal expertise could be mediated where firms had effective links with external sources of expertise, notably from regulators, peers or suppliers.

Policy implications: the different tasks of regulation

Figure 12.2, by differentiating the factors which might stimulate environmental responses, and cleaner technology in particular, also shows how different kinds of stimuli might be particularly relevant in improving the environmental responses of particular kinds of firm. This has important policy implications. It suggests that the tasks for regulation and policy intervention differ between sectors depending on their location on these two dimensions. Specific types of intervention may prove optimal in terms of improving environmental performance and integrating it with process improvements. We can recap these as follows:

> *In the* bottom right *segment, resource efficiency and environmental improvement are both well entrenched (though consideration should be given towards how to integrate these elements).* In this segment (occupied by our chemical industry sectors), economic and regulatory incentives both reinforce the pursuit of resource efficiency, to which end considerable internal expertise is deployed (though occupational and organizational barriers may impede integrated approaches).

In pharmaceuticals there are pressures to comply with regulation, but no generally recognized economic signals to orient these towards cleaner technology.

In the top left *segment, the aim of policy should be to both motivate environmental improvement and push it towards more resource efficient responses.* The low environmental pressures and lack of economic incentive to economize on low value waste streams provide little incentive to change. There may be a role for tougher regulation, both to *motivate* change and to *direct* this towards cleaner responses. Here, and in the other sectors with low value waste streams, such as paper and plating, increasing charges for resource use and waste disposal may be doubly effective, in motivating environmental improvement and pushing it towards resource efficiency.

In the top right *segment, the need to comply with regulation is becoming accepted, but environmental responses may need to be directed towards cleaner approaches.* For example, in the paper and plating sectors end-of-pipe solutions have often prevailed (in a context in which many small firms have lacked the technical resources and access to external knowledge to develop more innovative responses). Initiatives by regulators have succeeded in stimulating the adoption of cleaner technologies. In this segment there may be a need to consider how public policy might shift environmental responses towards the adoption of cleaner technologies, for example by considering how regulation is drafted and implemented as well as other public interventions to develop and disseminate alternatives to end-of-pipe solutions.

In the middle left *segment, a transition towards greater resource efficiency has begun, but this needs to be encouraged (eg by the catalyst of environmental regulation or waste disposal charges).* In sectors like dairying (and to a lesser extent sugar), where there have been some shifts towards product diversification and improved resource efficiency (in order to retain some of the value previously lost in waste streams), it would be helpful to reinforce and accelerate this process by measures such as consultancy and awareness initiatives.

Table 12.2 summarizes the situation in these various groups of sectors in terms of their responsiveness to environmental issues and the obstacles to change.

THE ORGANIZATION

Decision-making and the managerial division of labour and knowledge

The two preceding sections have demonstrated the importance of both direct and indirect regulatory pressures in stimulating environmental improvements, and the role of economic factors in shaping the selection of industrial processes

Table 12.2 *Responsiveness to environmental issues*

Proactive: resource efficiency institutionalized

Chemicals Fine Chemicals Petro-chemical Refining	Receptive to change if it can be incorporated into long-term planning. This encourages some firms to position themselves ahead of current regulatory requirements. Reputation and positioning are important and the sector responds to disasters. There is an established dynamic of technological development and improvement in process control and efficiency, particularly in the most competitive markets (eg refining). Large-scale capital-intensive operations and technical inseparability of processes can lead to technology lock in and inhibit incremental change. Some firm cultures have stabilized around end-of-pipe solutions

Proactive: measures needed to encourage resource efficiency

Pharmaceuticals	Little incentive to improve process efficiency as process costs are marginal and process change may lead to unwelcome interruption in production and uncertainties about product quality. Product quality is paramount (both because of market pressures and the emphasis of the regulatory regime) and many firms scale up laboratory procedures for production rather than re-optimizing. There is little incentive to incorporate environmental criteria in production

Reluctant: low regulatory pressure; economic incentives stimulate shift to improved resource efficiency

Dairy	A generally traditional sector, with a low level of public concern and low regulatory pressure. Competitive dynamics are starting to stimulating product diversification and improved resource efficiency, and some are looking to recover potentially high value from otherwise wasted streams. There is a lack of information about techniques and technologies Hygiene standards can discourage change

Reluctant: little economic or regulatory pressure

Brewing	Industry generally reluctant to change, due to the slow rate of equipment renewal of its capital-intensive operations, plus the low level of public concern and low regulatory pressures deriving from the traditional image of its products and processes (though the latter tends to engender a positive attitude to environmental issues). There are (relatively mild) economic pressures to improve efficiency eg of water-use. Opportunities for significant upgrades of equipment are rare, given the problems of retrofitting old plant and buildings, and the age of a plant is a major determinant of current resource efficiency
Sugar	Generally compliance-oriented. The sector has been under public pressure on smell and noise issues, and the waste water has high levels of silt, nitrogen, phosphorus and BOD. There are also economic incentives to improve process efficiency (eg of energy-intensive evaporation). Industrial concentration has created the basis for increasing the scale and improved technologies/process efficiency of plants.

Reactive: measures needed to encourage resource efficiency

Paper	Generally compliance-oriented. The sector is under considerable pressure from both regulators and the public to reduce its emissions to water; pulping and de-inking cause major problems. A relatively undynamic sector. There are problems of retrofitting in old plant and buildings. There is limited dissemination of ideas and techniques, leading to uneven uptake of available technologies.
Plating	Now under considerable pressure to reduce emissions of zinc, nickel, cyanide and other heavy metals. Poor environmental history; often bad relationships with regulators, with little dialogue. Many small companies in the sector, with limited internal R&D capacity

and the kinds of environmental response adopted. One of the most striking findings of the study, however, is that the ways in which firms respond to these pressures are not simply determined by these external stimuli, but are strongly mediated by the internal structures and decision-making processes of the firm. The behaviour of the firms studied could not be reduced to a simple economic or technical rationality, but was, for example, subject to internal politics and conditioned by the particular accounting procedures of the firm. Decision-making structures, the repertoire of existing management and engineering practices, and the availability of knowledge to support these shaped the ways in which decisions were made.

Thus although it is clear that regulatory pressure is critically important in initiating change and in shaping priorities, it is equally clear that this does not necessarily determine the outcome. Even with a dimension as apparently straightforward and well understood as economic considerations, for example, there were a number of ancillary issues as to how cost and market information was handled within the firm, depending on its internal structure and management practices. It is essential, therefore, to examine the structure and the detailed process of decision-making in the firm if we are to understand why regulatory and economic pressures stimulate proactive change and more innovative 'cleaner' solutions in some cases, but result in reactive or end-of-pipe solutions in others.

The decision-making process

We found that the *process* of organizational decision-making was the most immediate factor shaping a firm's response to a given challenge. Corporate decision-making is characterized by 'bounded rationality' (Simon, 1982). Decisions are made under circumstances of uncertainty and incomplete information. Ideas about the problems the firm faces and possible solutions are also incomplete and partial, and may be contested between different groups within the firm. We explore several related dimensions of this process: *information inductance* (the influence of existing information practices and decision criteria), the *entrenchment of practices, expertise structures* (the division of labour and knowledge), *organizational politics* (and the individuals and groups who support projects), *head office/ branch plant relationships* and the way this shapes *access to finance.*

The information inductance effect
Every firm has to make a number of decisions as to which performance indicators are important, and which it should therefore measure and which it should not. These decisions embody a number of conscious and unconscious assumptions about the firm and its business, and about the wider environment in which the firm operates. Evaluation and reporting procedures, once adopted, pattern the kind of information that is selected and reported in future. Similarly, decision-making structures and routines, developed in order to deal with a particular task, may tend to predispose to certain kinds of outcome. More fundamentally, evaluation and reporting procedures can create an 'information inductance' effect.

This means that the information that an individual or group is required to report will influence its behaviour as actors seek to produce actions which, when recorded by the information systems, will appear creditable.

One of the striking findings of the study was how much scope for highly cost-effective beneficial improvement had been overlooked, in many cases, simply because firms did not have the necessary information systems in place. These situations would tend to persist until some trigger event brought the situation to light and thus stimulated a re-evaluation of the cost of inaction and the potential benefits of change. There is no particular reason to believe that we are anywhere near the limit of the scope for such benign improvements in many sectors of industry.

At UK Dairy, for example, intervention by the sewage treatment authority set off a significant long-term process of change. A minor re-appraisal of the information systems led to the realization of a resource loss that had gone undetected and unrecognized for some time. This in turn led to the development of a more sophisticated information collection system, which then enabled further waste minimization. This process brought about a change in the behaviour of employees, as they were required to report on items that had previously been disregarded. *The introduction of better monitoring and control systems, helped to make a particular long-standing problem (the loss of large quantities of cheese and whey down the sewer) more salient.* This case provides a particularly clear example of a general phenomenon: as corporate reporting systems tend to select for certain categories of information, so other categories of information, and associated problem diagnoses and solutions, may become less visible. It is clearly possible for some problems – or at least the true extent of some problems – to remain invisible and undetected.

The importance of the internal reporting system can also be seen in the case of the Irish Brewery. A corporate benchmarking exercise, initiated by the parent company, highlighted the scope for improvement and stimulated a local exercise in water use reduction.

The entrenchment of practices
There is also a strong tendency for particular problem solving repertoires to become embedded (Clark and Staunton, 1989). Procedures developed many years ago, at a time when environmental issues were of less general concern, may continue to be followed until there is a sufficiently compelling reason to change. Our cases showed a number of factors which could overcome the organizational inertia and catalyse such a reassessment, including internal factors such as changes in ownership, or some external challenge, such as a change in the regulatory regime. At UK Fine Chemicals, established operating procedures embedded the priorities and values that prevailed when the production process was designed (in one case, several decades earlier) when resource costs and environmental concerns were both much lower. The plant had a huge range of products. Relatively dirty processes had run for many years. In this case the re-assessment of working practices was stimulated by a desire to reduce the cost of a planned waste water treatment plant. The true extent of the scope for

improvement only became apparent when the plant started monitoring its 600 different waste streams properly for the first time.

As this case shows, dirty practices and procedures may become entrenched and may then persist, unchallenged, until there is some trigger for change. This can be internally or externally generated. As we have seen, internal information can itself serve as a trigger for change (eg about the value of waste streams). External events can also provoke a reassessment of practices and assumptions (Pettigrew, 1985). For example several petro-chemical companies took relatively rapid steps to improve the environmental control systems in their own plants in the aftermath of the Exxon Valdez disaster. Events of this magnitude permeated the consciousness of the chemical industry as a whole, worldwide. They stimulated a wider change in public perception, and acquired a symbolic importance as milestones in changing awareness, attitudes and acceptance of certain industries and industrial practices. Such critical events may thus promote relatively radical change in the culture of the firms in that sector. Such visible events are rare; the impact of smaller-scale events tended to be more localized, and perhaps limited to the operating plant itself (for example UK Refinery's conspicuous environmental project in the form of an expensive waste treatment plant appeared to be related to earlier incidents on that site, including a spillage and a fire).

Conversely, the question arises about how cleaner technology approaches can be entrenched. Some firms appear to have developed a culture of innovation and a self-generating momentum for further improvement and change. Irish Dairy, for example, has a history of innovation and environmental improvement, which now appears to be institutionalized. Developments are driven proactively by internal strategy, and oriented to market opportunities, rather than being in reaction to external factors such as regulatory compliance. UK Dairy appears to be moving rapidly in the same direction, but is still in a process of transition from being reactive. What started with a limited response to regulatory pressure, has gradually developed into a more systematic process of re-evaluation of the firm's basic routines.

Expertise structures

The extent of internal expertise and its distribution across the corporate structure was a key influence upon organizational decision-making. This division of expert labour tends to vary by size. Large firms are more likely to have the necessary internal expertise to deal with most of their environmental challenges. They are also more likely to have the internal R&D capacity to develop solutions to particular problems. However this functional specialization can also cause internal barriers to flows of information within the organization (Burns and Stalker, 1961). Problems may be seen to 'belong' to particular groups. This may inhibit a more holistic and open search for solutions and may thus result in 'solution lock-in'. One example was the UK Refinery. It wanted a demonstrably 'green' solution. Its choice of an end-of-pipe solution was related to the fact that the company possessed world-class expertise in design of waste water treatment plants for refineries.

In contrast, small firms often have a lower internal division of labour and expertise, and greater reliance on sources of external expertise. Potentially, therefore, SMEs could be more open to novel approaches to environmental challenges, including the adoption of cleaner technologies.[11]

The content and organization of a firm's core expertise has important implications for the likelihood of cleaner technology being implemented. The core expertise of particular industrial sectors stems from the nature of the industrial processes carried out, as well as from the market conditions. Industrial activities differ in terms of their internal technical complexity. Changing highly complex operations – for example in the chemical industry – may require a considerable basis of technical knowledge. However the refineries and larger chemical industry operations have substantial internal research and development capacity. Moreover, the industry's core expertise in these sectors may incorporate precisely those skills needed to devise cleaner approaches. Chemical engineering is a case in point, involving sophisticated techniques for assessing and optimizing the resource efficiency of industrial processes as part of the normal requirements of ensuring commercial success. This body of expertise is also evolving, so that future generations of engineers are likely to be increasingly aware of the health and environmental implications of their activities.

An important issue concerns the way that different kinds of knowledge are deployed. If environmental concerns are not fully integrated with the core productive expertise then environmental improvement is likely to be sought from an end-of-pipe solution. In this way, the establishment of a separate environmental function within the firm may, paradoxically, inhibit cleaner approaches if that group's expertise lies in traditional environmental treatment methods and does not encompass detailed knowledge about the plant's processes. The search for cleaner technologies depends critically on knowledge of the existing activities of the firm and industry.[12]

Organizational politics and project champions
The firm can be understood as an alliance of groups and individuals, with diverse expertise and approaches to solving the firm's problems. Groups compete to consolidate their position in particular realms (eg technical specialisms) or to gain greater control over the overall corporate agenda. An important factor in the search for improved environmental performance, and cleaner technology in particular, concerns the extent to which these ideas are taken up within the occupational strategies, career and professional interests of particular individuals or groups.

Some interesting examples can be found in the dairy sector, which appears to have been undergoing a dual transition involving product diversification and growing awareness of the scope for better resource utilization and cleaner production. In the Irish dairy the specialized marketing department and R&D department were able to carry forward the search for new outlets for current waste products (milk minerals). In UK Dairy these approaches were not established at the outset. *However the local manager most closely involved saw an opportunity to generalize lessons from an initiative stimulated by the regulator into a more far-reaching programme of waste minimization and ultimately of Total Quality Management for the whole firm (in a context in which the Canadian-based owners were willing to allow considerable local autonomy).* In this way the individual concerned has consolidated his position, while cleaner approaches have been taken up and incorporated within the firm's agenda.

In larger firms, with more established divisions of labour, there may be less scope for an individual to exert such a span of control. An important factor is the extent to which cleaner approaches were taken up by particular occupational or organizational groups, or whether environmental issues were seen as a marginal. In UK Fine Chemicals, the search for clean technology was initiated by the Process Technology Department – a group whose role and expertise arguably would be enhanced by this addition to their competences. They seem to have been more influential than the Health Safety and Environment (HSE) function who continued to be more oriented towards waste water treatment.

Head office–branch relationships and corporate policy
Many of our cases were at the level of the operating branch plant of a larger (often multinational) enterprise, as this is the level at which cleaner options will be implemented. However, the relationship between the branch/plant and corporate headquarters had important implications for environmental policies and for access to technical resources and finance.

In some cases the environmental agenda for the firm was driven by corporate environmental policy. This tends to ensure that all the plants in a corporate group operate to a minimum standard (which may well be higher than strictly required in some regions). Changes in ownership were thus often associated with changes in approach to environmental issues (at DK Fine Chemicals, for example, the new American owners gave a higher priority and greater attention to meeting regulatory requirements which had been resisted by the old management regime, who had seen them as imposing additional costs). There may also be drawbacks from head office involvement. Headquarters staff are not always in the best position to be aware of local problems, opportunities and the reservoir of potential innovation within each plant. A degree of knowledge of local conditions is needed in order to be able to identify the scope for waste minimization and external recycling/industrial symbiosis. In comparison to end-of-pipe approaches, which can more readily be handled centrally,[13] the search for cleaner innovations imposes a greater decision-load and uncertainties (in so far as it is less well established and requires greater knowledge of local conditions). Where head office are setting the pace of environmental responses, this may tend to favour the certainty that can be offered by end-of-pipe solutions. The case of DK Fine Chemicals also provides some support for such a view. As part of its engagement in a clean technology programme it had been exempted by the regional regulator from fulfilling certain regulatory requirements. However they encountered difficulties in explaining this to their head office in the US who required all their plants, in the US and abroad, to provide a certificate of their environmental performance including their compliance with regulatory requirements.

Head office–branch plant relations have complex implications for environmental response. Some kinds of cleaner approach (such as low-cost improvements in housekeeping and changes in working practices to minimize waste and cut costs) were available to branch plants without requiring head office support (eg UK Dairy). But more substantial development (for example the search for radical changes in process technology in NL Chemicals 1 and NL Chemicals 2) generally requires more substantial top level commitment.

Access to finance

The relationship between the corporate structure and the individual plant also has significant implications for the access to finance. This turns out to be an important factor, but not necessarily in the way that might be predicted. Interestingly, lack of finance can promote waste minimization measures which can often be adopted with the expenditure of limited time and cost. Given the high costs of waste water treatment plants, capital shortages can have the apparently paradoxical effect of encouraging the adoption of waste minimization in preference to end-of-pipe controls. This was explicitly the case in the UK Dairy, where the search for waste minimization followed the refusal of the Canadian parent company to sanction investment in an expensive waste water treatment plant. Fiscal stringency, and the adoption of an internal market, also encouraged waste minimization in UK Fine Chemicals, where this could significantly cut operating costs, and reduce the size and cost of the planned waste water treatment plant.

Experiences in the nearby UK Refinery points to the complexity of the relationship between external economics and internal politics. The fact that Health Safety and Environment (HSE) investment was sourced from company-wide capital budgets, rather than branch plant operating costs, created an incentive for local managers to try to maximize investment in their plant thereby securing their plant's future in a context of global overcapacity and anticipated closures in the industry. Given that the company was seeking to enhance its environmental image, the result was 'conspicuous compliance': a large and expensive end-of-pipe treatment works, which had the advantage of being highly visible. This was pursued in preference to a number of potentially cost-effective good housekeeping measures and incremental changes in process technology. This course of action, while appearing to be irrational on technical or economic grounds, made sense in terms of both the internal politics and the public presentation of the organization.

The terrain for decision-making

The terrain for the decision-making process in the firm is also shaped by a set of features that we describe as structural factors, relating to the nature of the operations carried out in the firm/sector. Following on from this we also address the knowledge links between the firm and external players.

The cases studied were all process industries, with relatively large, and sometimes very large, amounts of fixed plant. There were however important differences between sectors (or, as already noted, between groups of sectors depending on the different scale of production across our chemical industry cases). These 'structural factors' include the capital intensity of the operation, the technical complexity of processes and the length of the capital renewal cycle, which in turn had important implications for the sophistication of the process of planning change, the depth and array of expertise involved.

Size and the position of small and medium sized enterprises (SMEs)

Even though process industries tend to be larger, capital-intensive operations, there were a number of SMEs in the sample of cases (DK and NL Plating, Irish Dairy, Irish Refinery, UK Pharmaceuticals, UK Paper Mill 2). Some operations, though owned by larger groups, were relatively autonomous and resembled SMEs in their situation and behaviour (eg UK Dairy).

The size of the plant or the parent company per se did not seem to favour cleaner or end-of-pipe approaches. Thus SMEs and branches of large multinational corporations are both represented amongst firms adopting more thoroughgoing cleaner technology initiatives, and amongst firms adopting more conventional end-of-pipe solutions. Firm size is correlated with a number of factors, without itself being causal. Size matters, but it matters in a number of different, contingent ways. In particular, as already noted, it has an important influence upon the extent of expertise resources, and upon divisions of labour, knowledge and power, and thus the internal politics of the firm. Lack of internal expertise resources, weak links with external sources of expertise, and shortages of capital were key issues for *some* SMEs (and some larger firms that resembled SMEs). However, other SMEs had acquired these resources where competitive conditions required them (eg Irish Refinery, Irish Dairy), despite being small.

Scale of process, technological complexity and capital intensity

Large-scale, capital intensive operations are more susceptible to technology lock-in, particularly where production equipment involves 'technological inseparabilities': where plant takes the form of large pieces of fixed capital which, in their design or their implemented configuration, are dedicated to particular processes and parameters. This may reduce the scope for reconfiguring the plant and its activities; for example to meet stricter environmental standards. Scope for change may be substantial during intermittent plant renewal (or in 'greenfield' developments), but is limited in between these periods. For example, in our brewing cases, a key influence over water use efficiency was how recently plant had been installed. And in the refinery sector, certain kinds of changes were seen as commercially and environmentally desirable (eg 'pinch' technologies to optimize energy and water efficiency), but could only be adopted to a limited degree within the physical constraints of existing fixed plant and layout.

Lock-in is not just a technical matter, but depends upon the range and depth of expertise deployed. Where large and complex operations call for a high level of functional specialization, organizational practices can become ossified around established methods and procedures and allocations of roles between specialist groups, resulting in 'solution-lock in'. This can serve to make them less flexible than smaller operations (with a lower division of labour) and might, for example, inhibit the search for more innovative and holistic cleaner solutions.

Large-scale, capital intensive operations also tend to have a longer capital equipment renewal cycle, which in turn necessitates a longer planning horizon.

The planning horizon and the capital renewal cycle

High fixed capital costs and the inherent delay entailed in significant plant upgrades or replacements may create a significant lag-time before regulatory and market pressures are fully reflected in plant design. These considerations apply particularly to the large-scale production end of the chemical sectors: oil refineries and petro-chemicals.

Differences between firms and sub-sectors in batch size, technological inseparabilities and the level of fixed capital affect the speed at which technological change is implemented, since it is often cheaper to implement changes, including improvements in environmental performance, when capital equipment is being renewed, rather than trying to retrofit existing fixed plant. The nature of the product market, and the dynamics of competition are critical here. For example, a specialist electronic engineering firm, operating in a dynamic product market, might change its capital equipment base over some four years. A distillery, in contrast, might still be using equipment dating from the last century.

These factors relate in turn to the planning horizon adopted by firms. In capital-intensive operations, particularly where this takes the form of pieces of large dedicated plant, the pace of change is more likely to be determined by the length of the capital renewal cycle. The enormous investment in fixed plant required in the refinery sector obliges firms to plan over 10 years ahead or more. The more sophisticated of these firms are already incorporating environmental factors into their long-term planning, particularly regarding anticipated regulatory change affecting product markets and future compliance requirements which may affect their ability to 'stay in business'. In contrast, firms in the dairy sector could operate with a planning horizon measured in months.[14]

The competitiveness and dynamism of the market were also important factors in this regard. Firms operating in dynamic and rapidly evolving markets devoted considerable resources to market intelligence, to monitoring technological developments and to modelling future conditions. Firms that engaged in such long-term planning of their technologies and markets (especially in sectors like refining, where even maintenance had to fit within infrequent planned shutdowns) were forced to carry out sophisticated economic and operational assessments of procedures. Processes were subject to detailed advance planning and assessment. As a result, resource efficiency (and increasingly environmental concerns) would be built-in to future solutions. However, as the refinery sector also indicates, long-term planning does not invariably mean that firms will adopt more radical cleaner solutions; where improvements were needed in environmental standards before the next plant upgrading the result could be the implementation of end-of-pipe solutions.

Knowledge networks

Firms operate within broader networks – of competing firms, customers, suppliers, regulators, broader publics – which are an important source of information and influence.

The extent to which firms sought to develop networks to keep informed of R&D and broader developments in other firms and countries seemed to depend largely on the extent and nature of competition in their product markets. For example, while the pharmaceutical sector as a whole showed a high level of networking and awareness of developments elsewhere, UK Pharmaceuticals, which had an established and protected market, was isolated and self-referential. It found little incentive to change its methods of operation and consequently sought little information. Similarly, though oil refining was largely dominated by large firms serving international markets and international in outlook, the one firm in the study that had a semi-protected domestic market (Irish Refinery) was more self-referential, with what resembled a small firm mentality. Size and industrial structure were important. Electroplating was the clearest example of a sector made up of relatively small operations, with no overall dominant operator. The firms studied lacked internal R&D capacity, had a limited range of internal expertise, and were largely self-referential in outlook.

Under these circumstances, external sources of trusted information, for example from suppliers or regulators, were potentially important. Here some sources of information were seen as more authoritative or credible than others. Most of the Scottish companies, for example, trusted their industry bodies, but were more sceptical about the information available from regulatory bodies or from the research and higher education sector. In comparison, their counterparts in the other regions studied (Denmark and The Netherlands in particular) tended to have more links to external sources of ideas and expertise (such as universities), while the Cork Cleaner Technology Centre in Ireland served as a forum for the development and exchange of ideas between companies and academics.

The importance of such networks in the search for innovative and cleaner technological solutions gives special emphasis to public initiatives in cleaner technology that revolve around collaboration between firms and academics (eg the Clean Technology Centre in Ireland, the PRISMA initiatives in The Netherlands, the INES (industrial ecosystem project) or the UK Catalyst Project), and between firms and regulators such as SPURT in Denmark and the Dutch sectoral covenants.

We return to these points in Chapter 13 in our discussion of the innovation system.

DECISION-MAKING IN THE FIRM

We now pull together some of these observations about factors shaping the behaviour of firms, to develop a model of the processes of decision-making in relation to its choice of production and environmental control strategies. This draws attention to *uncertainty avoidance*, which has important implications for understanding why firms may choose established 'end-of-pipe' controls, rather than more innovatory, cleaner responses. It in turn indicates the kind of policy setting which may favour one or other development.

Firms make a variety of more or less explicit trade-offs when planning their activities. In general we found a pattern of bounded rationality, with firms undertaking decisions in contexts of incomplete information, uncertainty and indeterminacy. As a result, firms cannot know, let alone pursue, technically and economically optimal solutions. Instead, firms, and groups within them, engage in *satisficing behaviour*. They deploy various strategies to handle the different types of uncertainties inherent in different courses of action, involving complex (often tacit) judgements about the risks and benefits that might be encountered. These have important implications for the firm's environmental responses, and in particular the choices between innovative cleaner technologies/waste minimization versus 'end-of-pipe' solutions.

On technical and economic grounds, cleaner technologies should be the preferred solution, as they seem to offer 'win–win' outcomes of reduced costs and improved environmental performance. This raises questions about why such technologies are not more widely adopted, and why firms continue to build 'end-of-pipe' waste treatment facilities which are expensive to install and run and offer no efficiency improvements.

One important factor is the extent to which (internal and external) costs are perceived and recognized. Within the firm, wastage of materials may not be systematically measured, and may not be internally costed. Thus managers may be unaware of the true costs of inefficiency and wastage, and hence the value of the wasted resources. Recognition of the latter may depend upon additional knowledge, needed, for example, to identify opportunities to market wastes as auxiliary products (as in Irish Dairy). These are real, internal monetary costs, but it is clearly possible for them to go unrecognized.

Fines and other financial costs imposed for breaches of environmental regulations will, on the other hand be clearly visible, even within firms which did not have effective information about the cost of wastes. However, as we saw in the case of UK Paper Mill 2, sewage disposal charges may be accepted as an unpleasant fact of life (until the authority pointed out its different components and how these could be reduced). On the other hand, this case and that of UK Dairy, show that such charges may increase the awareness of firms to the costs of wastes.

Non-monetarized costs are far less likely to be recognized than internalized financial costs in calculating the costs and benefits of different courses of action. Most corporate decision-making is done on a heuristic basis. Many elements are difficult to quantify, let alone put a financial value on. Firms are rarely, if ever, in a position to calculate the full costs and benefits of different courses of action and their inherent risks. Indeed, it should be remembered that cost-saving cleaner innovations represent just a small part of an array of potential improvements all offering a positive return on investment. This reinforces the point made earlier about the need to find mechanisms to improve the coupling between commercially and environmentally oriented improvements in the firm. In a context of uncertainty and incomplete information, traditional decision-making criteria may prevail. Engineers and managers may find it simplest to choose methods of operation on the basis of 'custom and practice', drawing upon a repertoire of established problem diagnoses and solutions. DK Fine Chemicals only recognized the scope to apply their *own* membrane separation technologies to reducing their waste emissions after they became involved in a cleaner technology programme initiated by the regulator. This shows how demonstrator projects and other kinds of initiative aimed at shifting accepted cultures and accepted practices (for example directed towards professional training) may have an important role.

It is also important to bear in mind that managers are juggling with a range of incommensurable considerations. They are forced to make trade-offs between various *non-equivalent* risks. In so doing they adopt de facto forms of risk management strategy. Some outcomes are thus given more prominence than others – for example where they have symbolic or political importance. Firms are likely to give disproportionate weight to the consequences of a highly visible environmental accident[15] or even a publicized failure to comply with regulatory requirements. In such contexts, decision-making will be biased towards the avoidance of uncertainty. There will also be a strong incentive to avoid risks of outcomes which are perceived as serious. This is important in this discussion as such considerations may well favour the continued adoption of tried and tested 'end-of-pipe' solutions.

The adoption of cleaner approaches may involve a number of risks for corporate managers. It may be hard to predict how long it will take to reduce discharges from process improvement. It can therefore be difficult to plan improvements – for example to fit in with impending changes in regulatory requirements. These uncertainties may be greatest where more innovative approaches are being sought. A firm might sponsor a radical R&D programme (for example to find a 'cleaner' synthesis route) but this may prove unsuccessful, forcing the firm to write off the investment without meeting its environmental requirements. These considerations provide a powerful rationale for opting for known solutions, which today will be largely end-of-pipe solutions, even when these might not appear to be the most cost-effective.

The scope and pace of change may, as already noted, be important. Some improvements may be immediately available, for example from good house-keeping and changes in technique. But where more substantial potential benefits have been identified from more comprehensive changes in production processes, this may require a greater innovative effort, taking a longer time and involving greater risks of failure and imposing 'opportunity costs' from the diversion of staff time. For the firm, tested end-of-pipe solutions may seem a safer bet than a potentially difficult and uncertain path towards cleaner approaches.

Under what circumstances would it be worthwhile for firms to seek to innovate cleaner technologies? As we have seen, regulation could be used to promote this directly, by extending the concept of best practice and by explicitly requiring firms to explore waste minimization options. The manner in which regulations are implemented could also be redesigned to help reduce the uncertainties involved. This may require regulators to offer some flexibility in implementing new standards, based on an understanding that the search for more radical innovation to minimize waste may involve uncertainties about how quickly improvements can be achieved. This may in turn require a willingness to offer waivers or temporary suspension of regulatory requirements, so that firms are not penalized if their search for more innovatory and beneficial cleaner processes does not yield results as quickly as had been hoped. Such developments will depend upon the establishment of a *dialogue*, and understanding *between regulators and firms* (and we saw different models of how this could be achieved in Denmark and The Netherlands). Equally, a *predictable regulatory regime* reduces the risk for firms of making an inappropriate investment in technology. It is the framework, rather than the precise standards, which should be stable. To stimulate progressive improvement, emission standards or resource charges could be set to rise steadily for some time ahead (and the lead-in would need to be considerable – say 10 years – for sectors such as refining with a long capital renewal cycle). This would help to shift the balance of costs and benefits for the firm and make more fundamental solutions – such as process redesign to eliminate wastes at source – more attractive. Such an approach could stimulate the firm to integrate environmental improvement into the process of planning its production processes and markets.

Public initiatives to promote flows of information about cleaner technologies and establishment of 'best practice' models could also help counter uncertainty. Both the costs and the risks of clean technology are clearly greatest for first movers in a particular industrial process. Where an innovation has more general applicability, other firms may be able to utilize these experiences, thus reducing their costs and risks. Collaboration between firms may be an important way of sharing the costs and risks of cleaner developments. There may be a case for public support for such R&D, in collaboration with or within industry.

On the other hand it is clear that in some circumstance (eg where resources and waste streams have high value) competitive dynamics already encourage innovation and resource efficiency – for example in sectors such as fine and petro-chemicals. The question then is how to ensure that regulation and public policy complement (rather than inhibit, as in the case of product regulation in pharmaceuticals) the positive dynamics already established within the sector. We return to these questions about the promotion of innovation in more detail in Chapter 13.

CONCLUSIONS

Our broad conclusion is that companies have to be understood as social organizations, operating in a complex arena of opportunities, constraints and pressures, utilizing various heuristics to deal with imperfect information about themselves, their market and their wider environment, and consisting of individuals and groups with their own agendas for change, both within the firm and beyond. If we are to unlock the reserves of latent innovation within firms and achieve a steadily increasing rate of improvement in energy and resource-use efficiency and a steadily diminishing level of environmental impact, we must modify our regulatory and market systems in ways that will both shape the environmental behaviour of firms and encourage the development and dissemination of cleaner solutions.

Our study has shown that regulatory pressure, underpinned by broader pressures within civil society, are the key to stimulating environmental improvements. However we have also shown that the effectiveness of the regulatory system in encouraging such innovation varies between firms and sectors, reflecting variations in regulatory pressure, as well as differences in economic contexts and the particular internal milieu of the firm (particularly its access to expertise). Indeed in some situations, the content and implementation of regulation seems to have impeded the adoption of cleaner responses, and further entrenched existing end-of-pipe solutions.

This further suggests that no single regulatory approach will be equally effective in all circumstances in promoting the innovation of more fundamental sustainable solutions. Instead, the most appropriate manner of encouraging industry to develop cleaner and more effective solutions in response to environmental pressures will vary according to the particular characteristics of the firm and sector. We showed that in some contexts the key issue is (still) to motivate improved environmental performance, while in others it may be to direct such change towards cleaner responses. The latter may depend upon the content of regulatory provision and the manner of its implementation and the role of the regulator. Other possible instruments include the application of increased charges for resource use or waste disposal, creating economic pressure to stimulate greater resource efficiency. In some cases an important constraint may be lack of access to expertise, or even lack of awareness of value of current wastes, suggesting that consultancy services or demonstrator programmes may be effective. The level of awareness of cleaner alternatives is another important factor, which indicates that more general educational programmes would also be helpful.

Different contexts produce different outcomes in terms of environmental response. The use of end-of-pipe engineering controls on environmental hazards remains deeply entrenched within the perceptions and decision criteria of industrialists and regulators alike. Although more radical changes in production processes (and perhaps in products) may hold out much greater long-term benefits – from reduced environmental impacts and reduced costs – these are still largely unproven, and subject to considerable uncertainties. This is a major disincentive to managers, whose desire to avoid the risks of failure may outweigh the benefits of innovatory solutions. Certain features of the regulatory setting and the corporate context could serve to ameliorate such uncertainties. This has important implications, especially for the ways in which regulations are implemented. The development of more collaborative relationships between regulator and firm could be particularly useful. Cooperation between firms and with regulators and public sector research may also help share costs and risks of development.

Cost saving pressure may be an important motive for cleaner innovations, and waste management may best be pursued as part of management efficiency and Quality Management initiatives, rather than environmental initiatives. In some sectors, in which resource efficiency is a major competitive feature, the search to improve resource efficiency may be deeply institutionalized in expertise and decision-making practices. Here the role of regulation may at best be to reinforce such pressures.

These considerations have some important policy implications. We consider first the lessons for the ways in which regulation and public policy are both designed and implemented, before going on finally to consider the differing contexts for public policy intervention.

The design and implementation of regulation

Regulation is the key stimulus to improved environmental performance, but does not necessarily lead to the adoption of cleaner solutions. In some circumstances, regulation may further entrench end-of-pipe approaches, for example through the rapid and inflexible implementation of more stringent emission standards, or through requirements to implement 'best available technology' where an end-of-pipe approach is considered to be the best currently available proven control technology.

Flexible implementation of stricter standards

Emission standards are an important feature of the regulatory armoury. However the manner of their implementation may require consideration if cleaner approaches are to be encouraged. In particular, their rapid and inflexible implementation may give firms little scope to amend existing processes to reduce waste, forcing them to resort to proven end-of-pipe solutions. Regulators need to be able to be flexible about the timescale of their imposition, where cleaner responses remain unproven, and recognize that the search for radical process improvements may be slow and sometimes unsuccessful.

Incorporate waste reduction in provisions for best available technology

Best available technology (BAT or BATNEEC) provisions should be elaborated to give explicit priority to waste minimization over end-of-pipe solutions, and to allow for potentially better clean technologies to be pursued in place of existing end-of-pipe technology. This would represent a significant extension of the concept from the traditional narrow focus on technology per se to include both management and infrastructural issues.

Long-term predictability of regulatory signals

To encourage firms to pursue the potentially greater improvements in environmental performance available from rethinking and redesigning their products and processes, the regulatory environment needs to combine powerful incentives *plus* predictability over time. This might involve announcing a timetable of phased increases in waste treatment charges or in the stringency of emission standards, thus allowing these criteria to be factored-in to the planning and design of new commercial developments. This is particularly relevant for capital intensive industries, with a long capital renewal cycle, where sunk investments and technological inseparabilities may lock firms in to particular plant and processes.

Develop new models for the role of the regulator

The above provisions will involve a more specifically tailored approach to particular firms and sectors. The regulator will need to have greater knowledge of their production technologies, practices and circumstances, in order to assess what is the best available technology, or to appraise a request from a firm for a delay in the implementation of new standards. An important feature of many of the cases of cleaner technology was the development of new kinds of relationship between the regulator and the industry. This involved a shift away from the traditional arms-length policing model of the regulator to a more *collaborative relationship* and one in which regulators saw it as their *mission* to promote cleaner responses.

Regulatory systems differ in structure and operation, and it would be inappropriate to propose a single model. However the *partnership model* that emerged between local authority regulator and firm in (some) Danish counties is particularly interesting. The collective system that has emerged in The Netherlands, based on implicit or formal covenants between the regulator and groups of firms in a sector, also appears to have several advantages, such as the particular benefit of allowing participants to *share the risks* and benefits of improvement overall, and to *trade off* success in some areas against slower progress in more intractable areas.

An important consideration about the relationship between the regulator and firm concerns the balance of expertise between the two. With small and isolated firms, with limited internal R&D capacity and weak knowledge networks, the regulator's expertise can be a valuable resource. In such a situation, a more engaged regulatory style is effective and productive, allowing the regulator to expand their role beyond a limited policing function to an advisory role. Conversely, where firms are large and operating in high-technology areas with strong internal R&D capacity and established knowledge networks, the information imbalance in favour of the regulated firm effectively precludes this option. Here the regulator may need to act as assessor, rather than participant, in the firm's environmental decision-making. The experience in The Netherlands suggests that the regulator can play an important role in determining benchmarks for particular sectors and in assessing movement towards the targets, even though the preponderance of expertise lies within the firms concerned.

Contexts for public policy intervention

Perhaps our most important finding concerns the interaction between regulatory and economic pressures and the supplementary influence of knowledge networks, particularly in relation to:

- the strength of formal and informal regulatory pressures and the extent to which these are institutionalized in the firm;
- the perceived value of resource and waste streams, and the salience of resource efficiency as a competitive dynamic; and
- the organizational context: decision-making structures, internal expertise and links with external sources of information.

These allow us to understand different kinds of cleaner technology and how they were adopted. It also suggests contexts in which particular types of public policy initiative will be most successful in promoting cleaner responses. We summarize these findings below and in Table 12.3.

- *Regulation is important. It may both stimulate environmental improvements and shape these towards cleaner approaches.*

The need for regulation to specifically emphasize cleaner approaches depends in part on the economic dynamics of the firm/sector. Where economic incentives to adopt cleaner responses are weaker, public policy intervention may need to be explicitly directed to encourage the adoption of cleaner technologies; to motivate such a development in areas (eg brewing) where regulatory pressures are moderate and, where regulatory pressures are stronger (such as pharmaceuticals, paper or plating), to channel change towards cleaner responses.

In areas where resource efficiency is an established competitive dynamic (such as the chemicals sectors), this may motivate change, and shape responses to regulatory pressures towards cleaner solutions. Public intervention may be needed where firms lack expertise to realise these possibilities.

- *Education and awareness initiatives may help firms, particularly in smaller and more traditional sectors, to recognize the economic benefits of implementing waste minimization.*

Where such economic pressures are weaker, because waste streams have a low value relative to the product cost, regulation and other policy interventions are crucial:

- *The content and implementation of regulation may need to be explicitly directed towards cleaner responses.*
- *Increasing water and waste disposal charges may help motivate environmental improvements, and channel such responses towards cleaner approaches.*

Access to information is important, but the purposes and manner of information support will vary:

In high-technology sectors, with strong internal expertise resources and external knowledge links, many improvements may be available on the basis of existing technical resources. However, where the search for radical improvements in process technology and products involves potentially large costs and uncertain outcomes, public sector initiatives may be needed to share the costs and risks.

Public sector research could absorb some of the costs and risks. However, such research needs to be closely related to industrial requirements and circumstances, which may best be ensured by collaborative research. Alternatively, public support or other incentives for pooled R&D would help to spread the cost and innovation risk across the participating firms. The regulatory models followed in Denmark and The Netherlands both have the effect of sharing the development costs.

Dissemination of recent developments. Many developments that were new to particular firms, had already been tried and implemented elsewhere. Sectoral level initiatives have an important contribution to spreading knowledge of currently available cleaner solutions. Important experiences in different regions and countries (for example the cyanide-free plating processes in the UK) suggest the need for European-wide arrangements.

In low-technology operations, particularly involving small and isolated firms, with limited internal expertise and poor knowledge networks, *help may be needed in providing* reliable *sources of external advice* to identify opportunities for cleaner technologies (eg the regulator, consultants etc).

The various policy interventions required are summarized in Table 12.3.

Table 12.3 *Differing contexts for policy intervention*

STRONG ECONOMIC INCENTIVES TOWARDS RESOURCE EFFICIENCY

Industries with high value products or feedstocks, in which resource efficiency is already a key competitive feature, such as the chemical industry. Here public policy should seek to augment and support these processes already under way. In the sectors studied, regulatory pressures were also strong and institutionalized within the responses of firms. The key policy concern might be to ensure that regulatory requirements did not inhibit, or divert resources away from, cleaner responses, but were integrated with the existing dynamism of the industry. Shortages of expertise were not a major constraint. Given the potentially high costs of developing cleaner technologies there might be a role for public initiatives to share the costs and risks of research and development, by promoting links with public sector research, or collaboration between firms, or even through public subsidies. Such arguments are likely to be most relevant in relation to radical changes in product and process technology, particularly where developments had broader potential application than a single firm.

Industries with high value wastes, products or feedstocks, but where resource efficiency has not been a key competitive feature to date. The economic incentives are there, but people are not always aware of them. This could arise, for example, where there was a lack of internal expertise, or of a competitive culture built on resource efficiency (as could be seen in *some* of our dairy cases, for example, involving small firms in a traditional sector). In these circumstances, awareness raising and training initiatives could be extremely effective ways of stimulating change.

WEAKER ECONOMIC INCENTIVES TOWARDS RESOURCE EFFICIENCY

In areas where the economic incentives towards resource efficiency are low, public policy intervention is crucial. More stringent regulation may be needed where regulatory pressures are weak. However regulation *per se* may just have the effect of promoting end-of-pipe solutions. Regulation and other policy instruments therefore need to be geared specifically towards encouraging cleaner responses.

Industries with wastes, products or feedstocks with low per unit value.
Where regulatory pressures are weak (such as brewing), increase their stringency, and ensure that the content of implementation of regulation favours cleaner responses – in the ways already discussed. Increasing water and waste disposal charges could be particularly effective in such areas, as these will give firms more incentive to adopt cleaner technologies for commercial reasons.

Firms which have managed to 'get by' despite low resource efficiency will often be in areas lacking technological dynamism. Here, smaller and more isolated firms may lack relevant internal expertise and may have few existing external links. Without sufficient expertise to assess external knowledge sources, they may fear dependence on particular, potentially partisan sources, suggesting a particular role for regulators and public sector experts.

Table 12.3 *Differing contexts for policy intervention (continued)*

Industries with very high value products, in which resource efficiency is a less important competitive factor than product quality. In this case, economic pressures may not be sufficient to motivate cleaner responses (even where augmented by, for example, increasing waste disposal charges). Public policy initiatives may be needed, either to motivate change or to direct responses towards cleaner technology. These circumstances were exemplified in this study by the pharmaceuticals sector. This highlighted the need for the regulatory environment to favour cleaner technology (and certainly not to inhibit process improvement – as seems to be the case in pharmaceuticals as an unintended consequence of strict product safety regulations, and the need to avoid delays in getting production going given the limited period of exploitation of patented drugs). As in the chemical industry, public policy initiatives which support collaborative technological development to share the costs and risks of uncertain developments may be needed.

WIDER IMPLICATIONS: UNDERSTANDING THE SCOPE FOR CLEANER TECHNOLGIES

Anthony Clayton, Graham Spinardi and Robin Williams

INTRODUCTION

The previous chapter pulled together a number of specific conclusions from our empirical studies about the economic and other factors (notably organizational and knowledge structures) that shape the environmental behaviour of firms. We were able to suggest ways in which public policy intervention might best promote the adoption of cleaner approaches in place of 'end-of-pipe' solutions to environmental problems. This raised issues around the design and implementation of environmental regulation and about particular contexts in which it might be applied.

The study also allows a number of more general observations about the nature of, and scope for, cleaner technology. This final chapter explores the broader implications of this research for our understanding of the nature of cleaner technology. A taxonomy of cleaner approaches is presented and applied to the projects encountered in this study. This highlights two issues of particular importance to the pursuit of more far reaching improvements in environmental performance: the *organization of change* across the product supply chain, and the *promotion of more radical innovation,* particularly where this relates to a wider range of players involved in technological innovation.

WHAT IS CLEAN TECHNOLOGY?

Does cleaner technology equal resource efficiency?

At the heart of the 'pollution prevention pays' axiom is the potential for financial savings through the use of cleaner technology. These savings can arise in two main ways. First, the cost of waste treatment can be eliminated or reduced if less or no waste is produced. Often, the cost of implementing waste minimization at source will be exceeded by the savings in treatment costs, thus producing an overall financial benefit to the firm (increases in disposal costs might provide an important trigger for such change). Second, in many instances at least part of the waste which requires treatment will consist of lost product or other valuable process materials. Less product or process materials lost into the waste stream not only means less need for treatment, but also more product that can be sold, or less materials that need to be purchased. Experience across a range of cleaner production projects in a number of European countries and beyond indicates that the value of saved materials can be an order of magnitude higher than saved pollution control costs.

To a large extent, then, cleaner technology can be equated with the efficiency of industrial processes. Many cleaner technology developments may thus occur as a result of attempts to improve process efficiency rather than because of environmental concerns. In practice, of course, this means that much cleaner technology may not be recognized as such because its development was not driven by environmental concerns. A survey of cleaner technology in the UK noted that:

> *Where activity in cleaner approaches has been found, the environmental benefits are rarely either the motivating force* or recognised *by the developer. The aim is usually to reduce the costs associated with energy and raw materials use and the disposal or treatment of wastes (PA Consulting Group, 1991, p5).*

Although the end result will be the same, cleaner technology can thus be driven in two main ways. As the sugar sector study showed, developments (cleaner beet harvesting) that arose in the UK primarily for commercial reasons were taken up in Denmark within the remit of environmental improvement. This forces us to consider questions about how technologies may come to be justified – in financial or environmental terms – and how these justifications may differ between contexts depending on the industrial, regulatory or broader political setting. How, and under what circumstances, do technologies come to be seen as cleaner? At the same time, cleaner technology provides a way for 'efficiency' and 'the environment' to be seen as compatible, rather than these being in competition.

As discussed in Chapter 12, resource efficiency is an important competitive priority in many industries. For example, in oil refining, the competitiveness of a plant depends on its efficiency in turning a relatively low value raw material (crude oil) into higher value products (such as petrol). Reducing the wastage of hydrocarbons – whether in the form of unwanted by-products, burning undue amounts for fuel or losses to the environment – means more product, as well as reducing the need to dispose of waste streams. Putting aside broader doubts about the long-term sustainability of petro-chemical use, the commercial success of refineries can be seen to revolve around cleaner refining using the most efficient plant and practices to split the crude oil into saleable products with the least waste. In this sense pressures towards process efficiency and environmental cleanness go hand in hand. As already noted, this is particularly notable in industries in which the relatively high value of feedstocks provides an immediate and powerful incentive to avoid wasting resources. Conversely, in sectors involving materials with low unit values – for example paper pulp – the spontaneous alignment of economics and the environment may not be so marked.[1]

Simply associating cleaner technology with process efficiency in this way does involve pitfalls. In particular, such a narrow approach does not take full account of the potential for recycling and reuse of materials outside as well as within the firm. Definitions of cleaner technology usually encompass recycling or reuse within an industrial process or 'on-site recycling' (see, for example, ACOST, 1992, p36). However, to limit the search for recycling to reuse within a firm is perhaps rather arbitrary; end-of-pipe waste may be unavoidable in some industries, and may not be in conflict with sustainability. Rather than focusing on the firm as the level for environmental control, it is argued, we should take a broader view of industrial ecology (Frosch, 1995) in which one company's waste stream could become another's feedstock. It is also possible that some wastes that cannot currently be recovered economically on a site by site basis would acquire sufficient economic value if they could be aggregated across a number of sites.

An economic account of waste

This example forces us to reconsider what counts as 'waste'. Ideally an industrial process would produce only products which can be sold at a profit. Take again the example of oil refining. As we have noted, this involves splitting crude oil into a range of products, a range which varies from one refinery to another, depending not just on the composition of the crude oil feedstock, but also on the technology used to convert low value hydrocarbons into higher value ones. However, crude oil also contains sulphur, heavy metals, salt, and nitrogen which must be removed from these products because of environmental regulations and other restrictions on product quality. Some of these contaminants have negligible commercial value (eg salt). Others have a marginal value in relation to recovery costs. Elemental sulphur, for example, can be recovered, but whether this sulphur then constitutes a waste product or a by-product depends on its current market price.

In relation to wastes of marginal commercial value, whether such recycling is financially viable (or for that matter, environmentally desirable) will depend in large part on the proximity of another industrial process into which it could be fed, thus avoiding significant transport costs. Again a key factor is the availability of a market for a product (and especially in the case of low-value products, a local market, resulting perhaps from the co-location of complementary industries).

Our definitions of what is waste, then are fundamentally tied up with the economics of production and disposal, as well as environmental costs and benefits. In economic terms we could see waste streams simply as process streams which produce something that cannot be sold. Waste is a by-product for which no market exists (or has been identified),[2] or more precisely, since everything notionally has some potential value, a waste arises where the costs of conversion into a finished product exceed its market price. It may therefore be cheaper for the firm to dispose of it as waste, particularly if waste disposal charges are low. On the other hand, increases in waste disposal costs would make it financially attractive for firms to treat 'wastes' as co-products. Similarly, overall increases in raw materials prices would be expected to mandate in favour of cleaner, more efficient processes.

There may be a difference between market values and use values, particularly from an environmental point of view. Production processes may give rise to by-products which though not profitably marketable, may still be useful. The case of the Danish biotechnology firm reminds us that firms may be willing to subsidize the use of such products (in this case, delivering biomass to local farms as a soil improver) to avoid being seen to create waste. Cultural and political values may be important here. Moreover the change not only reduced waste-disposal charges, it also increased the perceived long-term security of waste-disposal routes. This example also suggests that the distinction made at the outset between end-of-pipe and cleaner technologies may become less clear in the context of industrial symbiosis. Many end-of-pipe treatment plants produce biomass in one form or another: sometimes simply settled out from a waste stream; more typically in the form of a sludge from biological treatment. Where there is no viable alternative but to pay to send this biomass to landfill then it must be considered waste. However, in many instances (for example, UK Paper Mill 2) it may be possible to recycle the biomass as fertilizer or animal feed.

These considerations highlight two shortcomings of the economic approach to clean technology. First, simply accounting costs and benefits at the level of the individual trading unit – the firm – may lead to outcomes which are not optimal in terms of overall resource use and environmental performance. Second it would be unhelpful to restrict the search for cleaner approaches to such economic factors.

In relation to the former, a firm's products may give rise to environmental problems for those who consume or dispose of them. This points to the possibility of *market failure* leading to wasteful processes, that is, where the market fails to transfer correctly the full costs and benefits of industrial activities between different players. For example, environmental costs may be externalized, in so far as the firm is not required to pay the full costs of wastes it generates. This could arise because the control costs fall on other players (for example in the ultimate disposal of goods), or are distributed to society as a whole (through environmental damage and general burden of clean up). The optimal way of dealing with resources used and wastes generated may only be apparent from assessment of the whole life cycle of a product, encompassing extraction, processing, consumption and disposal, rather than just a single manufacturing process (Jackson, 1993a; Clift, 1995). We consider these points in more detail below in relation to *cleaner production systems*, where we highlight the problems in coordinating such shifts to cleaner technology across the product supply chain.

The second point is that the search for clean technology cannot be reduced to an economically driven search for process efficiency. Whilst such pressures can work hand in hand with environmental concerns, it is important to see the search for cleaner approaches as *risk minimization* as well as in narrow economic terms. Under this perspective, 'cleaner' may also imply adoption of materials which inherently threaten fewer potential problems for the environment (in terms of creating hazards or waste disposal problems); for example, avoiding the use of toxic heavy metals or halogenated hydrocarbons, or shifting to water-based solvent systems in place of hydrocarbons. Assessments of 'cleanliness' are thus strongly influenced by our understanding of the hazards (the known and potential risks) of particular processes and materials. This is reflected for example in the concern expressed by Danish Pharmaceuticals and UK Fine Chemicals to secure disposal routes for waste materials that were likely to be available for the foreseeable future, and robust to changing attitudes to waste.

Moreover, as we noted in Chapter 12, the key trigger to environmental improvement is regulation. The level of environmental regulation shapes the trade-off between the economic and environmental performance of a system. As regulatory standards become stricter, the costs of compliance may rise. However, these costs will rise more steeply with end-of-pipe controls than cleaner solutions, favouring the latter in the long-term (Clift, 1995). The implication is that the search for cleaner technology, which may have started for spontaneous commercial reasons (retaining value currently lost in waste streams) may increasingly be driven by the need to meet more stringent environmental standards (albeit in a cost-effective manner).

A TAXONOMY OF CLEANER APPROACHES

The range of actors involved

By extending the search for environmental improvements beyond the boundaries of the firm and its existing processes, an array of possible improvements can be identified which may benefit the environment more than improving a firm's process efficiency. However, whether such changes can readily be achieved is another question. In particular, those changes which affect players across the supply chain may be more difficult to implement than changes within an organization, which is a legal entity and subject to a single managerial authority and decision-making process. These difficulties are liable to be particularly acute in the case of mass marketed products, where the number of consumers is very large, and the relations between producers and consumers may be only indirect and impersonal, mediated through distributors. As the number of players increases, and the relations between them become more diffuse and indirect (eg moving from relations of managerial authority to the voluntarism of market relations) the 'social' difficulties in achieving change become greater. A significant change in new products, for example, might require consumers to learn new ways of using them. Such change may threaten to erode a firm's current customer links if consumers shift to competitors' products which have not been altered. It may thus be very difficult to achieve the necessary changes in behaviour – to motivate, agree or enforce such changes – especially where these changes impose costs upon some of the players, or where the benefits may not be particularly obvious or accrue directly to them.

Figure 13.1 presents a taxonomy which seeks to capture the kinds of change that might be involved in the shift to cleaner approaches. The horizontal dimension addresses this by distinguishing the *range of actors* involved in different kinds of cleaner environmental response, ranging from the local level of the work group or the firm to the broader nexus of players involved in supply chain, potentially encompassing the whole life cycle of a product. The vertical dimension addresses a parallel aspect, of *knowledge sources*, distinguishing a range of different approaches to cleaner technologies in terms of the sources and kinds of technological knowledge involved in their creation and implementation. The lower part of the diagram encompasses incremental improvements to current processes, which will tend to be based on existing knowledge; knowledge and expertise which is to a large degree local (including experience-based knowledge that may be widely distributed across the organization). At the other end of the spectrum of possible responses are the more radical shifts in the technical principles underlying a product or production process which may be possible with the application of new knowledge (for example from external suppliers or public R&D).

This schema allows us to classify a range of different responses which may contribute to cleaner industrial activities. At the bottom left sector we find improvements in housekeeping and changes in techniques and working practices; essentially local programmes of waste minimization, which, arguably, offer the most readily attainable improvements, and which can often be implemented by players within the firm using locally available knowledge. As we move up or to the right in Figure 13.1 we encounter a range of more profound responses, including more radical changes in process technology or product changes, and ultimately cleaner production systems. Though these may be more difficult to achieve, in terms of the problems of knowledge acquisition and dissemination, and the alignment of diverse players, they may offer more substantial environmental gains in the longer term.

This taxonomy allows us to locate our case-study findings in relation to the range of possible cleaner approaches. We have grouped these cases in terms of the categorization of cleaner technology approaches used in Table 12.2.[3] Figure 13.2 shows how the environmental projects in our 31 case studies were distributed between the various types of response. We must apply caution, as noted in Chapter 12, in interpreting these findings. They represent snapshots of particular projects within companies, selected for their interest, rather than because they were 'typical' of the sector or region. Despite these caveats, one aspect above all requires comment. Even though our sample of cases could be expected to encompass some of the most innovative examples of adoption of cleaner approaches, most of the projects involved only relatively modest searches for cleaner approaches – in terms of the level of innovation sought (with only about a quarter of the projects involving the development or application of new technological knowledge), and the range of players involved (with 90 per cent of our projects involving change within the boundaries of the firm itself).[4] This is not to deny the value of these initiatives. Indeed, it points to the immediately available opportunities for cleaner approaches based on local initiatives and local knowledge. However this finding also points to the potentially obdurate problems besetting attempts to stimulate and guide more far-reaching change across diverse players in the supply chain and in the innovation system.

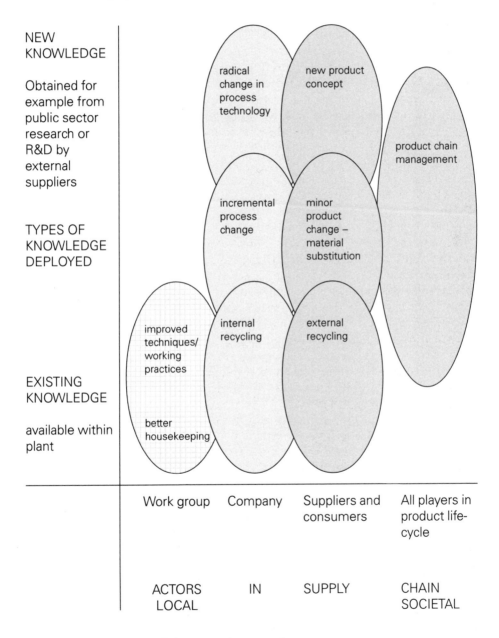

Figure 13.1 *Taxonomy of cleaner environmental responses*

Most of our cases of cleaner technology involved changes that were modest in their scope; in their resort to new technological knowledge or their involvement of other supply chain players. Almost half our projects (14) comprised improvements in techniques and working practice or internal recycling (in particular water reuse) and incremental changes in process technology. There were in addition seven projects involving end-of-pipe solutions (including reuse of sludge from waste water treatment) in which the overall production process remained largely unchanged.

TYPES OF KNOWLEDGE DEPLOYED	Work group	Company	Suppliers and consumers	All players in product life-cycle
NEW KNOWLEDGE — Obtained for example from public sector research or R&D by external suppliers		*radical change in process tech* NL Chem 1 NL Chem 2 NL Pharm NL Sugar DK Plating NL Plating	*new product concept* IRL Dairy	*product chain management* DK Sugar Co
		incremental process change IRL Pharm 1 IRL Pharm 2 UK Fine DK Sugar 1 UK Chems	*minor product change – material substitution*	
EXISTING KNOWLEDGE — available within plant	*improved techniques/ working practices* NL Dairy UK Dairy IRL Brew	*internal recycling* IRL Chems DK Refinery 2 NL Brew IRL Sugar UK Paper 2 DK Fine	*external recycling* IRL Fine DK Pharm	
sludge reuse UK Paper 1 DK Paper *end-of-pipe* UK Brew UK Pharm DK Refinery 1 IRL Refinery UK Refinery	ACTORS LOCAL	IN	SUPPLY	CHAIN SOCIETAL

Figure 13.2 *Classification of environmental responses of the selected projects*

A minority of our cases involved more innovative approaches along the two dimensions flagged in this taxonomy:

- the search for more radical changes in process technology;
- the search for improvements across the supply chain.

Radical changes in process technology

The most significant cases involving the development of radical change in process technology were mainly located in The Netherlands, in the chemical and pharmaceuticals sectors. This underlines the points made in Chapter 12 about the role of the regulatory regime and of sector level arrangements in providing a context that can promote longer-term research and development into cleaner technology.

Collaboration with external equipment suppliers was critical in the cases of radical changes in process technology in NL Sugar and in DK and NL Plating (ie cyanide-free electro-plating), though the supplier's lack of expertise in the Dutch case caused problems for the SME concerned. These all happened to be cases involving the transfer of a cleaner/more resource efficient technology developed in another country. Regulatory bodies and clean technology agencies were also important players in some cases. DK Sugar was supported in its search for a low waste/low water use sugar refining process by a grant from the Ministry of Environment under its Cleaner Technology programme – though the relatively small size of the grant makes it look more like a token of the close collaboration that developed between the firm and the Environmental Protection Agency. Intriguingly, none of our cases involved the application of new advanced generic cleaner technologies of the sort pursued by public sector research programmes such as that sponsored by the UK Cleaner Technology Unit. In all these cases the development of long-term linkages and knowledge flows (eg between firms and external sources of expertise) seem to have been key.

Another feature in these cases involving the search for radical change has been the way in which improving environmental performance and meeting regulatory requirements had become a critical issue for the future commercial development of the enterprise. In this setting we find a coupling of environmental demands and economic objectives; indeed, commercial triggers (plant expansion, quality improvements, cost savings) figured in four of the six cases!

The problem of promoting radical innovation may vary depending, among other things, on the size and internal technical competence of the firm. Thus there are big differences between SME's in low technology sectors which were strongly dependent on external knowledge sources from suppliers and the public sector and the larger, more technically advanced firms with their own R&D facilities. We return below to the issues this throws up in relation to the innovation system.

Initiatives across the supply chain

Danish Sugar Corporation is rather exceptional in that it involved collaboration along the supply chain with sugar beet farmers to promote beet cleaning on the farm, thereby reducing pollution problems in sugar refining. Equally, Irish Dairy is of special interest as it had a project to develop a new market in Japan, for a product (milk minerals) that had hitherto been seen as of marginal value. It thus represented a relatively radical product innovation. Two other cases involving coordination with external supply chain players fell under the heading external recycling, and one of these (DK Pharmaceuticals), in using waste biomass from its biotechnology processes as a soil conditioner, was not very different from various cases of disposal of sludge from biological treatment plants.

CLEANER PRODUCTION SYSTEMS: CHANGE ACROSS THE SUPPLY CHAIN

Our case study methodology based on the behaviour of single firms meant that we took improvements *within* the firm as our starting point. We found many instances of such improvements, but not much evidence of coordinated change across product supply chains. However, the search for cleaner technology cannot be understood fully in the context of one firm's activities. It is not clear why the scope for cleaner developments should be restricted by the boundaries of the firm, which, after all may vary somewhat arbitrarily depending on the size and level of vertical integration of the firm. Restricting the search for cleaner technology to process innovation within firms and sectors fails to encompass the full range of ways that industrial processes could be reshaped to improve environmental performance.

The previous chapter explored the many reasons why a firm may not implement cleaner technology – despite the fact that it would be financially beneficial – in terms of its existing information resources, culture and decision-making criteria. If we take a broader view of cleaner technology – say in the context of life cycle analysis of a product – then a further reason becomes apparent: that the benefits associated with a cleaner approach may not fall neatly within one firm's organizational and financial boundaries.[5] Thus, for example, focusing on measures to minimize waste within a plant may mean that environmentally sound external recycling routes are overlooked (Frosch, 1995). Another concern is the way that firms may avoid local environmental problems – by what appears locally to be a clean approach – by switching to different raw materials which simply transfer the environmental impact to another region (and possibly one with lower levels of regulation). The closure of most wood pulp processing facilities in our study countries and the import of pulp by paper mills is a case in point.

Such narrow, 'firm-level' approaches to cleaner technology exclude many important potential sources of environmental improvement – for example through a shift to cleaner products and cleaner production systems – which may be available if we address the entire life cycle of a product, from the extraction of materials through production to consumption and disposal. Further, focusing simply on process innovation to improve 'eco-efficiency' ignores the more fundamental issue of changing the patterns of consumption and lifestyles needed if we are to move towards a more ecologically sustainable industrial system.

Although valuable, there is a limit to how much reduction in environmental degradation can be gained from cleaner technology which seeks only to improve waste minimization within the context of making the same products. At the very least, cleaner technology needs to encompass product innovation, asking not just whether the same products can be made with less resource use, but whether products can be modified or substituted for further environmental gain. For example products could be changed to reduce their utilization of scarce or non-renewable resources, or designed for disassembly and reuse or to allow materials to be recycled.

This view of cleaner technology therefore involves the use of life cycle analysis to go beyond the level of any particular industrial process and to develop cleaner production systems. For example, what was formerly seen as a waste or by-product could be redesigned to enhance recycling or reuse. This could be done by co-locating another industry for which the waste would serve as a feedstock. One traditional example is the use of spent hops and barley from brewing as animal feed. This dates back to the 19th century, when brewing wastes were used to feed urban dairy herds before transport systems were sufficiently developed to remove these wastes from the city and bring in milk from the country.

The extension of the concept of cleaner technology into industrial ecology represents a significant increase in the number and range of options open to firms, but also introduces an apparent paradox. If the focus is exclusively on the individual firm, a strategy to eliminate a particular waste via process redesign might appear a good option. In a wider context, however, there might prove to be a market for the same waste material with another firm. In this context, it might be a better option to produce and sell more of the material previously classified as waste.

Baas and Silvester (1998) have argued that realizing industrial ecology in practice requires firms to undertake an internal re-optimization before looking to external recycling and industrial symbiosis, partly on the grounds that it is usually more efficient to eliminate problems than to solve them externally. But we must allow for the fact that this may not invariably be the case. As Clift (1995) has pointed out, it is only environmentally efficient to recycle some materials to a certain point. There may be both economic and environmental advantages in recycling valuable materials like aluminium, but there might not be an economic or environmental case for recycling materials with a low value to weight ratio, such as low-grade waste paper and packaging material. Once the costs involved in handling, de-inking, bleaching and pulping low-grade waste paper are taken into account, it can be a better economic and environmental option to use the material as fuel.

These considerations force us to examine the relationship of the concept of cleaner technology to wider discussions about industrial ecology. These suggest that we need to consider a number of steps as complementary components of an overall strategy.

The first step would be to encourage firms to adopt cleaner technologies and, where appropriate, to redesign processes or products to reduce or eliminate some categories of wastes at source. In so far as it is more efficient to eliminate wastes than to reprocess them, this would be the first priority. It is impossible, however, to eliminate all wastes; there are some that are intrinsic to various basic production processes, there are others that cannot be reduced beyond a certain point without prohibitive expense or without creating a new environmental problem (by, for example, requiring a large amount of energy to extract the last traces of contaminants from the outflows).

The second step would be to encourage firms to reconfigure their operations to make greater use of used components and recycled (rather than virgin) raw materials, and to disseminate this message up and down the supply chain. There is considerable scope, as these cases have shown, for internal recycling, thus closing the loop within the one manufacturing operation. Some materials, however, must go on to other manufacturing processes. Different processes have different degrees of tolerance, but, with the appropriate arrangements, materials could 'cascade' down a sequence of processes, from low to high-tolerance uses.[6] As industrial ecosystems develop, firms might find that they had an incentive to have the same regard to the quality of their wastes as they previously had to the quality of their inputs, as there might then be an economic advantage to being able to sell on for a high value, low-tolerance use rather than a low value high-tolerance use. This would depend, of course, on the market for such materials.

The third step would be to close loops by linking firms together into symbiotic pairs and groups. The 'ecology' of most supply chains today remains rather fragmented; resources flow through industrial operations with little regard to their origin or to the destination of wastes. This is very different from natural ecology, where energy and resources form both inputs and outputs as they flow though a wider set of interlocking processes. The ultimate goal of industrial ecology, therefore, is to eliminate all waste by capturing and utilizing the output from every operation as an input to another operation.

These steps are, of course, complementary and overlapping, and the third stage would inevitably start to feed back into the first two stages: once an industrial ecosystem has become self-sustaining, the cost-effectiveness of the various options open to each firm will change. It might become more economically attractive, for example, to produce more of a 'waste' that has acquired a market value than to try to eliminate it. This means that the whole process of moving to an industrial ecosystem is intrinsically dynamic, and likely – if successful – to generate some quite unexpected outcomes. It also means that the definition of 'waste' becomes less clear. In sectors where new uses and markets for products from waste have developed, some firms have redesignated some of their wastes as auxiliary products, which now form part of a recognized production flow.

Perhaps the most fundamental point, however, is that a transition to a more sustainable way of life may require us to make more far reaching changes in our lifestyles and societal organization. To take the example of transport, cleaner technology as now widely defined, at the level of firms or product market, would seek to reduce the resources used in petrol refinery or in car manufacturing. The difficulties with the idea of 'sustainable oil refining' have however already been discussed. A more radical application of the concept might seek instead to change the nature of cars produced, including perhaps a move to electrical power, as well as lightweight materials. However, even the development of new types of 'cleaner cars' may not by itself be sufficient to address some of the fundamental environmental concerns about the sustainability of transport systems. What might really be needed is to tackle the level of car use, which in turn relates not only to the availability and quality of public transport, but also to work and recreation patterns, urban design, and so on. To simply apply the concept of cleaner technology to production of existing car types might offer some immediate environmental gains, but at the expense of masking the more fundamental issues which will eventually have to be addressed (Schot, 1992; Schot et al, 1994).

Coordinating change across the supply chain

The limited number and scope of instances of product chain management in our sample point to the potential difficulties involved in coordinating change across the supply chain. For example suppliers may only have limited ability to encourage their customers to change their practices. On the other hand, as the sugar sector studies show, powerful customers do have scope to enlist change in the technology and working practices of their suppliers. This could be achieved through long-term contractual relationships with beet farmers, motivated by incentive payments and penalties. Where final consumers are highly disaggregated, it is less clear whether and how they might be in a position to evaluate the 'cleanliness' of the supply process. Moreover the messages from the consumer are often ambivalent, juggling as they do, very immediate concerns about price and product quality with more general concerns about the environment. Arguably, 'demand aggregators', such as retail chains, could be mobilized to play an important role in exercising environmental scrutiny. However, the lesson from some of the Dutch and Danish cases would seem to be that sectoral organizations and public agencies could play an extremely influential role in aligning expectations and catalysing the establishment of initiatives to coordinate cleaner development along the supply chain.

Any change beyond the level of the firm, going across a sector or up and down a supply-chain, has to be coordinated and managed if it is to be effective. Boons and Baas (1997), Baas (1998) and Baas et al (1997) have explored this issue in some detail. Baas et al have pointed out that there are two competing proposals in The Netherlands for implementing integrated chain management. In the one, more dirigiste approach, government and regulators would assume the role of chain directors and propose new legislation, draft new regulations based on life cycle analyses of flows of substances, and so on. In the other, more reformist approach, they would reconsider existing legislation and regulations, while adopting the concept of integrated chain management as a new policy principle. They add that:

> *Industrial ecology, as defined and analyzed by various authors, provides a somewhat different perspective by broadening the scope from (strictly) cooperation within chains to cooperation between chains (cascading, facility sharing, and so on)...Many articles on industrial ecology, however, focus largely on the physical flows of substances and the physical transformation processes. They do not address issues of coordination (mechanisms) within and between organizations, they ignore the institutional structures within which organizations operate. These may be markets, for raw materials, commodities, products, services, labour, capital and insurance. These may be legislative, addressing issues of competition, "right to know", fiscal incentives, environmental regulations and liability. They may also be cultural, social, historical or ethical.*

This emphasizes the need to see the behaviour of the firm in context – embedded in a set of diverse relationships with suppliers, customers, sources of technology and knowledge, regulatory bodies and other firms and actors – and to identify the range of actors involved in any significant supply-chain decision. It also indicates that any programme to stimulate research, innovation and the development of cleaner technologies will have to be able to address this inherently complex set of relationships.

THE INNOVATION SYSTEM

Cleaner technology and the stimulation of innovation

Implementation of cleaner technology depends on the firm's capacity for innovation; at the same time, the ability to innovate is central to the firm's competitiveness. As we have seen cleaner innovation can encompass a range of solutions, including small changes in working practices, to the introduction of radically different process technologies, and the redesign of wider production systems. The common thread linking all these cleaner solutions is not just that they improve environmental performance, but also that they are more efficient in the use of resources, and can therefore (although perhaps not immediately) be financially beneficial to the firm.

Innovation by firms is also likely to be directly related to the economic conditions and competitiveness of the market(s) in which they operate. In some cases, resource productivity may be deeply established as a concern of managers and corporate R&D. Conversely, in other sectors the competitive pressures may give this less salience; for example in protected markets or in high-value added sectors such as restricted or patented drugs, where the priorities of R&D revolve around product innovation rather than process innovation (PA Consulting Group 1991).

Better coupling between environmental protection and resource use can, as argued by Porter and van der Linde (1995), stimulate innovation and result in improved industrial competitiveness. Some environmental improvements may necessitate an unavoidable cost, but more often innovative cleaner solutions can increase competitiveness, with three provisos. First, although there are many immediate opportunities for low-cost improvements in techniques and operating procedures, more substantial changes may require significant investment in R&D or in capital equipment (particularly in high-technology, capital intensive industries).[7] Second, innovative cleaner technologies, which may be old ideas not originally implemented (Green et al, 1994), may take time to reach their full potential. Third, developments which eliminate problems at another part of the supply chain (for example, reducing final disposal problems) will not necessarily lead to savings in the short term but will depend upon price adjustments to take into account the change.

This indicates that regulation needs to protect environmental resources in a way which encourages (or at least does not stifle) firm innovation. Regulatory pressure can be an important stimulus for change; particularly since, as we have seen, innovation within firms is typically constrained by 'organizational inertia' and the shared assumptions about how to proceed. The challenge is to design ways of imposing regulatory pressures which encourage innovation geared towards more efficient use of resource *and* reduced environmental impact. As we have seen, for example in the plating sector, regulation may sometimes entrench end-of-pipe controls in several ways: directly, implicitly in the standards adopted, and in the manner of their implementation. In Chapter 12 we outlined various ways in which regulation could promote cleaner innovation: directly, by making the search for cleaner technology an explicit regulatory requirement; and indirectly, through, for example, the flexible implementation of (more stringent) emission standards to allow firms time and leeway to experiment with cleaner solutions, as well as by fiscal measures (waste disposal charges and resource (eg water) charges) to motivate more efficient use of resources.

We need to consider here the interaction between different forms of regulation, which may be geared towards other, more or less closely related goals. Some forms of regulation (for example, regulations about the composition of vehicle fuels, geared towards exhaust emissions) can have a major impact on the competitive strategies of firms, triggering important shifts in products and process technology alike. Equally, regulations geared to the health of workers may stimulate the shift to less environmentally hazardous materials (the shift to water-based paints in place of hydrocarbon-based solvent systems is a case in point (Meredith and Wolters, 1994)). Careful design and implementation of these various requirements may be needed to ensure that various societal goals are met, which complement rather than impede one another. Conversely, as our study indicated, FDA Regulations and approvals for pharmaceutical production may have the effect of inhibiting innovation in process technology in this sector.

Sources of technological knowledge

Large firms can often draw upon considerable internal expertise and R&D facilities. This, together with potentially greater access to finance, suggests that large companies could be better placed to develop and implement radical cleaner technology approaches, than SMEs with lower levels of in-house technical expertise (PA Consulting Group, 1991). High levels of internal expertise, however, may not always mandate in favour of cleaner approaches where environmental improvement has come to be associated with end-of-pipe treatment, and where the firm has established functions specializing in this. In larger firms, the more established division of labour and expertise may mean that existing traditional approaches can become institutionalized, and harder to change.

A key issue for public policy initiatives to promote cleaner technology is the extent to which innovation in firms can benefit from external sources of expertise, and in particular from publicly funded R&D. In the UK, for example, the Department of Trade and Industry, in collaboration with the Engineering and Physical Sciences Research Council, has supported university-based fundamental research into the development of advanced cleaner technologies. The attraction of this conception lies in the idea that this will give rise to generic cleaner technologies – 'black box' solutions – cleaner techniques or pieces of hardware which, once developed, could be widely diffused to industry. However the 'linear model' of innovation, which this initiative implicitly adopts, has been widely criticized (Williams and Edge, 1996) for its presumption that basic research will generate 'technical fixes' which can be readily inserted into existing industrial processes. There has been remarkably little evidence to date of the implementation of such approaches to cleaner technology. None of our case studies result from such science driven initiatives. Even if they produce useful innovations, the evidence from studies of other types of innovation suggests that their potential benefits may be difficult to exploit. One problem is that high-technology solutions emerging from public R&D may be far removed from the current circumstances and requirements of firms (for example if their use requires radical shifts in core process technologies, or new kinds of skill outside the range of core competences currently available within the industry). Moreover studies have shown that the adoption of such radical new technologies typically requires further, and often protracted, technological innovation (for example in introducing complementary technologies that may be needed to get them to work) as well as institutional change (eg acquisition of new bodies of technical expertise, retraining staff in new operating principles and so on) (Freeman, 1984).

Though public research into basic cleaner technologies might be helpful in increasing the range of potential solutions available to industry, their uptake and application may therefore be slow.[8] On the other hand many potential solutions already exist, and are not being implemented. There is a danger that such public sector research will be too far removed from the actual circumstances of firms to be of practical value. This is particularly relevant when we consider that cleaner technologies overlap strongly with commercial (eg resource efficient) technologies. It is generally argued today that public sector research has not had a good success rate in 'picking winners', that is in identifying those technological routes that will prove commercially important. Publicly directed research might turn out to have been directed to the wrong goals. To help offset these problems in future, such research should perhaps be conducted in collaboration with user firms in order to make use of their detailed knowledge of existing products and processes as well as of technical and commercial trends in the sector. This could help to reduce barriers to adoption and improve their uptake. This model has been adopted in other countries, notably Denmark. Rather than simply subsidizing technology acquisition or development (which may well unhelpfully distort decision-making, as we saw in the case of the subsidies for introducing end-of-pipe controls in the plating sector), support might be most productively targeted on promoting flows of knowledge between public sector research and private R&D, and cooperation and exchanges between firms. In this way, public sector support could help catalyse changes in the selection environment for corporate R&D (Green and Miles, 1996).

Several of the 'cleaner technologies' adopted in our case studies were already widely adopted in other countries (for example cyanide-free electroplating and farm-based cleaning of sugar beet extraction were both well established in the UK). One important implication of this research concerns the need for better exchange at the European level of experiences and practices in relation to cleaner technology, a development which could well yield dividends in terms of competitiveness as well as environmental performance.

Finally, regulatory agencies may also play an important role in stimulating the innovation of cleaner technology. In relation to smaller firms, with limited technical resources, regulators may provide an important resource of expertise, as we saw in the advisory role adopted by the sewage authorities with both UK Dairy and UK Paper Mill 2. More generally, we have seen how some regulators moved from simply policing standards and adopted a more proactive mission, advising the regulated industry and even collaborating with them in pursuing cleaner approaches. For such an approach to be successful, however, requires the regulator to address the particular conditions within each firm, either directly or through other sources of expertise such as trade associations and consultants. In relation to larger and technologically more advanced firms, the regulator's role may be somewhat limited by the information imbalance between regulator and regulated firm. In these circumstances, the regulator can only really comment on the process, rather than the substance, of the firm's cleaner technology innovation. Today we find environmental regulation mechanisms moving in two directions: towards increasing centralization in the UK and Ireland, and its decentralization in Denmark and The Netherlands. The latter would appear to be conducive to the development of a more collaborative relationship with local firms. However, the former would allow greater specialization within inspectorates, potentially redressing problems of unequal expertise. Reform of regulatory systems may need to consider this dilemma and how it could be resolved, for example, by improved information systems. Mechanisms for information exchange about cleaner technologies between agencies at European level could also prove helpful.

CONCLUSIONS AND ISSUES FOR THE FUTURE

This study of the factors shaping and promoting the implementation of cleaner technology has touched upon a set of issues central to the transition to a more sustainable economic system. Many writers have addressed these issues, notably from an environmental economics and policy perspective. Additional insights have been possible in this study, we argue, from the application of analytical perspectives from science and technology studies. Work from the social shaping of technology (broadly defined to include related constructivist perspectives and evolutionary economics (Williams and Edge, 1996)) has, in particular, provided tools for analysing both the factors which underpin the entrenchment within society of particular technological choices as well as the scope for transformation and change. Social shaping analyses draw attention to the way in which particular sets of priorities may become entrenched, not only in the design and configuration of material artefacts, but also in decision-making criteria, taken-for-granted methods of operation and the division of labour and knowledge. It also highlights the complex social processes involved in innovation, in achieving both technological change and the associated institutional change.

Questions of stability versus dynamism are extremely pertinent to attempts to move towards environmental sustainability; a move which will clearly require far-reaching social and technical change. This will call for a rethinking of the values underpinning trajectories of technological innovation, the design of current production processes and patterns of consumption (Schot, 1992). But how will these be achieved? Our study provides some pointers to the difficulties and opportunities in meeting this challenge.

First and foremost our study highlights the enormous opportunities for cleaner innovation that are immediately available, by adopting relatively modest changes in production processes, working practices and techniques. This observation provokes questions, explored in the previous chapter, about why such environmentally and economically beneficial changes were not more widely adopted. In addition to these incremental, local changes our survey also found a few striking examples where more fundamental changes were achieved. This chapter has examined the factors which support this dynamism, and considered the kinds of intervention that might bring about such a radical re-orientation of the priorities underpinning economic activities.

We now have a clear picture of the mechanisms by which cleaner innovation can be promoted, as well as the barriers in terms of organizational inertia and the entrenchment of traditional practices. The study has pointed to the role of market forces, as well as regulation, in promoting the shift towards waste minimization. Firms can make considerable financial savings by reducing the amount of valuable materials lost as waste and reducing waste disposal costs. There is also scope to retrieve value from waste streams by recycling materials internally or by finding alternative markets for these by-products. As a result of these kinds of pressures, competitive dynamics, particularly in mature product markets, will tend to make resource efficiency an intrinsic concern of organizations: incorporated within the expertise and methods of operation of the industry. However, cleaner technology is not just resource efficiency, and we cannot restrict it to developments motivated solely by economic factors. It also implies risk avoidance, and may, for example, involve a search for materials that are inherently less hazardous (it might, for instance, suggest avoiding materials such as heavy metals which may be ecotoxic or pose special disposal problems).

This brings us on to the key question of how commercial pressures for resource efficiency can be coupled to environmentally motivated initiatives in the search for industrial processes and products that minimize resource utilization and environmental hazards. In product markets in which cost structures favour resource efficiency, particularly where this has become institutionalized within plant operations, this will tend to channel environmental responses towards waste minimizing solutions. This happy coincidence will not, of course, prevail in relation to low-value wastes (or raw materials such as water), where the market may fail to promote environmental goals. In this situation, increasing waste disposal charges, or taxing raw materials could provide a means to offset such failures of the market to motivate waste minimization. Regulation can also be directly geared to encouraging cleaner technology, in the content of regulation (as is the case in Ireland where best available technology (BAT) requirements explicitly require exploration of cleaner technology possibilities). The role of regulators could also be changed from the traditional concept of simply policing the implementation of regulations towards a broader mission of encouraging greater awareness of the scope for cleaner approaches.

However, considering the extent of change needed to achieve sustainability, a crucial question is how environmental responses can be directed towards the more far-reaching benefits that can be expected from longer-term *research and development of cleaner processes and products*. One important finding from our study concerns the need to apply increasingly stringent environmental regulations over a *long-term time frame*, to allow environmental improvement to be incorporated into commercial planning (particularly in industries in which process changes require substantial, albeit infrequent, replacements of fixed capital equipment). Some flexibility in the time frame for implementing regulations could also reduce the risks for firms embarking on a search for as yet unproven opportunities for process improvement. These would provide a space for a more open-ended search for cleaner innovation, offsetting the tendencies of managers to avoid uncertainty by using tried and tested end-of-pipe solutions. Subsidies and other measures to offset or share the costs of cleaner research and development have also proved helpful.

There was little evidence in our study of improvements arising from 'science push'. Although some countries have launched public sector research programmes directed towards developing radical generic cleaner technologies (eg by changing the basic scientific principles underlying industrial processes), innovations arising from these programmes did not figure in our study. Some lag can, of course, be expected before such innovations can be adopted. On the other hand, basic scientific research conducted with little reference to industrial conditions may well result in innovations that are so far removed from the methods of operation and arrays of technological expertise available within industry as to have little scope for application, particularly in the short term. Innovation studies suggest that the adoption of radical innovations may depend upon further development work to bring new technological processes to industrial scale, as well as complementary technological innovations and institutional change (Freeman, 1984) and that these may constitute a considerable barrier to their adoption in the short term and may imperil their longer-term viability. More research may be needed into how publicly funded scientific research could best contribute to cleaner and more sustainable industrial systems. It would seem desirable to couple public sector research in this field closely to efforts within industry.

Industrial research and development of cleaner processes tended to involve (mainly larger) firms that already possessed research and development functions and expertise. Some smaller firms in more dynamic sectors had established greater in-house technical capacities in addition to well-developed linkages with external sources of knowledge, such as regulators and public sector research. However, many small and medium sized enterprises lacked the technical and financial resources for such a concerted development effort. In such contexts, equipment suppliers could potentially play a key role (though SMEs may be rather dependent upon their suppliers and, lacking expertise needed to assess supplier claims, may be vulnerable to their shortcomings). There is an international division of labour within Europe in research and development for equipment in various kinds of sector/process. This raises questions about the structure of the 'sectoral innovation systems' in different industries and how this may pose problems of access to technology and expertise by firms (particularly smaller firms).

These considerations bring us on to the knowledge and expertise issues which constitute an important intervening variable in patterning environmental responses. For example, many firms, especially smaller firms with limited technical resources, were not aware of the costs of waste, and did not have in place the information collection and evaluation mechanisms needed to monitor the situation. In a number of cases, external pressures (ranging from waste minimization demonstrator programmes to threatened penalties for excess discharges or charges for waste disposal from waste disposal authorities) catalysed a shift in firm culture, promoting a more far-reaching search for cleaner solutions. Knowledge flows seem to be critical. In some larger firms, bureaucratic barriers to knowledge flows within the organization prevented environmental protection specialists from learning about the opportunities for process improvement from process engineers, allowing traditional end-of-pipe engineering controls to continue unchallenged. In smaller firms, internal barriers to knowledge flow may be less of a problem. However in smaller firms with lower levels of internal expertise, access to external sources of knowledge – from other similar firms, equipment suppliers and regulators – may play a crucial role in allowing firms to find out the state-of-the-art and address the scope for cleaner solutions. What was at issue, however, was not necessarily access to specialized technical expertise. In some cases, access to new management techniques (eg to monitor and evaluate waste flows or to assess quality) was important. In others it was marketing knowledge (eg about the scope for selling-on current wastes as profitable products). New *combinations* of expertise could therefore prove more relevant to cleaner innovation than *high levels* of expertise in particular high technology solutions, especially since what is required often involves *integration* of environmental and process improvement, and an ability to rethink current taken-for-granted methods of operating. In the longer term, better training and clean technology awareness initiatives may well help to encourage a shift in corporate culture. In these ways, cleaner approaches are likely to become more institutionalized, better proven and more widely accepted over time.

Thus far we have mainly considered changes at the level of the individual firm or plant. This may not always be sensible. For example, improvements in process efficiency may only ever address a marginal part of the overall waste generated (especially in mass consumption products). It is therefore essential to consider the entire life cycle of a product from raw material extraction to ultimate disposal, and consider how the activities of a plant operates within a broader product chain. Such a broader perspective may identify opportunities not visible at the firm level. This may include, for example, changes in products that may reduce the volume or hazards of waste generated, or opportunities for 'industrial symbiosis', recycling wastes from one industrial process as feedstock for another (using biotechnology wastes as animal foodstuff as a case in point). In relation to low-value wastes in particular, the *local* availability of firms able to utilize waste products may be critical (by minimizing the energy and financial costs of transport) to the economic viability and ecological attractiveness of industrial symbiosis.

Our cases suggest that it may be difficult to achieve such far-reaching changes, not least because they require coordination between a wider range of players along the supply and disposal chain. These difficulties may be particularly intractable where the changes impose unwanted costs (eg from the need to change entrenched methods of working or to acquire new kinds of knowledge) especially where these fall on players who do not receive perceived benefits. Large, powerful consumers may be well placed to exert influence on their suppliers, but this is harder to achieve with more widely dispersed consumption (particularly, for example, in the case of mass-produced domestic goods).

In conclusion, although we can be optimistic about the increasing adoption of cleaner technology in existing industrial processes, more far-reaching change in our patterns of economic life and their environmental impacts will be harder to achieve. Our study has identified powerful potential stimuli for change, arising particularly from regulation (underpinned by growing societal awareness of environmental issues) and competitive issues towards increased resource efficiency. It has provided indicators about how these stimuli can best be mobilized to promote the search for environmental sustainability. The systematic comparison between regions and sectors has also made an important contribution to identifying the scope for change by revealing important differences between cases and settings that may often have been taken for granted by those directly involved. It has allowed us to gain some insights into the interplay between socio-political, economic, and technical/expertise factors patterning industrial processes and environmental responses.

However important questions remain, in particular, about how to apply these pressures beyond the level of the individual firm, to the supply chain, the innovation system and widespread patterns of consumption and social behaviour. Though the transition to environmental sustainability has often been seen as requiring revolutionary changes – radical shifts in technologies and patterns of economic life – we conclude that there are substantial prospects for improvement in environmental performance through sustained incremental change in industrial activities, through both endogenous innovations and the re-orientation of the existing system of production and consumption.

NOTES

CHAPTER 1

1   Filters can recover some of the solid matter content from a flow of waste water, for example, but the recovered solid matter still has to go somewhere – and usually ends up in a landfill.

2   Marx argued that removal of the parasitic *rentier* class would allow a more equitable distribution of wealth, thereby enabling a transition from the capitalist exploitation of human and natural resources to the disinterested scientific management of these resources.

3   For example, similarities are perhaps most obvious in early phases of industrialization, when primary and secondary industries – which tend to generate the largest flows of wastes – are being established.

4   This is approximately equivalent to 35 per cent of global aggregate GDP. It would not be possible to eliminate all this waste, but this estimate from Weizsäcker et al (1997) suggests that a sufficiently extensive efficiency programme could raise effective global GDP significantly.

5   For example, the notion of industrial ecology (Graedel and Allenby, 1995), is based upon the establishment of a web of interconnected industries, processing all residues currently classed as waste into further useful products, thus maximizing the overall efficiency of human resource use to an extent probably unachievable any other way.

6   As noted earlier, the increasing mobility of corporate operations and the ceding of real economic power to international product and capital markets give firms a number of such ways to evade effective regulation. This is why, of course, the environment is now a major issue in international trade and political relations. Over the next couple of years, there will probably be further moves to control these attempts to evade environmental regulation by developing and strengthening the environmental requirements for imports into the major European and North American markets, while the WTO is likely to move further to clarify its position on the extent to which environmental standards can be used as non-tariff barriers to trade, an issue that has, unfortunately, caused considerable controversy in the relationship between the developing nations and the advanced industrial and post-industrial nations.

7   For example, Rendan (1994) cites a number of definitions of cleaner technology in use in Denmark, Ireland and The Netherlands, all of which are similarly compatible with the approach taken here. Similarly, the US Office of Technology Assessment identifies 'five broad approaches to waste reduction' (OTA 1986, pp78–82), although it adopts some slightly different definitions and tends to regard pollution prevention technology and cleaner technology as virtually synonymous (OTA 1994, p229). The UK Department of Trade and Industry (DTI) also gives examples of technology which 'focuses on reducing demand for raw material and energy and on the prevention as distinct from the treatment or disposal, of pollution and other wastes' (ACOST, 1992),

although DTI tends to focus largely on innovative engineering solutions rather than management approaches.

8   This has led some advanced firms to develop a single, coherent management strategy that integrates the management of quality control, working conditions and environmental impact into a single framework, with the single goal of continuous improvement across all areas of activity (Zwetsloot, 1995).

9   Recycling refers to those cases where material is recovered and reintroduced to primary production process. Used paper, for example, can be collected and pulped. The pulp is then de-inked and bleached, if necessary, before being cycled into the paper-making process again, thus reducing the demand for virgin pulp. Scrap steel can be fed back into the steel production process in place of iron ore. The excess CO_2 generated during the brewing process can be captured and used to carbonate beer, thus replacing bought-in CO_2. Secondary recycling refers to those cases where material is recovered and introduced into a different production process. The term is usually used to refer to those cases where the second production process is managed by another firm, possibly in a different sector. The use of demolition rubble to form the foundation for roads, for example, which would involve a commercial transaction between two firms, would constitute secondary recycling. Some firms refer to such materials as 'auxiliary products', rather than wastes, as the distinction between 'product' and 'waste' starts to become blurred when both are being sold.

10   Similarly it has been argued that the energy and environmental costs of plastic bottles used once and incinerated for energy are lower than heavy glass bottles given their higher energy costs of production and transport for use and for recycling.

11   Different firms cannot be expected to react in the same way to external pressures and opportunities. Firms in the pollution abatement industry, for example, might well have a significant financial interest in promoting tougher environmental standards. Firms in heavily polluting industries, however, perhaps with a large sunk investment in obsolete plant, are more likely to be pushed into closure by rising environmental standards than into enhanced profits (Howes et al, 1997).

12   Christensen and Nielsen (1993) noted that an external environmental audit service might have been a possible solution, but the SMEs also made it clear that they would not be prepared to cover the cost of external audits. Christensen and Nielsen concluded that SMEs could not be relied on to act – even in their own interest – without some additional government assistance and funding!

13   Social shaping studies have, for example, demonstrated the variety of technical choices inherent in every stage in the development and implementation of technology, and shown how the options which are selected reflect an array of social, economic, cultural and political factors. This draws attention to the scope for alternative design approaches, and how particular choices could be encouraged by changes in the cultural, regulatory or policy context (Williams and Edge, 1996).

14   It was necessary to draw some cases from industries in adjacent regions in order to cross-match by sector. These instances are explained in the main text.

15   Paint-making was also investigated as a possible sector for study, but was rejected as in most countries and companies this only involved mixing brought-in materials and did not involve significant processing activities.

16   The closure of the refinery under study in The Netherlands during the course of the study reduced the number of cases in The Netherlands to seven, and the number of cases overall to 31.

17   DK Sugar Corporation is the parent company of DK Sugar 1. This case addresses corporate R&D into cleaner approaches.

CHAPTER 2

1   Most firms remain largely unaware of the more long-term, indirect and diffuse consequences of their actions. Very few firms have the capacity to monitor such effects, partly because consideration of these outcomes and long-term collective interests is generally seen to be the responsibility of governments. Moreover some of the less obvious effects could not have been predicted, particularly by industry, given the state of knowledge at the time.

2   Indeed one can trace back this kind of debate to the earliest days of industrial regulation in 19th century Britain (Marx, 1976 esp. pp625–6).

3   The cost that regulation imposes on industry is probably lower than has been claimed. For example ECOTEC Research and Consulting Ltd (1992) dispute the UK Department of the Environment estimate that total pollution control costs in the UK amount to some 1.5 per cent of GDP (1986 figures), suggesting on the basis of their practical operating experience that the figure is more likely to be in the range 0.75–1.0 per cent of GDP.

4   This is well illustrated in the study by the water-based emission limits for plants discharging into the Forth Estuary in the UK. Recipient-oriented limits were set in terms of the levels of pollutant that could be absorbed by the waterway without giving rise to evident (ie acute) environmental effects. As the Forth is a large, tidal estuary, its absorption capacity is relatively large, so these plants were under less onerous restraints than others in the study discharging into more enclosed water bodies.

5   These fall largely into three categories: price rationing (where a tax, charge or subsidy is used to increase either the cost or the opportunity cost of undesirable behaviour), quantity rationing (where tradable permits are used to allocate pollution quotas) and liability rules (where financial penalties are levied for breaches of acceptable behaviour) (Grasl, 1997).

6   Thus many plants in the Forth Estuary hitherto possessed only rather rudimentary systems for physical separation and chemical neutralization of effluents, and were only now installing the biological waste water treatment plants that their continental counterparts in this study had been forced to introduce a decade or more earlier.

7   The current arrangements have been under debate. It is likely that the existing system of environmental permits will be continued, although the procedure is to be somewhat simplified, with new permits linked to the development of 4-year Company Environmental Action Plans.

8   West-Zealand County (DK), for example, used their regional planning powers to construct a comprehensive plan for the cleaning and restoration of a lake and the reduction of the impact from nutrients on nearby shallow coastal waters. Though taking other substances into account, they decided to make the nutrient issue the top priority for some time to come. This policy was used to change the environmental consents whenever they came up for renewal or were otherwise 'open' for change under the EPA rules (companies are generally entitled to eight years of unchanged regulation unless there are major changes in their technology, in volume of their production etc).

   An example of this regulatory option arises in this study in relation to the Danish refineries, which were directly affected by the moves of the Regional Planning authorities to protect the coastal waters. They took a fairly comprehensive view of the companies' activities. Though stressing the need to reduce nutrient releases to a lake, the authorities were willing to 'trade', adopting a more relaxed attitude towards nutrient discharge in exchange for a reduction in another compound (such as a higher rate of phenol removal).

9   Allocation between these councils has been made on the basis of the potential risk, apart from those cases where waste water was discharged directly to surface waters, which remained the responsibility of the county councils. County councils, which are directly elected bodies, have the formal powers, while a regional / local council administrative body is charged with their implementation.

10 This may of course change with the re-establishment of a Scottish Parliament.

11 Dating back, for example, to Rachel Carson's book *Silent Spring* (1962) which documented the destruction of insect life by pesticides such as DDT that had hitherto been seen as wonder chemicals, and to the 1976 Seveso disaster when contaminated land had to be sealed off for decades after a Trichlorophenol plant exploded releasing highly toxic dioxins (Williams, Faulkner and Fleck, 1998).

12 The Brent Spar oil rig was installed in the North Sea in 1976 for use as a storage unit and as a tanker loading terminal. It was decommissioned in 1991. The owners, Shell, believed that the best disposal option – once human safety, environmental impact and costs were taken into account – was to clean up the rig and sink it at sea. The environmentalist group Greenpeace mounted a vigorous campaign against this decision, which achieved widespread and largely uncritical media coverage. This resulted in an international consumer boycott, and Shell was forced to abandon its original plans. However, scientific arguments seem to support Shell's original decision. After a number of further assessments, there is now a general agreement in the scientific community that disposal at sea may be the best environmental option for many of the obsolete North Sea installations. Though Shell's position has been largely vindicated, it has suffered significant losses, estimated at $500 million, mainly from lost sales, as well as damage to its reputation.

CHAPTER 3

1   About half the NOx will come from the fuel, and the other half from thermal reactions with atmospheric nitrogen.

2   The standards here are the emission limits set by the authorities.

3   The figures for the DK 1 are the actual discharge in total ton/year, based on the calculation of the quantity of fuel used for burning, multiplied with the average sulphur content.

4   State-of-the-art or 'Model' Refinery, Western Europe 1995, based on the experiences of the company working with refinery (re)construction, from Sieuwert HAVETHOEK (1995) *ZERO-Waste Refining, A Conceptual Approach* published by Raytheon Engineers & Constructors BV, PO Box 91, 2501 AK The Hague, The Netherlands, 24 pp, October 1995.

5   Set for oil. For gas it is 200 mg.

6   VOCs are too diverse probably to set any useful reference.

7   See note 4 to Table 3.1 (above). For the water based discharge, the reference model is shown with the same amount of throughput as the smallest refinery in this study, assumes the same level of water consumption per day, and also parallels the level found in the DK Refinery 1.

8 Phenol emissions are normally below 0.1 ppm, and are not detectable.
9 This represents a low figure and at the same time shows the interrelation – and possible trade-offs – between emissions to the air and to water as the Irish figure on NO_x is relatively higher, although in total still a good performance, if the all measures are correct.
10 The regulator is only concerned about ammoniacal nitrogen (shown here) rather than nitrate. UK Refinery are not even required to measure nitrate emissions.
11 The UK water use figures are rather high. Partly this is attributable to the complexity of the production process. It can also be seen in the light of the low water charges (currently 35 pence per tonne) which have provided little incentive for water recycling
12 There are few local firms using sulphur. There has been some evidence of a falling off of sulphur prices as refineries start to extract more, in the same way that the gypsum market is now becoming saturated as a consequence of increased production as a by-product of SO_2 scrubbing from power station flues.

CHAPTER 4

1 The EU criteria for large firms are: more than 500 employees; net annual turnover over ECU 38 million; more than one-third owned by a large company.

CHAPTER 6

1 The biomass was given away, rather than sold.

CHAPTER 7

1 The two other EU criteria for medium sized firms are:

■ *Annual turnover:* the net annual turnover has to be less than ECU 38 million. Only UK Dairy fits.
■ *Company ownership:* less than one-third should be owned by a large company. Only IRL Dairy fits.

2 These centres were established by the Ministry of Economics in 1989 in 18 industrial regions.

CHAPTER 8

1 Industrial symbiosis, a modern concept, has a long history in the brewing industry. Dairies were often located near breweries in city centres, for example, to allow the spent grains to go directly for cattle feed (UK Brewery produces some 30,000 tonnes

of spent grain per annum, which they are obliged to sell quickly and cheaply because it is perishable). Distilleries were also located beside maltings and breweries in order to share supplies of malt and to allow the surplus yeast from brewing (the volume of yeast increases three or fourfold during fermentation) to be used for distilling (the process of distilling kills the yeast, so fresh supplies are constantly required). Some more recent ideas include fish farming (using waste heat from brewing to warm ponds and accelerate fish growth). The way in which breweries have dealt with these 'auxiliary products' has, historically, been determined by the market value for these products.

2   In considering this sector, as others, it is important to have regard to the overall production and consumption system as a whole. Breweries are not the main consumers of energy in the larger process of the manufacture and consumption of beer and related products. The aggregated energy demand of the 90,000 pubs in the UK is about 10 times the total energy consumption of the breweries.

3   There is less need for cleaning with continuous as opposed to batch brewing. A number of brewers have found, however, that batch brewing gives a superior product.

4   Larger containers are both more energy and water-efficient. The choice of packaging, however, has several determinants. One is cost. The total tonnage of packaging used for shipping beer in the UK has remained fairly constant for two or three decades, but the composition of the packaging has altered to reduce the use of metal (which is both expensive and heavy). The weight of aluminium in cans has been reduced by 40 per cent in 20 years, and some metal has been replaced by plastic, which is cheaper and allows a higher shipment value to weight ratio. Another determinant is consumption patterns. The current trend in the UK to do more drinking at home and less in pubs, means that more beer has to be shipped in cans and less in tankers. In Ireland off-license sales grew by 37 per cent during 1995/96 and packaged sales grew by 15 per cent, reflecting a similar change in consumption patterns.

5   Some firms in rapidly evolving engineering sectors, by contrast, will replace the bulk of their capital equipment over four years.

6   The most significant emerging new technology in this field is reverse osmosis (microfiltration). It is now possible to manufacture membranes that are so fine that they can extract large organic molecules. This technique is already in use in UK Brewery's Nottingham brewery to reduce the nitrate level in the brewery's intake water. It may be possible to use microfilters to substitute for some forms of chemical cleaning, and to recover and reuse caustic from the waste stream. There would be an economic incentive, in that a brewery would save the money now spent on buying caustic (UK Brewery spends some £300,000 per annum on caustic), plus the money now spent on treatment and disposal. There would, however, be a trade-off, in terms of the energy required to run the high pressure pumps needed to force solutions through microfilters. One of the most important determinants of adoption will be the replacement cycle (how often it is necessary to stop the process and clean the filters), as down-time is expensive. The main driver for the adoption of this new technology would clearly be primarily economic, although the industry recognizes that there will be an important environmental bonus. This new technology would require some re-organization of plant, which means that take-up is likely to be slow unless the industry is placed under additional pressure to adopt such methods.

CHAPTER 10

1   Some potential pollutants arrive via the raw materials, eg from the pesticides used in forestry.
2   UK Paper Mill 1's 'sister' mill has also recently installed a treatment plant, again designed to treat existing effluent levels (Howard, 1991).

CHAPTER 12

1   There are obvious dangers in seeking to extrapolate from a limited number of cases, particularly since these cases were neither randomly selected, nor (necessarily) typical for each sector. Indeed many of the cases were chosen as exemplars of the adoption of cleaner technology approaches, and included firms which had taken part in initiatives such as the SPURT and PRISMA programmes in Denmark and the Netherlands, or who are subscribing partners of Cork RTC's Clean Technology Centre. Many of the firms in the study can therefore be expected to show considerably more awareness and attention to environmental issues, and to cleaner technology in particular. However the methodology adopted was not of the large-scale quantitative survey, but of detailed *qualitative* research. In this sense, *each case study is an investigation* that highlights the *processes* leading to the adoption of cleaner technology.
2   The focus on projects provides a 'snapshot' of developments that altered the environmental performance of our case study firms. Often these projects were part of a wider programme. The reader is invited to examine the more substantial summaries of the cases in the preceding chapters to see how these projects fitted within a broader picture.
3   Some of the projects involved a variety of initiatives. For the purposes of this comparative exercise, we have categorized each project according to the 'cleanest' and most innovative component. Thus UK Fine Chemicals involved process changes in the run up to the installation of an (end-of-pipe) waste water treatment plant, and is therefore classified here as incremental process change.
4   There are exceptions, in this as in other sectors. Danish Pharmaceutical's use of genetically manipulated organisms has brought them under particular scrutiny.
5   Here the Størstroms regulator set a long-term goal of achieving strict limits by using cleaner approaches (even though, at that time, end-of-pipe solutions presented the best available technology). Another sugar factory in a different county was forced to install such end-of-pipe treatment.
6   Only firms with a high profile or pollution potential are formally obliged to develop four-year environmental care plans, and are likely to come under such scrutiny.
7   Water is somewhat exceptional as a productive resource, in that it is mainly used as a carrier to wash, dissolve or emulsify materials rather than as a constituent. Charges for water supply have typically been low. Increasing water use charges and charges on the volume of sewage could be an important stimulus towards extending this kind of clean-up, effectively by providing a financial incentive to firms to economize on its use.

8   The Common Agricultural Policy may have been a significant stimulus for change here. It provides a floor for milk prices, and imposes a production ceiling, with stiff penalties for exceeding quotas. If a dairy wants to increase their profits they must become more efficient, move into higher value products or bid, at potentially inhibiting prices, for a higher milk supply.

9   In this connection we can also consider UK Fine Chemicals (discussed in the following section), in which industrial processes were carried forward from earlier stages in the company's history when resource efficiency and environmental pressures were less intense.

10 This characterization would apply to the UK. Its general implications hold true, even if some sectors might be slightly differently located in other countries with different regulatory histories.

11 As discussed earlier, there was some evidence that external agencies such as regulatory bodies were in a better position to influence SMEs. They were more willing to engage in a joint problem solving approach because they were relatively lacking in expertise, whereas large firms often possess more internal expertise than the regulators. It is also true, of course, that smaller firms are often short of capital, which may be an additional stimulus towards waste minimization (rather than expensive capital intensive treatment plants or radical technical change).

12 What is at issue is not just specialist knowledge, as all grades of staff can make a potentially important contribution in identifying and implementing local improvements in cleaner practices.

13 Although effective design even of end-of-pipe solutions such as waste water treatment plant does require some local knowledge of the nature of those wastes and how they may vary with the processes that are generating them.

14 This is another factor that tends to differentiate firms by size; the less sophisticated smaller firms were more likely to be reactive to external changes, including regulatory pressures and market forces. With shorter-term planning horizons they tended to focus on immediately available solutions.

15 Such as a major river spillage. Equally, unpleasant smells (Irish Refinery, Irish Pharmaceuticals 2) or strongly coloured discharges (UK Fine Chemicals) were given just as much attention by some of our firms as environmentally hazardous ones.

CHAPTER 13

1   And, as discussed in Chapter 12, the true extent of inefficiency and wastage, and thus the costs incurred – in the form of profits foregone by the firm's failure to reduce product loss or to market wastes as auxiliary products – may go unrecognized by managers grappling with a range of complex and pressing concerns in a context of incomplete information.

2   As we saw in the case of the Irish dairy, a very high-value market was identified for milk minerals; what had been hitherto a question of finding the cheapest disposal route had become an important source of profits. This brings us back to the point that firms may be unaware of the potential value of waste products; market knowledge may be as important as process knowledge in reducing waste.

3   For the purposes of this comparative exercise, we have categorized the selected projects that were studied in detail in each case. Where a case involved various elements, they are classified according to the 'cleanest' and most innovative component.

4   There is an important methodological issue here. Our survey took as its starting point a sample of firms in selected industries and, in particular, specific projects within those firms, identified as being significant in terms of environmental performance. As such it could be expected to have captured formal initiatives to tackle wastes through collaboration along the product supply chain, as we found for example in the Danish sugar industry. However the methodology may not have fully picked up de facto inter-organizational changes which may have affected the environment, albeit not necessarily consciously, for example mediated through the market, rather than through direct collaboration between firms. One example is the withdrawal of UK Fine Chemicals from producing certain older and 'dirtier' products (although in this case the environmental improvements achieved in the UK were offset by the fact that this (shrinking) product market was taken over by firms operating in developing nations to lower environmental standards). Another example was the resort of various firms in our study to solvent recycling, which involved sending contaminated solvent wastes to contractors for regeneration. In this case specialized firms were able to carry this out more efficiently and economically, and the market provided a mechanism for inter-organizational improvements in resource efficiency.

5   Similarly, from a life-cycle perspective, we can also see that many end-of-pipe solutions may represent a transfer of risk rather than a true minimization of risk. The solids that accumulate in an end-of-pipe filter may end up in a landfill, rather than in a river, but they have not been eliminated.

6   For example, the experience of the UK paper mills studied was that recycling of waste process water was possible for low-grade products such as packaging, but not for higher quality papers as it caused discoloration. Likewise, though it would not be acceptable to use shredded and reformed mixed thermoplastic wastes for low-tolerance uses (for food or medical packaging, for example), they might be quite suitable for high-tolerance uses (such as flooring material).

7   In contrast, traditional end-of-pipe approaches, though also typically capital intensive, do not offer any payback in improved resource productivity. Moreover, traditional end-of-pipe environmental solutions have benefited from a long learning curve compared to more recent, or as yet unused, approaches, making them seem cheaper and more reliable in the short term. Comparisons between the two may therefore be misleading.

8   This will not always be the case, of course. Indeed we can point, in principle, to certain types of basic innovation that could be adopted in a more 'linear' fashion, for example 'instrumentalities' in which the innovation, and the technical knowledge needed to operate it, could be 'black-boxed', that is designed to be widely adoptable without the need for local adjustment or expertise.

REFERENCES

ACOST (Advisory Council on Science and Technology), UK Cabinet Office, (1992) *Cleaner Technology*, HMSO, London

Adams, J (1995) *Risk*, UCL Press, London

Allen, M (1994) 'Ecosystems for Industry', *New Scientist*, vol 141, no 1911, pp21–22

Ashford, N A, Ayers C and Stone, R F (1985) 'Using regulation to change the market for innovation', *Harvard Environmental Law Review*, vol 9, no 359, pp443–462

Baas, L W (1996) 'An Integrated Approach to Cleaner Production', in K B Misra (ed) *Clean Production: Environmental and Economic Perspectives*, Springer Verlag, Heidelberg/Berlin, pp211–229

Baas, L W (1998) 'Cleaner Production and Industrial Ecosystems: A Dutch Experience', *Journal of Cleaner Production*, vol 6, no 3–4, pp189–197

Baas, L W and Silvester, S (1998) 'Industrial Ecology; learning from the INES project', *Journal of Industrial Ecology*, MIT, vol 2, forthcoming

Baas, L W, Hofman, H, Huisingh, D, Huisingh, J, Koppert, P and Neumann, F (1990) *Protection of the North Sea: Time for Clean Production*, Erasmus Centre for Environmental Studies, Erasmus University, Rotterdam, February

Baas, L W, Huisingh, D and Hafkamp, W (1997) *Schonere Produktie, Ketenbeheer en Industriele Ecosystemen*, RMNO-publikatie no 131, Den Haag, pp51–63

Ballance, R et al (1992) *World's Pharmaceutical Industries: an International Perspective on Innovation, Competition and Policy*, Edward Elgar, Cheltenham

Bonifant, B and Ratcliffe, I (1994) *Competitive Implications of Environmental Regulation of Chlorinated Organic Releases in the Pulp and Paper Industry*, Management Institute for Environment and Business Case Study, Washington, DC

Boons, F A A and Baas, L W (1997) 'Types of industrial ecology: the problem of coordination', *Journal of Cleaner Production, Special Issue*, vol 5, no 1–2, pp79–86

Brickman, R, Jasanoff, S and Ilgen, T (1985) *Controlling Chemicals: the Politics of Regulation in Europe and the United States*, Cornell University Press, Ithaca

Brown, L R, Flavin, C and French, H (1998) *State of the World 1998: A Worldwatch Institute Report on Progress Towards A Sustainable Society*, Earthscan, London

The Brundtland Report (World Commission on Environment and Development) (1987) *Our Common Future*, Oxford University Press, Oxford

Buriks, C (1989) 'Waste Reduction Technology: a Case Study in Resistance to Technical Change', unpublished thesis, Research Policy Institute, University of Lund, Sweden

Burns, T and Stalker, G M (1961) *The Management of Innovation*, Tavistock, London

Callon, M (1980) 'The State and Technical Innovation: a case-study of the electric vehicle in France', *Research Policy*, vol 9, pp358–76

Campina Melkunie bv (1995) 'A fascinating world of dairy products', Zaltbommel, brochure

Carson, R (1962) *Silent Spring*, Houghton Mifflin, New York

CEFIC (1994) *Responsible Care, a Chemical Industry Commitment to Improve Environmental Performance in Health, Safety, and the Environment*, CEFIC (European Chemical Industry Council), Brussels

Centre for Exploitation of Science and Technology (1995a) *Waste Minimisation – a Route to Profit and Cleaner Production: Final Report on the Aire and Calder Project*, CEST, London

Centre for Exploitation of Science and Technology (1995b) *Waste Minimisation and Cleaner Technology: An Assessment of Motivation*, CEST, London

Chadwick, M and Nilsson, J (1993) 'Environmental Quality Objectives; Assimilative Capacity and Critical Load Concepts in Environmental Management', in T Jackson (ed) *Clean Production Strategies: Developing Preventive Environmental Management in the Industrial Economy*, Lewis Publishers, Boca Raton, Florida, pp29–39

Christensen, P and Nielsen, E H (1993) 'Environmental Audits, Clean Technologies and Environmental Protection in Denmark', *European Environment*, vol 3, part 2

Clark, P and Staunton, N (1989) *Innovation in Technology and Organization*, Routledge, London

Clayton, A M H and Radcliffe, N J (1996) *Sustainability: a Systems Approach*, Earthscan, London

Clift, R (1995) 'Clean Technology – An Introduction', *Journal of Chemistry, Technology and Biotechnology*, vol 62, pp321–6

Cole, G (1990) *Pharmaceutical Production Facilities, Design & Applications*, Ellis Horwood, Hemel Hempstead

Coleman, A R (1993) 'CO_2 Recovery Systems', *The Brewer*, November, pp484–487

Commission of the European Communities (1990) 'Council Directive on freedom of access to information on the environment', CEC 90/313/EEC, *Official Journal*, L158/56, 23 June

Commission of the European Communities (1993) *Council Regulation* allowing voluntary participation by companies in the industrial sector in a Community Eco-Management and Audit Scheme, CEC 1836/93, 29 June

Commission of the European Communities (1996) 'Council Directive concerning integrated pollution prevention and control', CEC 96/61/EEC, *Official Journal*, L257/26, 10 October

Commission of the European Communities (1997) 'Amended Proposal for Directive on Volatile Organic Compounds (VOCs): Originally Proposed: 11/96 COM(96) 538, *Official Journal*, C 99/97. [This is not yet approved. See also Current Amendment to proposal: COM(98) 190, *Official Journal*, C 126/98.]

Commoner, B (1994) 'Pollution Prevention, Putting Comparative Risk Assessment in Its Place', in A M Finkel and D Golding (eds) *Worst Things First?: the debate over risk-based national environmental priorities*, Resources for the Future, Washington, DC

Conway, S and Steward, F (1998) 'R&D Networks in Environmental Innovation: A Comparative Study in the UK and Germany' Proceedings of COST A3 Conference on *Management and Technologies*, Madrid, June 1996, vol 5, Office for Official Publications of European Communities, European Commission, Directorate General Science Research and Development, Luxembourg

Cramer, J, Kok, M T J and Vermeulen, W J V (1994) 'Government Policies to promote Cleaner Products', paper presented at *Third International IACT Conference*, Vienna, 7 April

Cunningham, J D et al (1993) *Clean technologies for the fine chemicals / pharmaceutical industry*, Clean Technology Centre, Cork

Department of Environment (1993) *Access to Information on the Environment: Guidance Notes*, Department of Environment, Ireland

Department of Environment (1995) *Access to Information on the Environment: a Review*, Department of Environment, Ireland

Dieleman, J P C et al (1991) *Choosing for Prevention is Winning*, Dutch State Publisher, The Hague

Duncan, O F (1996) 'Sustainable Development, Cleaner Processes and Accounting: A Case Study Examination of the Role of Accounting in the Construction of Choice and Organisational Change', unpublished PhD thesis, Heriot-Watt University, Department of Accountancy and Finance

Dutch Government (1989) *National Environmental Policy Plan*, The Hague

Dutch Government (1990) *National Environmental Policy Plan Plus*, The Hague

Dutch Government and the Association of Dutch Chemical Industry (VNCI) (1993) *Declaration of Intent on the Implementation of Environmental Policy for the Chemical Industry*, The Hague, 2 April

ECOTEC Research and Consulting Ltd (1992) 'The Development of Cleaner Technologies: a Strategic Overview', *Business Strategy and the Environment*, vol 1, part 2, Summer, pp31–38

Environmental Protection Agency (EPA) [Ireland] (1994) *BATNEEC Guidance Note for Manufacture of Dairy Products*, Dublin (draft)

Fischer, K and Schot, J (eds) (1993) *Environmental Strategies of Industry*, Island Press, Washington, DC

Fleck, J, Webster, J and Williams, R (1990) 'The dynamics of I.T. implementation: a reassessment of paradigms and trajectories of development', *Futures*, vol 22, pp618–640

Freeman, C (1984) *The Economics of Innovation*, Penguin, Harmondsworth

Frosch, R A (1995) 'The Industrial Ecology of the 21st Century', *Scientific American*, 273 (no 3, September), pp144–47

Geffen, C (1995) 'Radical Innovation in Environmental Technologies: the Influence of Federal Policy', *Science and Public Policy*, vol 22, no 5, October, pp313–323

Goodstein, E (1999) *Economics and the Environment*, Prentice-Hall, New Jersey

Graedel, T E and Allenby, B R (1995) *Industrial Ecology*, Prentice Hall, New Jersey

Grasl, W (1997) 'Lessons Learnt in the Application of Economic Instruments: The OECD Experience', paper presented at the *Conference on Economic Instruments in Environmental Management*, Kingston, Jamaica, October

Green, K (1992) 'Creating Demand for Biotechnology: Shaping Technologies and Markets', in R Coombs, P Saviotti and V Walsh (eds) *Technical Change and Company Strategies: Economic and Sociological Perspectives*, Academic Press, London, pp164–184

Green, K and Miles, I (1996) 'A Clean Break? From Corporate Research and Development to Sustainable Technological Regimes', in R Welford and R Starkey (eds) *Reader on Business and the Environment*, Earthscan, London, pp129–143

Green, K, Irwin, A and McMeekin, A (1994) 'Technological Trajectories and R&D for Environmental Innovation in UK Firms' *Futures*, vol 26, no 10, pp1047–1059

Hawken, P (1994) *The Ecology of Commerce: How Business can Save the Planet*, Harper Business, New York

Hirschhorn, J, Jackson, T and Baas, L W (1993) 'Towards Prevention – the emerging environmental management paradigm', in T Jackson (ed) *Clean Production Strategies: Developing Preventive Environmental Management in the Industrial Economy*, Lewis Publishers, Boca Raton, Florida

Holm, J and Stauning, I (1994) 'The Changing Role of Regulation in the Development of Environmental Strategies in Firms', paper presented at the *Third Greening of Industry Conference*, Copenhagen, 13–15 November, (mimeo) Department of Environment, Technology and Social Studies, Roskilde University, Roskilde

Holm, J, Klemmensen, B and Stauning, I (1994) *Two Cases of Environmental Front-Runners in Relation to Regulation, Market and Innovation Network: A Story about Successful Resource Management and Eco-Auditing in Glass Wool Production and a Story about Cleaner Technology in Surface Treatment of Steel Constructions*, Department of Environment, Technology and Social Studies, Roskilde University, Roskilde, August

Howard, D W (1991) 'The right effluent treatment system for Guardbridge mill', *Paper Technology*, (February), vol 32, no 2, pp28–31

Howes, R, Skea, J and Whelan, B (1997) *Clean and Competitive? Motivating Environmental Performance in Industry*, Earthscan, London

Huisingh, D (1990) 'Waste reduction and pollution prevention at source: the imperative for sustainable societies' *Proceedings of Conference on Renewable Energy and Cleaner Technology*, 16–18 May 1990, Størstroms Amt (Council), Denmark, pp19–25

International Chamber of Commerce (ICC) (1990) *The ICC Business Charter for Sustainable Development*, April

Irish Government (1992) *Environmental Protection Agency Act*, Dublin

Irwin, A and Hooper, P D (1992) 'Clean Technology, Successful Innovation and the Greening of Industry: a Case-Study Analysis', *Business Strategy and the Environment*, vol 1, part 2, Summer, pp1–11

Jackson, T (1993a) 'Principles of Clean Production – Developing an Operational Approach to the Preventative Paradigm', in T Jackson (ed) *Clean Production Strategies: Developing Preventative Environmental Management in the Industrial Economy*, Lewis Publishers, Boca Raton, Florida, pp143–164

Jackson, T (ed) (1993b) *Clean Production Strategies: Developing Preventive Environmental Management in the Industrial Ecology*, Lewis Publishers, Boca Raton, Florida

Johnston, N (1992) 'Industrial Wastewater', in *Water: Summary Report*, Proceedings of the CEST Water Resources and Opportunity Conference, London, March

Kemp, R, Schot, J and Hoogma, R (1998) 'Regime shifts to Sustainability through processes of niche formation: the approach of strategic niche management', *Technology Analysis and Strategic Management*, vol 10, no 2, June, pp175–196

Larsen, I and Olsen, K O (1989) 'Furthering Cleaner Technology: The role of the decentral authorities' paper presented at the ISWA Conference *Waste Minimisation and Clean Technology: Moving Towards the 21st Century*, Geneva, 29 May–1 June

Laughlin, R C (1991) 'Environmental Disturbances and Organizational Transitions and Transformations: Some Alternative Models', *Organization Studies*, 12/2, pp209–232

Löfstedt, R and Renn, O (1997) 'The Brent Spar Controversy: an example of Risk Communication Gone Wrong', *Risk Analysis*, vol 17, no 2, pp131–6

McMeekin, A and Green, K (1994) 'Defining Clean Technology', paper presented at the International Conference on the Environment *Towards a Sustainable Future: Promoting Sustainable Development*, Manchester, 29 June–1 July, (mimeo) CROMTEC, UMIST, Manchester

Marx, K (1976) *Capital volume 1*, Penguin, Harmondsworth

Meredith, S and Wolters, T (1994) *Proactive Environmental Strategies in the Paint and Coatings Industry in Great Britain and the Netherlands*, TNO Report STB/94/022, TNO Centre for Technology and Policy Studies, Apeldoorn

Miles, I and Green, K (1994) 'A Clean Break? The Role of Corporate Research and Development in Creating Sustainable Technological Regimes', paper presented at the *International Conference on the Environment: Towards a Sustainable Future: Promoting Sustainable Development*, Manchester, 29 June–1 July

Ministry of Public Housing, Physical Planning and the Environment & the 'Stichting Verpakking en Milieu' (1991) *Packaging Covenant*, The Hague

Mnatsakanian, R (1992) *Environmental Legacy of the Former Soviet Republics*, University of Edinburgh Centre for Human Ecology

National Academy of Science (1984) *Toxicity Testing: Strategies to Determine Needs and Priorities*, National Academy Press, Washington, DC

OECD (1985) *Environmental Policy and Technical Change*, OECD, Paris

Office of Technology Assessment, US Congress (1986) *Serious Reduction of Hazardous Waste for Pollution and Industrial Efficiency*, OTA-ITE-317, Washington, DC, September

Office of Technology Assessment, US Congress (1994) *Industry, Technology, and the Environment: Competitive Challenges and Business Opportunities*, OTA-ITE-586, Washington, DC, January

PA Consulting Group (1991) *Cleaner Technology in the UK*, HMSO, London

Partidario, P (1997) *Environmentally Sound Technology Development and Innovation in SME's*, IPTS Report no 19, November, IPTS–JRC, Seville

Pettigrew, A M (1985) *The Awakening Giant: Continuity and Change in Imperial Chemical Industries*, Blackwell, Oxford

Porter, M E and van der Linde, C (1995) 'Green and Competitive: Ending the Stalemate', *Harvard Business Review*, vol 73 (no 5, September–October), pp120–134

Remmen, A (1995) 'Pollution Prevention, Cleaner Technologies and Industry', in A Rip, T Misa and J Schot (eds) *Managing Technology in Society: The Approach of Constructive Technology Assessment*, Pinter, London, pp199–224

Rendan A/S DK, Kruger AS, DK, & TME NL (1994) *Waste Management: Clean Technologies: up-date on the situation in member states*, Commission of the European Union, Directorate General for Environment, Nuclear Safety, and Civil Protection (DG XI), June

Renn, O (1990) 'Risk Perception and Risk Management: A review (Part I: Risk perceptions)', *Risk Abstracts*, vol 7, pp1–9

Rogers, A M (1983) *Diffusion of Innovations*, 3rd edition, Free Press, New York

Rothwell, R (1992) 'Industrial Innovation and Government Environmental Regulation: Some Lessons from the Past', *Technovation*, 12:7, pp447–458

The Royal Society (1992) *Risk: Analyses, Perceptions and Management*, Report of a Royal Society Study Group, The Royal Society, London

Schot, J (1992) 'Constructive Technology Assessment and Technology Dynamics: the Case of Clean Technologies', *Science, Technology, & Human Values*, vol 17, no 1 (Winter), pp36–56

Schot, J, Hoogma, R and Elzen, B (1994) 'Strategies for Shifting Technological Systems: The case of the Automobile System', *Futures*, vol 26, December, pp1060–1076

Simon, H A (1982) *Models of Bounded Rationality* (2 vols), MIT Press, Cambridge, Massachusetts

Sørensen, K (ed) (1994) *The Car and its Environments – The Past, Present and Future of the Motorcar in Europe*, Proceedings of the COST A4 Workshop, May 1993, vol 2, European Commission/COST, Office of Official Publications of the European Communities, Luxembourg

Storstrøm County (1993) *SPURT: Storstrøm County's Programme for the Dissemination of Cleaner Production*, Storstrøm County

Sweeney, M and Mega, V (1996) *The Enterprise and the Environment: Highlights of the Research and Case-study in Ireland*, European Foundation for the Improvement of Living and Working Conditions, Loughlinstown, Ireland

Tait, J, Brown S and Carl, S (1991) 'Pesticide Innovation and Public Acceptability: The Role of Regulation' in L Roberts and A Weale (eds) *Innovation and Environmental Risk*, Balham Press, London

The Scotsman (1996) Business and Recruitment Supplement, 07/03/1996

US Food & Drugs Administration (1995) *From Test Tube to Patient: New Drug Development in the United States*, 2nd edition, January

Van Weenen, J C (1990) *Waste Prevention: Theory and Practice*, Den Haag

Veld, R J (1992) in 't, J A de Bruijn, E F ten Heuvelhof, A Niemeijer, R W Hommes, L W Baas and D Huisingh *Recommendations for a PROCESS STANDARD; concerning the environmental and feasibility analysis as laid out in the Dutch Covenant for Packaging*, Erasmus University Rotterdam Press, Rotterdam

Wallace, D (1995) *Environmental Policy and Industrial Innovation*, The Royal Institute of International Affairs: Energy and Environmental Programme series, Earthscan, London

Walsh, V (1993) 'Demand, Public Markets and Innovation in Biotechnology', *Science and Public Policy*, vol 20, no 3, pp138–156

Webb, L (1993) *Pollution Control for Paper and Pulp Processes*, UK Department of the Environment [DoE] report no DoE/HMIP/RR/93/036 prepared for Her Majesty's Inspectorate of Pollution, Department of the Environment by Mott MacDonald Environment, September

Weizsäcker, E von, Lovins, A B and Lovins, L H (1997) *Factor Four: Doubling Wealth, Halving Resource Use*, Earthscan, London

Welford, R (1997) *Hijacking Environmentalism: Corporate Responses to Sustainable Development*, Earthscan, London

Williams, R (1984) 'The Regulation of Industrial Hazards', unpublished PhD thesis, The University of Aston, Technology Policy Unit, Birmingham

Williams, R and Edge, D (1996) 'The Social Shaping of Technology', *Research Policy*, vol 25, pp865–99

Williams, R, Faulkner, W and Fleck, J (1998) *Exploring Expertise*, Macmillan, Basingstoke

Zwetsloot, G I J M (1995) 'Improving cleaner production by integration into the management of quality, environment and working conditions', *Journal of Cleaner Production*, vol 3, no 1–2, pp61–66

GLOSSARY OF TECHNICAL TERMS, ACRONYMS AND ABBREVIATIONS

BAT	best available technology
BATNEEC	best available technology not entailing excessive cost
BOD	biological oxygen demand
BS	British Standard
CEAP	Company Environmental Care Plan
CEC	Commission of the European Communities
CHP	combined heat and power
CO_2	carbon dioxide
COD	chemical oxygen demand
DG XII	Directorate-General for Science, Research and Development (European Commission)
DK	Denmark
DTI	Department of Trade and Industry (UK)
EC	European Community
ECF	elemental chlorine free
ECU	European Currency Unit
EMAS	Eco-Management and Audit Scheme
EPA	Environmental Protection Agency
EU	European Union
FDA	Food and Drug Administration (US)
FRPB	Forth River Purification Board (Scotland)
GDP	gross domestic product
GMP	good manufacturing practice
H_2S	hydrogen sulphide
HMIPI	Her Majesty's Industrial Pollution Inspectorate (UK)
HMSO	Her Majesty's Stationery Office (UK)
HSE	health, safety and environment
ICC – BCSD	International Chamber of Commerce – Business Charter for Sustainable Development
IE	inhabitant equivalent, a unit for expressing the environmental load of diverse water emissions in relation to the waste produced by one domestic consumer
IPC	integrated pollution control
IPPC	integrated pollution prevention and control
IRL	Republic of Ireland
ISO	International Organization for Standardization

LPG	liquefied petroleum gas
LRC	Lothian Regional Council (Scotland)
MNC	multinational corporation
N	nitrogen
NAFTA	North American Free Trade Association
NEPP	Dutch National Environmental Policy Plan of 1989
NEPP+	Dutch National Environmental Policy Plan of 1990
NL	The Netherlands
NOx	nitrogen oxides
NWA	National Water Authority (The Netherlands)
OECD	Organisation for Economic Co-operation and Development
ONO	a form of processing that removes most of the heavy metals from waste water, leaving a concentrated chemical waste than can go to special landfill
R&D	research and development
RCF	recycled fibre
PAH	polycyclic aromatic hydrocarbon
recipient oriented	standards based on the capacity of the disposal medium (such as a waterway) to absorb, dilute and disperse pollution without undue harm. Such standards therefore vary – for example between inland and estuarine waterways, which have very different capacities to absorb and dilute pollutants. They can be contrasted with 'source oriented' standards, which are based on estimates of the extent to which industrial processes can be cleaned up
RTD	research and technological development
SHE	safety, health and environment
SME	small to medium sized enterprise
SO_2	sulphur dioxide
source oriented	see recipient oriented
TQM	total quality management
UK	United Kingdom
UNEP	United Nations Environment Programme
US	United States of America
VOC	volatile organic compound
WTO	World Trade Organization

INDEX

Figures in **bold** indicate figures; figures in *italic* indicate tables or boxed text